The Collection Program in Schools

The Collection Program in Schools

Concepts and Practices

SEVENTH EDITION

Marcia A. Mardis

Library and Information Science Text Series

LIBRARIES UNLIMITED®
An Imprint of ABC-CLIO, LLC
Santa Barbara, California • Denver, Colorado

Library of Congress Cataloging-in-Publication Data

Names: Mardis, Marcia A., author.
Title: The collection program in schools : concepts and practices / Marcia A. Mardis.
Description: Seventh edition. | Santa Barbara, California : Libraries Unlimited, 2021. |
    Series: Library and information science text series | Includes bibliographical
    references and index.
Identifiers: LCCN 2021007769 (print) | LCCN 2021007770 (ebook) |
    ISBN 9781440878725 (hardcover ; acid-free paper) | ISBN 9781440876639
    (paper ; acid-free paper) | ISBN 9781440876646 (ebook)
Subjects: LCSH: School libraries—Collection development—United States. |
    Instructional materials centers—Collection development—United States.
Classification: LCC Z675.S3 V334 2021 (print) | LCC Z675.S3 (ebook) |
    DDC 025.2/1878—dc23
LC record available at https://lccn.loc.gov/2021007769
LC ebook record available at https://lccn.loc.gov/2021007770

ISBN: 978-1-4408-7872-5 (hardcover)
        978-1-4408-7663-9 (paperback)
        978-1-4408-7664-6 (ebook)

25   24   23   22   21   1   2   3   4   5

This book is also available as an eBook.

Libraries Unlimited
An Imprint of ABC-CLIO, LLC

ABC-CLIO, LLC
147 Castilian Drive
Santa Barbara, California 93117
www.abc-clio.com

This book is printed on acid-free paper ∞

Manufactured in the United States of America

Contents

Introduction

The collection is at the core: it's at the center of everything we do as information professionals, and its development is the unique role that school librarians play within the learning community. Collection development is a responsibility that entails curating resources that must reflect larger trends in society such the explosion of digital content and the inclusion of content creation as well as content consumption in the learning process. No longer simply repositories for books and other print and audiovisual materials, school libraries have both a physical and a virtual face that allows students, teachers, and parents to access digital and physical information from home, school, and myriad other sites. The school library can be as ubiquitous as personal information devices we use if the collection is current, relevant, and flexible.

While many principles and techniques for collection development are applicable to most school library settings, the unique characteristics of each school and its library program generate new and changing demands that require translation and adaptation to a local context. To help professionals face these dual challenges, this text will help preparing and/or practicing school librarians to:

- become aware of and describe the learning environment in which the school library collection exists;
- learn principles, techniques, and common practices of collection development and management;
- be conversant issues that affect all collections, but that must be resolved in accordance with the goals and needs of a particular collection;
- develop best practices and strategies for handling collection management situations and demands; and
- identify helpful resources, including suggested readings, websites, and selection aids.

This introductory textbook provides an overview of the processes and procedures associated with developing, maintaining, and evaluating (i.e., curating) a collection of curriculum and personal learning resources at the school level. Throughout this book, I link collection development to leadership; as the only educators whose primary responsibility is to build and maintain the school's resource base, the school librarian is inherently the collection *leader* who develops and orchestrates all steps of the process in a systematic, cyclical pattern guided by clearly articulated and transparent policies and procedures that reflect a range of issues including accessibility and diversity, intellectual freedom, copyright and fair-use, and acceptable use of Internet materials.

Chapter 1 focuses on definitions and characteristics of the collection and provides a brief overview of collection development activities, while Chapter 2 explores the impact of the curriculum on the collection and Chapters 3–12 discuss specific collection development activities in more detail, focusing on policies and procedures that need to be addressed for each activity. Chapter 13 deals with issues and ethics related to the development and management of school library collections. Chapter 14 looks at how building and promoting the collection are central to a school librarian's leadership role. Fiscal issues that relate to the collection, such as licensing, raising funds, and writing grants, are discussed in Chapter 15. Chapter 16 emphasizes the relationship of the collection to school library facilities and the learning environment. Information related to creating, moving, and closing collections and responding to disaster scenarios is included in Chapter 17.

The Appendix is an annotated bibliography of resources that can be used for various collection development activities. Items listed in the Additional Readings at the end of each chapter are usually not also included in the Appendix; refer to the listings in Additional Readings and Helpful Multimedia at the end of each chapter to obtain other valuable information on the topics covered in the chapters. Care was taken to provide a variety of articles in the Additional Readings, including primarily short practical information, but also (when available) a few articles that discuss research studies relating to the chapter topics. Articles and websites from other English-speaking countries (especially Canada) are sometimes included, and articles from other types of libraries, such as academic or public libraries, are listed when the information in them also applies to school library settings.

NEW AND UPDATED FEATURES

Since the last revision of this textbook (Mardis, 2016), K–12 education in the United States has continued to experience fundamental shifts. The common standards movement has continued to gain ground and is now the basis for learning standards in 41 states and the District of Columbia that have formally adopted the Common Core State Standards (CCSS) (Achieve, 2020). In 2020, 44 states (representing 71 percent of U.S. students) have education standards influenced by the *Framework for K–12 Science Education* and/or the *Next Generation Science Standards* (NSTA, 2020). The NGSS has recently been expanded to include a framework for engineering. In Chapter 14, I explore these movements and how their conceptual shift will affect collection development and management.

Perhaps the most dramatic impact on school libraries over the last few years has been the global COVID-19 pandemic. Suddenly, school librarians and educators had to pivot to virtual learning on a mass scale and help their learners and communities improvise high-quality learning in an unknown environment. School librarians stepped up and exhibited leadership in big and small ways, delivering support, resources, and distributed versions of their collections and services; instead of allowing the crisis to overtake them and mute their essential role, school librarians used their collections to further a conversation about accessible education. Chapter 17 and Chapter 18 will include a discussion of school libraries and their collections in crisis situations, including public health and natural disasters.

Long-time users of this textbook have built dynamic, exciting courses around its structure, so in this edition, I have strived to preserve chapter and content order with additions and revisions. Chapter 15, "Equity, Diversity, and Inclusion and the Collection"; Chapter 17, "Learning Environment"; and Chapter 18, "Opening, Reclassifying, Moving, or Closing the Collection" are substantial revisions to this seventh edition of *The Collection Program in Schools*. Additionally, the discussion of new technologies, digital resources, and tools has been integrated into the other chapters. Many new resources have been added to the text of chapters, particularly in Chapter 14, "The Curriculum." The impact of the CCSS and NGSS on the curriculum and collections in school libraries is also included in Chapter 14. Because long-time users of this book recognize that it is a class text that students might keep as a professional reference throughout their career, I have curated a selection of anecdotes, scenarios, lessons learned, and best practices from state school librarian email lists and the LM_NET (n.d.) e-mail list archives. LM_NET represents one of the most established and widely engaged school librarian communities; the LM_NET archives represent decades of the profession's captured wisdom.

References to the information in the American Association of School Librarians' (AASL) *National School Library Standards for Learners, School Librarians, and School Librarians* (2018) are made in many of the book chapters. Where possible and relevant, chapters also include references to the complementary Future Ready School Libraries movement, as well as National Board Certification standards. Additional recent documents, such as the American Library Association's position statements and handbooks are also discussed in the book. Suggested readings and websites at the end of chapters have been updated with more recent sources. However, this does not indicate that many of the outstanding articles and books from older editions of the book should not be used. In this seventh edition of the book, I have included updated titles and multimedia from the global school library community. My heartiest thanks to Casey Brant for her help with these updates.

Many figures and tables in the book have been revised, and some new ones have been added. The Appendix has been revised to include only items in print and published within the last decade, with many new titles added.

The opportunity to take on the responsibility for a text that is used in many courses for preservice school librarians as well as by practitioners throughout the United States and in other countries is bittersweet. Prior to her passing in January 2013, Dr. Kay Bishop had arranged for me to take on the sixth edition and I honor her legacy by maintaining and updating this work. I always welcome feedback from university faculty and from practicing school librarians. My sincere desire is that this text will continue to serve as a useful primary source for all readers who are interested in the exciting, dynamic practice of collection development in school libraries.

REFERENCES

Achieve. (2020). Standards in your state. Retrieved from http://www.corestandards.org/standards
-in-your-state/

American Association of School Librarians. (2018). *National school library standards for learners, school librarians, and school libraries.* Chicago, IL: American Library Association.

LM_NET Home. (n.d.). Retrieved from http://lmnet.wordpress.com/

Mardis, M. A. (2016). *The collection program in schools: Concepts and practices.* 6th edition. Santa Barbara, CA: Libraries Unlimited.

National Science Teachers Association (NSTA). 2020. K–12 Science Standards Adoption. Retrieved from https://ngss.nsta.org/About.aspx

CHAPTER 1

The Collection

Key Learnings
- The definition of "collection" has expanded over time.
- The collection includes materials the school librarian identifies, organizes, and promotes.
- The collection is influenced by many levels of policy and practice.

What constitutes a school library collection? Before the 1990s, it would have been fairly easy to answer this question: a collection describes the resources (mainly print, but also some audiovisual items) that are housed in a single room of a school, the library. *Tangibility* (the physical presence of an item) and library *ownership* were two basic concepts of a traditional school library collection.

Today, however, it is much more difficult to define a school library collection. Does it include the online databases to which a school library subscribes? Are websites that a school librarian *marks* or *collects* for learner use considered to be in the library's collection? If a school librarian provides links to digital resources, are these resources part of the school library collection? If a librarian can access titles on a union catalog (a catalog combining the bibliographic records of more than one library) and obtain those titles for learners through interlibrary loan, are they considered part of the school library collection? And if a learner can access thousands of websites while seated at a computer in a school library, are all those sites included in a library collection? Advances in information technology have significantly changed and expanded the concept of the school library collection. The collection now undoubtedly goes beyond the walls of a single room in a school.

In 1931, S. R. Ranganathan proposed the five laws of library science, detailing the principles that should guide all library collections. These laws are:

1. Books are for use.
2. Every reader, his [or her] book.
3. Every book, its reader.
4. Save the time of the reader.
5. The library is a growing organism.

These laws emphasize the library is a space in which resources and users are brought together for learning and enrichment purposes. Connaway and Faniel (2014, p. 5) noted that the laws "are still an enormously helpful way to link the values of librarianship with concrete programs and activities . . . In an increasingly abundant information environment, the laws of nature may not have changed, even though nature itself has."

Although the laws seem to focus only on print materials, they do apply to the richness of today's school library collection. For the purposes of this book, a school library collection is defined as a group of information sources (print, nonprint, and digital) selected, organized, and managed by the school librarian for a defined user community (learners, faculty, and sometimes parents and community members). This definition excludes the thousands of websites learners locate while conducting searches on school library computers, but does include online databases to which a school subscribes; lists of websites that are selected and managed (i.e., curated) by a school librarian; materials in digital libraries that can be accessed by the librarian and users; and items provided in a union catalog through interlibrary loan. In respect to Connaway and Faniel's illustration of Ranganathan's five laws: Original vs. new conceptions (2014, p. 3), Figure 1.1 reflects a reconception of Ranganathan's five laws of library science (1931) from a school library perspective.

As the figure suggests, school librarians' collection tasks encompass a wide range of media and applications. If we ascribe to this definition, which includes viewing school librarians as both collection builders and managers, the concept of collection development policies becomes all-important since one needs guidelines to develop and manage a collection. Information about writing and implementing collection development policies and procedures for school libraries constitutes a major portion of this book. Several chapters provide tools to assist school librarians in writing and implementing effective collection development policies.

Ranganathan Law	Original Conception	New Conceptions in the Current Environment		
First Law	Books are for use.	E-books are for reading.	Digital video is for watching.	Online courses are for learning.
Second Law	Every person his or her book.	Every listener her media player.	Every artist his graphics editor.	Every student her citation tool.
Third Law	Every book its reader.	Every blog its reader.	Every data set, its analyzer.	Every online database its researcher.
Fourth Law	Save the time of the reader.	Save the time of the listener.	Save the time of the creator.	Save the time of the researcher.
Fifth Law	A library is a growing organism.			

Figure 1.1. Reconceptualization of Ranganathan's Five Laws of Library Science for School Libraries

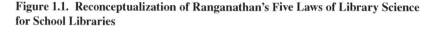

PHYSICAL ENTITY AND ACCESSIBILITY

The collection housed in the school library is a physical entity composed of individual items that collectively create a whole. In collection development and management, the value of a single item must be viewed in relation to other items in the collection. When deciding whether to add or withdraw a specific item from the physical collection, school librarians should consider the following questions:

- Is the same information already in the collection, but in a different format?
- Will an alternative format make the information accessible to more people?
- Is the same or a similar item quickly accessible through a resource-sharing network or the Internet?
- Does this item uniquely fill a particular user's need?

Questions like these help identify the relationship of one item to another in the collection and are explored in greater depth in later chapters of this book.

With access to information through resource sharing and digital means, school librarians have moved from ownership to accessibility, or "from having things" to "looking things up." The immediate physical collection provides a starting point for learners as they begin to search for information. Through online catalogs, learners can learn about information resources in other libraries or information collections. Although answers to learners' questions were traditionally found in the collection housed in the school library, the answers today may or may not be located with its physical space. The collection goes beyond the walls of the immediate school library to a far-reaching world of resources and information. The collection as a physical entity provides an initial point for coordinated collection development practices and resource sharing with other school libraries and institutions.

Many barriers can limit access to information: physical, intellectual, and cultural barriers and a lack of policies and practices that demonstrate a commitment to intellectual freedom. Examples of potential physical barriers are height of shelving, width of aisles, and lack of necessary equipment for using or accessing materials. Intellectual barriers may involve circulation policies that do not allow challenged readers to take extra time with materials. Cultural barriers may be reflected in a fiction collection that that does not reflect equity, diversity, and inclusion among its subject matter.

A key principle for information access and delivery is centered intellectual freedom. This commitment is not new; it is part of school librarianship's history. The position is significant today as we help learners become critical thinkers and competent problem solvers who can contribute in a democracy. This topic is explored throughout this book, but in depth in Chapter 15.

THE SCHOOL LIBRARY PROGRAM AND THE COLLECTION

In the *National School Library Standards for Learners, School Librarians, and School Libraries,* the American Association of School Librarians (AASL) (2018) emphasized that the school librarian guides learners to "make meaning for oneself and others by collecting, organizing, and sharing resources of personal relevance" (AASL, 2018, p. 96). These activities are linked to the shared foundation, that is, the cornerstone set of beliefs, of "curate." Learners, school libraries, and school libraries manifest curation in four cognitive domains of think, create, share, and grow, as Table 1.1 illustrates.

TABLE 1.1. CURATE FRAMEWORK FROM NATIONAL SCHOOL LIBRARY STANDARDS (AASL, 2018)

Learner Domains and Competencies	School Librarian Domains and Competencies
A. Think: Learners act on an information need by: 1. Determining the need to gather information. 2. Identifying possible sources of information. 3. Making critical choices about information sources to use.	**A. Think:** School librarians challenge learners to act on an information need by: 1. Modeling the response to a need to gather and organize information. 2. Designing opportunities for learners to explore possible information sources. 3. Guiding learners to make critical choices about information sources to use.
B. Create: Learners gather information appropriate to the task by: 1. Seeking a variety of sources. 2. Collecting information representing diverse perspectives. 3. Systematically questioning and assessing the validity and accuracy of information. 4. Organizing information by priority, topic, or other systematic scheme.	**B. Create:** School librarians promote information gathering appropriate to the task by: 1. Sharing a variety of sources. 2. Encouraging the use of information representing diverse perspectives. 3. Fostering the questioning and assessing of validity and accuracy of information. 4. Providing tools and strategies to organize information by priority, topic, or other systematic scheme.
C. Share: Learners exchange information resources within and beyond their learning community by: 1. Accessing and evaluating collaboratively constructed information sites. 2. Contributing to collaboratively constructed information sites by ethically using and reproducing others' work. 3. Joining with others to compare and contrast information derived from collaboratively constructed information sites.	**C. Share:** School librarians contribute to and guide information resource exchange within and beyond the school learning community by: 1. Facilitating opportunities to access and evaluate collaboratively constructed information sites. 2. Devising pathways for learners to contribute to collaboratively constructed information sites by ethically using and reproducing others' work. 3. Directing learners to join others to compare and contrast information derived from collaboratively constructed information sites.
D. Grow: Learners select and organize information for a variety of audiences by: 1. Performing ongoing analysis of and reflection on the quality, usefulness, and accuracy of curated resources. 2. Integrating and depicting in a conceptual knowledge network their understanding gained from resources. 3. Openly communicating curation processes for others to use, interpret, and validate.	**D. Grow:** School librarians show learners how to select and organize information for a variety of audiences by: 1. Engaging learners in ongoing analysis of and reflection on the quality, usefulness, and accuracy of curated resources. 2. Formulating tasks that help learners to integrate and depict in a conceptual knowledge network learners' understanding gained from resources. 3. Making opportunities for learners to openly communicate curation processes for others to use, interpret, and validate.

(Continued)

TABLE 1.1. CONTINUED

School Library Domains and Alignments

The school library facilitates the key commitment to and competencies of **Curate** by:

A. **Think:** The school library provides problem-based learning experiences and environments by:
1. Using resources and technology to foster inquiry and scaffold mastery of skills necessary for learning to progress.
2. Adopting a dynamic collection-development plan to ensure that adequate resources reflect current and in-depth knowledge.
3. Focusing on the effective use of a wide range of resources to foster information skills appropriate to content areas.

B. **Create:** The school library promotes selection of appropriate resources and tools for information use by:
1. Demonstrating and documenting how resources and technology are used to address information needs.
2. Providing opportunities for all members of the school community to develop information and technology skills needed to promote the transfer of information-related problem-solving strategies across all disciplines.
3. Employing a dynamic collection policy that includes selection and retention criteria for all materials within the collection.
4. Implementing an administratively approved and endorsed policy that clearly addresses procedures for handling material challenges.
5. Designing and providing adequate, appropriate space for library resources, services, and activities.

C. **Share:** The school library facilitates the contribution and exchange of information within and among learning communities by:
1. Providing an environment in which resources that support the school's curriculum and learning goals can be collaboratively selected and developed.
2. Including and tracking collection materials in a system that uses standardized approaches to description and location.
3. Establishing policies that promote effective acquisition, description, circulation, sharing, and access to resources within and beyond the school day.
4. Maintaining procedures that ensure user confidentiality and promote unimpeded access to materials by staff members and learners.

D. **Grow:** The school library engages the learning community in exploring resources by:
1. Describing, organizing, and promoting the collection for maximum and effective uses for multiple learning applications.
2. Maintaining a collection of sufficient breadth and currency to be pertinent to the school's program of studies.
3. Supporting access through a schedule that allows use by learners and staff at time of need.
4. Using local and external data to inform ongoing adjustments to the scope of the resource collection, and its audiences, formats, and applications.

As Table 1.1 suggests, the school librarian has an important role in ensuring that the school library is integrated into the overall learning environment and in providing access to information both inside and outside the school. To meet the school's information and media needs effectively, the school librarian needs to:

- be a vital part of the total school program;
- respond to the curricular needs and interests of educators, administrators, and other staff members;
- include the multicultural diversity of the learner population, the developmental levels and learning styles of learners, and the needs of learners with disabilities;
- guide the use of and access to a full range of resources—print, nonprint, and digital;
- cooperate with other institutions to provide the widest possible access to information, which may involve interlibrary loan, coordinated collection development, and other forms of resource sharing;
- exemplify the total media concept, providing access to materials in a variety of formats, appropriate equipment, trained personnel, and resources housed inside and outside the school library; and
- manage a staff that adequately plans and carries out the selection, maintenance, and evaluation of resources.

The school librarian is the primary person in the school community responsible for ensuring that these conditions exist and these functions take place.

Effective school librarians support the school's philosophy, goals, and objectives by collaborating with educators and administrators to ensure that the library program is an integral part of the school program, manage the library program's operations, select materials and other resources (including digital formats), and instruct learners and educators. A school librarian who understands the value of the school library to learning advocates by offering informational, instructional, consultative, and production services; evaluating the services and collection; and promoting the program through public relations activities. All educators share responsibility for the school library; a school librarian cannot run a dynamic, integrated program alone. The school librarian exercises leadership involve others in the program, by partnering with classroom educators in curricular planning, and, by this example, encouraging educators to collaborate with the librarian in planning and evaluating the library program. A school librarian may find it difficult to involve administrators, educators, and learners in planning, implementing, and evaluating the library media program or collection. However, collection-related activities provide a range of opportunities for involvement. The school librarian can increase participation in collection development by

- identifying the characteristics of the school library users and the demands of the curriculum;
- taking documented steps to involve administrators, educators, and learners in the development of school library policies;
- inviting learners and educators to participate in the selection of materials and online resources for the collection;
- facilitating interagency borrowing and lending of materials; and
- involving educators, learners, and administrators in the evaluation of the materials and policies.

The school librarian makes many decisions about the collection: what to add, what to access online or through resource sharing, and what to remove. While others can help with these decisions, it is the school librarian who must develop an overview of the total program, take responsibility for the decisions, and manage a responsive collection while involving others in the planning and evaluation process.

ROLES OF THE SCHOOL LIBRARIAN AND THE COLLECTION

The American Association of School Librarians developed and published professional standards in 1960, 1969, 1975, 1988, 1998, and 2009, often in collaboration with other organizations (Roscello, 2004). The most recent iteration of the professional standards, *National School Library Standards for Learners, School Librarians, and School Libraries* (AASL, 2018), affirmed the following key roles of the school librarian as they relate to the total learning program:

- Leader: The school librarian is "a teacher and a learner who listens to and acts upon good ideas from peers, educators, and learners. Leadership also requires increased professional commitment and thorough knowledge of the challenges and opportunities facing the profession. By becoming an active member of the local and global learning community, the school librarian can build relationships with organizations and stakeholders to develop an effective school library program and advocate for student learning" (AASL, 2018, p. 14).
- Instructional Partner: "The school librarian collaborates with classroom teachers to develop assignments that are matched to academic standards and include key critical-thinking skills, technology and information literacy skills, and core social skills and cultural competencies. The school librarian guides instructional design by working with the classroom teacher to establish learning objectives and goals, and by implementing assessment strategies before, during, and after assigned units of study . . . [C]ommunication with classroom teachers and learners now takes place virtually, as well as face-to-face" (AASL, 2018, p. 14).
- Information Specialist: "As an information specialist, the school librarian uses technology tools to supplement school resources, assist in the creation of engaging learning tasks, connect the school with the global learning community, communicate with students and classroom teachers at any time, and provide [continuous] access to library services. The school librarian introduces and models emerging technologies, as well as strategies for finding, assessing, and using information. He or she is a leader in software and hardware evaluation, establishing the processes for such evaluation to take place . . . [The] school librarian must be versed in the theoretical grounding and practical application of [copyright and fair use] laws in order to teach the ethical use of information to the learning community" (AASL, 2018, p. 14).
- Teacher: "As teacher the school librarian empowers learners to become critical thinkers, enthusiastic readers, skillful researchers, and ethical users of information. The school librarian supports students' success by guiding them to read for understanding, breadth, and pleasure; use information for defined and self-defined purposes; build on prior knowledge and construct new knowledge; embrace the world of information and all its formats; work with each other in successful collaborations for learning; constructively assess their own work and the work of their peers; [and] become their own best critics (AASL, 2018, pp. 14–15).
- Program Administrator: "As program administrator, the school librarian ensures that all members of the learning community have access to resources that meet a variety of needs and interests. The implementation of a successful school library program requires the collaborative development of the program mission, strategic plan, and policies, as well as the effective management of staff, the program budget, and the

physical and virtual spaces. To augment information resources available to the learning community, the school librarian works actively to form partnerships with stakeholders and sister organizations at local and global levels. The school librarian also addresses broader educational issues with other teachers in the building, at the district level, and at the professional association level" (AASL, 2018, p. 15).

These five roles are essential to a dynamic, relevant school library. Leadership is the central important factor that contributes to a successful school library media program. Increased professional commitment and active participation in local, state, and national organizations not only strengthen the skills of the school librarian, but also help advance the profession (AASL, 2009). Effective school librarians take the lead in embracing model innovations in learning.

The collection is also the central element of the school library's purpose and function. The collection is a constant in the school environment that supports teaching and learning through indirect and direct roles and activities of the school librarian. The roles operate in a cyclical and interconnected pattern as shown in Figure 1.2.

As Figure 1.2 illustrates, the school librarian's direct roles involve interaction with library users and include teaching and acting as an instructional partner for learners, educators, staff, parents, and community members. In the educator's role, librarians impart skills for helping learners locate, assess, use, and communicate information in all formats. School librarians also teach the school's community how to use the collection to meet their instructional and learning needs. As an instructional partner, school librarians

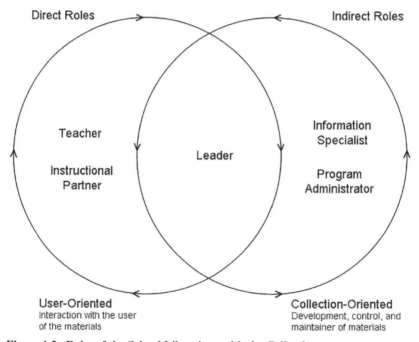

Figure 1.2. Roles of the School Librarians with the Collection

engage educators with resources and expertise that allow the collection to be maximized in teaching and learning processes. The school librarian's indirect roles provide the means for carrying out the direct roles. In these roles, the school librarian serves as an information specialist and a program administrator of the school library program, including developer and evaluator of a responsive, current, and appropriate collection. These direct roles and indirect roles are interdependent, but at the center of them is bold leadership that engages and supports the school community with cutting-edge tools, materials, and implementation.

The leader role brings the roles together in dynamic professional practice through following and communicating trends, proactively seeking materials and skills, communicating the purpose and impact of the library collection, and building relationships that leverage and support the best use of exciting and appropriate resources for teaching and learning. In any particular setting, the collection must support the school librarian's roles as teacher, instructional partner, information specialist, and leader advocate for the effective use of information and information technology. Today's school librarian uses collection development as a leadership opportunity, not a clerical task.

EXTERNAL RELATIONSHIPS THAT INFLUENCE THE COLLECTION IN SCHOOLS

District Level

Many building-level library programs (those designed to meet the needs of a single school) are units of a school district library program. The district's goals and objectives apply to the building-level library program, and the district-level library program personnel provide a wide range of resources and services to the building-level library program. The district may provide centralized purchasing and processing of materials. The online public access catalog or union catalog may include bibliographic and location information about items owned by the district and housed in school libraries throughout the system.

Collections housed in the school district library often include items that supplement materials owned by individual schools. District collections may contain materials that are expensive or heavily used at limited intervals, museum items with curricular value, and backup equipment. They also may include streaming video libraries, professional collections, and materials examination collections. District-level collections are available to all school personnel within the district. Some districts also provide the transportation of items in their collections to individual schools.

Many school district libraries are overseen by a school library supervisor. In service to the district through collection-related and other activities, this school librarian enacts a professional developer/educator role as well as the roles of leader, administrator, communicator, and facilitator, ensuring that the district's library services are meeting teaching and learning needs on an overall coordinated basis. School district librarians also interface with the local community as well as cognizant regional, state, and national organizations (AASL, 2012).

Regional Level

The school library program and the school librarian have formal and informal relationships with groups and agencies within the county and regions of the state. County-level and regional-level professional associations provide programs and contacts useful to the school librarian. Some states, such as New York, with its several separate boards of cooperative education services (BOCES), or Michigan, with its regional educational media centers (REMC), provide shared educational programs and services to school districts. School library systems function within these regional entities, providing access to information and library resources and conducting professional development activities.

State Level

In the United States, education is the responsibility of each state, guided by national requirements. Each state has its own philosophy, goals, standards, and objectives for its educational programs. These responsibilities are assigned to the state education agency. The agency staff may serve as consultants and information disseminators, and their products and services may include printed publications; e-mail lists, websites, or other electronic services; statewide online catalogs for the holdings of all the schools in the state; and the maintenance of instructional and library materials examination centers. For school librarians working without the benefit of a district-level library program, the state school library consultant is a key contact. In addition to consultants, state educational agencies may offer recommendations and standards for the library program and collection, as well as other useful guidelines for school librarians.

Other state agencies are information resources. They provide information about all aspects of the state, sponsor websites, or offer lists of resources available from the state.

National Level

In the United States, school library programs, just like other areas of schools, are influenced greatly by national issues and legislation. For instance, society's concerns about people with physical disabilities spawned several pieces of federal legislation that affect library programs and collections. In 1990, the Americans with Disabilities Act (ADA) mandated that public services and facilities be accessible to people with disabilities. This act has had additional amendments during the past few years. It is important for school librarians to be knowledgeable about ADA and to assess whether their libraries fulfill the mandates of ADA.

Other pieces of legislation that directly affect the operation of a school library include the Copyright Act of 1976 and the amendments to the act made by the Copyright, Clarification, and Corrections Act of 2010; the Digital Millennium Copyright Act passed by the U.S. Congress in 1998; and the Teach Act passed in 2002. Designed to balance the interests of authors and artists with the user's ability to access information, these laws guide librarians in carrying out their responsibilities.

The U.S. Congress also passes legislation that affects K–12 education and consequently impacts school library programs and collections. In 2016, the Every Student Succeeds Act (ESSA) replaced prior legislation entitled "No Child Left Behind" (NCLB). Like NCLB, ESSA is a reauthorization of the Elementary and Secondary Education Act (ESEA); unlike NCLB, ESSA includes the phrase "effective school library programs." Although school libraries and school librarians are eligible for ESSA funding (for resources and professional development, for example), the legislation does not mandate support for school libraries. School librarians can access support through ESSA implementation plans at the state, district, and local level (Norton, 2016).

Some grant programs are also part of the current ESEA legislation. Programs that especially affect school libraries include Innovative Approaches to Literacy (IAL), a U.S. Department of Education grant program that supports high-quality programs designed to develop and improve literacy skills for children and learners from birth through 12th grade in high-need local educational agencies and schools. IAL aims to support innovative programs that promote early literacy for young children, motivate older children to read, and increase learner achievement by using school libraries as partners to improve literacy, distributing free books to children and their families, and offering high-quality literacy activities. It does allow for the limited support of school librarians (U.S. Department of Education, 2014): Preschool Development Grants support states to (1) build or enhance a preschool program infrastructure that would enable the delivery of high-quality preschool services to children, and (2) expand high-quality preschool programs in targeted communities that would serve as models for expanding preschool to all four-year-olds from low- and moderate-income families (U.S. Department of Education, 2015); and Reading First Title I, through which states and districts receive support to apply scientifically based reading research—and the proven instructional and assessment tools consistent with this research—to ensure that all children learn to read well by the end of third grade (U.S. Department of Education, 2010).

The U.S. Congress signed the Libraries and Services Technology Act (LSTA) in 1996. Originally known as the Library Services Act, the LSTA program has been in existence in various forms since 1956. Funds are available to school libraries, public libraries, academic libraries, qualified private/research libraries, special libraries, library consortia, and libraries in correctional institutions to improve patron services. LSTA emphasizes improving library services to the underserved, especially to children living in poverty (American Library Association, 2014). The Institute of Museum and Library Services, a federal agency, administers LSTA.

National professional associations also provide guidance and information to school librarians. Two professional associations directly involved with school library programs are the AASL, a division of the American Library Association, and the Association for

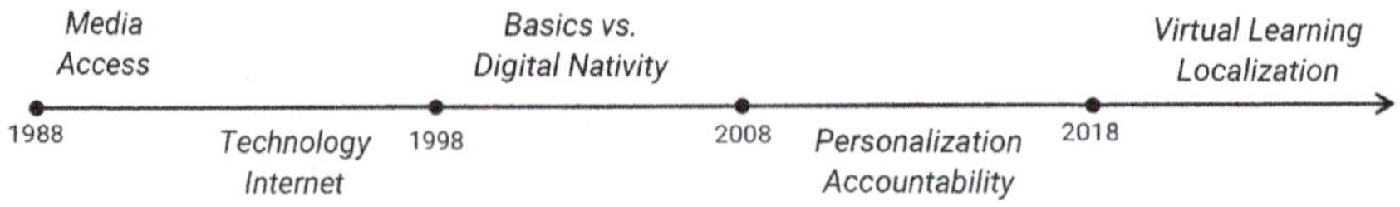

Figure 1.3. Interplay Between Recent National Education Themes

Educational Communications and Technology School Media and Technology Committee. The joint efforts of these two associations led to the publication of two past national standards for school librarians: *Information Power: Guidelines for School Libraries* and *Information Power: Building Partnerships for Learning* (American Association of School Librarians & Association for Educational Communications and Technology, 1988, 1998).

The interplay between national education themes is reflected in AASL's standards, as Figure 1.3 depicts.

When *Information Power: Guidelines for School Libraries* (also known as *Information Power I*) was introduced in 1988, a time marked by a need to increase access to instructional resources and create spaces in which interdisciplinary connections could be made; during this time, the name "school library media center" was forged. *Information Power I* was focused on the library facility and a collection that was large enough to serve a diverse learning community. Then, in 1998, the advent of widespread Internet availability led to *Information Power: Building Partnerships for Learning* (also known as *Information Power II)*, which positioned the school library as a place to access digital and physical information and the school librarian as a tech-savvy information specialist. This tech-forward approach was in tension with previous emphasis on testing, accountability, and basic skills, thus, *Empowering Learners* (2009) reflected the integration of digital and physical information resources and multimedia literacy as a means for achieving documentable learner outcomes. In 2017, AASL completed the next revision of its learner learning and professional standards, by identifying six Shared Foundations, or "core values that learners, school librarians, and school libraries should reflect and promote" (AASL, 2018, p. 16) in the *National School Library Standards for Learners, School Librarians, and School Libraries.* As mentioned in an earlier section of this chapter, the Shared Foundations are Inquire, Include, Collaborate, Curate, Explore, and Engage. While Engage is the Shared Foundation most obviously linked to collection development, acquiring, organizing, and promoting high-quality learning materials cross-cuts every Shared Foundation.

Global Level

Educators and learners can search the Internet for information and learning resources from across the globe. School librarians can also use the Internet to build an international professional community. LM_NET, a library community with a large and established e-mail list of over 10,000 members, is dedicated to school librarians worldwide and to people involved with the school library field. School librarians can join this group and discuss various topics that focus on topics of interest to the school library community; many of the discussions are archived online (LM_NET, n.d.).

The International Association of School Librarianship shares information about school library programs and materials for children and youth throughout the international community. Its website includes information and documents that are helpful to school librarians (International Association of School Librarianship, 2021). The Schools Section of the International Federation of Library Associations (IFLA) provides guidelines, standards, networking opportunities, and research from and to school libraries and librarians in established and emerging school librarianship cultures.

CONCLUSION

Access to a range of high-quality learning resources has a significant impact on learner outcomes (Chingos & Whitehurst, 2012; Maull, Saldivar, & Sumner, 2010). From this perspective, an expertly built and managed school library collection is an essential component of an exemplary learning environment. The concept of the school library collection has changed dramatically in recent years. Accessibility, rather than just ownership, now constitutes the school library collection. Not only is there a physical collection owned by the school library, but the school library collection also includes materials that are available on databases, resources that are accessible through resource sharing, and items found online that are selected by school librarians for learner use. By being a leader and serving in the roles of educator, instructional partner, information specialist, and program administrator, the school librarian can align the school library collection with the needs of its users and with the school's mission and curriculum.

DISCUSSION QUESTIONS

1. What do you identify as major educational trends that will influence the library collection? How should these trends be reflected in professional standards?
2. How do you define "leadership"? How does this definition apply to the school librarian's role in collection development?
3. Choose a school librarian role (educator, instructional partner, information specialist, program administrator, leader) at which you feel you would excel? Why do you feel you would excel in this role? How do you feel this role influences the collection?

REFERENCES

American Association of School Librarians. (2009). *Empowering learners: Guidelines for school library media programs*. Chicago, IL: American Library Association.
American Association of School Librarians. (2012). Position statement on the school library supervisor. Retrieved from http://www.ala.org/aasl/advocacy/resources/statements/supervisor
American Association of School Librarians. (2018). *National school library standards for learners, school librarians, and school libraries*. Chicago, IL: American Library Association.
American Association of School Librarians & Association for Educational Communications and Technology. (1988). *Information power: Guidelines for school library media programs*. Chicago, IL: American Library Association.
American Association of School Librarians & Association for Educational Communications and Technology. (1998). *Information power: Building partnerships for learning*. Chicago, IL: American Library Association.

American Library Association. (2014). Library Services and Technology Act (LSTA). Retrieved from http://www.ala.org/advocacy/advleg/federallegislation/lsta

Chingos, M. M., & Whitehurst, G. J. (2012, April). Choosing blindly: Instructional materials, educator effectiveness, and the common core. Retrieved from http://www.brookings.edu/~/media/research/files/reports/2012/4/10-curriculum-chingos-whitehurst/0410_curriculum_chingos_whitehurst.pdf

Connaway, L. S., & Faniel, I. M. (2014). *Reordering Ranganathan: Shifting user behaviors, shifting priorities.* Dublin, OH: OCLC Research. International Association of School Librarianship. http://www.iasl-online.org/

International Association of School Librarianship. (2021). Retrieved from https://www.iasl-online.org/

LM_NET *Home* (n.d.). Retrieved from http://lmnet.wordpress.com/

Maull, K. E., Saldivar, M. G., & Sumner, T. (2010). Observing the online behavior of educators: From internet usage to personalization for pedagogical practice. Paper presented at the Association for Computing Machinery Conference on Human Factors in Computing Systems, Atlanta, GA. Retrieved from http://communication.ucsd.edu/barry/chiws10/maull_position paper_chi2010ws.pdf

Norton, S. (2016, November 1). ESSA and school libraries: ALA/AASL sessions train librarians on the fundamentals. *American Libraries.* Retrieved from https://americanlibrariesmagazine.org/2016/11/01/essa-school-libraries-training/

Ranganathan, S. R. (1931). *The five laws of library science.* London, England: E. Goldston.

Roscello, F. (2004). President's column. *Knowledge Quest, 32*(4), 6–8.

U.S. Department of Education. (2010). NCLB. Retrieved from http://www2.cd.gov/policy/elsec/leg/esea02/index.html

U.S. Department of Education. (2014). Innovative approached to literacy. Retrieved from http://www2.ed.gov/programs/innovapproaches-literacy/index.html

U.S. Department of Education. (2015). *Preschool development grants.* Retrieved from http://www2.ed.gov/programs/preschooldevelopmentgrants/index.html

ADDITIONAL READINGS

Bush, G. (2006). The changing role of the school librarian. *Principal, 85*(4), 56–58.

Dickinson, G. K. (2015). Change and the school librarian: An experience in evolution. *Knowledge Quest, 43*(4), 22–27.

Hamilton, B. J. (2011). The school librarian as educator: What kind of educator are you? *Knowledge Quest, 39*(5), 34–40.

Hand, D. (2011). The school librarian as instructional partner: Up with educators to guide learner learning. *Knowledge Quest, 39*(5), 22–26.

Harris, H. J. (2011). The school librarian as information specialist: A vibrant species. *Knowledge Quest, 39*(5), 28–32.

Kimmel, S. C. (2014). *Developing collections to empower learners.* Chicago, IL: American Library Association.

Lamb, A. (2015). A century of change: The evolution of school library resources, 1915–2015. *Knowledge Quest, 43*(4), 62–70.

Martin, A. M. (2013). *Empowering leadership developing behaviors for success.* Chicago, IL: American Association of School Librarians.

Purcell, M. (2010). All librarians do is check out books, right? A look at the roles of a school library media specialist. *Library Media Connection, 29*(3), 30–33.

Steadman, W. S. (2011). The school librarian as leader: Out of the middle, into the foreground. *Knowledge Quest, 39*(5), 18–21.

Yates, S. D. (2011). The school librarian as program administrator: Just-in-time librarianship. *Knowledge Quest, 39*(5), 42–44.

HELPFUL MULTIMEDIA

ABC-CLIOLive. (2010). Mike Eisenberg vodcast #4—The role of the educator-librarian and the school library program. Retrieved from https://www.youtube.com/watch?v=nE2MpvByblc

Capstone Publishers. (2014). School libraries matter: The changing role of the school librarian. Retrieved from https://www.youtube.com/watch?v=6eilZJp3_h8

Hamilton, B. (2010). It's broken; let's fix it: The traditional model of school librarianship. Retrieved from https://theunquietlibrarian.wordpress.com/2010/04/27/its-broken-lets-fix-it-the-traditional -model-of-school-librarianship/

O'Connell, J. (2009). 21c school libraries leading learning. Retrieved from http://www.slideshare .net/heyjudeonline/21c-school-libraries-leading-learning

Oberg, Diane. (n.d.). Changing school culture: The role of the 21st century educator-librarian. Retrieved from http://tmcanada.pbworks.com/f/TM+Canadasz+org+culture+and+chg+Apr +2010.pdf

CHAPTER 2

Collection Development

Key Learnings
- Collection development is composed of many activities that interact with one another.
- School librarians should be prepared to make alterations to policies and procedures in order to meet changing needs.
- A range of external factors can also impact collection development.

Collection development comprises numerous activities that are dependent upon one another. As we saw in the previous chapter, often, collection content and development activities are driven by a variety of influences that may lead a school librarian to adopt either a collection-oriented or a user-centered perspective on building, maintaining, and promoting the collection (Pattee, 2014). The collection-oriented perspective centers on the nature and extent of the materials within the collection. Collection decisions are driven by factors such as the age and subject coverage of its content and informed by published lists of materials. In contrast, the user-centered perspective involves a focus on the creation of a collection for a specific purpose, such as supporting curriculum standards or increasing independent reading. Library mission statements often reflect one orientation or the other, but in practice, school librarians likely use a blend of both approaches in the activities they perform to maintain and develop an effective library collection by:

- Becoming knowledgeable about an existing collection
- Becoming familiar with the school and community
- Assessing the needs of the school's curriculum and other programs
- Assessing the specific needs of the users
- Establishing collection development policies and procedures
- Identifying criteria for selection of materials

- Planning for and implementing the selection process
- Acquiring and processing materials
- Participating in resource sharing
- Maintaining and preserving the collection
- Providing physical and intellectual access to materials
- Evaluating the collection

This chapter provides an overview of collection development activities. Many of these activities will be addressed in more depth in subsequent chapters.

LEARNING ABOUT THE EXISTING COLLECTION

Although it is possible that you will have the opportunity to build a collection from the beginning, most often you will take on the development of an existing collection. If a collection is to serve as a resource base for the entire school, the school librarian should investigate how the users' needs compare to the collection's available resources. Browsing is a quick way to learn about a collection. Walk through a collection and note whether you recognize titles and equipment. Ask yourself the following types of questions:

- What is your general impression when you enter the library? Are materials displayed in inviting ways?
- Do signs clearly and accurately point users to materials and services?
- Are materials housed in unusual areas?
- Are there materials that are inaccessible to users—for example, require a special request or are kept in a restricted area?
- How does the online catalog help learners locate items?
- Do materials appear to be old or worn?
- Are reference sources available in print and/or online?
- How do users access digitally delivered information?
- Is there a content filter through which online information must be accessed? If so, can the school librarian override the filter to access sites?
- Did the previous school librarian collect and mark websites for learner use? If so, how were digital materials described and organized?
- Is the collection accessible only in the school library or does the library website allow learners and educators remotely access it from classrooms and outside of the school?

While browsing, try out the library catalog and make notes about materials or formats that are new to you. Think of the library catalog is a local online repository (database) that lists all the materials held by a library. Create a list of areas that need signs to make materials easier to find. Note whether equipment is housed in an area convenient to the materials that require it. Look to see if there is a ready reference area and note whether any of the reference materials are duplicated in the circulating collection.

Remember that some collections extend to materials housed outside the school library but are still on the school campus. Professional journals or other materials may be located in the educators' lounge or department offices. Check other resources in the school. Does the counseling center collect vocational materials or materials about colleges? Do educators have classroom collections? Are there other departmental collections? Does the library catalog indicate the storage locations of these materials throughout the school?

As you gather these first impressions, examine the library's procedures manual for explanations of unusual situations. For example, ten copies of one book title may seem unusual, but perhaps the books are used in classrooms that conduct literature-based reading programs.

Although these procedures will help you gain information about the collection, remember that it is impossible to become familiar with all items in a collection in your first semester or even in your first year as a school librarian. However, as you participate in the day-to-day operations of the school library (circulating materials, shelving books, and other frequent activities) and become involved with educators and learners, you will gain valuable knowledge about the collection.

KNOWING THE COMMUNITY

A basic consideration of all collection development activities is the interaction of the library program with the school, other educational or informational institutions and agencies, and the external environment. The community (its geographical, political, economic, cultural, and social characteristics) influences the collection. Changes in a school's mission or goals, in access to other collections, or in citizens' attitudes about education will influence decisions about the collection.

Today, the global community is a key resource. Learners have computers in their homes and access to computers at school and in their public libraries. Educators electronically communicate with colleagues around the world. Internet access can speed the delivery of an article for a learner's report. All these factors affect a school library's collection development activities. See Chapter 3, "Community Analysis, Environmental Scanning, and Needs Assessment," for more discussion of community analysis.

ASSESSING NEEDS

To ensure that the collection fulfills the informational and instructional needs of its users, the school librarian must identify those needs. Whom does the collection serve? What are the users' informational needs? What are the subjects taught in the school? What are the educators' instructional needs? Are there groups of learners with special needs?

You can begin to find the answers to these questions by accessing the school's website for pertinent information, examining curriculum guides, asking the administrative staff for learner demographic statistics, and attending departmental meetings. Analyzing past school library reports, such as circulation statistics or interlibrary loan requests, will also help provide information about the needs of the users. Conducting a survey or organizing a focus group of learners and educators to determine how a collection can assist in meeting specific needs is also a valuable means of assessing user needs.

More information on assessing needs is included in Chapter 3, "Community Analysis, Environmental Scanning, and Needs Assessment."

DESCRIBING THE PROGRAM

Learners and educators need to know when they will be able to physically access the materials in the collection. Both outside the library and on the library's website clearly post the school library's hours of operation for your users. Let users know how the school library is scheduled. Do you have flexible scheduling, fixed scheduling, or a combination of flexible and fixed scheduling? Is the school library open before or after school hours? Can learners access the collection from classrooms and from home? Is that access restricted by hours or the number of learners who can access the collection simultaneously?

You should also note whether there are special reading programs that the collection supports, such as "Battle of the Books," Scholastic's *Reading Counts*, Renaissance Learning's *Accelerated Reader*, or state-focused reading contests. You can answer numerous other program questions in a policies and procedures manual:

- Does the school library sponsor special programs, such as author visits or National Library Week?
- Does the library have volunteer or learner assistant staff?
- Do the library personnel conduct book fairs?
- Are there orientations for learners and new faculty members?
- Are there opportunities for learners to serve as volunteers or aides?
- How does the library assist with learner or faculty research?
- Are copying and printing services available?
- Are there provisions or materials for learners with special needs?
- Do school library personnel conduct professional development workshops for educators?
- How are the library program and services evaluated?

All of these areas of the program may not relate directly to the collection (although many do), but it is important to have this type of information included in a school library manual or in a publication that is available to learners and educators. Chapter 4, "The School Library Program," includes more information about library programs and services that impact the collection.

SELECTING MATERIALS

Selection policies articulate the library program's commitment to the right of intellectual freedom, and they reflect professional ethics, rights of users, and concern for intellectual property. These policies are carried out using specific selection procedures.

Criteria, or the standards used to evaluate items, are a major component of selecting print, nonprint, and electronic resources. One must establish criteria for assessing each item and its relationship to the collection as a whole. Generally, criteria used to evaluate materials include literary quality, currency, accuracy of information, appeal and value to learners, application within the curriculum, quality of presentation, and format. You will also need to establish selection criteria and policies relating to specific formats, including electronic formats that are accessed online through the Internet.

Selection is the process of deciding whether an item will be a valuable addition to the collection. During this process, keep the set criteria in mind and make decisions within established policies. Personal examination and favorable reviews can provide the basis for selection decisions. Sources that provide reviews of a variety of formats include selection tools and reviewing journals. Some of the most useful selection tools for school librarians are listed and described in the Appendix to this book.

Use the same criteria for accepting donated materials that you use for purchasing collection items. Some materials that you select, such as eBooks, require equipment. Therefore, it is necessary for you to also establish criteria and procedures for the purchase of equipment. Many school districts provide guidelines for such purchases.

Established criteria, policies, and procedures are not the only factors that can influence a school librarian's choices. It is possible that one's values, interests, and even prejudices may influence selection decisions. To make sound decisions, you must set aside personal biases and make objective choices. Soliciting and gathering input from educators, administrators, and learners can also assist in the selection process.

The selection of materials is a major portion of collection development and includes establishing criteria for selection of many types of formats. Chapter 6, "Selection," Chapter 7, "General Selection Criteria," and Chapter 8, "Criteria by Format" address this topic.

ACQUIRING AND PROCESSING MATERIALS

After selecting materials and equipment to add to the collection, you must then make decisions relating to the process of acquiring and processing these items. In schools where clerical assistance is available in the library, an aide or clerk can be very helpful in these activities. Frequently, a school bookkeeper or financial officer is also involved in the acquisitions process.

For items such as books or magazines you may want to acquire your materials through a jobber. A *jobber* is a company that handles titles from several publishers. Using jobbers has many advantages including saving money and time spent by school library personnel. You may also decide to order some items directly from publishers or local bookstores. Some audiovisual vendors handle and distribute materials from several companies. For some selections, such as reference databases, you may need to make decisions about whether to purchase the item through an online subscription. Purchases that involve online access are generally more complex than acquiring a physical item and often involve price negotiation and licensing issues.

Many items can be purchased already processed, including catalog records, spine labels, barcodes, security strips, plastic book jackets, and school library stamp identification. Purchasing *shelf-ready items* (those that are processed by the jobber or publisher) can save you and your staff an enormous amount of time. The cost is affordable and varies due to the number of items purchased and the extent to which the items are processed. If you choose to do some of the processing on your own, there are also many sources of free catalog records that can ease cataloging effort and you will need some written procedures detailing the process for this activity. More detailed discussions of acquisition and processing activities can be found in Chapter 9, "Acquisitions and Processing."

RESOURCE SHARING

Participation in resource sharing will influence your selection and acquisition decisions. Networks involving more than one library provide access to information materials and services housed outside the school's facility. A school that participates in a cooperative network has access to a plethora of resources and services; however, participation carries with it certain responsibilities and perhaps financial obligations. Some networks offer cooperative purchasing programs, cataloging and processing, computerized databases, delivery systems, production services, examination centers, serials cooperatives, and other forms of resource sharing. Generally, there are policies and procedures that are written cooperatively by representatives from the libraries involved in this type of resource sharing. These should be included in your library's policies and procedures manual. You can also participate in informal resource sharing, such as inquiring by phone or e-mail as to the availability of a particular item in another school in your district or perhaps scanning and sending a journal article from one school library to another or hand delivering an item that is needed in a nearby school.

Fitting resource sharing into a continuum of collection development activities is somewhat difficult since resource sharing can impact multiple collection development activities, including selection, acquisitions, and circulation. More information relating to resource sharing can be found in Chapter 9, "Acquisitions and Processing," and in Chapter 16, "Fiscal Issues Relating to the Collection."

MAINTAINING AND PRESERVING MATERIALS

Collection maintenance is an important and often neglected function of collection development. The school librarian must make decisions about removing (deselecting or weeding), mending, rebinding, and replacing materials. Equipment must also be kept in working condition. Website locations will change, so those listing should be checked frequently.

You can do many things to help preserve and maintain your collection and equipment. These include teaching learners the proper handling of materials, providing copy machine access, using a security system, and maintaining appropriate temperature and humidity in the school library, to name just a few. Conducting systematic inventories of materials also helps maintain a usable collection. It is important to establish policies and procedures for these maintenance and preservation activities. Chapter 10, "Maintenance and Preservation," provides additional information about how to effectively maintain a collection.

ACCESSING AND CIRCULATING MATERIALS

While some librarians may not consider accessing and circulating materials as collection development activities, they are the reasons that the other activities take place. The ultimate purpose of collection development is to make materials accessible to users. As mentioned in Chapter 1, school librarians need to provide physical and intellectual access to materials. Physical access includes having work hours (during school, before school, or after school) when learners and educators are able to use the collection.

You will also need to develop circulation policies and procedures to provide some guidelines for the use of the collection. Some questions to consider are as follows:

- Which types of formats circulate and to whom?
- How long can learners check out materials?
- Is there a limit on the number of items that can be checked out?
- Does the limit on items vary depending on a learner's grade level?
- How do the checkout policies differ for educators?
- Are fines charged for overdue items?
- Do learners need to pay for materials that are damaged during the time the materials are checked out?

Learners and educators also need access to digital materials. It is the librarian's responsibility to provide and manage this access. This may involve working closely with the person responsible for setting up the school's network and with the school's technology committee. It is also important that acceptable use policies be written for the use of digital materials. If there is not such a policy in place, then you should take the initiative to develop a policy. Educators and administrators should be involved in developing an acceptable use policy since it is a policy that needs to be adopted and utilized throughout the school.

Your policies and procedures manual should contain a statement endorsing intellectual freedom. Some official documents, such as the *Library Bill of Rights* written and amended by the American Library Association Council, are valuable additions to your manual, either in the text of the manual itself or in an appendix. Such documents will be beneficial if you receive complaints about materials in your collection and you need to defend intellectual freedom. Your manual should also include a list of specific procedures to follow if an item is formally challenged. This list should be a part of your policies and procedures manual before a challenge occurs.

Copyright issues also affect access. Acquaint yourself with copyright and use policies like Creative Commons so that you can ensure that both physical and digital materials are used and reused properly. Your manual should include a statement noting that school library personnel uphold the U.S. copyright laws and fair use guidelines. In most schools, the librarian is responsible for enforcing those laws and guidelines within the school library and is responsible for providing information to the faculty and learners regarding copyright. School librarians should not serve as *"the copyright police"* outside the school library (this is a responsibility of school administrators); however, the school library manual should include how copyright information is provided to users. It is imperative to have a list of guidelines that affect educators and learners.

In some instances, intellectual freedom and copyright issues are addressed in the selection portion of a policies and procedures manual. Exact placement of them within the manual does not matter, but it is essential that they be included.

Circulation of materials is covered in more detail in Chapter 11, "Circulation and Promotion of the Collection." Certain intellectual freedom and copyright issues are also discussed in Chapter 13, "Legal and Ethical Issues with the Collection."

EVALUATING THE COLLECTION

Gathering information on how learners and educators use the materials will assist you in evaluating the collection. Some evaluation techniques that involve users include examining circulation statistics, auditing the catalog for subject area extent and age of books, determining the in-house use of materials, and conducting surveys. Collection-centered techniques, such as directly examining the collection and comparing the materials to lists or bibliographies, can also be used to evaluate a collection. From a user-centered perspective, you will want to acquaint yourself with the curriculum standards used in your school and consider your collection's content in light of them. You may adopt a policy of including curriculum standards in your catalog or creating lists of resources that meet standards is certain areas. Your manual should include a plan for systematically evaluating the collection, including who conducts the evaluation, what types of measures are used, and how often the collection is evaluated. More information related to how to carry out evaluation of a collection is found in Chapter 12, "Evaluation of the Collection."

INTERACTION OF COLLECTION DEVELOPMENT ACTIVITIES

You can view collection development activities as a continuum in which one activity depends upon and influences the others (see Figure 2.1). Activities are not isolated; rather, their interactions are cyclical. Thus, a change in one activity affects others. For instance, if there is a change in the curriculum (part of the community analysis) and several science courses are added, this will affect selection. You should establish policies that provide guidance, but also remember that policies may need to be altered to meet changes. With the rapid developments in technology, librarians can expect to add new formats to the collection; selection criteria for these formats will then need to be incorporated into the policy.

Figure 2.1. Interaction of Collection Development Activities

OTHER FACTORS THAT AFFECT COLLECTION DEVELOPMENT

The school librarian is responsible for developing and implementing collection development activities. However, the librarian cannot control all the factors that influence collection development activities. The library program must operate within policies that the local board of education adopts and must also meet the goals of the district and of the school. The attendance districts established by the school board may change yearly and impact the composition of the learner body or potential users of the collection. State or federal legislation may dictate requirements about the learner population, the curriculum, and other school programs. Shifts in the learner population will impose new demands on the collection that collection development activities must accommodate. The changing availability of digital access creates continual shifts in the equipment needed and requires librarians to update their skills.

District School Library Program

A building-level school library program that is part of a district library program offers many advantages to the entry-level school librarian. The system's school library program coordinator or director is someone you can turn to for guidance. The district-level guidelines for school library programs and the selection policy also aid the school librarian. District-level school library programs may offer services to help establish and maintain the collection program. For example, there may be opportunities to examine new materials or view exhibits and demonstrations at district-level library program meetings.

Regional centers also provide personnel and services, including consultants or technicians, cooperative collections, examination centers, staff development workshops, and clearinghouses for information about new technology. Providing distance-learning opportunities is another way these centers can extend the resources of the building school library.

Although district and regional programs offer many benefits, they may also impose constraints on a school library program. An approved buying list generated by a district-wide committee or state purchase agreements may limit the equipment that a librarian can purchase or the librarian may be allowed to order from only specific jobbers. If you encounter these situations, you should ask district-level personnel if there are procedures for ordering other items. In some districts, you must also order resources at specified times of the academic year.

VOICES FROM THE FIELD

I've tinkered with Makerspaces in our library. But wouldn't you know it: my kids love coming to the library for books! I've set out mini-stations, and only the drawing books get regularly used. My class time with each grade is very short, only 30 minutes, so after any instruction there's precious time for books. And all they want to do is look/read/discuss/share books! In some ways, it's validated my role as a librarian and collection development specialist.

—Liz White

Financial Support and Control

The school's and district's funding policies, including policies regulating use of outside funding sources, impose constraints on collection development. Accrediting agencies may also make budget demands. School librarians operate within the limits set by budget allocations. In addition to the size of the budget, the accounting system can affect collection activities. For example, funds designated for equipment cannot be used for books. Collection development is more successful when budgeting allows program objectives and needs to determine priorities.

The school board's or administrator's position regarding the use of outside funding also affects the collection. Some school districts opt not to use outside funds; others encourage school librarians to seek grants or endowments. Such grants or endowments may specify materials to be purchased or may limit the type of use or user for whom materials may be purchased. For example, some funding may be used only for materials for learner use.

At some point in your career as a school librarian, a school official may inform you that you must spend a large sum of money earmarked for materials for special uses within 7 to 10 days. This situation does not encourage thoughtful planning or selection, but it sometimes occurs with outside funding opportunities. Try to be knowledgeable regarding what materials can be funded by outside sources and be aware when the funding will occur. You should maintain a *consideration file,* a listing of materials (with ordering information included) that you are currently considering for purchase; such a file will be a great asset in these situations.

School Facilities

Limitations of the physical plant or the physical facilities of the library can affect the collection. For instance, the lack of adequate number of safe electrical outlets limits the use of some media or development of a makerspace. School library usage by after-school programs, summer school, or programs for preschoolers may influence collection development activities. Many formats in the collection (such as picture books, art prints, and maps) require specialized storage units. As school libraries change from predominately print collections to ones with digital collections, less shelving space is needed, but more computing devices and greater bandwidth are required. In some instances, such as a lack of an adequate number of electrical outlets, you may need to advocate for additional wiring to be put into the library or ask for wireless access. You may need to find funding to provide the additional computer workstations or laptops that are required for electronic resources.

CONCLUSION

Collection development comprises many activities that interact with one another. Changes in one activity often affect other collection development activities. Policies and procedures should be written to address each of the activities, but school librarians should be prepared to make alterations in order to meet changing needs. Other factors, such as district-wide policies and services, financial support, and school facilities, can also impact collection development.

GROUP ACTIVITY: TEDX JAM!

Each member of a group of four should visit the TED Talks website (https://www.ted .com/talks) and search for the word "library." Each group member should choose a different video and watch it while considering these questions:

- What is the title of the talk?
- When and where was it recorded?
- Who was the speaker?
- What aspects of collections were discussed?

Then, assemble as a group and summarize the TED Talk you watched. Share your responses to discussion questions, and then consider:

- What new ideas appealed to you?
- Were there any ideas that seemed off base? Why?

REFERENCE

Pattee, A. (2014). *Developing library collections for today's young adults.* Lanham, MD: Scarecrow Press, Inc.

ADDITIONAL READINGS

Craver, K. W. (2021). *School libraries in a time of change: How to survive and thrive.* Santa Barbara, CA: Libraries Unlimited.
Stephens, C. G., & Franklin, P. (2015). *Library 101: A handbook for the school librarian,* 2nd edition. Santa Barbara, CA: Libraries Unlimited.
Woolls, B. and Coatney, S. (2017). *The school library manager: Surviving and thriving,* 6th edition. Santa Barbara, CA: Libraries Unlimited.

HELPFUL MULTIMEDIA

Alliance for Excellence in Education (2017). Future Ready Librarians. Retrieved from https:// www.youtube.com/watch?v=rQZBOJCVTiA
FollettLearning (2018). The Library: Journey to the Future. Retrieved from https://www.youtube .com/watch?v=Ldaz4V2W8Rs
National Institutes of Education Office of Education Research (Singapore). (2019). Moving Ahead: Developing a Future Ready School Library Collection for Adolescents. Retrieved from https://www.youtube.com/watch?v=LK9y1hwTGmA

CHAPTER 3

Community Analysis, Environmental Scanning, and Needs Assessment

---

Key Learnings

- Community analysis, often referred to as environmental scanning, can identify external forces that may impact collection decisions.
- Knowledge of the community can also identify community collaborators and competitors.
- User needs assessments provide important information about the learners and educators' interests and needs.

Every school library is influenced by economic, social, political, regulatory, and technological forces that are constantly evolving. Effective collection development must be based on reliable knowledge about the collection's users (in the case of a school library: the learners, educators, administrators, and parents being served). The gathering of information about a population that a library serves is generally called *community analysis,* and is related to *environmental scanning,* which includes collecting information about external trends, opportunities, and threats affecting the school library and/or community, and *needs assessment,* which takes into account community composition and external factors and translates them to school community needs. Figure 3.1 illustrates the interplay between these three activities.

By collecting and reflecting on information about the school library's user community, librarians are able to more precisely align library resources and services with changing teaching and learning needs.

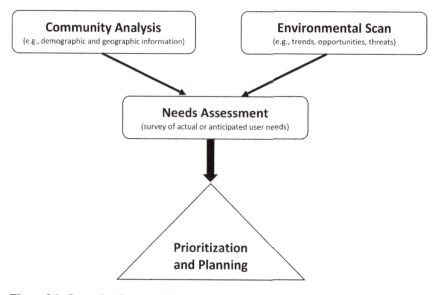

Figure 3.1. Interplay Between Planning Activities

LEARNING ABOUT THE COMMUNITY

Begin your community analysis by understanding the type of environment in which the school is placed. Locale, socioeconomic status, population distribution, and community resources shape opportunities and needs the library's users have.

How do you learn about the community? Good sources of information include the U.S. Census Bureau, the local chamber of commerce, the news media, government agencies, service and civic clubs, government census data, and the public library. These sources can provide maps, surveys, brochures, community profiles, lists of local activities, and projections for future population shifts. They can also lead you to other information sources, such as planning commissions or historical societies, and other tools, such as geographic information systems. Almost all communities have official websites that can provide some of the information you will need to collect, and many of the groups and institutions often have their own websites. If the public library has recently surveyed the community's information needs, its findings can be helpful. U.S. census data, which are available online, provide much information for a community analysis. With similar databases available at the state, county, and city levels, school librarians would simply need to seek out the expertise of their local data professionals, which most school districts rely on to manage school redistricting and bus routes (Johnston & Bishop, 2011).

A geographical information system (GIS) is a tool that many librarians are using to anticipate who needs library services the most, what libraries should offer to best impact communities, and where to spend limited human and financial resources to meet users' changing needs. GIS analyses can be conducted using proprietary tools like Tapestry or

COOL TOOL: DATA.GOV

Data.gov is a federal initiative to provide easy access to data created with taxpayer dollars. The Geospatial portion of the Data.gov site provides access to spatial data and maps for novice and advanced users of geographic and geospatial information systems (GIS). The portal includes the ability to view maps, spatial data sets, and other visualization services from state, local, and tribal governments, as well as from the private sector and higher education.

open source, and free tools like QGIS. For example, clear sense of users' demographic profiles can help school librarians to evaluate and adjust collections to fit closely with their information preferences and needs. GIS helps to identify potential growth areas in collections based on changing community composition. GIS analyses make emerging trends to be tangible and located (Sharma, 2016).

The following information is helpful to include in a community analysis:

- Geographic setting
- Topographic features (near mountains, oceans, or rivers)
- Population
- Age distribution of the population
- Ethnic and racial groups
- Educational levels of the population
- Economic levels of the population
- Employment opportunities
- Businesses
- Political activities
- Modes of transportation
- Educational institutions
- Availability of libraries and museums
- Information agencies (newspapers, radio stations, or TV stations)
- Technological resources (availability of Internet via cable TV, fiber-optic cable to the home, high-tech industries)
- Recreational facilities
- Religious institutions
- Housing
- Governmental units
- Medical care facilities and organizations

In addition to the topics listed above, a community analysis might also include information that is unique to the community, such as historical development or cultural data.

LEARNING ABOUT THE SCHOOL

Your community analysis should also include a detailed description of the school itself. It is extremely important to have knowledge about the learners, educators, and administrators who use the school library. The best sources for such information include the school website, the guidance office, and the school secretary or administrative assistant. The U.S. Department of Education and many states also maintain websites with data about individual schools. These websites can provide you with information such as learner enrollment, the number of learners on free or reduced lunches, and learner test scores. The following is information to be included in a school analysis:

- Enrollment
- Grade levels
- Ethnic makeup of the learner body
- Number of learners whose second language is English
- Socioeconomic status of the learners
- Number of learners on free or reduced lunches
- Dropout rate
- Number of learners enrolled in advanced courses
- Percentage of learners going to college
- Special education population
- Standardized test scores
- Courses or units of study emphasized in the curriculum
- Extracurricular activities available
- Number of faculty members
- Background of faculty members (Do the educators live in local neighborhoods? Do they have advanced degrees? Do they come from diverse backgrounds?)

Other types of information, such as the number of high school learners who have jobs or the number of transient learners in a school, can also influence collection development. The purpose of a school has implications for the collection. If you are a librarian in a magnet school, such as a performing arts or technical school, or in a parochial school where specific religious beliefs are taught, certain titles may need to be included in the collection (or perhaps excluded).

Schools with a high percentage of learners in advanced placement classes will have demands different from those schools where learners are entering the military or job force, rather than going on to higher education. Learners taking courses through advanced placement or international baccalaureate programs are likely to need materials available through interlibrary loan or on the Internet. On the other hand, learners who attend vocational programs for a part of the school day will need specialized materials, such as car repair or hair fashions, that support their vocational curriculum. If an elementary school has many learners whose first language is not English, you will want to include many bilingual materials in the collection. If learners in a school are enrolled in distance education courses, their information needs will also need to be considered, especially if the courses they are taking are not those offered in the on-campus facility.

LEARNING ABOUT THE ENVIRONMENT

Every school reflects not only its immediately surrounding community, but also larger trends in society. Tracking external forces is an excellent way to anticipate future school library collection and service needs.

Some of your most valuable allies and potential competitors may be the public library's collection, programs, and young adult specialists. If you are a new school librarian, investigate the following: What services do libraries and other information agencies offer to learners? Is there a branch library near your school, or do learners use a bookmobile? Do learners have access to the Internet at the public library? Can they access the public library's online catalog from their home or from the school? Do school and public libraries offer cooperative programs or services? Can you borrow public library materials for classroom use? Has the school established a procedure for alerting the public library of forthcoming assignments? Do the two libraries participate in resource sharing plans? Have the libraries jointly applied for grant funds?

Visit local community college, college, and university libraries. Their collections probably include reference materials, bibliographies, and selection tools too expensive for the school's collection. If special libraries (industry, hospital, or government) in the community are open to learner use, their resources can be of particular interest to high school learners completing research papers or school projects.

TRANSLATING DATA TO SCHOOL COMMUNITY NEEDS

Demographics can provide guidance for collection development and programming. Census data about racial, ethnic, and language backgrounds indicate some types of materials the collection needs. Community demographics must also be considered in the selection of resources to address the specific needs of diverse learners. These groups may include those with different language needs, differing cultural traditions, and social needs resulting from socioeconomic status. It is essential that the school library collection not only serve the teaching and learning needs of the school, but also reflect the unique composition of all stakeholders.

In communities with large populations of refugees and immigrants, you will also need materials that help learners, parents, and educators understand the new members of their community. The people of a community have a vested interest in schools and represent possible sources of funding and support. Educating the community with data and maps to more concretely represent the space and the school library's place within the community may help them understand why school libraries are important to the communities they serve.

Stability of the population also affects the collection. A community without an influx of young families may face a decline in learner population, leading to closing or consolidating schools. If you are in a school with low-income workforces, there is likely to be a certain amount of transience. Children of inner-city factory workers or migrant farm workers may spend only a few weeks in your school. When working with children from such families, you may need materials in less permanent formats. In these situations, consider selecting less costly paperback books, and try not to fret about the loss of materials.

The location of the community, its climate, and its recreational patterns also make demands on the collection. Schools in areas where skiing, snowmobiling, water sports, or other outdoor activities are common need appropriate related materials in the school library collection.

Many communities support recreational and educational programs. Young people may regularly participate in functions at museums, zoological gardens, and concert venues. These interests result in demands on the collection. For instance, if a community has a planetarium that is open to learners, the collection will need stronger astronomy resources than one in a community without such a facility. Active scout or 4-H programs may also indicate a need for specialized materials in the collection.

A community of young families may be more likely to support educational programs than a community of fixed-income people. The educational level of the population may be

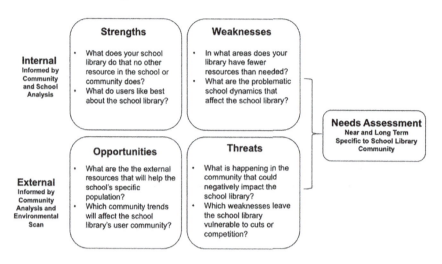

Figure 3.2. Sample SWOT Analysis of Data for Needs Assessment

another clue to the willingness of citizens to financially support schools. Active participants in community groups might be more receptive to the importance of a school library program. Remember that neighborhoods in large school districts differ drastically. You may find pockets of support, or opposition, in various neighborhoods.

As a school librarian, you also should assess the needs of the educators in your school. A well-selected professional library will be greatly appreciated by the faculty, as will instruction in accessing online materials for their courses. It could be beneficial to determine whether there are educators in the school who are working on advanced degrees. They may need your assistance in locating print or online materials to help them complete requirements for the courses in which they are enrolled.

Figure 3.2 provides an example of how to bring together data from environment scanning and community analyses into a Strengths, Weaknesses, Opportunities, and Threats (SWOT) analysis to inform a school library needs assessment (adapted from ALA, n.d.)

As Figure 3.2 suggests, strengths and weaknesses tend to be more locally focused, while opportunities and threats are external. Each SWOT area will be informed by the community and environmental data you gather, and may also be informed by feedback from library stakeholders, perhaps based on the sample driving questions provided in each quadrant. To ensure a representative SWOT analysis, remember to include many voices as you gather your data.

ASSESSING USER NEEDS

While a community and school analysis can provide valuable information for collection development, other means of assessing learner and faculty needs should also be used. Conducting separate surveys for learners and educators can be helpful. These surveys should include questions relating to the needs of the users and to the collection. The questions on a learner survey should be written so that learners can clearly understand them.

The wording of questions will vary greatly, depending on grade levels included in a school. Sample survey questions for classroom educators might include the following:

- What units of study are you planning for this school year?
- Does the library currently have adequate materials to support your curriculum?
- Do learners in your courses need materials from the library to complete assignments?
- Will you be bringing learners to the library for research?
- How can I help your learners with their research?
- What areas of professional development are of particular interest to you?
- Are you currently working on an advanced degree? If so, in what area of study?

Figure 3.3 illustrates a sample needs assessment for learners that can be used to gather learner interests that may need to reflect in the school library's collection and programs.

Check the topics you like to read about:

Action / Adventure / True adventure / Survival	
Animals / Animal stories	
Art	
Books on Facts / Trivia	
Cars	
Comics / Graphic Novels	
Cooking / Cookbooks / Diet / Food and nutrition	
Crime / Detective / Mystery stories	
Famous people / Biographies	
Fantasy / Vampires	
Fashion	
Games	
Ghost stories / Supernatural	
Health and fitness	
"How To" books	
Joke books / Humor / Funny books	
Monsters	
Movies	
Music / Singers	
Plays / Theater	
Poetry	
Romance / Relationships	
Science fiction / Aliens	
Short stories	
Sports stories / Sports / Sports people	
Stories about the past / Historical fiction	

Figure 3.3. Sample Learner Needs Assessment

The data from surveys should be analyzed and presented in a report that includes some graphic representations so that survey results can easily be understood, not only by a librarian, but also by other interested parties. In your report include collection recommendations based on the survey results. For instance, if survey findings indicate a large percentage of learners whose first language is Spanish, consider applying for a grant to add bilingual materials to your collection. If you find the eighth-grade science educators are beginning a new unit of study on oceanography, include in your budget funds for materials to help strengthen that area of the collection. If learners indicated they were not able to find enough materials about gay rights, then you may want to add related print resources or collect and mark relevant websites. Consider creating *pathfinders* (curated and organized lists of materials on particular topics). The pathfinders should include print, nonprint, and online resources; they are especially helpful to learners who are beginning research projects.

To conducting formal surveys that can impact collection development, you should also use informal means to assess user needs. One informal way to gather this information is to attend grade-level or department meetings to learn about what types of projects, assignments, or units of study are being planned by classroom educators. In the library, at lunch in the cafeteria, or at faculty meetings, chat with educators about the types of materials and services they would like to see in the school library. Provide a suggestion box on the circulation desk where learners or educators can comment on materials they are not able to locate in the collection.

CONCLUSION

In order to determine the needs of the users of a school library, a librarian should conduct a community analysis, including demographics relating to both the community and the school itself. Carefully designed and administered surveys can also provide accurate and reliable data about user needs. Librarians can assess the needs of learners and educators through informal means, such as attending department or grade-level meetings. Information gathered in a community analysis and through needs assessments should be major influences for collection development and the school library program.

INDEPENDENT ACTIVITY

Visit the National Center for Education Statistics (http://nces.ed.gov) and look around the site. What sorts of data are available that might be helpful for school library collection planning? Then, under "School Search," choose a school or district near you. What sorts of data are available for you to better understand the community the school or district serves?

REFERENCES

American Library Association (ALA). (n.d.). Your Library Media Center's Strengths, Weaknesses, Opportunities, Threats. Retrieved from http://www.ala.org/advocacy/files/advleg/advocacy university/frontline_advocacy/frontline_school/swot.pdf

Johnston, M. P., & Bishop, B. W. (2011). The potential and possibilities for utilizing geographic information systems to inform school library as place. *School Libraries Worldwide, 17*(1), 1–12.

Sharma, D. M. (2016, January 7). Using GIS to assess public libraries. *The Wired Library.* Retrieved from http://publiclibrariesonline.org/2016/01/using-gis-to-assess-public-libraries/

ADDITIONAL READINGS

James, C. (2008). Environmental scanning: An essential tool for twenty-first century librarianship. *Library Review, 57*(7), 528–536. doi: 10.1108/0024253081089

Young, T. (2010). Aligning collection development with instructional and learning needs. *School Library Monthly, 26*(10), 20–22.

HELPFUL MULTIMEDIA

ALA Map and Geography Round Table. (2010, June). GIS in every library: Making it happen. Retrieved from http://www.ala.org/rt/sites/ala.org.rt/files/content/publicationsab/GIS_Program_Top_5_Re.pdf

Conway, M. (2014). Environmental scanning: What it is and how to do it. Geospatial data. Retrieved from http://geo.data.gov

Library of Michigan. (2015). Community analysis resources. Retrieved from https://www.michigan.gov/libraryofmichigan/0,9327,7-381-88855_89739_90014-52763—,00.html

National Library of New Zealand. (2019). Working out your collection' requirements. Retrieved from https://natlib.govt.nz/schools/school-libraries/collections-and-resources/your-collection-management-plan/working-out-your-librarys-collection-requirements

North Carolina Library Advocacy. (2018). School library strategic planning resources. Retrieved from https://nclibraryadvocacy.org/nc-library-stories/strategic-planning-resources/

QGIS (free GIS tool). https://qgis.org/en/site/

Tapestry (proprietary GIS tool). https://www.esri.com/en-us/arcgis/products/tapestry-segmentation/overview

University of Kansas. (2014). Community toolbox. http://ctb.ku.edu/en/table-of-contents/assessment/assessing-community-needs-and-resources/conducting-needs-assessment-surveys/main

U.S. Department of Education. National Center for Education Statistics (NCES). http://nces.ed.gov

The School Library Program

Many research studies clearly concluded that in order to succeed, learners need strong school libraries (Lance & Kachel, 2018). Through the school library, all learners need access to current, quality, high interest, and extensive collections (American Association of School Librarians, 2018). The school library provides a setting where learners can develop essential information skills: being able to locate, evaluate, organize, use, and create information. Here learners will not only access the traditional print and nonprint resources, but they will also access needed information via virtual learning environments.

SCHEDULING OF THE SCHOOL LIBRARY

Patrons need to be informed of the operating hours of the school library, including the times they can check out materials or use the school library computers. These hours are generally affected by the librarian's employment contract, the number of professional school librarians in a school, and the presence of clerical or paraprofessional assistants.

Having more school library personnel usually makes it possible to have expanded hours of access for patrons. For instance, in a high school setting where at least two professional librarians are on staff, it may be possible to stagger work hours so the library can be open to learners before classes begin and after school. The operating hours of the school library should be specified in your policies and procedures manual, in a learner handbook, and on or near the entrance to the school library. Additionally, patrons need to know if online materials are accessible from classrooms or from learners' homes, and whether there is around-the-clock access to the online resources.

According to American Association of School Librarians (AASL) past president Carl Harvey, points you will need to consider as you decide upon a scheduling approach include:

- Do instruction and circulation have to be connected? How can it be ensured that instruction in the library connects to what is happening in the classroom?
- If the educator is not part of the planning, delivering, and assessing, how can communication be maintained between the librarian and the classroom educator?
- How can it be ensured that all learners have the opportunity to work with the librarian?
- How is the librarian part of planning and curriculum design if he/she is working with fixed classes all day?
- What is the size of the library? Are there opportunities for multiple things to be happening at once?
- What "spaces" are available in library? For example, is there a story area, instructional areas, conference rooms? How can that space best be utilized?
- How is scheduling handled for the spaces that are available for others to use? Would a Google Calendar work as a central calendar?
- Should the library facility have other uses? (Harvey, 2014).

You might be able to decide whether your school library will operate on a fixed, flexible, or mixed schedule. Each of these types of schedules has advantages and disadvantages. Table 4.1 summarizes these aspects of each scheduling approach.

Fixed (or rigid) schedules are sometimes utilized in elementary schools. In this type of schedule, each class is provided a prescribed time (usually once a week for a set duration) to visit the library for story hours, library instruction, or materials checkout. In a school that uses fixed scheduling, the visits to the library are often part of a master schedule that provides classroom educators with planning time. Music, art, physical education, and computer are generally in the same master schedule to provide planning time for classroom educators. Often in a fixed schedule only one class is allowed into the school library at a time.

In flexible (or open) scheduling, classes are scheduled as classroom educators and the librarian define a need. For example, in one week a classroom educator may have the learners working on research projects and schedule a 40-minute block of time every day of that week. The classroom educator accompanies learners to the library and plans cooperatively with the school librarian. The schedule for teaching information literacy skills is based on need and is integrated into research activities; thus, the schedule varies each week. With a flexible schedule, individuals and small groups of learners use the library as often as needed. Although the AASL strongly recommends flexible scheduling, some school librarians note disadvantages.

Some elementary school libraries use mixed scheduling, which is a combination of fixed and flexible scheduling. For instance, the librarian could have fixed classes in the

TABLE 4.1. COMPARISON OF SCHOOL LIBRARY SCHEDULING APPROACHES

Schedule Type	Fixed		Flexible		Hybrid (Mixed)	
	Pro	**Con**	**Pro**	**Con**	**Pro**	**Con**
	• All students have access to the library resources during their scheduled library time. • The school librarian has the opportunity to teach information literacy skills to all students in the school. • Teachers are provided with a planning period.	• Information literacy skills are often taught in isolation and may soon be forgotten by the students. • The school library is treated as a subject, rather than a center for resources and learning. • Students cannot visit the library at times when they may have specific needs for resources. • Teachers may not be able to send individual students or small groups of students for check-out or research activities. • A fixed schedule can occupy almost all of a librarian's day, leaving little time for other management responsibilities or collaborative opportunities.	• Students have access to resources at the time of need or interest. • Library visits and the teaching of information literacy skills are related to classroom activities and assignments. • The librarian has time to collaborate with classroom teachers, thus improving communication, increasing curriculum awareness, and knowledge of resources are available in the school library. • Students become more independent users of resources and gain information literacy skills for lifelong learning.	• It is possible that some students never or infrequently visit the school library and thus do not get opportunities to check out materials for either research or pleasure. • Some teachers may send their problem students to the library frequently, simply to get them out of the classroom. • The librarian may feel as if there is not time to take care of other management responsibilities, such as ordering or cataloging, when there are students and teachers constantly using the library resources and needing assistance.	• Good for small student populations • Allows responsiveness to changing learning and teaching needs • Allows tailoring to student developmental levels • Offers consistent access to the library • Model allows for the best of fixed scheduling to be combined with best of flexible scheduling.	• Ineffective if follow-up time does not occur • Limited by facility size • May be confusing for teachers and students • Model allows for the drawbacks of fixed scheduling to be compounded by the drawbacks of flexible scheduling.

morning and flexible access during the afternoon. Another frequently used mixed schedule involves having fixed classes for the lower grades and flexible access for the upper elementary grades. If a full-time clerk is available in the library, the librarian might teach classes in a fixed schedule, while the clerk assists small groups of learners or individuals who come to the library from other classes. Fixed and flexible scheduling has many possible combinations. Some elementary librarians consider the mixed scheduling to be the ideal school library.

Libraries in secondary schools usually operate on a flexible schedule in which educators sign up with the librarian for times to bring their classes to the library. Other times they are allowed to send individual learners or small groups of learners to the library. Some middle school librarians choose to use a mixed schedule, generally scheduling fixed classes through English or social studies educators, with specific times for learners to check out books or work on special projects, while the library remains open for small groups of learners or individuals. Regardless of which type of scheduling is used in a library, learners and educators must be made fully aware of the schedule and how it affects their access to the library.

The type of scheduling used in a school library can impact the collection. If you are in a school where flexible or mixed scheduling is present, you will most likely find there is more use of the library for both personal reading and research activities; thus, you need to develop a collection that includes the materials needed to support such activities. You need to become familiar with the curriculum, possible research assignments, and the times of the year there will likely be a demand for particular resources. Additionally, you need to work collaboratively with your classroom educators to provide integration of the teaching of information skills into the curriculum, and at the same time develop a collection tailored to the needs of the learners and educators.

Beyond the support or constraints of the physical space, scheduling considerations must also reflect the library's and school's teaching and learning philosophy. School librarians should take the lead in ensuring that school libraries embrace a model to provide unrestricted access to learners and educators so that they can use the library when resources are necessary. Librarians, principals, and faculty must have a shared philosophy, develop a policy, and enact a plan in order to provide equitable access to the library and its collection (Moreillon, 2014).

GENERAL SERVICES

What general services are included in a school library? This may vary according to the number of school library personnel, learner body enrollment, grade levels included in the school, and school library facilities. General services provided to learners and educators could include the following:

- Providing orientation sessions for learners and educators
- Providing copy machines so learners and educators can make copies of library materials
- Providing access to online databases
- Making it possible to print Internet resources
- Collaborating on research projects
- Providing reading and viewing guidance for learners and educators
- Providing book talks for classes
- Preparing bibliographies and pathfinders

- Providing style sheets for learners
- Bookmarking Internet sites for classroom assignments
- Providing resources and equipment for learners with special needs
- Conducting professional development workshops for educators

How are these services related to the school library collection? The collection is inescapably intertwined with the school library's offerings. Providing the services listed and a collection that reflects the needs of the learners and educators will help create an effective, high-quality school library.

Effective school libraries engage learners and provide services that contribute to authentic learning with prior knowledge as a baseline and value beyond being a single school assignment. This school library provides learning opportunities through technology; thus, it is important to have emerging technologies available to all learners. In turn, school librarians need to base their technology-related instruction on learner learning, rather than the technologies themselves.

SPECIAL PROGRAMS

Many opportunities are available to provide special programs in a school library. Traditionally, a high priority of school libraries has been the promotion of reading. With the current emphasis on increasing standardized reading test scores, this priority has become even more of a focus and has served to closely link classrooms and the school library. In some schools, special reading programs, such as computer reading programs (Renaissance Learning's *Accelerated Reader* and Scholastic's *Reading Counts*) or the "Battle of the Books" (a reading competition program), are school-wide activities and are closely connected to the reading curriculum. In other schools, reading programs are used as reading motivational tools and are administered only through the library. These programs are discussed in more depth in Chapter 14, "The Curriculum." Many librarians continue to design their own reading motivation programs and contests.

Although school librarians are not reading educators, they can complement and collaborate with classroom educators to reinforce strategies and techniques used to teach reading. Such strategies include pointing out rhyming words in a poem, defining unfamiliar words, predicting what will happen next in a story, or determining an author's message. Introducing learners to various genres and imparting a love for literature will also help learners enjoy reading and become lifelong readers for both pleasure and information.

Other special programs that are sometimes part of a school library program include computer clubs, book discussion groups, and learner library aides. Many school librarians also plan programs for special events held in the library. These include author visits, book fairs, career days, speakers, storytelling, read-ins (famous local persons or parents are invited to the library to read a book aloud), and National Library Week or Children's Book Week celebrations. For many learners, these special programs give a social network and outlet to express themselves beyond class participation. Indeed, as Figure 4.1 shows, the collection, at the core of the library's programs and services, not only facilitates learning and exploration, but also provides programs and opportunities for extensive use of the program instigate even further learning.

An appropriate, well-promoted, and high-quality collection is at the center of the cycle of learning facilitation and learning facilitation.

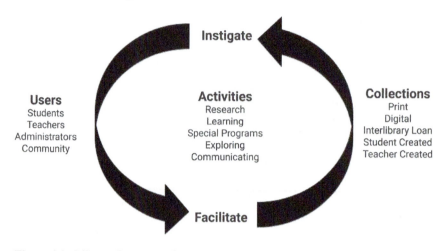

Figure 4.1. Library Programming Instigation/Facilitation Cycle

EVALUATION OF PROGRAMS

Every school library program should frequently use varied means of evaluation. Initially, a school librarian should perform some type of self-assessment of a program. One way to evaluate a program is to put in written format the mission, goals, and objectives of the school library and then compare the current program to those items.

Using a rubric will provide a more thorough evaluation and present an overall picture of the current status of your program and the areas in which you would like the program to move forward. Several school districts and states have developed program evaluation rubrics that can be used for this purpose. Check with your school district or state department of education to see if such a rubric is available for your use. If there is not already a rubric that you can use for this purpose, you can adapt other rubrics to accommodate the objectives and needs of your library. In some instances, state departments of education issue "certifications" that denote that a library has met the state requirements to an exemplary standard. At the end of this chapter, you will find website listings of some valuable program evaluation rubrics. In your rubric be sure to include items that will evaluate how well the program is developing critical problem solvers and how the program contributes to learner achievement.

Provide opportunities for your community to evaluate the school library by interviewing learners and educators or by creating surveys in which patrons can indicate their present usage of the library and share useful feedback for improvement. Surveys should provide anonymity, be relatively brief (very short for younger learners), and be written in clear, concise language.

Figure 4.2 is an example of a learner survey appropriate for a school library. Different questions might need to be used depending on the grade levels of learners. You can also choose to utilize a different format for learner responses.

Classroom educators can provide valuable information about the school library, particularly if you are using a flexible schedule and educators are accompanying their

[SCHOOL NAME | SCHOOL DISTRICT HERE]

Dear Students:
This survey is being conducted to help us understand how you use the school library and how the library program may be Improved. Please complete the survey below and return it to your school librarian. Thank you for taking the time to provide us with this valuable information.

~Your School Library Staff

How often do you visit the School Library?   □ Daily   □Weekly   □Monthly   □Never
When do you generally visit the School Library?   _____Before School _____At Lunch _____With Classes _____ After School
Please list your grade: _____

Indicate your level of agreement by putting a check mark in the box that most closely represents your response. If this item doesn't apply, please leave the answer blank. Thank	QUALITY RATING					
	Strongly Agree	Agree	Neutral	Disagree	Strongly Disagree	Don't Know
SCHOOL LIBRARY RESOURCES						
The School Library provides the resources I need to complete my assignments.						
The School Library provides the resources I need for my school interests.						
The School Library promotes reading.						
The School Library Catalog/OPAC is easy to						
The School Library Web Site is useful.						
I feel well prepared to locate resources in the School Library because of the training I						
The skills I learned in the School Library help me to locate electronic resources through the						
The School Library has books and other resources that are of interest to me.						
The atmosphere in the School Library is conducive to learning the skills I need.						
TECHNOLOGY RESOURCES						
Please complete the following questions by writing your response:						

Do you use any of the digital subscriptions that are part of our library collection?	□ Yes □No
If you utilize e-readers, would you like to see more e-books as part of our library collection?	□ Yes □No
What, if any, technologies would you like to see added to our library?	
How often do you utilize e-readers and/or e-books?	□ Daily □Weekly □Monthly □Never
What other technology/applications would you like to see utilized in our school library (e.g. social network applications, podcasts, blogs, wikis)?	

Figure 4.2. Student School Library Survey

learners to the library. Figure 4.3 is a sample of a survey that could be used for classroom educators to help evaluate the technology resources in the school library. While paper surveys are portable and easy to distribute, you may wish to investigate using a free online survey tool like SurveyMonkey (https://surveymonkey.com) to create a digital survey by which you can quickly visualize and share results.

FACULTY LIBRARY TECHNOLOGY SURVEY

This survey is intended to help us meet the needs of the teachers in our school. Please answer each question as completely as you can and then return the survey to school librarian. Thank you for taking the time to provide us with your valuable input!

~ Your School Library Staff

Indicate your level of agreement by putting a check mark in the box that most closely represents your response. If this item doesn't apply, please leave the answer blank. Thank you.	QUALITY RATING					
	Strongly Agree	Agree	Neutral	Disagree	Strongly Disagree	Don't Know
LIBRARY RESOURCES						
The school library contains the print resources I need to assist me with planning and teaching.						
The school library contains materials that are of interest to my students and promote information literacy skills.						
The school library staff advises me of new additions to the library collection that would be beneficial to me.						
The school library staff solicits my input when adding resources to the library collection.						
TECHNOLOGY RESOURCES						
The school library has access to the digital and other non-print resources I need to support my classroom.						
There are sufficient computers, online subscriptions, whiteboard, and other technology resources in the school library to meet my classroom needs.						
The school library provides resources to encourage students' 21st Century learning skills.						
SCHOOL LIBRARY AVAILABILITY						
The school library hours of operation are sufficient to meet my needs.						
The school library staff is available to answer questions and meet my needs.						
The school library staff assists me in the use of the library resources.						

Please complete the following by checking off or writing in your response:

What technologies or other resources would you like to see added to the school library collection?

Do you utilize the library's digital subscriptions?   ☐ Yes   ☐ No

If you answered "no" above, why not?

Do you utilize the library's access to e-books?   ☐ Yes   ☐ No

If you answered "no" above, why not?

Would you support the purchase of additional e-books for the school library collection? ☐ Yes   ☐ No

What e-books would you like to see added to the school library collection?

Would you support the purchase of e-readers for the school library collection? ☐ Yes   ☐ No   ☐ Maybe

Do you support the use of social applications like Facebook, Twitter, etc. for learning?

☐ Yes   ☐ No   ☐ Maybe

If you answered "no" above, why not?

OTHER COMMENTS OR SUGGESTIONS? If you have additional comments or would like to clarify any responses, please feel free to do so below. Thank you!

Figure 4.3. Faculty School Library Survey

CONCLUSION

Research has shown that strong libraries and access to information in a variety of formats contribute to authentic learner learning and achievement. Effective school libraries are dependent on a collection that is responsive to the needs of learners and educators and are integrated into the curriculum through resource-based instruction of information literacy skills. A school library should be evaluated frequently, both through self-assessments by the school librarian and by its users. School librarians must strive to ensure that the relevancy of their school libraries and instructional impact of information literacy skills are understood by administrators, educators, parents, and the community in general.

DISCUSSION QUESTIONS

1. Locate the school library standards for your state. If your state does not have standards, use the Oregon standards at https://www.olaweb.org/school-library-standards. After you review your chosen standards, respond to these questions:
2. Which areas of the rubric do you feel relate to development activities? Which areas do you feel most school librarians are well prepared to address through their collections?
3. In which areas do you feel they should receive more professional development, training, and/or experience to achieve exemplary status in their school library collections?
4. And, importantly, given your own professional vision, which aspects of the state collection standards are in line with your strengths and preferences?

REFERENCES

Harvey, C. A. (2014). The schedule spectrum. *School Library Monthly, 31*(3), 17.

Lance, K. C., & Kachel, D. (2018, May 26). Why school librarians matter: What years of research tell us. *Phi Delta Kappan*. Retrieved from https://kappanonline.org/lance-kachel-school-librarians-matter-years-research/

Moreillon, J. (2014). Leadership: Fixed, flexible, and mixed library scheduling. *School Library Monthly, 30*(7), 25–26.

ADDITIONAL READINGS

American Association of School Librarians. (2018). *National school library standards for learners, school librarians, and school libraries.* Chicago, IL: American Library Association.

American Association of School Librarians. (2020, January 25). *The school librarians role in reading.* Retrieved from http://www.ala.org/aasl/sites/ala.org.aasl/files/content/advocacy/statements/docs/AASL_Position_Statement_RoleinReading_2020-01-25.pdf

Everhart, N. (2020). *Evaluating the school library: Analysis, techniques, and research practices,* 2nd edition. Santa Barbara, CA: Libraries Unlimited.

Woolls, B., & Coatney, S. (2017). *The school library media manager,* 6th edition. Santa Barbara, CA: Libraries Unlimited.

HELPFUL MULTIMEDIA

American Association of School Librarians. (2019, June). School library scheduling. Retrieved from http://www.ala.org/aasl/sites/ala.org.aasl/files/content/advocacy/statements/docs/AASL _Scheduling_Position_Statement.pdf

Florida Department of Education. (2014). ExC3EL—Expectations for collaboration, collections, and connections to enhance learning: Florida's K–12 library program evaluation tool. Retrieved from http://www.fldoe.org/core/fileparse.php/7564/urlt/evaluationrubric.pdf

Library of Michigan. (2015). School libraries in the 21st century. https://www.michigan.gov /libraryofmichigan/0,9264,7-381-88855_89742_90263—,00.html

Maryland State Department of Education. (2020, January 6). Maryland school library media standards for learners, librarians and libraries. Retrieved from http://marylandpublicschools.org /programs/Documents/ITSLM/slm/MD_SLM_Standards.pdf

Ohio Department of Education. (2020). Ohio guidelines for effective school media programs. Retrieved from http://education.ohio.gov/Topics/Learning-in-Ohio/Library-Guidelines

Utah Educational Library Media Association, Utah Library Media Supervisors, & Utah State Office of Education. (n.d.). Utah Core Standards. Retrieved from https://www.schools.utah .gov/curr/librarymedia?mid=1005&tid=1

CHAPTER 5

Policies and Procedures

Key Learnings
- Clear, up-to-date policies are essential to guide collection activities.
- Policies created by other librarians provide a valuable starting point for your own policy.
- Include key stakeholders in policy drafting, revision, and approval.

One of the most important responsibilities of a school librarian is to develop or maintain an updated policies and procedures manual. Written policies and procedures are critical to the efficient management of a school library program and collection. Such policies and procedures have numerous purposes:

- Ensure a degree of consistency
- Define the scope and coverage of the collection
- Assign selection responsibility
- Facilitate quality selection
- Provide guidance in the acquisition, processing, and cataloging of materials
- Provide for maintenance of materials and equipment
- Aid in weeding or deselection of the collection
- Impart information dealing with the circulation and promotion of the collection
- Guide evaluation of the collection
- Acknowledge the rights of individuals to ask for reconsideration of materials
- Guide staff in handling complaints
- Protect intellectual freedom
- Promote fair use of copyrighted materials
- Ensure equitable student access to materials, including those on the Internet
- Provide guidelines to protect the confidentiality of library users

- Serve as a training tool for new staff or volunteers
- Provide a road map for your successor
- Create a public relations document to inform the public of the purposes of the program and collection
- Provide a means of assessing overall performance of the school library program
- Provide a model for other libraries

Having written policies can save time, help avoid confusion, and provide guidance. For instance, if you are absent from your position for a long period of time due to illness or perhaps maternity leave, a policies and procedures manual will be invaluable to the person who is substituting in your position. If you leave your position to take another, your replacement will be able to have background on your program and collection, including a clear understanding of what policies and procedures have been in place. In difficult situations such as a materials complaint being made by an emotional parent, the written procedures for handling a challenge can provide guidance, consistency, and support. Written policies and procedures demonstrate to a reader that the program is run in a professional manner, decisions are not arbitrarily made, and overall planning is taking place.

POLICY VERSUS PROCEDURE STATEMENTS

Policy statements and procedure statements guide the activities of the collection program and tell why the collection exists. They state goals in general terms, allowing for flexibility and change. Policies establish the basis for all the collection activities by identifying who will use the collection and what will be in the collection. They need to be in place before procedures are developed. Policy documents are known by various terms including *collection policy*, *collection development policy*, and *materials policy*.

Procedure statements direct the implementation of policies. They should be concrete and measurable. By defining *what*, *how*, and *when* questions, they address the tasks or processes for attaining the policy goals. Procedure statements explain how policies will be put into practice and identify the people responsible for their implementation. Procedures are specific and should be reviewed and updated on a regular basis. Examples of policies and procedures for specific school libraries can be found using the Helpful Multimedia listed at the end of this chapter.

As you examine documents, try to determine whether the policies and procedures are clearly distinguished. Figure 5.1 contrasts policy and procedure statements.

Policy	Procedure
Address the purpose of the collection?	Explain how the collection will be created
State who is responsible for the collection development	Describe the steps for maintaining the collection
Identify the types of materials that will be included	Describe how items will be described to enable location and use
Identify who (students, teachers) will be involved in the selection process	Explain the basis for adding or withdrawing materials from the collection
Identify student responsibilities for ethical and educational use of resources	Describe how stakeholders will be involved in the selection process

Figure 5.1. Policy Statements versus Procedure Statements

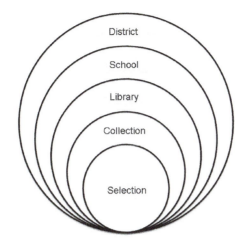

Figure 5.2. Layers of Library Policy

FORMULATING AND ADOPTING POLICIES

Policies need to reflect the goals and needs of the individual school library program and its institution. To be effective and responsive to these specific goals and needs, policy statements should be created at both district and building levels. Figure 5.2 illustrates the layers of policy that guide library collection activities.

As Figure 5.2 shows, district-wide policies provide a framework for school-wide policies. A portion of school-wide policy drives library policy. Within overall library policy, a portion will pertain to the collection. Finally, a selection policy is one aspect of collection policy. Other collection policies might pertain to cataloging or circulation. For all levels of policy, procedures are concrete steps used to enact the policy.

For example, usually the school district's stance on intellectual freedom and fair use is developed at the district level; however, questions dealing with the level of collecting materials on specific subjects would be at the building level. The diversity of building-level educational programs and the changing needs of users limits the effectiveness of adopting another school's policy statement. Nonetheless, it is helpful to examine statements from various sources. Doing so can prevent omissions, provide guidance for the outline, and offer suggestions for wording.

VOICES FROM THE FIELD

In terms of content standards, demonstrating adequate yearly progress, NCLB, etc. I think it's vital that we're able to show how integral the library's collection is in our building. There are many ways to do this, but the policy can lend credibility to us due to the fact that it's a written document, approved by the school board.

—School librarian, Michigan

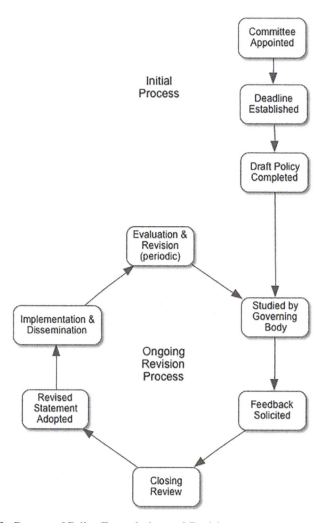

Figure 5.3. Process of Policy Formulation and Revision

You should obtain input from others when writing specific policies for your school library. A library advisory board comprising teachers, administrators, parents, and perhaps students can assist with the development, approval, and implementation of both policies and procedures. Each school will have its own process for approving policies. In some schools, the policy is approved only at building level. For instance, in a school using site-based management, a school advisory board composed of administrators, classroom teachers, and parents might be the group to whom policies are submitted for approval. In other school districts, there is a defined procedure that terminates with school board approval. Consult your school administrators to plan for the steps to obtain formal approval of your policies. A graphical representation of this process can be found in Figure 5.3.

The following is a sample of the steps that might be followed by a governing body in formally formulating and adopting a policy:

- Decides to establish and adopt a policy.
- Appoints an ad hoc committee composed of representatives of the school community.
- Includes parents, students, certified school librarians, administrators, people from other libraries and educational institutions, and community members. If the policy is to cover all instructional materials, including textbooks, then the body should also include subject specialists.
- Determines who will use the policy.
- Identifies when the statement might be used for evaluating the collection, preparing funding proposals, generating accreditation reports, or guiding cooperative resource sharing agreements.
- Charges the committee with the responsibility of developing the policy and establishes a deadline for the presentation of a draft.
- Distributes general guidelines to the committee to facilitate its work.
- Studies the draft before discussing it with the committee.
- Determines whether and how the policy can be easily updated.
- Solicits discussion and suggestions from legal counsel, personnel within the school (such as department heads or curriculum committees), and groups such as parent-teacher associations and teachers' associations.
- Conducts a closing review of the committee's recommendations and the comments expressed by others who studied the draft.
- Adopts a formal written statement as the approved policy of the issuing agency.
- Provides for implementation of the newly adopted policy. This involves disseminating the policy to all staff members involved in the evaluation, selection, and use of materials covered in the policy. A meeting or staff development program should familiarize the staff with the policy so they can respond to inquiries about it. Library personnel and teachers are likely to be the ones who receive requests that materials in the collection or used in classrooms be reconsidered.
- Disseminates the policy to the community.
- Plans and conducts school and community activities to make people aware of the importance of the freedom to read, speak, view, listen, evaluate, and learn.
- Establishes periodic evaluation and revision of the policy. Reviews should be scheduled on a regular basis with intervals of one to three years.
- Formally adopts changes. Dates of the original adoption and sequential revisions recorded on the document are helpful indicators of the document's history.

WRITING A POLICIES AND PROCEDURES MANUAL

If you take a position in a school library that does not have written policies and procedures, one of your initial responsibilities should be to begin the development of a manual that includes the policies from the district level, plus any policies and procedures specific to your school library. Policies and procedures can be integrated into one manual or you may choose to separate them into two different manuals.

Your manual should be written in third person, and proper names of persons should not be included. Instead of naming the person who performs a task or has a specific responsibility, use terms such as *the school librarian* or *the library assistant* or *the principal*. These terms should not be capitalized. Using such terms will create a more professional manual and will avoid having to make frequent revisions when personnel changes are made. Other helpful hints for creating a professional manual include the following:

- Be concise; use a minimum of verbiage.
- If you use acronyms, spell them out the first time they are utilized.
- Include step-by-step instructions for describing procedures.
- Do not be too technical; make the manual simple enough to be understood by a lay person or a new employee.
- Make generous use of white space.
- Be factual; double-check for accuracy.

If desired, the manual can be created and maintained digitally; thus, it is much easier to revise the information in the manual and make it available to others. A table of contents should be included in the beginning of the manual to make it possible to easily find a particular policy or procedure. If you are maintaining a hard copy of the manual, then it is wise to put each policy and procedure on separate pages and place your manual in a sturdy loose-leaf binder, with various topics presented in separate sections (perhaps denoted by labeled tabs or color-coded division pages). This will make it easier for you to make revisions or additions when you want to update the manual. If at a later date you choose to add or delete a few paragraphs, printing out a couple of revised pages of a section is much more efficient than having to reprint the entire manual. When you make revisions, be sure to note the date of the revision (e.g., 11/12) in the footer of the page. Ideally, the manual should be reviewed annually, although completed revisions may not be necessary each year. Be sure to note these review and revision dates on the manual document. If the manual is only in a digital format, then it may be necessary in some instances to print out particular pages when needed (e.g., a printed page that lists the steps for processing a book might be needed for a volunteer who is assisting in the procedure). Often, digital document creators forget to add creation, review, and revision dates—be sure to add this information to your digital documents and web pages!

You do not need to recreate the wheel when you are writing a manual, but if you take a substantial amount of wording from another document, you should provide a citation for the original document. This can easily be done by placing an asterisk after the original wording and putting a citation in the footer of the page. You might want to adopt a certain style (MLA, Turabian, or APA) for your citations, but no matter what style you decide to utilize, the citations need to have enough information for the reader to access the original documents. If you are including a district-level policy or procedure in your manual, you might choose to place it in an appendix and cite the item in the text of your manual (e.g., "See Appendix A for the district policy on intellectual freedom"). You can then add into the text any other information that is specific to your school library, such as where a complainant can obtain a copy of a form for reconsideration of a challenged material. If the

VOICES FROM THE FIELD

We created our handbook in wiki format and about six people participated in the committee. We started with an old document for ideas of topics, but we also surveyed our [school librarians] for suggestions and we got plenty to start with. One other part that is critical is as one learns of new procedures or policies you have to be sure to update the handbook. As our handbook is overseen by volunteers, it is easy to let things slide.

—Anonymous posting to LM_NET

library in which you take a position as a librarian already has written policies and procedures, you need to carefully read and follow them until any revisions are made.

You will be extremely busy as a new school librarian, so having already carefully
considered all the aspects of collection development and management and having a model
to follow for written policies and procedures will be a huge timesaver in the future.

CONTENTS OF A MANUAL

Numerous topics can be included in a policies and procedures manual. The following are
suggested items for all library manuals:

- Title page with date
- Table of contents
- Date signature page for librarian, principal, and school board members
- Community and school analyses
- Library philosophy or mission statement
- School library goals and objectives
- Description of programs and services
- Personnel job descriptions
- Formats collected
- Selection policies and procedures
- Acquisition, processing, and cataloging of materials
- Gifts
- Maintaining materials and equipment
- Inventory of materials
- Weeding materials
- Circulation
- Confidentiality of library records
- Collection evaluation
- Internet or technology (including an Internet use policy)
- Copyright and fair use compliance
- Intellectual freedom

These items do not need to be in the order listed, but they should be in a logical order. For
instance, a community and school analysis should be at the beginning of a manual since
the policies and procedures are supposed to be based on the needs of the users.

Other topics or items that can be helpful to include in the text of a manual or in an
appendix are: resource sharing, behavior guidelines and classroom management techniques,
budget and fund-raising, public relations, evaluation of the library media program, evaluation of personnel, a student handbook, a manual for volunteers, and any useful forms or
surveys. As you can see, there are many policies and procedures to remember when developing a collection and managing a program. You will not want to carry all this information
around in your head, and it will not serve others adequately if it is not in a written format.

CONCLUSION

In order to efficiently develop and manage collection activities, policies and procedures
need to be developed by the school librarian, with input from others who utilize the materials. District-level policies that relate to a school library must be considered and

followed. Additionally, policies should go through an approval process. All policies and procedures should be organized in a written format so that consistency can be maintained, and a clear understanding of collection activities and the library program is available. Policies and procedures should be regularly reviewed for possible revisions to make certain they are meeting the mission and goals of the library.

DISCUSSION QUESTIONS

Scenario: You have been asked to write a policy and procedures manual for a neighboring school in your district that has replaced its qualified school librarian with community volunteers.

1.   Do you accept this assignment? If so, why? If not, why not?
2.   If you accept this assignment, what should you be sure to include to help someone with no formal education in librarianship?

INDEPENDENT OR GROUP ACTIVITY

Part A. Locate a Policy

Option 1: If you work in a school district or library currently, find out if a collection development (or management) policy (or instructional materials development policy) exists. Base your responses for this activity on that policy.

Option 2: If you either do not work in a library or school district currently OR if your organization does not have an accessible collection development (or management) policy (or instructional materials development policy), then locate another policy using one of the websites listed in the Helpful Multimedia section or try searching "library collection development policy" (without quotes) in any search engine.

Part B. Gather Supplementary Materials

(1)   ALA (American Library Association) Workbook for Selection Policy Writing
(2)   ALA Intellectual Freedom Statements and Guidelines
(3)   AASL's (American Association of School Librarians) Position on Intellectual Freedom   http://www.ala.org/aasl/sites/ala.org.aasl/files/content/aaslissues/intellectual_freedom_brochure0212.pdf

Part C. Evaluate Your Policy

Prepare a written evaluation of your policy with a separate section for each of these criteria:

Criterion 1. Introduction/goals/philosophy.
    Assess the introduction or beginning of your policy. How does it stack up against ALA and AASL recommendation? How could it be improved? Does it go beyond the ALA and AASL recommendations in any way? If so, how? Give specific examples.

Criterion 2. Responsibility for selection.

Assess your policy in terms of stating responsibility for selection. How does it stack up against these recommendations? How could it be improved? Does it go beyond the ALA and AASL recommendations in any way? If so, how? Give specific examples.

Criterion 3. General and specific criteria.

Read what ALA says. Read what textbooks and/or professional resources say. Assess your policy in terms of both general and specific criteria. How does it stack up against these recommendations? Give specific examples.

Criterion 4. Position on intellectual freedom and confidentiality of patron records.

Assess your policy in terms of intellectual freedom. Specifically state if the policy mentions confidentiality, controversial materials, and sensitive topics in the criteria and what it says. How could the policy be improved in these areas? Does it go beyond the ALA's and AASL's policies on controversial materials and textbook recommendations in any way? If so, how? Give specific examples.

Criterion 5. Special areas.

Assess your policy in terms of multimedia, serials, digital resources, gifts, consortia, interlibrary lending, and other special collection. How does it stack up against ALA recommendations? Does the policy mention any special areas? How could it be improved? Does it go beyond the ALA and textbook recommendations in any way? If so, how? Give specific examples.

Criterion 6. Reconsideration of materials.

Assess your policy in terms of reconsideration of materials. Is it approved by the school board? Does it have the proper forms? Does it give procedures? How could it be improved? Does it go beyond the ALA and AASL recommendations in any way? If so, how? Give specific examples.

Criterion 7. Selection procedures.

Assess your policy in terms of selection procedures, including deselection (weeding). How does it stack up against these recommendations? How specific is it? How could it be improved? Does it go beyond the ALA and AASL recommendations in any way? If so, how? Give specific examples.

Criterion 8. Other.

Does your policy have any sections that go beyond those sections recommended by ALA or AASL? Is so, what are they? Describe them. Evaluate them. Do not repeat information given elsewhere in your evaluation. Give specific examples.

Criterion 9. Recommendations.

Summarize recommendations for policy improvement. Include a time estimate for current and future revisions with reasoning. Include ways in which you will prioritize the sections to be updated. Refer to ALA, AASL, or your own ideas as sources of recommendations. Give specific examples.

ADDITIONAL READINGS

Downs, E. (2010). *The school library media specialist's policy and procedures writer.* New York: Neil Schuman.

Hoffman, F. W., & Wood, R. J. (2007). *Library collection development policies: School libraries and learning resource centers.* Lanham, MD: Scarecrow Press.

HELPFUL MULTIMEDIA

Acedo, S. (2014). Collection development: The blended collections of the 21st century library. Retrieved from http://www.slideshare.net/AcedoShannon/collection-development-isacs-oct -2014-39953201

American Association of School Librarians (AASL). (n.d.). Position statements. Retrieved from http://www.ala.org/aasl/advocacy/resources/statements

American Library Association. (1998, October). Workbook for selection policy writing. Retrieved from http://www.ala.org/Template.cfm?Section=dealing&Template/ContenManagement/Content Display.cfm&ContentID=11173

American Library Association. (1999). Intellectual freedom statements and guidelines. Retrieved from http://www.ala.org/aboutala/governance/policymanual/updatedpolicymanual/section2 /53intellfreedom

American Library Association. (2018, December). Selection & reconsideration policy toolkit for public, school, & academic libraries. Retrieved from http://www.ala.org/tools/challengesupport /selectionpolicytoolkit

Resources for School Librarians. (n.d.). Retrieved from http://www.sldirectory.com/

Suffolk School Library Media Association. (n.d.). What should be included in collection develop- ment policies? Retrieved from https://suffolkslma.weebly.com/collection-development -policies.html

CHAPTER 6

Selection

Key Learnings

- Selection policies provide guidance for consistent, appropriate materials selection choices.
- Include a detailed materials challenge policy in your selection policy in the event that you are asked to reconsider an item in the school library collection.
- Published and crowdsourced reviews, along with your knowledge of the school environment, are key sources of information to guide collection decisions.

As a school librarian you will be involved in updating a selection policy for your school. If one is not in place, you should take the lead in creating a selection policy, including guidelines and procedures that relate to requests for reconsideration of materials. As discussed in Chapter 5 "Policies and Procedures," policy statements are stronger and more effective when formulated by a group. The school librarian's professional responsibility is to ensure that appropriate policies are in place. Involving educators, administrators, learners, and members of the community is vital to the process. A major benefit to this is the participants' advocacy and support of the principles on which the policy is based. This process presents an opportunity to explain the school library's role in the educational process, to emphasize the importance of a commitment to intellectual freedom, and to discuss the concept of providing access to information.

Some states have mandates for school library selection policies that include procedures for reconsideration of challenged materials. In other states, similar mandates are present at the school district level. You should contact your state department of education or department of public instruction for information about such mandates.

ELEMENTS OF A SELECTION POLICY

If you include your library's selection policy in a larger manual that deals with all policies and procedures for the library, then statements that address philosophy might be covered in an earlier section of your manual. However, if your selection policy is issued as a separate document, several elements need to be included. The following section discusses each of these elements.

Statement of Philosophy

This brief statement presents the school district's values and beliefs. It can refer to the school's mission and goals statement or language from that document. The statement of philosophy should also address how the educational resources help the school achieve its goals.

Other relevant documents can be duplicated in this section. A statement referring to the U.S. Constitution's First Amendment's protection of learners' rights to access information to read, listen, view, and evaluate is important to include. Readers can be directed to copies of documents in an appendix that support these principles. Such documents include the American Library Association's *Library Bill of Rights* and *Freedom to Read Statement*, the National Council of Teachers of English's *Students' Right to Read*, and the American Film and Video's Association's *Freedom to View Statement*.

Sample phrases in this section generally start with "The Board of [school district's name] through its professional staff 'shall provide,' 'will provide,' or 'is committed to facilitating teaching and learning by providing' . . ." One or more of the following phrases could be used to complete sentences:

- "library collections that meet both the curricular needs and personal needs of learners"
- "resources in various formats and varying levels of difficulty"
- "materials that provide a global perspective and promote diversity"
- "resources that reflect the basic humanity of all people and are free of stereotypes"
- "library materials that present different points of view in an objective manner"
- "materials that will help learners develop critical thinking skills and aesthetic appreciation"

Selection Objectives

This element of the policy translates the school district's philosophy and goals into collection objectives. The statements show how the collection helps the school meet its goals. Objectives identify the materials that will be in the collection, present a rationale for using a variety of resources in the school, and describe the basis for judging the educational suitability of the materials for use by learners and educators. Examples of main objective statements are:

- To make available to faculty and learners a collection of materials that will support, supplement, and enrich the curriculum
- To provide a wide range of the best materials available on appropriate levels of difficulty

- To enhance the curriculum with materials representative of the points of view of the religious, cultural, ethnic, and social groupings within the community
- To select materials that present various sides of controversial issues so that learners have an opportunity to develop skills in critical analysis and in making informed judgments in their daily lives
- To place principle above personal opinion or prejudice in order to assure a comprehensive collection that is appropriate to the school community
- To provide materials in a variety of formats, including both print and electronic materials, to support the learners' learning needs
- To select materials that stimulate growth in factual knowledge, literary appreciation, aesthetic values, and societal standards

Responsibility for Selection

An important element of the selection policy is stating who is responsible for selection decisions. If the policy applies to all instructional materials, this statement should distinguish between those who are responsible for text materials and those responsible for library program materials.

These statements usually acknowledge that the school board is legally responsible and delegates to school librarians the authority to select. The term *school librarians* can be defined as "professional, certified personnel employed by the district."

A statement that identifies who participates in the selection process should also be included. This statement indicates the role and level of involvement of educators, learners, administrators, staff, and community members in the selection process. Some questions that might be addressed include the following: Does a committee make selection decisions? Do school librarians work independently? Is a combination of committee selections and librarian selections utilized? How is responsibility delegated? How is input for selection gathered from educators and learners?

Selection Criteria

Selection criteria generally consist of two or more parts. The first is a list of general criteria that apply to all materials and relate to the district or school goals. A statement that these criteria apply to all materials, including gifts and loans, can eliminate the need to write a separate section about such items.

General criteria commonly used include literary qualities, technical qualities, qualifications of authors or producers, and appropriateness for audience. You can obtain additional assistance for this section by consulting Chapter 7, "General Selection Criteria." Criteria that are often used for general selection indicate that the materials should do the following:

- Contribute to the instructional program's objectives.
- Be consistent with and support the general educational goals of the state and district.
- Help learners gain an awareness of our pluralistic society.
- Be relevant to today's world.
- Reflect the problems, aspirations, attitudes, and ideals of society.
- Be appropriate for the age, ability level, learning style, and social and emotional development of the intended users.
- Be appropriate for the subject area.

- Meet quality standards in terms of content, format, and presentation.
- Be selected for their strengths, rather than rejected for their weaknesses.
- Reflect value commensurate with cost and/or need.
- Not represent a personal bias.
- Represent artistic, historic, and literary qualities
- Have a high degree of potential user appeal.
- Motivate learners to examine their own attitudes; to understand their rights, duties, and responsibilities as citizens; and to make informed judgments in their daily lives.

In selecting formats for possible purchase, the school librarian should consider the following general criteria:

- Reputation of the author, illustrator, publisher, and producer
- Overall content quality and accuracy
- Currency and appropriateness of the content
- Value in relation to cost and need
- Value to the collection (ALA, 2018a).

The second part of selection criteria can address criteria for specific formats of materials, including electronic formats and equipment. If you want to address the criteria for specific formats, the contents of Chapter 8, "Criteria by Format," will be especially helpful.

Some policies identify selection sources to consult and then specify that two or more favorable reviews must appear in the selection tools before an item can be considered for selection. This practice has several disadvantages that may prove to be restrictive. First, reviewing journals and selection tools often do not review the same titles. Second, a dearth of reviews exists for some formats. Third, a specific list of selection tools may not be comprehensive or may not identify sources actually used. This policy creates a problem if none of the cited sources has reviewed a particular item. The requirement of having two reviews in particular selection tools limits selections made by librarians and should not be included in policies.

While selection aids can be helpful in identifying titles to be considered for purchase, using reviews as a criterion for selection focuses on the review, rather than on the professional judgment of the school librarian. However, if you choose to include procedures relating to selection of materials, you might want to list the selection tools that are recommended as consultation aids. Possible wording could be: "The following recommended lists can be consulted in the selection of materials, but selection is not limited to their listing." An annotated listing of some selection aids that could be included in such a list can be found in the "Appendix: Resources and Further Reading."

Gifts

If the acceptance of gifts is not included in the general criteria section of your selection policy, statements addressing criteria used for the acceptance or rejection of gifts need to be included in a separate section. Most schools apply the same criteria for acceptance of gifts as they do for purchases. However, you might want to also consider how you will handle items that are donated by businesses or commercial concerns. It is useful to note that no advertising beyond the name of the contributing company be included and that donations must relate to the curriculum. You might also wish to include a statement relating to the currency of donated materials. This may eliminate the need of having to deal with boxes of donated *National Geographic* magazines from the 1960s and 1970s. While some of the articles in those magazines might have interesting information, most of the information will be quite outdated, and your available space to put them on your shelves will most likely be limited.

Some school librarians also include a statement relating to the fact that all gifts become the property of the school district and when declared surplus can be dispensed as deemed appropriate by the librarian. This might include transferring the surplus items to another school or weeding them from the collection. A statement could read: "The library does not accept gifts with restrictions or conditions relating to their final use, disposition, or location."

Policies relating to the acceptance of monetary gifts to purchase materials should also be addressed. If accepting monetary gifts, specific procedures should be written and carefully followed.

You might also want to address some procedures relating to gifts made to the school library. The provision of letters and/or receipts to acknowledge gifts to a library should be part of such procedures. The letter or receipt should note the number and types of materials donated, but should not specify a dollar amount, unless the gift was monetary.

Other procedures might include whether notations of donated resources are included in the catalog entry and whether a bookplate or notation is added to the material itself.

Policies on Controversial Materials

You should include a section in your policy that deals with intellectual freedom and the handling of controversial materials. Most school districts have written policies that address this topic not only in regard to materials present in the library, but also for books or other formats used in classroom lessons. Thus, it is important for you to include in your selection policy any school district policies that relate to controversial materials in a school library. This can be done in the text of your selection policy, or the school district policy can be placed in an appendix and referred to from the text.

You need to include a statement that your school library supports the principle of intellectual freedom and explain why it is important to maintain. If you have not already referred to the First Amendment to the U.S. Constitution, or to other documents that address intellectual freedom, you should do so in this section. Wording in this section might read as follows: "The Lincoln School Library supports the principles of intellectual freedom inherent in the First Amendment to the United States Constitution as expressed in official statements of professional associations. These include [identify statement(s)] and form a part of this policy."

VOICES FROM THE FIELD

Both of our [book] challenges that went to committee were with administrators new to the district. The superintendent in each case asked me to select the committee members as per the policy and the administrators simply went along with the process. The books were successfully defended in both cases. The complainant was treated respectfully, the discussion was open, the tone was tense, but compassionate. We could focus on the book and on caring for the people because the other details were spelled out.

—School librarian from Michigan

Request for Reconsideration of Materials

Most selection policies also include procedures for handling complaints and for focusing the complainant's attention on the principles of intellectual freedom, rather than on the material itself. A school district may have specific procedures for dealing with challenged materials. In such a case, you will need to place these procedures in your policies and procedures document and make certain they are implemented correctly.

If the steps to follow for challenged materials are not specified by the school district, then you should meet with an advisory board at your school, develop the procedures, and put them through an approval process. Possible steps to consider in your reconsideration of materials in your school library include the following:

1. Listen calmly and with courtesy to the complainant.
2. Explain to the complainant the selection criteria used for materials that are in the library and try to resolve the issue informally by discussing the educational uses of the material in question and noting relevant sections of the American Library Association's *Access to Resources and Services in the School Library Program: An Interpretation of the Library Bill of Rights.*
3. If the complainant wants to proceed with a formal request for reconsideration of a material, provide a copy of the policies and procedures related to the handling of challenged materials, as well as a copy of the school's *Request for Reconsideration of Library Resources* form.
4. Instruct the complainant that the form must be completed before a formal complaint proceeds.
5. Inform the principal of the challenge and the identity of the complainant. If the complaint is resolved informally, keep the identity of the complainant confidential.
6. When the complainant returns the completed form, the principal will inform the superintendent of schools of a request for formal reconsideration.
7. Provide the principal with a formal response to the complaint referencing library selection criteria and policy.
8. Contact the established library advisory committee, which should include a building administrator, a classroom educator from the appropriate grade level or subject area, the school librarian, an objective member of the community, and a learner (if the challenged material is in a secondary school).
9. Appoint a chairperson for the committee.
10. Have the chairperson arrange a meeting of the committee to be held within 10 working days after the form is returned to the school by the complainant.
11. At the first meeting, instruct all members of the committee to read the completed *Request for Reconsideration of Library Resources* form and to read, view, or listen to the material in question. The librarian may need to obtain additional copies of the challenged material (book, video, DVD, CD, or audiocassette) through interlibrary loan or through informal means before time for the next meeting can be set.
12. At a second meeting when all committee members have had ample opportunity to examine and evaluate the challenged material, discuss the item that has been questioned.
13. Instruct the committee members to form opinions on the material as a whole, not on specific passages or selections.
14. Have the committee reach a decision, using majority rules, to retain or remove the item.
15. Have the chairperson complete a report of the committee's procedures and its decision regarding the challenged material and submit the report to the principal.

16. Instruct the principal to send a copy of the report to the complainant and discuss it with the complainant if so requested. Remind the principal to also submit a copy of the report to the superintendent of school.
17. If the complainant continues to be dissatisfied with the process, inform that person that he has the right to appeal the decision of the committee to the superintendent of schools and the district school board.
18. Keep challenged materials in circulation until the process is complete.

Figure 6.1 is a sample of a form for requesting the reconsideration of a library resource. You should make certain that the form that you use meets the needs of your particular school setting and has been approved. In some schools the same form is used for challenging materials in a classroom setting as for the reconsideration of materials in a library; thus, in those cases some adaptation of this sample form would be needed.

Generally speaking, procedures are written for internal use and are not necessarily available for public use; however, in the case of challenged materials, a single document for the public's use should combine both the policies and procedures for handling the challenge. This document should be readily available to the public, with a copy kept at the circulation desk. Sharing this information in a forthright manner can alleviate some of the tension that can occur in situations where materials are challenged.

Most challenges can be settled informally if one takes the time to calmly listen to the complainant's concerns and then explain the library's criteria for selection, emphasizing the principle of intellectual freedom. Assuring parents that you respect the interest that they have in their own child's reading or viewing can often satisfy the needs of parents to voice their concerns. It is also in your best interest to establish a library advisory board to advise you on a number of policy matters, and also to act as your reconsideration committee. As one school librarian from Michigan pointed out, "It is vital to have the committee requirements in place to avoid charges of 'stacking' the committee by a disgruntled community member."

Challenges to materials are to be expected in most schools. The challenges may come from parents, community members, educators, principals, or organized groups. Having a written procedure to follow and knowing how to respond to a challenge will alleviate the emotional upset that sometimes is experienced by school librarians when faced with an irate parent or an outspoken member of an organized group that challenges library materials. To ensure that all queries, whether internal or external, are treated in the same manner, each individual's complaint should be treated according to the written procedures. Be aware that grassroots organizations may challenge library materials in schools to which they have no connection for religious, political, or other reasons. Your policy should make clear that only members of the school community may initiate the reconsideration policy.

SELECTION PROCEDURES

In choosing materials, a school librarian plans and carries out certain activities that culminate in selection decisions. These activities include identifying and assessing evaluative information about materials, arranging for examining materials either through visiting exhibits or through examination centers, and providing ways to involve others in the process. These steps lead to the direct acquisition of materials or obtaining materials and information through resource sharing and electronic means. For a listing of resources that can assist in the selection process, see the "Appendix: Resources and Further Reading."

REQUEST FOR RECONSIDERATION OF LIBRARY MATERIAL

The School Board of XYZ School has delegated the responsibilities of selection of books and other resources to the school librarian, and has established reconsideration procedures to address concerns about any of the selected materials. If you wish to request reconsideration of a book or other library resource, please return the completed form to the principal of XYZ School.

Title: _____

Author: _____

Publisher:_____   Copyright Date: _____

Person Initiating Request:_____   Date of Request: _____

Address:_____   Phone Number: _____
Email Address:_____

Please answer the following questions completely. Use additional pages if necessary:

1. Are you representing yourself?   Organization?
    Name?_____

2. Resource Type: ☐ Book   ☐ Textbook   ☐ DVD   ☐ Magazine   ☐ Newspaper
                    ☐ Electronic Resource   ☐ Other

3. What brought this book/resource to your attention?

4. What concerns do you have about this book/resource?

5. Have you examined the entire book/resource? If not, what parts did you examine?

6. What other resource(s) would you suggest to provide additional information on this specific issue or topic?

7. What action would you like the library to take regarding this book/resource?

8. Would you like to make a presentation to the Reconsideration of Library Resources Committee and/or School Board regarding this material? ☐ Yes   ☐ No

9. Other comments?

Figure 6.1. Request Form for Reconsideration of Library Resources

Overview of the Selection Process

Selection is the process of deciding what materials to add to the collection. Librarians can identify potential materials through many sources. For example, administrators, educators, and learners request specific items or types of materials. The librarian learns about new materials by reading reviews, viewing the announcements of publishers and producers, and previewing materials.

You need to keep a record of suggestions and requests to purchase materials. This can be done electronically in a computer file, in a card file, or simply by keeping written notes; this record is called a *consideration file*. You should record as much bibliographic and purchasing information about the item as you can obtain, including the identifying source and the person who requested the item. The next step is to determine whether the item is already in the collection or on order. Some librarians enter the information in the online catalog, so users will be aware that the item is being considered or on order.

Once an item is fully identified, the librarian must decide to include or exclude it from the collection. The librarian bases this selection decision on several considerations, including collection policy; budget; and content, format, use, and immediacy of need. After the librarian has decided to purchase the item, the status of the record for the item is changed from *consideration file* to *order file*. The actions following this step compose the acquisition process.

Sources of Information about Resources

Bibliographic tools provide information about the availability of materials, their cost, and whether they are recommended. Trade bibliographies, such as *Books in Print* (R. R. Bowker), Bowker's online *New Books in Print*, and *Canadian Books in Print* (University of Toronto Press), provide information about the existence of materials, but do not evaluate them. Selection tools, such as *Senior High Core Collection* (H. W. Wilson), *Middle and Junior High School Core Collection* (H. W. Wilson), and *Children's Core Collection* (H. W. Wilson), evaluate materials and may include purchasing information. They are available electronically and in print format and are especially useful if you are developing a library collection from scratch.

When considering a bibliography or selection tool for use or purchase, read the introduction and examine several entries. This will help answer the following questions about the work:

- *Purpose of the bibliography*: Does it meet your need?
- *Directions for use*: Are they clear? Does the work give sample entries with explanations?
- *Format*: Is the bibliography available in print, CD-ROM, or online?
- *Extent of coverage*: Does the resource include information about a variety of formats?
- Does it provide information for many items, or is coverage limited? Does it include materials for a wide range of audiences, preschool through adult? What periods of publication and production does the work include?
- *Method for collecting the information and designated responsibility*: Who wrote the entries? What are the writers' qualifications? Are reviews signed?
- *Criteria for inclusion*: On what basis are items included? Are the criteria stated? Is the selection policy provided?

- *Form and content of entry*: Does the work present information clearly? Does it use symbols and abbreviations? Symbols may indicate levels of recommendation, reviewing sources, interest level, readability, and type of media. What ordering and bibliographic information does the work give? Are the annotations descriptive, evaluative, or both? Are all items recommended equally? Are items recommended for specific situations, uses, or audiences? Are there comparisons with other titles or formats? Does the work include only materials that have received favorable reviews in other tools?
- *Organization of entries*: Are the indexes necessary to locate an item? Do cross-references direct the user to related items? Do indexes provide access by author, title, series titles, audience, reading level, and subject? Does the index include analytical entries? For example, the selection tools by H. W. Wilson Company include analytical entries for individual folktales in anthologies, biographical sketches (not limited to collective biographies), subjects, and short stories in collections. This information is helpful in locating these materials for learners and educators.
- *Date of publication*: Does the work provide the compiler's closing date? How often is the bibliography revised or cumulated? Does it provide supplements? What time lag exists between compiling the information and the issuing of the bibliography?
- *Special features*: Does the bibliography include directories for sources of materials? Does the work include appendices? If so, what is included?
- *Cost*: Does the tool provide sufficient information for a variety of users to merit the expenditure for it?

Digital resources have similar, but specific selection criteria, which are detailed in Chapter 7, "General Selection Criteria," and Chapter 8, "Criteria by Format."

Selection Tools

Selection tools exist in a variety of formats: books, reviewing periodicals, and bibliographic essays. These tools can be in print or electronic format.

Books

Commonly used general selection tools that appear in book and electronic format are the H. W. Wilson series (*Children's Core Collection, Middle and Junior High School Core Collection*, and *Senior High Core Collection*). The lead time required to produce printed formats of these books creates a time gap between the publication of the last item reviewed and the publication date of the bibliography itself. Subscribing to the online versions of these tools can lessen this time gap. Even if published in electronic formats, the bibliographies are sometimes not as current as reviewing journals. Other print and electronic selection tools list recommended materials for specific subjects, audiences, or formats. See the "Appendix: Resources and Further Reading" for titles of these books.

Reviewing Journals

Reviewing journals evaluate currently published and produced materials. There is a wide range of these journals, each with unique and valuable features. Commercial firms, professional associations, education agencies, and other publishers produce reviewing journals. Generally, they are written for a specific audience, such as school librarians or classroom educators. The coverage of materials that journals review is often limited by format, potential users, subjects, or particular perspectives. The reviews are written by journal staff members or by professionals in the field. Signed reviews sometimes provide information about the reviewer's position or background.

The content of some journals such as *Booklist* are primarily reviews of materials. However, many reviewing journals, such as *School Library Connection, Voice of Youth Advocates (VOYA),* and *School Library Journal,* also include articles or columns of interest to school librarians. Some professional journals, such as the American Association of School Librarians' *Knowledge Quest,* limit their reviews to materials that could be a part of a professional collection.

Journal editors have legitimate reasons for why their journals might not review a specific title. Some do not have a work reviewed unless it can be reviewed within a specific time after its publication. Some titles may be outside a journal's scope, or they might simply fail to meet other criteria set up by the journal. A huge number of juvenile resources are produced each year so it is impossible for a single journal to review all of them.

Locating reviews for audiovisual materials, computer software, electronic materials, websites, and online databases can be more challenging than finding book reviews. However, more review journals are including these formats than in past years. Cumulated indexes that appear in the back pages of some journals can be helpful in the search for reviews, but a more comprehensive approach to review indexing can be found in tools such as *Book Review Index* and *Book Review Digest.* These tools are available in print format and online. The cost of such tools may require that all school libraries in the district share them.

Bibliographic Essays

Bibliographic essays that describe and recommend materials about a subject, a theme, a specific use, or an audience can be found in journals such as *Teacher Librarian, School Library Journal,* and *Book Links.* These essays can be very helpful, but they require careful analysis. Readers do not know whether the writer simply overlooked an omitted item or whether the writer deliberately omitted that item. Usually, bibliographic essays focus on a specific topic and do not provide overall assessments of the resources.

Best, Notable, and Recommended Materials

Some professional journals contain articles listing materials that have been selected as *best, notable,* or *recommended* for particular years. Some lists are annotated, while others simply contain the bibliographic information. Such lists can also be found online. It is important to consider authority (who has chosen the materials) when using such lists as selection aids. For instance, resources compiled by national professional library associations can generally be considered reliable since they are selections made by committees that include several librarians and library educators. ALA's Selection Policy Toolkit (2018a) includes an excellent compilation of book award and recommended lists; lists found on individuals' or publishers' websites may need to be examined more closely to ensure that the lists are assembled without bias.

Relying on Reviewing Media

School librarians use reviewing media on a regular basis. If no selection committee exists, the entire burden of selection rests with the librarian. To examine every item published or produced within a given year would be an impossible task.

What should school librarians expect from reviews? Brock (2019) wrote, "The best reviews include a brief summary of the book and critical comments to help librarians decide if a book is worth purchasing. Most reviews will also include the most appropriate grades or age range for its readers" (p. 20). Remember that reviews reflect the writer's opinion, based on the reviewers' knowledge of materials and learners.

A variety of sources provide reviews. In addition to the ones noted earlier in this chapter, reviews can be *found* on websites of individuals, professional groups, and commercial organizations, such as Amazon.com. Like with other review sources, you should try to determine the authority and background of the reviewer and whether there are guidelines for the reviewers.

Evaluate reviews by examining the following:

- Bibliographic information
- Purchasing information
- Cataloging information
- Description and evaluation of literary characteristics: plot, character, theme, setting, point of view, and style
- Description and evaluation of usability: authority, appropriateness, scope, accuracy, arrangement, and organization
- Description and evaluation of visual characteristics: shape, line, edge, color, proportion, detail, composition, and medium style
- Description and evaluation of comparison: author, illustrator, and other works
- Description and evaluation of sociological factors: controversial or popular
- Description and evaluation of other considerations: total artistic appearance, book design, use, and audience

School Library Connection, School Library Journal, and *Teacher Librarian* are three professional journals published specifically for school librarians. Each of the journals reviews a variety of formats. A summary of their reviewing coverage is as follows:

School Library Connection

- Bibliographic information: author, title, illustrator, year of publication, number of pages, cost, publisher or producer, ISBN, URL for web items
- Formats: books (fiction, nonfiction, reference, biography, poetry, graphic novels, Spanish language, and professional reading); free web; subscription web; software-CD-ROM; mobile learning
- Grade-level divisions: picture books; fiction K–5; fiction 6–8; fiction 9–12; nonfiction (listed by subjects, with grade levels at the end of the bibliographic information)
- Grade-level symbols (placed in small circles at the beginning of the review text): green K–5; blue 6–8; red 9–12
- Ratings: highly recommended (large gold star in front of the red highlighted title of the material); recommended; additional selection; not recommended
- Reviewer information: name of reviewer and place of employment at the end of review

School Library Journal

- Bibliographic information: author, title, illustrator, number of pages, publisher (producer and distributor for multimedia), cost, ISBN, LC (when available); URL for websites; miscellaneous information (number of hours for audio cassettes, CDs, and DVDs; educator's guide included or available online)

- Formats: books (fiction, nonfiction, reference, professional); multimedia (video and audio); digital resources (covered in separate articles)
- Grade levels: provided at the beginning of the text of the review, no grade-level divisions, no grade-level symbols
- Grade-level symbols: none
- Ratings: highly recommended materials in yellow highlighted boxes with a large red star placed at the beginning of the bibliographic information
- Reviewer information: name of reviewer and place of employment at the end of the review
- Online reviews: some reviews are available at the *School Library Journal* website

Teacher Librarian

All reviews appear in various colored highlighted sidebars in different locations throughout the journal.

- Bibliographic information: title, author, publisher, date of publication, ISBN, cost, grade levels, URL for websites
- Formats: books (junior fiction, young adult [YA] fiction, adult books for teens, picture books, graphic novels, junior nonfiction, YA nonfiction); websites; software, professional resources included in separate articles
- Grade levels: provided at the end of the bibliographic information, no grade-level divisions, no grade-level symbols
- Ratings: none
- Reviewer information: name and photo of reviewer at the top of the sidebar; same reviewers for every issue

Other journals frequently used by school librarians for reviews of materials include *Booklist*, *Horn Book Magazine*, *Kliatt*, *Library Journal*, and *VOYA*.

Personal Examination

The ideal way to select resources for your school library is by personal examination. Depending on your school district's policies, you may be able to personally examine materials. The most practical ways include visits by sales representatives, formal previewing arrangements, visiting examination centers, and attending conferences.

Previewing is one of the most efficient ways to examine materials prior to purchasing. This is the practice of borrowing materials from an examination center, a producer, a distributor, or a jobber for a specific time for the purpose of evaluation. Previewing is an effective way to involve learners and educators in the selection process. Previewing is not a free way to supplement the collection, nor should several educators within one building request the same item for examination at different times. The librarian is responsible for returning previewing materials in good condition within the specified time. Some companies will not allow preview of certain formats, such as databases or computer software. Also, some school districts do not allow the request of materials for preview. However, requesting materials you are seriously considering for purchase is an excellent way to make informed selection decisions.

When attending conferences, you should always set aside ample time to examine the materials in the exhibit areas. This is an excellent opportunity to not only view the materials, but to also ask company representatives questions or to provide them with suggestions. Vendors are interested in the opinions of school librarians and welcome their input into ways to improve their products. Some vendors arrange focus groups at conferences and present their new products; they then ask librarians to provide comments about the products.

Some school district staff arrange for exhibits of materials in a central location during the preopening school activities. These exhibits allow librarians and educators to compare a wide range of materials. If your school district sponsors such exhibits, invite educators to examine the materials with you.

Another way to personally evaluate materials is to visit an examination or preview center. These centers may serve at district, regional, or state levels. They can be housed in the district school library center, at a university, or in a state agency. Often the materials in a preview center cannot be checked out, but can be examined only within the center.

Whether your evaluation involves personal examination of items or relies on reviews, some materials will, for one reason or another, remain unused or prove to be inappropriate. You should consider these situations as learning experiences. Schomberg (1993) observed, "There seems to be no way to avoid the occasional 'lemon.' Selection of materials based upon reviews cannot be expected to be successful 100% of the time" (p. 42).

Other Sources of Information

Information about materials can also be obtained from publishers, producers, distributors, vendors, and wholesalers. The information appears in catalogs, on flyers, on television, and on the Internet. However, you should always be cautious about making selections from only these types of sources since their main objective is to sell their products.

Follett Titlewave

Titlewave is a website for Pre-K–12 school library collection development and assessment. Registration for Titlewave is free to anyone associated with a school. With Titlewave, you can:

- Search more than 1.5 million print and digital educational materials
- Quickly refine results with a variety of categories like release date, product type, interest level, reading level, classification, reading program, and language
- Explore title details including valuable information such as sets, series, full-text reviews, award information, and more
- Find books organized by reading program, including Accelerated Reader, Fountas & Pinnell, Lexile, and Reading Counts!
- Enjoy customized educational content professionally curated to meet your curriculum need
- Search by Follett's curriculum tags to find educationally relevant content

Titlewave also includes ordering and processing tools.

Mackin Compendium

Compendium is a professionally compiled collection of the most recent, highly reviewed Pre-K–12 titles. All selections have been culled from the leading review sources. Compendium content is published as quarterly issues for elementary, middle school, high school, nonprint, professional, and reference. All titles have a full-color book image, in-depth summary, review sources, author and publisher, ISBN, available bindings, subject heading, and more. Compendium is also available as an app for your smartphone or tablet.

Crowdsourced Reviews

Using the power of the "crowd" to rate and review resources has been a major innovation of the digital world. While Amazon's users provide many reviews of books and other materials that are helpful, crowdsourced sites like LibraryThing and GoodReads bring together millions of readers to provide feedback on current and classic books, eBooks, audio books, and movies. Common to all of the sites are user-submitted reviews that can be directly accessed via search, but they also use sophisticated recommending algorithms based on your search and browse behavior to "push" titles to your attention that you might otherwise overlook.

LibraryThing

LibraryThing has over 1 million users and more than 58 million books in its database. It gets book information from Amazon as well as from libraries. Recommendations are a central service of LibraryThing, as straightforwardly seen in its BookSuggester recommender feature. LibraryThing provides guidance in a host of other ways, too. For example, members can get recommendations from other members, or use tags to find specific types of books.

GoodReads

GoodReads is the largest crowdsourced review site with 5 million users, many of whom identify as librarians, and a staggering 130 million books in its database. Many libraries run reading groups through the site, including the San Diego Public Library and Salt Lake County Library Services, so the site's strength may be in identifying popular materials for older readers.

Although they may not provide objective evaluations of materials, crowdsources sites can be good ways of tracking trends in reading material and popular interest as well as communities' learners can join to extend their reading interests beyond the school day.

Involving Others in Selection

The idea that educators, learners, and administrators should participate in making selection decisions is not new, but the practice is not always utilized. Common ways to involve others in the process include:

- Routing bibliographies and reviewing journals to educators and administrators
- Attending faculty, departmental, or grade-level meetings to learn about curriculum changes and to discuss future purchases
- Conducting interest inventories with learners
- Sending out forms to educators and administrators to ask them what materials they would like purchased
- Providing a materials suggestion box at the circulation desk

School library advisory committees are another way to involve others. Teachers, community members, and learners can be members of the advisory committee. In some districts, the advisory committee's responsibilities are limited to policy issues and to establishing priorities for acquisition. In other districts, the advisory committee may be involved in the selection process or in making decisions about which materials to remove or replace.

SOURCES OF ASSISTANCE

Information regarding selection of materials is available from a variety of sources, including professional colleagues and professional associations. Several school districts and individual schools have placed their selection policies online. A selected list of such policies can be found at the end of this chapter under Helpful Multimedia. The American Library Association website, which includes a workbook for selection policy writing (ALA, 2018b), will be particularly helpful to you if you are creating a new selection policy for a school.

A list of suggested readings dealing with selection policies, intellectual freedom, censorship, and handling challenges can be found at the end of this chapter. Additional discussion of intellectual freedom appears in Chapter 13, "Legal and Ethical Issues with the Collection." Other organizations, besides the American Library Association, offer valuable assistance in handling censorship disputes. These include the American Association of University Women, American Booksellers Association for Freedom of Expression, American Civil Liberties Union, American Federation of Teachers, Association for Supervision and Curriculum Development, Association of American Publishers, Electronic Frontier Foundation, Freedom Forum, Freedom to Read Foundation, International Reading Association, Lamda Legal, Media Coalition, National Association of Elementary School Principals, National Coalition against Censorship, National Council of Teachers of English, National Education Association, National School Boards Association, and People for the American Way Foundation. Contact information for these groups can be located easily by using the title of the organization in an online search on the Internet.

CONCLUSION

Written selection policies for materials can be a separate document or part of a larger policies and procedures manual. Many school districts have selection policies for school library materials, as well as for textbooks. It is important to include in an individual school library's policies and procedures manual any portions of the school district's policies that relate to school library materials. Selection policies should include who is responsible for selection, criteria for selecting materials, and how to handle controversial materials. Having written policies and procedures for challenged materials can ease tensions for a school librarian, as well as provide an objective process for those persons who register concerns about specific materials in a collection. Be sure to have your school and district administrators sign the policies or officially record them in some other way.

The ideal way to make selections of materials is to personally examine the resources. This can be done at conferences, special exhibits, examination centers, and by requesting materials for preview. Reading reviews of items and referring to bibliographies and special selection aids are other valuable means of selecting materials for school libraries. Teachers, administrators, and learners should also be involved in the selection process.

GROUP ACTIVITY

Establish a free account at Follett Library Resource's Titlewave (http://www.titlewave .com). Then, use Titlewave to analyze a frequently challenged book and consider the ways in which Titlewave might help you defend against a challenge. Choose a book from the American Library Association's list of the most frequently challenged books (see list at http://www.ala.org/bbooks/frequentlychallengedbooks) and locate reviews for it in Title- wave. Then, consider these questions:

- Who might challenge the book and why?
- Locate review(s) of the book in Titlewave.
- Which publication(s) reviewed the book? Were the reviews positive or negative?
- Based on the reviews alone, would you purchase the book? Why or why not?
- How might the review(s) be used to defend against a book challenge? What is missing from the reviews that would help you handle a challenge situation?
- What other features could Titlewave add that would help you in a challenge situation?

As a group, discuss your title choices and experience locating reviews. Compare the rea- sons the books were challenged. How might your selection policy allow you to prepare for the challenge?

REFERENCES

American Library Association (ALA). (2018a, January). Review resources. Retrieved from http:// www.ala.org/tools/challengesupport/selectionpolicytoolkit/reviewresources

American Library Association (ALA). (2018b, January). Selection & reconsideration policy toolkit for public, school, & academic libraries. Retrieved from http://www.ala.org/tools/challenge support/selectionpolicytoolkit

American Library Association (ALA). (2018c, January). Selection criteria. Retrieved from http:// www.ala.org/tools/challengesupport/selectionpolicytoolkit/criteria

Brock, R. (2019). *Young adult literature in action.* Santa Barbara, CA: Libraries Unlimited.

Schomberg, J. (1993). Tools of the trade: School library media specialists, reviews, and collection development. In B. Hearne and R. Sutton (eds). *Evaluating children's books: A critical look: Aesthetic, social, and political aspects of analyzing and using children's books* (pp. 37–46). Champaign–Urbana, IL: University of Illinois Graduate School of Library and Information Science.

HELPFUL MULTIMEDIA

American Library Association (ALA). (2017). Conducting a challenge hearing. Retrieved from http://www.ala.org/tools/challengesupport/hearing

Mackin Compendium. https://www.mackin.com/corp/services/programs/compendium/

CHAPTER 7

General Selection Criteria

Key Learnings
- Quality is a universal selection criterion.
- Different formats may require different criteria.
- Legacy collections of obsolete media may be maintained to meet local needs and preferences.

Selection is a complex, decision-making process that benefits from consistent application of defined, appropriate, and tailored criteria. For example, the American Library Association (2018) recommends that school librarians consider these general criteria, prior to considering resource-specific elements. Does the resource:

- Support and enrich the curriculum and/or learners' personal interests and learning;
- Meet high standards in literary, artistic, and aesthetic quality; technical aspects; and physical format;
- Be appropriate for the subject area and for the age, emotional development, ability level, learning styles, and social, emotional, and intellectual development of the learners for whom the materials are selected;
- Incorporate accurate and authentic factual content from authoritative sources;
- Earn favorable reviews in standard reviewing sources and/or favorable recommendations based on preview and examination of materials by professional personnel;
- Exhibit a high degree of potential user appeal and interest;
- Represent differing viewpoints on controversial issues;
- Provide a global perspective and promote diversity by including materials by authors and illustrators of all cultures;

- Include a variety of resources in physical and virtual formats including print and non-print such as electronic and multimedia (including subscription databases and other online products, eBooks, educational games, and other forms of emerging technologies);
- Demonstrate physical format, appearance, and durability suitable to their intended use; and
- Balance cost with need?

Responsible collection development requires that broad considerations govern the evaluation and choice of a single item. A school librarian is responsible for the collection as an entity, as well as for individual items. Base evaluation on the item's relationship to the collection and school community. All types of materials for use with learners need to be evaluated: print, nonprint, and digital, including websites and virtual libraries. Justify the choice of an item by assessing its contribution to the policies and goals of the collection program.

When making selection decisions, the essential criterion is quality, determined by whether the format appropriate for the content and the presentation effectively addresses the users' needs. The criteria that are provided in this chapter are guides, not absolutes; the collection, the users, resource-sharing plans, and outside resources influence the applicability of each criterion to specific items. Selection decisions require the evaluator to judge materials within the framework of given criteria. These criteria relate to the content, physical form, or potential value of materials to users or to programs. A school librarian must consider all the criteria as appropriate.

The first part of this chapter describes general criteria that one may apply to all types of materials in a school library. The second portion of the chapter discusses the purchase of equipment. For assistance in selecting specific formats of resources, see Chapter 8, "Criteria by Format."

INTELLECTUAL CONTENT AND ITS PRESENTATION

How can one evaluate the idea, or intellectual content, of a work? Criteria to help one do so include the following: (1) authority, (2) appropriateness and audience, (3) scope, (4) authenticity, (5) treatment, (6) arrangement and organization, (7) instructional design, (8) special features, (9) materials available on the subject, and (10) value to the collection.

Authority

The basis for the criterion of authority addresses the qualifications and credibility of the people who created the work. This includes authors, illustrators, editors, directors, publishers, producers, and anyone else involved in the creation of a work. Judge authority by considering the qualifications of the author, illustrator, or director; the quality and acceptance of other works by the same person; and the dependability and reputation of the publisher or the producer. Authority is also expressed by favorable reviews from professional selection sources.

Appropriateness and Audience

Appropriateness of content focuses on the intellectual content of a resource in relation to its intended use and audience. The concept must be appropriate to the users' developmental level. In other words, the presentation should be geared to the maturity and interest level of the intended users. Whether the content is factual or imaginative, it should not be presented in a condescending manner, nor should it supersede the users' capacity to understand. An item should be appropriate for the learners who will use it and not for some arbitrary standard established by adults. Items should have educational significance and make a contribution to the curriculum and to the interest of learners

Scope

Scope refers to the content's overall purpose and depth of coverage. Examine the introduction, teacher's guide, or other documentation for an item to learn the intended purpose and coverage. Then, evaluate whether the stated purpose meets a need of the collection and, if so, then decide whether the resource itself actually fulfills the stated purpose. When the content of the item duplicates content in other materials in a collection, consider whether the item presents content from a unique perspective. If it does, it may be a valuable addition that broadens the scope of the collection. Consider also whether the material may make to the breadth of representative viewpoints on issues.

Authenticity

Information presented in materials should be valid, reliable, complete, and current. Opinions need to be distinguished from facts and, as much as possible, impartially presented. Accuracy is often linked to timeliness, or how recently an item was published or produced, especially in technological subjects where changes occur rapidly. Check with a subject area specialist, if necessary, to be sure the information is timely. Remember, however, that a recent publication date does not necessarily show that the material itself is current or accurate.

Treatment

The treatment or presentation style can affect an item's potential value. It must be appropriate for the subject and use. In the best items, the presentation catches and holds the users' attention, draws on a typical experience, and stimulates further learning or creativity. Asking the following questions can help to evaluate the presentation of an item:

- Are the material's signs (pictures, visuals) and symbols (words, abstractions) necessary to the content and helpful to the user?
- Are the graphics, color, and sound well integrated into the presentation?
- Is the presentation free of bias and stereotyping?
- Does the material reflect our multicultural society?
- Is the information accessible to those who have physical limitations?
- Does the user control the rate and sequence of the content presentation?
- With electronic information, can the user easily enter, use, and exit the program or site?

The treatment of an item must be appropriate to the situation in which it will be used. Some materials require an adult to guide the learner's use of material; other materials require use of a teacher's guide to present the information fully. Treatment may present very practical limitations. For example, consider whether the length is appropriate to class periods as generally scheduled. The use of a 60-minute DVD may be problematic if the longest possible viewing period is 55 minutes.

Arrangement and Organization

Presentation of the material in terms of sequences and development of ideas influences comprehension. Content should be presented clearly and develop logically, flowing from one section to another and emphasizing important elements. The arrangement of information needs to facilitate its use. Content should be divided by headings, and information should be easy to locate. The presence of a summary or review of major points enhances effectiveness and helps users understand the work.

Instructional Design

Some materials are intended to meet certain instructional objectives. This is particularly true of textbooks, but can also apply to other books and formats. These materials need to meet the expectations of the learner or teacher. The following general questions can be asked to help evaluate such resources:

- Does the material encourage problem solving and creativity?
- Does the resource promote the understanding of ideas?
- Will users have the necessary capabilities (reading ability, vocabulary level, or computational skills) to learn from the material?
- Will the presentation arouse and motivate interest?
- With electronic materials, is direct access to specific parts of the program possible?
- Does the presentation simulate interaction?
- Are instructions clear?
- Is there effective use of color, text, sound, and graphics?
- Are there suitable instructional support resources provided?

Special Features

Some works have special or unique features that are absent from other resources on the same topic and thus they could have value to a collection. Some of these features may be peripheral to the main content of a work but still add to the collection. Visuals (maps, charts, graphs, or other illustrations) or added items, such as glossaries or listings of award-winning children's books, can serve particular reference needs in a school library. A teacher's guide to the resource may offer suggestions for follow-up activities or contain a bibliography of related materials. These special features can be a decisive factor in selection decisions that are not clear-cut.

Materials Available on the Subject

In selecting materials to fill a need for a particular subject, program, or user, availability may outweigh other criteria. This occurs frequently with current events, such as the election of a new U.S. president. Biographical information may be needed immediately and yet little may be available for young users. By the end of a U.S. president's first four-year term, there is most likely a wide range of titles and formats from which to select, but at this time the attention to the information may be on the wane. Other examples of information that may have initially limited availability of materials for young people include new scientific discoveries, creation of new nations from former countries, and diseases that suddenly become a threat.

Value to the Collection

After evaluating the specific qualities of the item, the librarian needs to consider it in relation to the collection by asking some of the following questions:

- Does the item meet the needs of the school program or the users?
- Can the resource serve more than one purpose?
- Who are the likely users? How often would they use the item?
- Could a teacher in an instructional situation use the item for informational or recreational purposes?
- Is the item readily available through interlibrary loan?

Other Considerations

Series

Deciding whether to select items in a series can sometimes be problematic. It may be tempting to order an entire series produced by a company, but a school librarian should judge each item within a series independently in terms of its value and known needs. Several authors may write books in a series, but not all the authors may be equally skilled. Even if one author writes the entire series, consider whether that person is knowledgeable about all the subjects presented in the series. Authors of fiction may not be able to sustain the readers' interest throughout a series. Thus, consider whether the works function independently of each other, or whether sequential use is required. In the case of nonfiction series, readers may not need all the topics that are covered in the series. The library collection may already have sufficient coverage in other materials for some of those topics.

Sponsored Materials

Particular organizations may produce and distribute materials often referred to as *free or inexpensive*. They include books, computer programs, games, maps, multimedia kits, posters, DVDs, and realia. The materials may provide more up-to-date and in-depth information than you will find in other materials. Sponsors include local, state, national, and international groups, such as government agencies, community groups, private businesses, and trade and professional associations. For example, obtain posters about foreign countries from airline and cruise ship companies. Embassies can provide information about their countries. The U.S. Government Printing Office and the National Audiovisual Center identify free and inexpensive materials that are available on a wide range of subjects. Some of the materials from both of these agencies are available digitally online.

In addition to applying general selection criteria and format-related criteria when evaluating these materials, one needs to also assess whether the information presents a one-sided or biased view of the topic. Advertising and references to the company or organization should be extremely limited and not dominate the content.

PHYSICAL FORM

Although content is one basis on which to evaluate an item, examine the packaging of the information, or its physical form. The quality of the content can be weakened if it is not presented through the appropriate medium. Criteria to consider in this area are (1) technical quality, (2) aesthetic quality, (3) durability, (4) safety and health considerations, and (5) accessibility and/or adaptability to ensure use by all users.

Technical Quality

To judge the technical qualities of items, some of the following questions may need to be considered:

- Are illustrations and photographs clear and eye catching?
- Is the balance of illustrations to text appropriate to the content and prospective user?
- Does the use of sound, visual materials, and narrative help focus attention?
- Is there a balance of music, narration, and dialogue?
- Are sound elements synchronized?
- Is the speech clear and effectively paced?
- Is the sound clearly audible?
- Is closed captioning available?
- Are the mobility of subjects, expressiveness of presenters, camera work, resolution, and clarity used effectively?

Aesthetic Quality

Aesthetics refer to a resource's appeal to the intellect, senses, and imagination. Both the external design of an item and the presentation of the content need to be aesthetically pleasing. Book jackets and CD and DVD covers should appeal to the potential user, but they also need to be appropriate. For instance, book jackets for teen romance novels should have illustrations that are vibrant and interesting, but they should not be racy or depict characters that are much older than the main characters in the story.

Durability

It is important to consider the quality of a resource in relation to its durability (how long an item will remain in usable condition with frequent use). Unfortunately, many resources produced today do not compare in durability to materials that were produced many years ago. For instance, the paper and binding in many books today are far inferior to those produced in the early and mid-20th century. The types of bindings used to make book covers and the quality of materials used to make videocassettes, DVDs, and CDs can all affect durability. Items that are going to be frequently used, such as those in a reference collection, should be especially durable. Print encyclopedia sets and books in elementary schools can often be ordered in special library binding, which will help them stay in good condition through heavy usage. Since most items in a school library collection circulate and leave the library itself, resources should be as durable as possible.

Safety and Health Considerations

While safety and health features are particularly important when selecting tactile materials, consider these issues for all materials. When dealing with items in a kit, such as puppets or stuffed animals, consider whether the items are constructed with nonflammable materials and whether they can be cleaned. Some real objects present a special challenge in terms of cleanliness. What about a piece of salt from the Great Salt Lake that probably will be licked by most of the 1,000 learners in an elementary school? Materials with movable parts can also pose problems, possibly with loss of integral parts. Models and kits may have parts that can cut fingers or be swallowed, while architectural models may collapse.

Accessibility and Adaptability

To ensure an inclusive learning environment, school librarians need to consider the usefulness of the resource to all members of the learning community. For example, when possible, choose items that are adjustable, have customizable displays, and/or is adaptable to low vision or low mobility users. Accessible and adaptable school library collections reflect three principles of Universal Design for Learning (Sturge, 2020):

- Multiple means of representation—give learners options for acquiring knowledge;
- Multiple means of action and expression—for learners to demonstrate what they know; and
- Multiple means of engagement—to tap into learners' interest.

Cost

Cost is an item that must be analyzed in relationship to both intellectual content and technical qualities. Once the criteria discussed previously have been sufficiently applied to an item that you are considering adding to a collection, you must then decide whether the price of the item is commensurate with the intellectual content and technical qualities of the item, the value to the collection, and the monies available in your budget. These factors, of course, are important and will greatly affect your decision on whether to purchase an item. If you determine that the contemplated item for purchase is of high quality and you are in need of the resource for your particular collection, but you do not have sufficient funds in your budget, then you should consider some other options for obtaining the item: interlibrary loan, shared collection development with another library, or fundraising projects. These options will be discussed in more detail in later chapters.

SPECIAL CONSIDERATIONS FOR DIGITAL RESOURCES

Digital resources and physical resources have many of the same considerations that relate to the validity, accuracy, authority, uniqueness, completeness, coverage, currency, and audience of a resource. These considerations ensure that the resource is appropriate for the community and collection areas identified in the needs assessment. Accessibility and technical considerations relate to the implementation of the resource: sites that host digital resources must be well organized, have terms and conditions that permit the intended uses, and be accessible to learners with special considerations such as diverse language and physical access needs. Additional considerations common to one or more of the criteria checklists include contemporary considerations such as standards alignment, ability to view and contribute ratings and reviews, support for deep learning, and reusability present new considerations.

Some digital resources are subscription or fee-based; however, open educational resources (OER), which can be used, adapted, edited, and shared, are increasingly a mainstay of classroom learning, and therefore of interest for the school librarian to evaluate, curate, and organize. OER are appealing because they have the potential to:

- Increase Equity—All students have access to high-quality learning materials that have the most up-to-date and relevant content because openly licensed educational resources can be freely distributed to anyone.
- Keep Content Relevant and High Quality—Traditional textbooks force districts to invest significant portions of their budgets on updating and replacing them. The terms of use of openly licensed educational resources allows educators to maintain the quality and relevance of their materials through continuous updates.
- Empower Teachers—Openly licensed educational resources empower teachers as creative professionals by giving them the ability to adapt and customize learning materials to meet the needs of their students without breaking copyright laws.
- Save Money—Openly licensed materials enable school librarians to redirect funding spent on static materials for other pressing needs, such as investing in the transition to digital learning (AASL Vision for Implementing ESSA, 2017).

Granularity

"Granularity" refers to the size or level of the resource. Librarians should be comfortable with the notion of granularity because, as shown in Figure 7.1, it is a concept much like the notational hierarchy of the Dewey Decimal Classification System.

The challenge for librarians is to match their collection development practices to the level of granularity that best serves the learning task. If a learner has a question about the biomes of a specific location, for example, it might not be appropriate to point the learner to a collection of interactive digital resources that relates to biomes; instead, the learners will benefit from a resource about biomes in the target region. School librarians might find multiple levels of granularity appropriate for their collection needs.

Resource Type

Moreover, the growing array of resource types demands expertise not only in identifying high-quality or trustworthy resources, curating also means recommending the right resource in both content and format. The levels of discernment required by curators are unprecedented and lead to niche expertise tailored to a particular information market and the needs of a unique audience (Rosenbaum, 2011).

School librarians can aid learning personalization by matching learners with resource types appropriate for their needs. Resource types provide a useful starting point for thinking about the range of digital resources available. Relevant digital resources could be in the form of animations; assessments; audio files; eBooks; eBook chapters; data sets; games; learning modules; reference materials; texts; tutorials; simulations; worksheets; and video files (Shank, 2014). Note that this list includes items at varying levels of

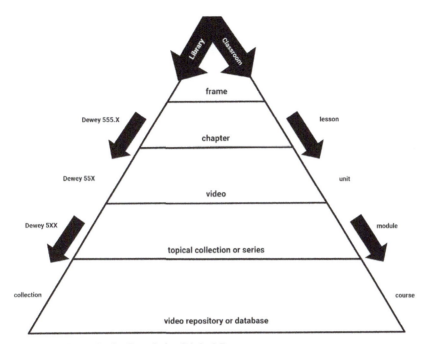

Figure 7.1. Granularity Levels for Digital Resources

granularity; the resource type and level of granularity must be considered in relation to the learning task. Figure 7.2 provides an overview of some possible combinations of these factors.

As Figure 7.2 suggests, in many instances, levels of learning can involve combinations of library resources to create learning products. The collection undoubtedly will favor some resource types over others. Genota (2018) reported that contemporary learners learned better through highly visual presentation, and multimodal learning helped to activate essential prior knowledge, the platform upon which subsequent learning takes place (Bransford, Brown, & Cocking, 2000; Hirsch, 2006; Roschelle, 1995).

Rights

Open educational resources might not be fee-based, but that does not mean that they can be used without any consideration of attribution and reuse restrictions. Tools such as the OER Commons authoring tool enable users to combine some digital resources into new and personalized resources, but these new combinations might not always respect the use conditions of the individual resources. As a result, many collection providers include rights information about the use of their resources. As Table 7.1 shows, for example, rights statements from two digital resource collections, OER Commons and PBS LearningMedia, reflect a range of restriction levels.

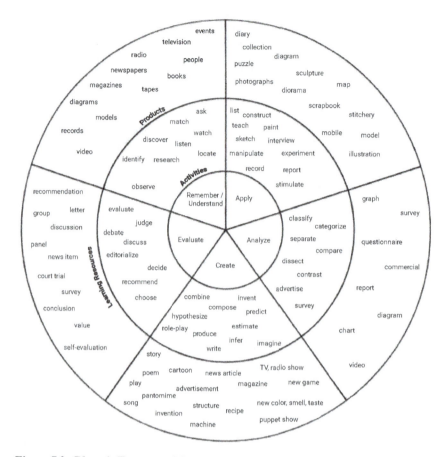

Figure 7.2. Bloom's Taxonomy Mapped to Activities, Products, and Learning Resources

As learners become information creators as well as information consumers, ensuring that available resources are used appropriately is an aspect of the school librarian's role that will remain important and likely will gain prominence.

EQUIPMENT

The majority of the school community considers school librarians to be technology leaders, and rely on them to make purchase decisions, select apps, maintain and troubleshoot equipment, and provide professional development and training. (SLJ, 2019). School librarians may be asked to help select equipment that is housed in classrooms, as well as equipment that circulates to classrooms, such as laptop computers. Fortunately, many classrooms have their own installed equipment. However, there are still several types of equipment that need to be purchased for the school library, such as computers, eReaders, interactive

TABLE 7.1. OER COMMONS AND PBS LEARNINGMEDIA OER RIGHTS STATEMENTS

OER Commons (2019)[*]	PBS LearningMedia (n.d.)[**]
No Strings Attached—No restrictions on remixing, redistributing, or making derivative works. Give credit to the author, as required.	**Stream, Download, Share, and Modify**—Users are permitted to download, edit, distribute, and make derivative works of the content. Users must attribute the content as indicated in the attribution file.
Remix and Share—Remixing, redistributing, or making derivative works comes with some restrictions, including how it is shared.	**Stream, Download, and Share**—Users are permitted to download the content, make verbatim copies of the content, incorporate the content unmodified into a presentation (such as an essay or web page), and distribute verbatim copies of the content, but you may not edit or alter the content or create any derivative works of the content. Users must attribute the content as indicated in the attribution file.
Share Only—Redistribution comes with some restrictions. Do not remix or make derivative works.	**Stream and Download**—Users are permitted to download the content to view it on a computer or other digital video device for your own personal use. Users may not modify, redistribute, reproduce, edit, retransmit, or in any way repurpose the content. Use of the content must conform to restrictions indicated in the associated attribution file.
Read the Fine Print—All Rights Reserved. U.S.-based educators have certain permissions under Fair Use and the TEACH Act that include educational and personal uses of copyrighted materials, custom licenses and terms, permission to print only, unknown restrictions, and any other redistribution restrictions.	**Stream Only**—Users are permitted only to stream the content from the site. Users may save links to the content in their PBS LearningMedia accounts and may also incorporate html links to the URLs of the resource pages for this content. You are not permitted to download this content.

[*] OER Commons (2014). Conditions of use. Retrieved from https://www.oercommons.org/help#conditions-of-use2
[**] PBS LearningMedia (2014). Terms of use. Retrieved from http://www.pbslearningmedia.org/help/terms-of-use/

whiteboards, digital cameras, and projectors. One-to-one (1:1) are also becoming increasingly popular ways to ensure that each child can access learning via a digital device during the school day. Often, the school librarian is asked to take on responsibility for selecting and managing these devices.

Many school districts put the purchase of equipment above a certain cost (sometimes $100) through a bid process in which they generally accept the lowest bid for each type of equipment. If this is the case in your school district, someone at the administrative office of the school district can provide you with a listing of the equipment and the companies from which you are allowed to purchase certain types of equipment. In your policies and procedure manual, you should include the selection criteria and procedure for obtaining equipment, noting whether certain types of equipment are put through a bid process.

Criteria that should be considered when selecting equipment include (1) quality and durability; (2) performance, compatibility, and versatility; (3) ease of operation; (4) safety; (5) maintenance and service; (6) reputation of manufacturer and dealer; and (7) cost.

Quality and Durability

Quality and durability are very important criteria to consider when selecting equipment. You should choose equipment that is constructed of strong materials and will remain intact through heavy and sometimes fairly abusive use. If a piece of equipment will circulate outside of a building, it needs to have a weatherproof carrying case. Straps and handles used to aid in moving the equipment should be strong enough to withstand the weight of the item when carried any distance.

Performance, Compatibility, and Versatility

Equipment should operate efficiently and consistently at a high level of performance. Poor quality projection or sound reproduction can negate the technical quality of carefully-selected materials. The noise or light from the equipment should not interfere with its use, nor should the equipment be easily subject to overheating.

Equipment needs to be compatible with other equipment and materials in the collection. This is especially true when selecting computers. You should not purchase equipment for which use is limited to materials produced by the manufacturer or a device that must be connected via outputs not present in existing library equipment or computers.

Ease of Use

If equipment is too complex, it will discourage use; thus, select equipment that has only the needed features and has clearly written, easy to follow directions. If possible, try to examine the equipment that you are considering for purchase. The following questions will help to determine how easy it is to operate the equipment:

- What level of manual dexterity must one have to operate the equipment?
- How many steps must one follow to run the equipment?
- Does the equipment have many controls?
- Does the equipment operate efficiently with minimum delay?
- Are there parts that can be easily removed and possibly misplaced?
- Are automatic operations dependable?
- Are there options for manual and remote control?
- Are shutoff or cooling-down features automatic?
- Does the size, weight, or design of the equipment require that you use and store it in one location?
- Does the item require special cables, cords, batteries, or adapters?
- Can one easily move the equipment to a cart or another location?
- How much time will be needed to teach learners and educators to use the equipment?

Safety

Safety features demand consideration, especially when young children will use equipment. The school librarian should choose equipment that has no rough or protruding edges that could injure the user. Equipment should be balanced so that it will not topple easily. Also, it should not be easy for users to come into contact with potentially dangerous components, such as a fan or a heated element.

Equipment needs to meet established safety regulations. Look for seals from the Underwriters Laboratory or the National Standards Foundation to help determine whether equipment meets safety standards.

Maintenance and Service

Although school library equipment should be built to withstand hard use, plan for regular maintenance and service, although you may be able to perform some of the easy maintenance, such as cleaning the equipment on a regular basis.

Examine warranties and guarantees to see what conditions are covered. Also, try to determine how easy it will be for minor repairs to be made or for parts to be replaced quickly and efficiently. Inquire as to whether the distributor or manufacturer offers in-service training on operating or repairing the equipment. Some distributors and manufacturers provide on-the-spot repairs, whereas others require that the purchasers send the item to a factory. Thus, it might be important to ask whether the manufacturer, vendor, or repair center provides replacement or rental equipment while they are servicing the equipment that needs repair. Finally, if the district or school has a staff person assigned to do repairs, consult the person regarding whether they will service the equipment that being considered for purchase.

Reputation of Manufacturer and Dealer

Ask other librarians who they regard as the most reputable manufacturers and distributors with whom to deal:

- Does the manufacturer have a reputation for honoring warranties?
- Is delivery prompt?
- Does the manufacturer handle requests for assistance pleasantly and efficiently?
- Does the dealer have outlets near the school?
- Does the manufacturer provide support service through e-mail, telephone hotlines, toll-free numbers, backups, preview opportunities, updates, refunds, and replacements?
- Is the support assistance readily available?
- Are the service hours convenient?

Cost

Educators agree that school technology spending is low and mis-prioritized (Promethean, 2020); for this reason, school librarians must weigh the financial investment required to acquire and maintain a piece of equipment carefully. When selecting equipment, a school librarian should weigh quality over cost, but also consider budget constraints. Try to determine whether a competitor offers a similar item at less cost. Ask if trade-ins are allowed. When purchasing a very expensive item, such as a large copy machine for the library, determine if it most cost effective to purchase or lease the equipment by considering how much use the copy machine will have, whether fees will be taken for copies, and from where the financial support for items such as paper and ink cartridges will come.

CONCLUSION

Several general criteria can be addressed when selecting items for a school library. For print and electronic resources, the intellectual content and its presentation, as well as the physical form of an item, should be considered. When selecting equipment for the school library or classrooms, specific criteria need to be addressed, but one needs also to be aware of any school district policies that deal with equipment selection and maintenance. For all purchases that are being considered, a librarian should strive to get the best quality within the constraints of the library budget.

DISCUSSION QUESTIONS

1. To what extent do these criteria apply to all media formats? Which formats require special consideration and what should those considerations be?
2. What do you see as the advantages and disadvantages of the library circulating equipment?
3. How might the considerations in this chapter apply to a "bring your own device" (BYOD) environment in which learners supply their own computers and other devices?

REFERENCES

AASL Vision for Implementing ESSA. (2017, March 17). Open educational resources and school librarians—The right fit! *Knowledge Quest.* https://knowledgequest.aasl.org/open -educational-resources-school-librarians-right-fit/

American Library Association. (2018, January). Selection criteria. Selection & reconsideration policy toolkit for public, school, & academic libraries. Retrieved from http://www.ala.org /tools/challengesupport/selectionpolicytoolkit/criteria

Bransford, J., Brown, A. L., & Cocking, R. R., eds. (2000). *How people learn: Brain, mind, experience, and school.* Washington, DC: National Academy Press.

Genota, J. (2018, September 11). Why Generation Z learners prefer YouTube lessons over printed books. *Education Week.* Retrieved from https://www.edweek.org/teaching-learning/why -generation-z-learners-prefer-youtube-lessons-over-printed-books/2018/09

Hirsch, E. D. (2006). Building knowledge: The case for bringing content into the language arts block and for a knowledge-rich curriculum core for all children. *American Educator, 30*(1), 8–17.

OER Commons. (2019, January 3). Usage rights. Retrieved from https://help.oercommons.org /support/solutions/articles/42000046845-usage-rights

PBS LearningMedia. (n.d.). Terms of use. Retrieved from http://www.pbslearningmedia.org/help /terms-of-use/

Promethean. (2020). The state of technology in education 2020/21. Retrieved from https:// resourced.prometheanworld.com/technology-education-industry-report/

Roschelle, J. (1995). Learning in interactive environments: Prior knowledge and new experience. In J. H. Falk and L. D. Dierking (eds.), *Public institutions for personal learning: Establishing a research agenda*. Washington, DC: American Association of Museums.

Rosenbaum, S. (2011). *Curation nation: Why the future of content is context*. New York: McGraw Hill.

School Library Journal (SLJ). (2019). School technology survey: U.S. school libraries. Retrieved from https://s3.amazonaws.com/WebVault/SLJ/School%20Technology%20report%202019.pdf

Shank, J. D. (2014). *Interactive open educational resources: A guide to finding, choosing, and using what's out there to transform college teaching*. San Francisco, CA: Jossey-Bass.

Sturge, J. (2020, June 2). School libraries and UDL in the time of learning from home. *Knowledge Quest*. Retrieved from https://knowledgequest.aasl.org/school-libraries-and-udl-in-the-time-of-learning-from-home/

ADDITIONAL READING

Smaldino, S., Lowther, D., & Mims, C. (2019). *Instructional technology and media for learning*, 12th edition. New York: Pearson.

HELPFUL MULTIMEDIA

American Library Association. (2018, January). Review resources. Retrieved from http://www.ala.org/tools/challengesupport/selectionpolicytoolkit/reviewresources

Bellamy, S. (2020, November 8). Best E-readers for digital book lovers. Retrieved from https://www.pcworld.com/article/3144037/best-e-readers.html

Evaluating the Quality of and Impact of Mobile Apps. (n.d.). Retrieved from http://itecideas.pbworks.com/w/page/82039871/Evaluating%20the%20Quality%20and%20Impact%20of%20Mobile%20Apps

Future Ready Schools. (2018, December 11). Future ready librarians: Investing strategically in digital resources. Retrieved from https://all4ed.org/webinar-event/future-ready-librarians-investing-strategically-in-digital-resources/

LaGarde, J., & Hudgins, D. (2020, February 4). It's time to go mobile while teaching news literacy. Retrieved from https://www.slj.com/?detailStory=teaching-news-literacy-jennifer-lagarde-darren-hudgins-fake-biased-news-reporting

Managing School Technology. (2018). Retrieved from http://itecideas.pbworks.com/w/page/129470907/Managing%20School%20Technologies%2C%20Fall%2C%202018

OER Commons. (n.d.). Collection development for school librarians in the era of open. Retrieved from https://www.oercommons.org/courseware/module/15950/overview

Pelletier, M. (n.d.). Libraries are a vital educational technology resource. *Education World*. Retrieved from https://www.educationworld.com/libraries-are-vital-educational-technology-resource

Schrock, K. (n.d.). iPad app evaluation forms. Retrieved from http://www.kathyschrock.net/storage.html

Teachers with Apps. (n.d.). Retrieved from https://www.teacherswithapps.com/

Vincent, T. (2012, March 4). Educational app evaluation checklist. Retrieved from http://learninginhand.com/blog/ways-to-evaluate-educational-apps.html

CHAPTER 8

Criteria by Format

Key Learnings
- While general principles apply to almost all items in the library collection, each media type has special considerations.
- Some media become obsolete, but may be retained in the school library collection due to appeal and ease of use, especially in times when other technologies are not available.
- Many media types are transitioning from physical formats to digital formats and these changes must be considered in selection.

People gather information through their senses and have different learning styles depending on how they utilize those senses. Although most people learn through a variety of sensory inputs, they usually have a predominant learning style: visual, auditory, or kinetic. Students learn better from media formats that incorporate their predominant learning style. Moreover, our information-rich learning environments demand that learners and educators be fluent in a variety of media (Bryan, 2018). Thus, a variety of media need to be included in a school library collection in order to meet the learning styles of all students.

Your school library's policies and procedures manual should include a list of all the media formats that are in your collection. This can be a separate listing or it can be included in your circulation section with a possible indication of which formats can be checked out by students and/or by faculty.

This chapter focuses on the characteristics of different formats and how school librarians should consider them in selection decisions. The formats are grouped into two categories: current and legacy. The "Current Materials" category includes materials that school librarians may acquire new and/or that likely have recent creation dates. The "Legacy Materials" category includes materials that school librarians may have had in a collection for some time or inherit from another collection or teacher. These materials require technologies to use them that are obsolete. Nonetheless, these materials still have value within the school library collection because they are valued by users and there may be occasions, such as Internet outages, in which legacy materials may be the only usable formats.

Within these categories, the formats are arranged in alphabetical order. Each description includes physical characteristics, advantages, disadvantages, selection criteria, implications for collection development, and copyright considerations. Although some of the formats are being phased out, if they are still available for purchase, they are included to accommodate all types of school libraries, regardless of their technology capabilities or budgets. In addition to the selection criteria listed for each format, you should consider whether the item has received awards or favorable reviews. The general selection criteria from Chapter 7 should also be applied.

You can refer to the "Appendix: Resources and Further Reading" of this book to locate materials that will provide reviews or other guidance for selection of particular formats. The Additional Readings and Helpful Multimedia listed at the end of this chapter are primarily those that relate to the newer formats that are being collected in school libraries.

CURRENT MATERIALS

ART PRINTS (*SEE* GRAPHIC MATERIALS)

AUDIOBOOKS

Audiobooks allow users to listen to a narrated version of a book via a range of media. As the use of smartphones and tablets has increased, for many users, downloadable audio files via services like OverDrive or Audible are the format of choice. However, due to personal device and downloading restrictions in many schools, audiobooks delivered via physical media remain popular. Some audiobooks are even installed on devices that play nothing but a single audiobook title—this format is especially useful for younger library users. Instead of presenting the considerations in narrative format as we have done with other media types, Table 8.1 compares the advantages, disadvantages, and selection considerations for various audiobook format.

Audiobooks require special considerations for promotion, too. For example, librarians will want to be sure to add audio titles to their library catalogs as both independent records as well as to the records for print versions of the title. Physical media audiobooks will need to be placed where users can browse them and downloadable audiobooks may need to be promoted with posters, displays, or workshops.

BOOKS

Most school libraries contain more books than any other format, although they are not always the most popular format among students, particularly in high school settings. Hardback and paperback books share similar characteristics, but often fulfill different needs in genre, topic, and content presentation. For an in-depth treatment of selection considerations for various audiences and genres for young adults, consult Chapter 5 of *Developing Library Collections for Young Adults* (Pattee, 2014).

TABLE 8.1. AUDIOBOOK FORMATS AND CONSIDERATIONS

Delivery Method	Advantages	Disadvantages	Selection Considerations
Audiocassette	• Easy to use • Individual experience	• Devices may be hard to find or replace • Only one user per cassette	• Storage • Shelving • Maintenance • Replacement
Audio File	• Easy to add titles to collection • Multiple users supported	• Requires software • Requires downloading • Subscription cost • Producer may limit number of downloads	• Subscription required
CD	• Easy to use • Individual experience	• Devices may be hard to find or replace • Only one user per CD	• Storage • Shelving • Maintenance
Preloaded Device	• Easy to use device	• Only one user per device	• Storage • Maintenance

Hardback books with special library bindings are frequently purchased for very young patrons, while paperback books are especially appealing to teenagers. eBooks, which are becoming more popular, are discussed in a separate section.

Advantages

- Books are usually designed for individual users.
- Users can set their own pace and stop in the process to recheck information or reread a section.
- The table of contents and index can provide ready access to information.
- Books are portable.
- A wide range of subjects and genres are available in books.
- Books do not require equipment.
- They are relatively inexpensive.

Disadvantages

- Use of colored artwork or photography, although adding to appeal or clarity of text, increases the cost.
- Compared to digital formats, movement is more difficult to illustrate on the printed page.
- Large group viewing of the same material is difficult, except with *big books* (oversized paperback books).
- Interaction and feedback for students is difficult to achieve except in programmed texts.
- Students must have the appropriate reading and comprehension level skills.
- It usually takes several months to get a book published; thus, the information may not be as current as that in digital formats.

Selection Criteria

- Are the shape and weight of the book appropriate for the intended audience?
- How opaque is the paper? Print that shows through the page may be confusing to a young or disadvantaged reader.
- Is the typeface suitable for the intended audience?
- Is the spacing between words and between lines adequate for the young or reluctant reader?
- Is the book jacket attractive? Does it reflect the content of the book?
- Are the illustrations placed throughout the text where readers can view them easily, or are they placed all together in an inconvenient location?
- Is the medium used for illustrations (e.g., pen-and-ink drawings, block prints, or oil paints) appropriate to the setting and mood of the story?
- Do the page layouts and color add appeal and clarity to the book?
- When a readability formula, such as Fry or Spache, is applied, is the text appropriate for the intended audience?
- Is the content accurate and current?

Additional Criteria for Hardbacks

- Are the bindings durable and the covers attractive and easy to clean?
- Are reinforced bindings available for titles that very young children will use or titles that will circulate frequently?
- Will the hardcover books lie flat when open?

Implications for Collection Development

Even though selections should cover a wide range of subjects and genres, one should also consider the reading and maturity levels of students. You should order additional copies of popular books; paperbacks are an inexpensive way to meet these demands. A paperback book may appeal to some users more than would the same title in hardback. Policies should address questions such as what foreign languages to purchase and whether there is a need for large-print books.

Copyright Considerations

Copyright law defines print materials as books, periodicals, pamphlets, newspapers, and similar items. A teacher may make a single copy of a chapter in a book, a short story, short essay, short poem, chart, graph, diagram, cartoon, or picture to use in teaching. Multiple copies are limited by specific guidelines:

- If a poem is less than 250 words and is not on more than two pages, the entire poem can be copied. For poems longer than 250 words, only 250 words can be copied.
- An article, story, or essay can be copied in its entirety if it is less than 2,500 words. Other types of prose are limited to 1,000 words or 10 percent of the whole, whichever is less.
- Creation of anthologies, compilations, and collective works is prohibited.

COMICS

Comic books, or the shortened form *comics*, tell a narrative by depicting sequential art. Although sometimes humorous, the subject matter varies. Popular genres include superheroes, fantasy, horror or supernatural, action or adventure, science fiction, and manga (Japanese comics). The majority of comic books are marketed to teenagers, with the two largest U.S. publishers being Marvel and DC Comics.

Advantages

- Comic books are particularly appealing to teens and will attract students to the school library.
- Reluctant readers of books will often read comic books.
- Visual learners like the graphic format, which can assist them in understanding a narrative.
- Comic books can lead readers to explore other literature.
- Comic books can help students develop an appreciation for art and different artistic styles.
- Many comic books address themes that are important to teens and preteens, including acceptance, prejudice, social issues, and triumph over adversity.
- Comic books are inexpensive.

Disadvantages

- Some comic books are not very durable.
- School librarians may not be very familiar with comic books and might need assistance in selecting the best ones for a collection.
- Some teachers, administrators, and parents may think that comic books do not have educational value and thus should not be included in a school library collection.

Selection Criteria

- Can you obtain sample copies to help you in selection?
- Is the content appropriate for the intended audience?
- What is the reputation of the publisher?
- Is the writing and art of good quality?
- Have the comic books won any awards?
- Will the selected titles be popular with students?
- Are the comic books available as trade paperback collections?

Implications for Collection Development

Comic books are particularly appealing to preteens and teenagers and will attract them to the school library. Since they are not very durable, it is wise to treat comic books similarly to magazine subscriptions where use is generally limited to the library and the materials are often placed in protective or laminated covers. If you wish to circulate comic books, you can purchase trade comics (stories collected in paperback format). Specialized comic book subscription agents and mail order services offer subscription plans for comic books. Subscriptions can also sometimes be arranged through local comic book stores, or are sometimes available from the major magazine subscription agencies like EBSCO. You should preview materials before placing them on the shelves and be prepared to address possible censorship issues.

Copyright Considerations

Although not specifically addressed in fair use guidelines, comic books would most likely be similar to picture books. Two pages of picture books may be copied as long as the two pages do not make up more than 10 percent of the book.

COMPUTER SOFTWARE

Computer software is available through educational institutes and consortia, commercial vendors, software companies, and textbook publishers. Shareware (courseware available at no cost or more often on a trial basis) is available from the educational agency or other body that produced it. After the software has been evaluated and retained, the user is expected to register the program and pay a voluntary fee. Open source (public domain) software is a computer program that the author has released and can be copied by anyone. Such software is often on Internet websites dedicated to public domain use. The title screen of the program indicates that the program is in public domain.

Most computer software is currently available via download or CD-ROM. See the selection criteria under CD-ROMs in addition to the following section, which emphasizes instructional software.

Advantages

- Software can be used for creative problem solving, drill and practice, testing, recreation, and guidance.
- Individual and self-paced interactions are special instructional features of computer software.
- Programs can provide the reinforcement and stimulation needed by students who have learning disabilities.
- Programs with branching allow the student with correct answers to move into more difficult questions, while allowing those who need to review and repeat responses opportunities to do so.
- Software available via download offers quick response to collection need.
- Use of computer software can be highly motivating for many students.
- Software is available for virtually every teaching and learning need.

Disadvantages

- Incompatibility of software and equipment can limit use.
- Some software can contain poor computer programming.
- Students and teachers may have unreasonably high expectations of how quickly mastery of the software will happen.
- School librarians may not have privileges to install and maintain software on school computers.

Selection Criteria

- Are the software and equipment compatible?
- Is content more appropriate for presentation on a computer than on other instructional media?

- Is the program designed to run on the user's computer? The computer's brand, model, memory size, operating system, storage format, display technology (monitor and graphics system), and accessories (mouse, game paddles, etc.) must be compatible.
- Is the computer's disk operating system compatible with the software program?
- Does the user control the rate and sequences of the content presentation (unless timing is an integral part of the program)?
- Is the student able to enter, use, and exit the program with relative ease and independence?
- Are the responses or feedback to answers (both correct and incorrect) appropriate?
- Are updates to the software included in the purchase price?
- Are on-screen instructions clear and easy to understand?
- Does the program require students to be familiar with special terms or symbols related to computers?

Implications for Collection Development

As mentioned previously, many computer software programs are now available on CD-ROM format or online. You will need to consider the scope of the software collection and whether it will circulate, and to whom it will circulate (only teachers or to both teachers and students). Some software has limited licensing; in such cases, it may only be used in the library or installed on a limited number of computers. It is wise to obtain teachers' opinions in deciding purchases.

Copyright Considerations

One archival or backup copy of each program is permitted. It may not be used at the same time as the original. For use at more than one computer, such as on a LAN (local area network) or WAN (wide area network), a site license agreement must be obtained. Any computer software programs that circulate should have copyright warning stickers placed on them.

DVDs

DVDs (digital versatile discs) are compact optical discs read by laser beams. DVD discs are the same diameter and thickness as compact discs, but are capable of storing up to 13 times the data contained on one side of a CD. Both sides of a DVD can be utilized for storage data; thus, it offers 26 times the power of a compact disc. Movies, documentaries, and music are all available in DVD format. DVDs are rapidly replacing videos, laser discs, CDs, and CD-ROMs.

Advantages

- DVDs can deliver video that is near studio quality and audio that is better than CD quality. The pictures are characterized by more color detail and color resolution than videos.
- Content can be easily searched and specific sections can be quickly accessed.
- Interactive menus are available.
- Many DVDs have extra features, such as additional footage, interviews, commentaries, links to online resources, and biographical materials.

- Some DVDs have additional materials, such as accompanying booklets or viewers' guides.
- The compact size is easy to store, and portable players are available.
- Discs are durable.
- Wear does not occur from playing, only from physical damage.
- DVDs do not deteriorate in quality over time.
- Unlike videos, DVDs are not affected by magnetic fields.
- DVDs can be played on a computer that has a DVD drive.
- DVDs are inexpensive.

Disadvantages

- Careless production can create visible artifacts (anything that was not originally present in the picture), such as banding, blurriness, fuzzy dots, and missing details.
- The production of materials has centered mostly on the home entertainment center; however, the production of DVDs designed for educational and instructional purposes is growing.
- Most DVD players must be connected to a television set.
- Some television sets need to have the controls adjusted to take advantage of the DVD's capabilities.

Selection Criteria

Criteria applied to video, audiocassettes, and computer software should be applied to materials on DVDs. As with other media, there are additional questions to consider:

- Is the content connected to the curriculum?
- Is the standard used to judge the content the same as for other materials in the collection?
- Do users have convenient access to a player?
- Would purchase of the item duplicate something easily available in public libraries?
- Is a DVD the best format for the message?
- DVDs produced outside of North America may not be in a format compatible with all players.

Implications for Collection Development

Development and availability of DVDs should be monitored for its replacement of audiocassettes, CDs, videotapes, laser discs, and CD-ROMs. When you add DVD drives to your systems, look for those that are designed to play CD-ROM titles, as well as DVDs.

Copyright Considerations

A number of copy protection schemes are used with DVDs. One is the SCMS (serial copy generation management system), which is designed to prevent copying. The copy generation management system (CGMS) is embedded in the outgoing video signal, and one must use equipment that recognizes the CGMS. The U.S. Digital Millennium Copyright Act (DMCA), in which *don't copy flags* are incorporated by the producers, became law in October 1998. Although perfect reproductions can be made of a DVD, copyright restrictions do not allow archival copies to be made of DVDs. DVDs bought in stores are protected by the copyright law and are not intended for use outside the home. However, fair-use guidelines permit the use of the DVDs in face-to-face instruction if they are part of the curriculum. Any movies that are to be shown in a school for entertainment purposes require a Movie Copyright Compliance Site License.

EBOOKS

Many different types of digital books (eBooks) are available. Some can be accessed digitally and are meant to be printed out for reading; others are distributed digitally but are intended to be read on a computer or on eBook readers. Most eBooks use EPUB, a free and open standard created by the International Digital Publishing Forum. Some school librarians have been fairly reluctant to purchase eBooks, but this has been changing as younger library users are comfortable accessing all types of information through digital formats. The Additional Readings and Helpful Multimedia sections include helpful guides for developing your own eBooks policy.

Advantages

- Books are available 24 hours of the day.
- Subscriptions to eBook libraries can be purchased from vendors with whom the school librarian already works such as library database companies, jobbers, and other library software suppliers.
- Free eBook sources can cut costs of adding new titles to the collection.
- If allowed by the licensing agreement, several students can access a digital book at the same time.
- Since some eBooks also include sound files and moving images, they are particularly interesting to reluctant readers.
- eBooks save shelf space in a library and do not have to be transported.
- The books cannot be lost or damaged by users.
- Books can be rapidly added to the collection.
- Search functions can be used to locate specific parts of the book.
- In some eBook formats, notes can be inserted right into the text, thus providing instructional features for a classroom teacher.
- eReaders allow adjustments to size and contrast and thus aid students with visual impairments.

Disadvantages

- Special software and hardware are required to access and read eBooks.
- eBook reading devices are more expensive than books.
- Some users prefer a physical book, rather than a digital version.
- Some book titles are not available in the eBook format.

- eBooks can cause eye strain in some users.
- eBooks do not have a defined life span. Paper has a longer life span than most digital forms of storage.
- Due to copyright constraints, eBooks may have time limits for availability and suddenly disappear.

Selection Criteria

When evaluating eBooks, school librarians should apply traditional criteria and also consider both the licensing arrangement and the equipment necessary for using them. As with other developing technology, basic questions are whether the library will circulate the materials and whether the library will provide the equipment needed to use the materials. Some additional questions that should be asked are as follows:

- What titles are available in eBook format?
- Will students and teachers use the eBooks?
- How much will the books cost in comparison to purchasing print versions of the titles?

Implications for Collection Development

Many book titles are already in public domain and available for free. The Project Gutenberg website has a large collection of public domain eBooks as does the University of Virginia website and the Internet Public Library. The International Children's Digital Library, which was developed by a team at the University of Maryland, provides free access to children's books from around the world. Before purchasing eBooks, a school librarian should promote the use of these sites and then determine whether teachers and students want or need access to additional titles.

Copyright Considerations

Copyright restrictions introduced by the DMCA in 1998 apply to eBooks, as well as to other digital technologies. It may be necessary to sign a licensing agreement for eBooks that are purchased and abide by the copyright restrictions of the agreement. Some agreements limit the number of users who can access the eBook simultaneously, the number of pages that can be printed within a certain time limit, the amount of cut-and-paste that a user can perform, and the amount of time an item can be checked out.

EJOURNALS

eJournals or digital journals are serial publications that are in digital format. Some eJournals are free of charge and are published only on the Internet. Such journals are generally referred to as open access journals. Other journals appear only in digital format and are available by subscription, while still others appear in both digital format (on Internet or on a CD-ROM) and also have print versions. Some digital journals are peer-reviewed scholarly journals, while others are not quality controlled. Thus, the term *eJournal* is not always specific. There are even more eJournals (many thousands) than eZines. In many states, eJournals are accessible through free online databases available statewide. A list of these databases in available in the Helpful Multimedia section of this chapter.

Advantages

- eJournals can be read anytime from any location that has Internet access.
- They can be delivered to one's computer desktop.
- More than one person can read an eJournal at a time.
- They can be published much more quickly than print versions of journals.
- eJournals can be searched.
- Articles can be downloaded and printed for offline reading.
- Many databases include citation information to ensure proper attribution.
- They can be retrieved directly through links when accessed through an indexing database.
- Hyperlinks to information can be inserted into articles.
- eJournals do not take up space on the library shelves.
- Statewide online eJournal databases save school libraries thousands of dollars each year while providing content far beyond what the school library could ever accommodate.

Disadvantages

- The main disadvantage is that one must have a computer to access eJournals and often also have a subscription.
- Some journals do not include illustrations, and if they do, the illustrations may not be in color or as clear as the print version.

Selection Criteria

The selection criteria for eJournals are similar to those of print periodicals (see Periodicals). Additional selection questions include the following:

- Does your state provide free online databases of eJournal content? If so, is access to these databases permitted from the school library?
- How does the cost compare to the print version of the periodical?
- Can you negotiate the cost of the eJournal according to the number of students in your school or the number of users who will access the eJournal?
- Is the journal title included in vendor databases, such as ProQuest or EBSCO?
- Is the journal easily available to students in informational databases provided by the state or by a public library?
- Will enough students use the journal to make the cost of its digital access feasible?
- Are back issues of the journals available?

Implications for Collection Development

One must carefully consider whether to purchase periodicals in print version or digitally. Few school libraries purchase the same title in both formats. Students in secondary schools enjoy reading print versions of popular periodicals such as *Sports Illustrated* or *Seventeen* so you should consider having these types of periodicals available on shelves in the library. Digital access to periodicals can be provided for those journals that are used primarily for research purposes. This will save enormous amounts of shelf space in a middle or high school library.

VOICES FROM THE FIELD

This year I started games in the library—not cards, but checkers, chess, and a jigsaw puzzle. Open to anyone to use anytime the library is open. The students love it . . . For the most part, they are quiet, respectful, and appreciate the break from sitting in a row and studying all day. My goal is to make the library THE place you want to be. . . . while they are here they are exposed to books, newspapers, movies, magazines, etc.—and often leave with library materials!

—Anonymous LM_NET poster

Copyright Considerations

Students can make one copy of an article for research purposes. Teachers should not make multiple copies of an article for classroom use unless they obtain copyright permission from the publisher of the journal or the need meets the spontaneity guideline (not enough time to get a timely reply to a request for permission to copy).

EZINES

eZines are publications (magazines or newsletters) that are distributed by e-mail, in small printed batches, or posted on a website. They usually focus on a particular subject and are free. Often one person or a small group of people who have special interest in a topic publish eZines on the web. Some eZines are updated constantly so do not have regular distribution, while others are periodically updated. Far too many eZines are available (thousands) to try to include them in OPACs, but if you want to help students locate eZines, the following sites are helpful: http://www.zinebook.com/directory/zine -directories.html and http://www.ezine-dir.com/.

GAMES

Games are recreational or educational activities involving one or more persons. They involve either reaching some type of goal or following a set of rules. Games can be categorized by those that involve skill, those that require strategy, and those that rely on chance. Many games involve a combination of skill, strategy, and chance. Some games require using a computer or other special equipment. Educational games in classrooms have become quite popular in many schools.

Advantages

- Participants become involved in solving problems.
- Some games simulate realistic environments.
- Participation usually generates a high degree of interest.
- Students receive immediate feedback.
- Some games contribute to effective learning by motivating and supporting learning and attitudinal changes.

Disadvantages

- Games can be very time consuming.
- The limited number of players can create problems if others want to participate.
- Some games have parts that can be easily lost or damaged.
- Students may gamble or dispute wins or losses.
- Some teachers may not be aware of the learning value of games, and thus may not understand why they are included in a collection.

Selection Criteria

- Is the packaging designed to store and quickly identify missing parts?
- Can lost pieces be easily replaced?
- Are the items durable?
- Are the directions clear?
- Are the content, reading level, time requirements, and required dexterity appropriate for the intended audience?
- Does the game require a computer? Will it run on the school library's equipment?
- Is the game too costly or elaborate for its intended use?

Implications for Collection Development

Games can serve many purposes, but it is wise to get input from teachers and administrators on the inclusion of games in the collection and whether to make them available for use in a library. Be sure to check your school and district policy to make sure that game playing is permitted during the school day. You should also carefully consider whether to circulate games to students, particularly if the games have many parts that can be easily lost. More elementary libraries than secondary school libraries tend to have games available for student use. However, some secondary libraries have chess or checker sets, board games, or computer games available.

Copyright Considerations

Generally copyright considerations are not involved with games, unless the games are in a different format, such as on computer software. In those cases, the same copyright considerations apply as to computer software (see Computer Software and CD-ROMs).

GRAPHIC NOVELS

Graphic novels' popularity with young people has certainly earned them a definite place in school libraries. It is important to remember that graphic novels are not a genre, but rather a separate format. They are stories in a comic form that are published as books. While usually called "graphic novels," often these graphic works include nonfiction. Storylines in graphic novels are longer than those found in comic books and are often more complex and serious. The modern types of graphic novels began in the 1970s, but in recent years they have become extremely popular and many librarians include them in their collections. The majority of the titles come in trade paperback versions.

Advantages

- Visual learners are able to connect with graphic novels.
- Graphic novels can lead students to explore other types of literature.
- Boys who are reluctant readers are often attracted to graphic novels.
- They are useful for ESL (English as a Second Language) students or students who read below grade level.
- Having graphic novels in a collection will attract young people to a library.

Disadvantages

- Some teachers and parents may think that graphic novels do not belong in a school library collection.
- Some titles are not available through jobbers.
- The contents of some graphic novels are not appropriate for young people.
- Some school librarians are not familiar with the format and may need assistance in selecting titles for the collection.

Selection Criteria

Standard selection criteria apply, but graphic novels and nonfiction also require some special consideration (Crews, Petersen, & Weaver, n.d.):

- Genre: Does the story and genre appeal to a broad range of readers and their interests?
- Quality and quantity: If you are buying a popular graphic novel title, will you need multiple copies or the whole series?
- Artistic merit: Will the artistic portrayal of characters, story, and cover art attract your readers?
- Reputation: The reputation of the title, author, or illustrator may determine the reader reception.
- Durability: Highly circulating graphic novels may need to be hardback or durabound binding. You may need to reinforce covers.
- Placement: Accessibility is key to placement of this collection. It can either be intermixed in fiction or be in a section all by itself.
- Use of text and illustrations: What is the story about? How do the comic book elements (like facial expression, clothing, background details, lettering and panel composition) help to portray the story?

- Layout of graphic novel: Are the panels easy for a reader to follow? Use of blank space (gutters) this comic book paneling does it give or detract from the readers understanding of the story and illustrations?

Copyright Considerations

Graphic novels were not invented when the fair use guidelines were written; however, they most likely would be considered as picture books. Two pages of picture books can be copied as long as the two pages do not comprise more than 10 percent of the book.

KITS

A kit contains a variety of formats in one package. In some kits the materials are preselected to present information in a fixed sequence. Other kits and packages are less structured, such as a collection of related materials that can be used singly or in any combination by an individual or a group.

Advantages

- Various formats relating to a specific subject are combined in one package.
- The various formats can meet different student learning styles.
- One kit may include material designed for several grade levels.
- Kits that include sound recordings of accompanying text materials can help learners who have difficulty reading.

Disadvantages

- Some kits may include materials that duplicate items in the collection.
- Kits can be expensive.
- Lost nonreplaceable parts may render a kit unusable.
- Storing kits may require special furniture.

Selection Criteria

- Does the kit create a unified whole? Is there a relationship among its parts?
- Is special equipment needed to use the materials in the kit?
- Does each item in the kit meet the criteria for that particular format?
- Is the kit easy to use?
- Are the directions clear?
- Is adult guidance needed?
- Does the kit fulfill a unique purpose that other materials in the collection do not meet?
- Is there sufficient space to store the kit?

Implications for Collection Development

Select kits on the basis of their potential use and appeal. Students and teachers may prefer to create kits using materials from the collection.

MAPS AND GLOBES

Materials included are flat maps, wall maps, and globes. When a map is published in an atlas or in a book, evaluate it in light of the criteria listed under that format.

Advantages

- Maps can provide a wide range of information: place locations and spellings; significant surface features; distances between places; and scientific, social, cultural, political, historical, literary, and economic data.
- Several people can simultaneously study wall and large maps.
- Unlabeled outline maps or globes encourage children to learn the names, shapes, and locations of political and topographical features.
- Maps are readily available at a wide range of prices.

Disadvantages

- If a group of students need to examine the same detail in a map, multiple copies or a transparency may be needed.
- Cartographic details, especially those on geographic, scientific, or political topics, quickly become outdated.
- Wall maps take up wall space that might be needed for book shelves or displays.
- Some maps can become out of date due to political or geographic changes.

Selection Criteria

- Does the color code help the user interpret the information?
- Is the map up to date?
- Is the depth of detail suitable for the intended audience?
- Are symbols representational and clearly designed?
- Is the item durable?
- Is a laminated surface that allows erasable writing for instruction available on large wall maps?
- Is the map aesthetically pleasing?

Implications for Collection Development

The collection should include maps of various sizes to meet the different needs of individuals and groups. Maps and globes should be easily accessible. Because geographic names of countries tend to change fairly frequently, you should set aside monies in your budget to replace maps and globes on a regular basis.

Copyright Considerations

Wall maps, globes, and flat maps are usually copyrighted by the company that produces them. Simple flat outline maps are not eligible for copyright and may be copied. More complex maps require the same criteria as graphics.

MODELS (*SEE ALSO* REALIA)

Models and dioramas are representations of real things. A model is a three-dimensional representation of an object and may be smaller or larger than the real object. Cutaway models show the inside of an object. Dioramas provide an impression of depth, with three-dimensional foreground against a flat background.

Advantages

- These formats offer a sense of depth, thickness, height, and width.
- They can reduce or enlarge objects to an observable size.
- They can simplify complex objects.
- The model can be disassembled and reassembled to show relationships among parts.

Disadvantages

- The size of models may limit their use with a group.
- Some models are difficult to reassemble.
- Loose parts are easy to misplace or lose.
- Specially designed shelving and storage units may be needed.

Selection Criteria

- Are size relationships of the part to the whole accurately portrayed?
- Are parts clearly labeled?
- Are color and composition used to stress important features?
- Will the construction withstand handling?

Implications for Collection Development

The size of many of these materials creates storage and distribution problems. Packaging models for circulation may also be difficult. Materials produced by staff and students may lack the durability needed for permanent inclusion in the collection.

NEWSPAPERS

Newspapers, especially local newspapers, are commonly found in library collections. Today, many newspapers are also available online and can be used for current events, as well as for research purposes.

Advantages

- Newspapers are a familiar format as a source of information to students.
- Having print copies of newspapers in a school library frequently draws students and teachers into the library.
- The information in newspapers is current.
- Some newspapers, such as *USA Today,* pictorially display data, making them accessible to those comfortable with figures and graphs.

- Local newspapers may provide community information not available elsewhere.
- More than one user can simultaneously access online formats of newspapers.

Disadvantages

- Storage of print newspapers can be difficult.
- Only one person at a time can read a print newspaper, unless the newspaper is separated into sections.
- Many users tend to not leave the print newspaper in its original order and condition.

Selection Criteria

- Is the content of interest to students and teachers?
- Are subjects treated clearly in a well-organized manner?
- Are illustrations pertinent and adequately reproduced?
- Do the strengths of the newspaper fulfill a need within the school?
- Is the paper directed to a local, regional, national, or an international audience?
- Does the newspaper feature visual materials with attention-getting pictorial information and clear graphics?
- In which formats (print or online) are the newspapers available?
- Is the content the same in all formats of the newspaper?
- How frequently is information updated?
- How easily can one retrieve back issues?

Implications for Collection Development

Local, state, and national newspapers should be represented in school library collections through print subscriptions or through access on the Internet. Elementary schools should have at least a local newspaper available in the library. If classes subscribe to instructional newspapers, the school librarian may find it useful to have a copy of the teacher's edition in the library.

Copyright Considerations

A teacher can copy a chart, graph, diagram, cartoon, picture, or an article from a newspaper for instructional use. Word limits for multiple copies for classroom use are 250 words for poetry and 2,500 words for articles. A copyright warning notice should appear on each copy. Online newspapers that require subscriptions may be subject to licensing agreements.

OPEN EDUCATIONAL RESOURCES

Open educational resources (OER) are teaching and learning materials in the public domain or released under a license that permits no-cost use, adaptation and redistribution. OER enable personalized learning experiences because through open licensing, materials can be used, adapted, localized, and shared across learning communities. Chapter 13, "Legal and Ethical Issues with the Collection," addresses OER licensing in more depth.

Most school librarians follow local criteria to guide their selection of digital learning resources, which often address the resource's accuracy, currency, and appropriateness. When OER are part of the curation process, additional criteria may be important (adapted from ISKME, 2019).

- **Licensing**. There is a statement indicating that the work is in the public domain, or the resource is a U.S. federal government work prepared by an officer or employee as part of that person's official duties, and is thus free to use without restrictions, or there is a symbol or statement that indicates it is licensed under one of the six Creative Commons (CC) licenses, or if there is no Creative Commons or other open license listed, there is a clear statement (for example, on the terms of use page) that the resource may be used and adapted.
- **Editability**. The resource is offered in an editable format, such as .docx or Google Doc (as opposed to PDF or other static formats);
- **Modularity**. The resource is modular and can be broken down into distinct pieces for remixing purposes;
- **Aligned**. The resource has been aligned to learning standards that are relevant and applicable to your context; and
- **Reusability**. The format of the resource supports reuse and adaptation; user reviews or other metadata about the resource indicate how the resource was used by others, or user satisfaction with the resource; there are multiple versions of the resource available in the repository or collection, due to adaptations and re-sharing of the resource by prior users.

In addition to selecting resources, school librarians will need to have a strategy to organize and make available OER through curated lists, records in the library catalog, or other means. As with all resources, OER pose advantages and disadvantages for school libraries:

Advantages

- OER enable match between learner need and learner resource.
- OER allow for a range of uses, including editing, remixing, and sharing.
- Collaborative collection development is easy with these resources.
- OER are free or low cost.
- OER cannot be lost or stolen.

Disadvantages

- Users may need access to download and/or browser extensions to use resources.
- Learners must have access to their own devices or the school library will have to maintain a device inventory.
- Resources may disappear without notice or replacement; and
- Use terms may not be apparent on resource; and

Selection Criteria

- Is the content of interest to students and teachers?
- Are subjects treated clearly in a well-organized manner?
- Is the sound quality good?
- Is the content accurate? How do you know?
- How easy is it to access OER? Is the server slow or does it require additional or special browser extensions or applications?

School librarians may also find a tool like the EQuIP rubric (see inset box) useful for evaluating OER, especially collaboratively.

EQuIP Rubric for Evaluating OER (Achieve, 2011).

	3=Superior	2=Strong	1=Limited	0=Very Weak	Not Applicable for this Resource
Degree of Alignment to Standards—How closely aligned to the learning standard is this resource? Standards could be Common Core, Next Generation Science Standards, or other.					
Opportunities for Deeper Learning—Are students engaged in any of the deeper learning skill areas?					
Quality of Explanation of the Subject Matter—How thoroughly is the subject matter explained in this resource?					
Quality of Instructional and Practice Exercises—Are exercises designed to provide an opportunity to practice and strengthen specific skills and knowledge?					
Utility of Materials Designed to Support Teaching—Is this resource designed to support teachers in planning and presenting the resource? Is it easy for teachers to understand and use?					
Quality of Technological Interactivity—Is technological interactivity included in this resource?					
Quality of Assessment—Are there assessments included in this resource that determine what a student knows before, during, and after the subject is taught?					

ONLINE DATABASES (*SEE ALSO* EJOURNALS)

Online databases provide digital access to organized collections of data through the use of a computer that is connected to the Internet. Numerous databases are available to libraries. Some contain data of special formats, such as indexes to periodicals, and others provide information from more than one format. Some vendors provide *bundled databases* or *aggregated databases*. Aggregated databases are databases selected by a vendor and put together as a package to which you can subscribe. Gale, ProQuest, and EBSCO are examples of vendors who provide bundled databases to libraries. Types of databases are the following:

1. Full text: includes all the information available for a certain record. Examples are encyclopedias, journal articles, and entire newspapers.
2. Bibliographic: provides citations and may include abstracts. An example is a magazine index or *Books in Print*.
3. Directory: provides a list of information. An example is a faculty and staff directory.
4. Numeric: contains numbers. Examples are population and census figures provided by the government.
5. Mixed: includes a mixture of the other types of databases.

Advantages

- Many states provide databases to school, libraries, and taxpayers for free.
- Information is current.
- Users can easily and quickly locate information.
- Users can modify searches during the process.
- Federated search features allow users to simultaneously multiple databases at once.
- Immediate feedback lets users know whether information is available and whether their search strategy was too narrow or too broad.
- The information provides complete citations.
- Bibliographies are easy to generate.
- Users can save search strategies.
- Many students prefer to access information digitally, rather than use print formats.

Disadvantages

- Not all the subjects in the curriculum may be included.
- Databases may contain content beyond users' reading levels.
- Users may need training in developing search strategies.
- Users may need training in evaluating and selecting information.
- Users may need training in interpreting bibliographic information.
- Teachers and librarians may be unable to quickly determine whether students are downloading information without analyzing it, evaluating it, or synthesizing information from several sources.
- Teachers may need assistance in designing assignments that call for evaluation of information, rather than merely locating a predetermined number of sources on a topic.
- Materials cited may not be available locally, and interlibrary loan requests may increase.
- Information generated before 1970 might not be included, limiting historical searches.

- Full-text information might not include graphics from the original work.
- Monographs are not covered as adequately as periodical articles and newspapers.
- Downtime and malfunctions that occur on a network may frustrate users.

Selection Criteria

- Which databases does your state provide for free? Focus your expenditures only on what is not provided to you at low or no cost.
- Are the intellectual level and the reading level appropriate for the intended users?
- Will students use the disciplines covered in the database?
- How is the database indexed?
- Can students conduct searches using title, author, and keywords?
- Can searchers use Boolean logic, connecting search terms with *and*, *or*, and *not*?
- Are cross-references provided?
- How frequently is the database updated? Is this appropriate for the curriculum needs?
- How accurate is the information?
- What years does the database cover?
- What services does the vendor offer?
- How clear is the written documentation? Does it include sample screens and other aids?
- If there is a print version, is the online search time less than that required for searching the print version?
- Is the screen easy to read and are directions clear?
- What criteria or standards were used in creating the database?
- Can the users access the database from home after school hours?
- Is the vendor willing to negotiate cost and having the database available during after-school hours?
- If the databases are bundled, can you search simultaneously through more than one database?

Implications for Collection Development

Important questions arise when making a decision on whether to subscribe to online data-bases beyond what may be available to you through statewide digital libraries (see this chapter's "Additional Readings" for more information about locating the databases pro-vided by your state). Costs for subscriptions can usually be negotiated with a vendor. The costs may vary depending on a school's enrollment, number of persons able to simultane-ously access the database, and whether the students have around-the-clock access to the databases. These are all parts of the licensing agreement that you will sign when subscrib-ing to a database or to bundled databases. Agreements with such vendors can affect use. The number of interlibrary loan requests may increase as searchers identify resources not available in the library and not available in full text in the databases. Future funding con-cerns may necessitate the formation of resource-sharing plans to accommodate the increase in requests for resources the school library does not own.

Copyright Considerations

License agreements usually define what the publisher considers to be fair use of the prod-uct. Limitations may include the amount of information that users can download or the number of users who may access the service at the same time.

PERIODICALS (*SEE ALSO* EJOURNALS AND NEWSPAPERS)

A periodical is a magazine or other publication that is issued on a regular basis. The following section deals only with magazines. Hundreds of magazines are available that can be included in a school library collection. Some popular magazines that are read primarily for entertainment are *Ranger Rick, Rolling Stone,* and *People.* Others, such as *Scientific American, U.S. News and World Report,* and *American Heritage,* are used heavily for research. Many of the professional magazines are referred to as journals. Examples of ones that you might have in your professional library are *Reading Teacher, School Library Journal,* and *Journal of Science Education and Technology.*

Advantages

- Periodicals offer short stories, participatory activities for young users, and extensive illustrations.
- Some magazines solicit contributions of writing or illustrations from students.
- Many periodicals suggest activities that adults can use with students.
- Reluctant book readers often enjoy reading magazines.
- Having a collection of popular magazines will attract teen users to the school library.

Disadvantages

- Circulation controls are difficult to establish.
- Periodicals lend themselves to theft and mutilation.
- When a large number of children are involved, reader participation activities (such as fill in the blanks, connect the dots, or puzzles) need to be copied or laminated so they can be used more than once. Copying is subject to copyright restrictions.
- Storage space that provides easy access to several volumes of a journal may be difficult or expensive to provide.
- If foldouts and cutouts are removed from periodicals, portions of the text may be eliminated.
- The number of advertisements in journals may detract from their usefulness.

Selection Criteria

- Is the content of interest to students and teachers?
- Are subjects treated clearly in a well-organized manner?
- Are the illustrations pertinent and adequately reproduced?
- Is the format appropriate for the purpose of the magazine and the intended audience?
- Do any users need large print items?
- Is the journal indexed?
- Does the digital version have the same coverage as the print version?
- How easy is it to access back issues?
- How is the digital version updated?
- Does the digital version provide links to other digital sources?
- How easy is it to download articles?

Implications for Collection Development

The length of time one keeps print versions of periodicals depends on their use and the availability of storage facilities. Anticipated use plus cost are key factors in deciding whether to obtain periodicals in print, online, or in CD-ROM formats.

Copyright Considerations

A teacher can copy a chart, graph, diagram, cartoon, picture, or article from a periodical or newspaper for instructional use. Word limits for multiple copies for classroom use are 250 words for poetry and 2,500 words for articles. A copyright warning notice should appear on each copy. Creation of anthologies, compilations, and collective works are prohibited.

PODCASTS

In this time of streaming media, learners have vast choices about what to listen to, learn, and discover. There are podcasts for academics, such as science, math, history, and English. There are podcasts for specific topics related to hobbies and interests, such as photography, animals, and astronomy. There are podcasts for young entrepreneurs. One of the most useful topics revolves around motivation and inspiration. School can be tough for some learners and kids can feel down and overwhelmed. Listening to an uplifting podcast could really change a young person's life!

Advantages

- Podcasts give students a way to experience information in addition to reading.
- Some podcasts are created by children for children.
- The range of podcast topics is large, linking to almost any academic and personal interest a learner may have.
- Podcasts are free or low cost.
- Podcasts cannot be lost or stolen.

Disadvantages

- Download issues may prevent updates.
- Learners must have access to their own devices or the school library will have to maintain a device inventory.
- While some podcasts release content on a regular, scheduled basis, some are infrequently updated, potentially leading to listener disappointment.
- Many podcasts are reviewed, but to date, there is no systematic review for language, accuracy, quality, or other selection criteria; and
- Locating and downloading podcasts may require a special app like Stitcher (http://stitcher.com) or Pocket Casts (http://pocketcasts.com).`

Selection Criteria

- Is the content of interest to students and teachers?
- Are subjects treated clearly in a well-organized manner?
- Is the sound quality good?
- Is the content accurate? How do you know?
- Do any users need large print items?
- Is the journal indexed?
- Does the digital version have the same coverage as the print version?
- How easy is it to access back issues?
- How is the digital version updated?

- Does the digital version provide links to other digital sources?
- How easy is it to download podcasts?

Implications for Collection Development

The length of time one keeps print versions of podcasts depends on their use and the availability of storage facilities.

Copyright Considerations

A teacher can excerpt a podcast instructional use. A copyright notice should appear on the web page accompanying the excerpted audio.

POSTERS (*SEE* GRAPHIC MATERIALS)

REALIA (*SEE ALSO* GAMES, MODELS, AND TOYS)

Realia are three-dimensional objects from real life that can be used for classroom instruction. Coins, tools, stamps, postcards, and fossils are examples of realia. They bring the real world into the hands of inquisitive users.

Advantages

- Students can handle and closely examine real objects.
- One can inexpensively acquire some objects, such as stamps and postcards, from a wide range of sources, including the students themselves.
- Teachers can check out realia and use them in classroom lessons.

Disadvantages

- Students can easily drop and break some realia.
- Some items may be too fragile or too small for more than one person to use at a time.
- Other items are hard to keep clean or to retain the original shape.

Selection Criteria

- Does the item serve an instructional purpose?
- Is the item durable?
- Is there a display area where several students can observe one item at the same time?
- Are items safe to handle?
- Is the item easy to clean?

Implications for Collection Development

You should avoid duplicating specimens found in other departments of the school, such as the science laboratory. Items should not be put in the collection unless they can potentially serve an instructional purpose. Realia may require special storage facilities.

SOFTWARE (*SEE* COMPUTER SOFTWARE)

TEXTBOOKS AND RELATED MATERIALS

Materials include textbooks (basic and supplementary), workbooks, and multimedia items. Commercial companies and educational agencies develop these materials. Textbooks may be used as chief sources of information or as supplementary information sources. Some school districts are moving to the use of online textbooks, which eliminates some of the disadvantages of print textbooks such as the need for storage space on shelves. Articles relating to the use of online textbooks can be found in "Additional Readings" at the end of this chapter.

Advantages

- Instruction is in a fixed sequence but is usually flexible enough for the instructor to reorganize.
- The table of contents and index facilitate rapid access to information.
- Each student can have a copy.
- The teacher's editions offer suggestions for related materials and activities.
- Textbooks are field tested, and one may request and evaluate the results of those tests.
- Users can move at their individual pace.

Disadvantages

- Textbooks can limit a teacher's creativity.
- Textbooks can encourage rote learning rather than stimulate exploration.
- A textbook's bibliographies may cite out-of-print materials or fail to reflect appropriate resources in the collection.
- Textbooks take up much shelf space if they have to be housed in the library.
- Adoption of textbooks often implies they will be used over a number of years.

Selection Criteria

Teachers, in consultation with librarians, usually select the textbooks or other instructional systems. In some situations, the librarian may not participate, but the criteria presented here provide basic information necessary to consider in making selection decisions. A librarian may want to buy a single copy of a particular text for its informational content, even though it is not used in a classroom.

- Is this item on the state's approved materials list?
- Is the content accurate and objective?
- Does the content represent a broad spectrum of viewpoints on a given topic?
- Are the visual materials keyed to the text?
- Are bibliographies up to date? Do they include a wide range of formats?
- Is the treatment appropriate for the intended purpose and audience?
- Is the arrangement chronological or systematic?
- Is the presentation free of racial or sexual stereotyping?
- Is the type clear and are the pages uncrowded?

Implications for Collection Development

In some schools, librarians are responsible for the organization, storage, distribution, and inventory of textbooks. Regardless of whether you have this responsibility, you need to be aware of the content, the materials recommended in the bibliographies, and the potential use of textbooks as information sources. Individual titles may be useful as information works or for anthologies of short stories or poetry. You may want to include textbooks in the professional collection. Most states publish selection criteria for textbooks that should be used to guide decisions.

Copyright Considerations

Users may not copy workbooks, exercises, test booklets, and other consumable works.

TOYS

Toys (dolls, stuffed animals, puppets, cars, etc.) allow students opportunities to develop coordination and to learn through touch, manipulation, and sight.

Advantages

- Play is a way of exploring natural laws and relationships.
- Toys can help develop perceptual motor skills.
- Dolls and stuffed animals can help develop affective skills.
- Toys are inexpensive.

Disadvantages

- Parts can be lost.
- The various shapes of toys can create storage problems.
- Germs and lice can be spread through the use of toys. Toys need to be cleaned and sanitized.
- Safety requirements must be observed.
- Toys can be used by a limited number of people.

Selection Criteria

- Can a student play with the toy independently or is adult guidance needed?
- Has the user's developmental stage been considered in the selection of the toy?
- Is the toy durable?
- Will the toy withstand use by children?
- Can one buy replacement parts or make them in-house?
- Is the material nonflammable?
- Can one wash or clean the toy?
- Are the parts of the toy safe for children to use without injuring themselves?

Implications for Collection Development

Selection should be based on knowledge of children's developmental needs. You may need to provide duplicate items so more than one student can use the same toy or so that the toy can be used in the library and can also be circulated. You will need to consider carefully whether you want to collect and circulate toys.

WEBSITES

Website refers to a collection of pages of documents accessible on the World Wide Web (WWW or the web). This environment on the global computer network allows access to documents that can include text, data, sound, and video. The user can move from one location to another within the website or use *links* to move to related websites. Access is by the website's address or by the *uniform resource locator* (URL). The URL identifies the name of the host computer, the server, the name of the directory, the domain, the directory or server, and the web page or the actual filename. The domain is identified by three letters describing the sponsoring organization: .com for commercial site, .edu for educational, .k12 for a school, .org for a nonprofit organization, .gov for a government agency, and .net for an Internet Service Provider, among others. The tilde symbol (~) designates a personal web page. These letters and symbols give a clue as to the author (and authority) of the information.

Advantages

- The web provides access to information on a global basis.
- The web allows for self-directed discovery.
- Websites can be accessed via computer, tablet, and smartphone.
- The links connect related sources of information.
- The information may be presented through text, sound, graphics, animation, video, and downloadable software.
- Users can interact with the website at their own pace.

Disadvantages

- Sometimes searching for information takes place without the guidance of an index or a classification scheme.
- The content of some websites, including the identified links, are not updated on a regular basis.
- Cataloging websites can be challenging.
- The advertising on some websites can be distracting.
- Content may not be age appropriate.
- Students can easily get lost or lose focus when accessing numerous links.
- Students can download a file, alter it, and (illegally) claim it is their own work.
- Internet safety and literacy must be taught to ensure proper and effective use.

Selection Criteria

- Is the following information provided: name of sponsoring organization or individual, their qualifications, the full mailing address, the e-mail address, the date the page was created, the date the information was updated, and copyright information?
- Is the content and vocabulary appropriate for the intended audience?
- Is the purpose clearly stated?
- Does the website fulfill its purpose?

- How long does it take to access the website?
- Is it easy to navigate through the various pages of the website?
- Are the links updated so that one does not get an error message indicating that the link no longer exists?
- Does the design add to the appeal for the intended audience?
- Does the type and background make the pages readable?
- Is there a link back to the home page on each page?
- Is a table of contents or outline provided for longer documents?
- Does the website have its own search engine for searching all the pages?
- Has the site been reviewed? If so, what did the reviewer say?
- If the website offers a fee-based service, is it a justified and reasonable price?

Implications for Collection Development

School librarians should curate a selection of websites for assignments, rather than having users rely solely on search tools. The school library's website can be one way that users learn of links to selected sites related to their needs and interests. The library's own website should be updated on a regular basis. If you are subscribing to a fee-based website, you may be able to negotiate the cost. Websites can also be cataloged so that users can locate them via the library catalog. See the Helpful Multimedia section of this chapter for helpful cataloging tools.

Copyright Considerations

All web pages are copyrighted. The design of the page, the HTML code, the graphics, and the collections of links are copyrightable. A notice will inform users if they may copy the materials. If you do not find a notice that you can reproduce the material, you must obtain permission to make more than one copy for personal use. If you are subscribing to a website, you will need to adhere to the licensing agreement.

LEGACY MATERIALS

While legacy materials may be slated for disposal, consider your community before you send them to the trash. If your learning environment has low or no Internet or is susceptible to natural disasters that may knock out Internet connections, then maintaining a small collection of legacy devices and content may make sense for times when learners and educators need content, but streaming or using the Internet is not an option.

AUDIOCASSETTES

Although not a new technology, audiocassettes remain popular in some school libraries today. Combination kits of books and audiocassettes are frequently found in elementary school libraries, whereas middle school and high school students enjoy digital audiobooks that stream or can be downloaded. Audiobooks are also extremely appealing to students who are visually impaired. Audiocassettes require tape recorders; thus, if teachers check out audiocassettes for classroom use, you should also provide quality tape recorders that make it possible for large groups of students to easily listen to the audiocassettes.

Advantages

- Tapes are portable and easy to use.
- A wide range of content is available.
- Equipment is easy to use and inexpensive.
- Information is locked into a fixed sequence, and specific sections can be easily located through use of counters on tape recorders.

Disadvantages

- Listening for an extended period of time may induce boredom with some students.
- Use with large groups requires high-quality tape recorders, with adequate amplification.
- Cassette players are becoming more expensive to buy or fix and require more maintenance.
- Cassettes must be rewound before circulating if a previous user did not rewind them.
- Cassettes are small and can easily be lost or stolen.
- Cassette cases break easily; thus a supply of empty cases may need to be purchased.

Selection Criteria

- Is the sound free of distortion?
- Are the length and quality of the performance appropriate to the intended audience?
- Do labels provide enough information to distinguish one item from another (cassette #1, cassette #2, etc.)?
- Do labels provide the time required to listen to the tape?
- If the recording is based on a book, is the recording true to the original?
- Does the recording engage the listener's attention?
- Does narration begin with attention-getting words to capture the listener's interest? Are keywords or key statements emphasized to help the listener?
- Are accompanying materials, such as a teacher's guide, appropriate and useful?

VOICES FROM THE FIELD

You wouldn't think we need these anymore, with everything that's available online. But I'm glad we still have our "pamphlet file" because it gives me a place to file things that I don't want to lose but have no other place to keep. We no longer file articles that are retrievable from periodical databases, but we do like to hang on to articles that feature current or past students or other people associated in some way to our school. Also, articles from local papers or pamphlets about local organizations are worthy for the file. Sometimes I pick up maps or brochures on local parks, museums, recreation areas, etc. For example, if your school has a regular school trip to Washington DC or Montreal, it might be useful to keep a travel guide or map of walking tours for those cities. Ephemera like that is useful and easily replaceable. It might also be important to archive school publications or documents of any kind just to have a current hard copy readily accessible.

—Anonymous LM_NET poster

Implications for Collection Development

The items should provide for individual and group use of narrative presentations, as well as for music and documentaries. Consider whether digital files and digital media players might not be better delivery mechanisms for audio content.

Copyright Considerations

Although it is easy to do, it is not legal to make copies of audiocassette tapes. Converting cassette tapes to another format requires written permission from the copyright holder.

CDs

A CD is an optical disc used to store and provide digital data. The disc is covered with a transparent coating and is read by a laser beam. CDs reached library markets in the mid-1980s. Originally, they were developed as music formats, but they grew to encompass other applications, such as audiobooks.

Advantages

- CDs take up little storage space.
- CDs are small, lightweight, and portable.
- Equipment used to play CDs is inexpensive.
- CD players are easy to use, and many students are familiar with them.
- Sound on CDs is generally of good quality.
- Because a track system is used on CDs, it is possible to access certain parts of a CD.
- Since nothing touches the encoding on the disc, CDs are not worn out in the playing process.
- CDs retain superb sound for hundreds of hours.
- Blank CDs can be used to record and store data.

Disadvantages

- It is relatively easy to scratch a CD, thus ruining parts of the CD. The top side (label side) is particularly vulnerable and is difficult to repair.
- CDs are sensitive to heat and exposure to heat may render them unplayable.
- If using a CD with a large group, the CD player must have adequate amplification.
- Capacity is fairly limited compared to some other formats, such as digital or online space.
- CDs are small and therefore easy to steal.
- As with audiocassettes, cases are easily broken; thus, it is wise to have extra cases on hand.

Selection Criteria

- Is the sound of high quality?
- Is the content appropriate for the intended audience?
- Will the content be appealing for more than just a few months?

- Are there accompanying materials, such as the words to the songs or the time to play each track?
- Does the label provide information on the time required for playback?

Implications for Collection Development

You need to consider whether you wish to collect and circulate CDs that contain music. Although they are popular items with teenagers, they can be easily damaged and copied (thus violating copyright). Some lyrics of songs may not be appropriate for a school setting. Musical CDs for preschool and elementary level students are also becoming increasingly popular. If you have a generous library budget, CDs will undoubtedly be a popular format. So many selections are available that it may be difficult to decide which items to purchase. Also, some of the musical CDs (particularly pop music) may be popular for only short periods of time.

Copyright Considerations

It is illegal to make copies of any sound recordings; even archival copies may not be made. Converting CDs to another format requires written permission from the copyright owner. It is a good idea to place appropriate copyright warning stickers on CDs that circulate.

CD-ROMs

A CD-ROM is a form of a compact disc that is read by using a CD-ROM drive on a computer. CD-ROMs can provide access to very large quantities of digitally encoded information at relatively low cost. Graphics, sound, and other nontext items can mix with text. This format is used for encyclopedias, reference sources, databases, multimedia products, interactive books, games, music, OPACs, computer software, clip art, and graphics. CDs are becoming increasingly less common as content providers use Internet-based cloud storage for their data. Still, because CDs can be used to record and store data as well as display data, their use is likely to persist into the near future. Accessing the information online makes it easier for several users to access the information simultaneously.

Advantages

- A single CD-ROM can store the equivalent of 1,000 short books.
- A single disc can hold more than 650 megabytes of text, graphics, and sound.
- With a good index, information retrieval is flexible.
- Use of CD-ROMs helps students learn search strategies before going online.
- The quality of images is high, and they do not fade as photographic images do. The images take less storage space than if they were individual slides or photographs.
- CD-ROM discs are small, lightweight, and portable.
- The discs are durable and resistant to fingerprints.
- The laser beam reader does not come into direct contact with the disc so the disc does not wear out with play.
- Graphics may be better and faster than on websites.
- The format is appealing to students.

Disadvantages

- A CD-ROM drive on a computer is required.
- Some CD-ROM discs require specific methods of retrieval.
- Scratching on the label side makes the disc unusable.
- Capacity is limited compared to online databases.
- Information cannot be updated or changed.
- Use of a single CD-ROM is limited to one student or a small group, creating scheduling and teacher planning difficulties. Networking CD-ROMs can alleviate these problems.

Selection Criteria

Criteria for CD-ROMs and software are similar (see the discussion in the Computer Software section). Additional questions to consider are the following:

- How frequently is the CD-ROM updated?
- Does the cost of a subscription include the update?
- Is there an annual fee?
- Are on-screen tutorials provided? Are they simple and easy to understand?
- Is the menu system easy to use?
- How fast is access to the information?
- What is the quality of the video and audio production?
- What is the technical quality of the underlying program, the manual, and the support personnel?
- Does the CD-ROM contain a large amount of high-quality information?
- Are the advertisement and promotional materials accurate about the number of minutes or hours of full-motion video, high-fidelity audio, number of photographic images, and amount of text?
- Is the CD-ROM truly interactive in the sense that users can explore options?
- Would online access to the information, rather than an individual CD-ROM, better serve your needs?

Implications for Collection Development

You should plan procedures to establish (1) time limits for individual student use of a CD-ROM workstation, (2) number of printouts allowed, (3) fee if applicable, (4) security for discs, and (5) whether to have a dedicated machine for each disc. Plans should also include how to obtain appropriate licenses and how to ensure adherence to copyright issues. These plans must be flexible and are best designed in conjunction with teachers. Administrators may be involved in setting fees, if students are to be charged for printouts.

When you find recommended titles you want to consider, find out whether you can obtain a copy of the CD-ROM for a trial period on your equipment. During the trial, evaluate the technical support found in the documentation, user manuals, and telephone or online help lines. It is important to remember that free demos can supply you with a look at the content of the CD-ROM, but the demos may be technically different from the CD-ROM itself. Use of previews (often with slide shows making a marketing pitch) can give you a sense of the possible interest to your users.

Copyright Considerations

Unlike books, audiocassettes, maps, and some other formats, the physical medium (CD-ROM) is purchased, but the content is often licensed for use. For multiple users or multiple copies of the disc at multiple workstations, you will need to obtain a site or network license.

PAMPHLETS

Pamphlets are multiple-page, printed materials that are frequently housed in the vertical file, rather than shelved as books. Local, state, and national governments, as well as associations or businesses, publish them. Pamphlets and other vertical file materials can provide a wealth of current information and special treatment of timely subjects. Government documents frequently provide concise and up-to-date information about a topic, although the vocabulary may be beyond the elementary school pupils' comprehension.

Advantages

- Pamphlets are inexpensive or free; librarians can readily obtain duplicate copies for topics of high interest.
- Often information found in pamphlets is more current than that in other print media, except magazines and newspapers.
- Pamphlets can provide a variety of viewpoints on a subject.
- Pamphlets often discuss subjects unavailable elsewhere in the collection. Their treatment is usually brief, focusing on a specific subject.

Disadvantages

- Because of their size and format, pamphlets are easily misfiled.
- The flimsy construction of pamphlets limits repeated use.
- Free pamphlets issued by organizations or corporations may take a specific position on issues or contain a great deal of advertising.
- It takes much time to set up and maintain a vertical file containing pamphlets.

Selection Criteria

- Because groups or businesses sponsor many pamphlets, school librarians must consider the extent of advertising. Does advertising dominate the presentation and distract from or distort the information?
- Regardless of whether the item contains advertising, is the message presented without bias and propaganda?
- Is the information provided elsewhere in the collection?

Implications for Collection Development

Since much of the information that is contained in pamphlets is now available through Internet access, many school librarians have eliminated collecting pamphlets and setting up vertical files. However, if you decide to collect pamphlets, they are an inexpensive way to provide balanced information on controversial issues. Materials should be readily accessible, and librarians should review them periodically for timeliness. Because many pamphlets are undated, librarians find it helpful to date them as they file them. This simplifies the reevaluation process. As new versions of pamphlets arrive, the old ones should be removed.

Copyright Considerations

Some pamphlets have copyright limitations. Others, particularly those that government agencies produce, frequently have no copyright restrictions. The user needs to examine each pamphlet for copyright information.

SLIDES

Two types of slides are (1) two-by-two-inch slides used with projectors with trays, carousels, or cartridges, on slide sorters, or in individual viewers and (2) microslides of biological specimens used with a microprojector.

Advantages

- The size of slides permits compact packaging and storage, with ease of distribution and circulation.
- Instructors can adapt sequencing and can edit according to their needs.
- Slides can be projected for an indefinite time to accommodate discussion.

Disadvantages

- Single slides are difficult to access rapidly.
- Slide quality degrades with time and temperature.
- Although slides are inexpensive to process or duplicate, this takes time and depends on the quality and speed of local laboratory services. Copyright restrictions apply to duplication.
- Older technologies, such as overhead projectors, must be kept in order to use slides.

Selection Criteria

- Are art slides faithful to the original?
- Are mountings durable?
- Is there continuity to the set of slides?

Implications for Collection Development

Effective group use of slides requires projectors with remote-control features and lenses of appropriate focal length. Newer technologies, such as digital photos and digital slide presentations like PowerPoint and Keynote, have replaced most of the use of slides in schools. Students and teachers are now able to access photographs of art and science specimens via the Internet. They can also develop their own slide presentations through the use of digital photos and presentation software.

Copyright Considerations

Copying slide sets in their entirety, altering a program, or transferring a program to another format requires written permission.

VIDEOCASSETTES

Videocassettes contain magnetic tapes on which both audio and video can be recorded simultaneously. They were first developed in the 1970s so movement in addition to sound could be recorded. The two major standard for videocassettes is JVC's VHS format. Although videocassettes can sometimes still be purchased today, the DVD format has overcome VHS as the most popular for playback of recorded video.

Advantages

- The videocassette can be stopped or replayed.
- Videocassettes are easy to store, maintain, and use without damage.
- The format is familiar to users.
- Several people can view a video at the same time.
- Showing videos over closed-circuit televisions can make a presentation accessible to a large number of viewers in different locations.

Disadvantages

- Small monitors limit the size of the audience, unless one can provide multiple monitors or video projector systems.
- One cannot jump to specific sections as easily as in DVDs.
- Compatible equipment is necessary.
- DVDs produce a clearer image than videocassettes, and many producers have moved to DVDs, rather than videos.
- Videocassette quality degrades with time and temperature.

Selection Criteria

- Is the content of the video appropriate for the intended audience?
- Are there reviews available for the video?
- Is the video content available online or via DVD?
- Is the case protective?

Implications for Collection Development

This format became popular because of its ease of use and range of selections. Due to the lifespan of videocassettes, one the quality has degraded, they may not be replaceable. Likewise, videocassette players are getting more difficult to find and repair, so equipment may be an ongoing challenge.

Copyright Considerations

Although there are devices available for transferring videos to DVDs, it is illegal to transfer any copyrighted materials to another format. Thus, school librarians need to retain video playing equipment for any videos that they have in their collections.

CONCLUSION

[I]n this increasingly digital age, content rather than format should be the criteria.
—Kate MacMillan, November 14, 2018

Include a variety of formats in a school library to meet the needs of all users. When selecting materials, librarians should consider who will use the materials, what formats they prefer, how they will use the materials, and whether appropriate equipment is available. Few collections will include every format described. Some materials may be outside the scope of a school's collection policy; others may not be suitable for a particular group of users. Each format has advantages, disadvantages, and selection criteria that may be specific to that particular media format. School librarians should also be familiar with copyright laws and fair-use guidelines and how they relate to each format. Advances in technology will continue to bring new formats to the market. As new materials and formats appear, librarians need to consider their relevance to the collection.

DISCUSSION QUESTIONS

1. Which other formats do you feel are nearing obsolescence? What do you see as replacement media for superseded media? How will you determine when it is time to remove the media from your collection?
2. What do you see as media types school library collections will need to include in the future? What are the advantages, disadvantages, selection criteria, and implications for collection development?
3. How do you view the role of materials that are created by members of the school community in the collection?

REFERENCES

Achieve. (2011). Rubrics for evaluating open education resource (OER) objects. Retrieved from http://www.achieve.org/files/AchieveOERRubrics.pdf

Bryan, L. (2018, November 8). How can school librarians teach media literacy in today's highly charged media landscape? Retrieved from https://knowledgequest.aasl.org/how-can-school -librarians-teach-media-literacy-in-todays-highly-charged-media-landscape/

Castellanos, L. (2015). The startup that lets you add scents to texts now offers scents with e-books. Retrieved from http://www.bizjournals.com/boston/blog/startups/2015/04/the-startup-that -lets-you-add-scents-to-texts-now.html

Crews, L., Petersen, R., & Weaver, A. (n.d.). Selection and evaluation: 6 areas to consider for making a graphic novel. Retrieved from https://sites.google.com/site/graphicnovelcriteria/

Institute for the Study of Knowledge Management in Education [ISKME]. (2019, July). The role of school librarians in OER curation: A framework to guide practice. https://iskme.libguides .com/SL-OER-Curation/

MacMillan, K. (2018, November 14). Revisiting collection development in a digital age. *KQ Blog*. Retrieved from https://knowledgequest.aasl.org/revisiting-collection-development-in-a-digital -age/

Pattee, A. (2014). *Developing library collections for today's young adults.* Lanham, MD: Scarecrow Press.

ADDITIONAL READINGS

Maxwell, L. (2020). *Podcasting with youth: A quick guide for librarians and educators.* Santa Barbara, CA: Libraries Unlimited.

Phoenix, J. (2020). *Maximizing the impact of comics in your library: Graphic novels, manga, and more.* Santa Barbara, CA: Libraries Unlimited.

Robison, M., & Shedd, L. (eds). (2017). *Audio recorders to zucchini seeds: Building a library of things.* Santa Barbara, CA: Libraries Unlimited.

HELPFUL MULTIMEDIA

Best of the Web (BOTW). (n.d.) Magazines and e-zines for teens. Retrieved from https://botw.org/top/Kids_and_Teens/Arts_and_Entertainment/Magazines_and_E-zines/For_Teens/

Buffalo & Erie County Public Library. (n.d.). Get graphic. Retrieved from http://www.getgraphic.org/

Copyright Website. (2020). Welcome to the copyright website. Retrieved from http://www.benedict.com

Director of Open Access Journals. (2020). Find open access journals & articles. Retrieved from https://doaj.org/

Kowalczyk, P. (2017). 25 sources of free e-books. Retrieved from http://ebookfriendly.com/free-public-domain-books-sources/

OverDrive. (2020). The 2019 K–12 digital content report: E-book and audiobook trends for the Classroom and School Library. Retrieved from https://companyoverdrive.cdn.overdrive.com/wp-content/uploads/2019/10/2019-K12-Digital-Content-Report_compressed.pdf

Schrock, K. (2015). Infographics as a creative assessment. Retrieved from http://www.schrockguide.net/infographics-as-an-assessment.html

Stafford, P. (2017, May 4). K-12 ebook business models and why you should care about them. Retrieved from http://www.noshelfrequired.com/k-12-ebook-business-models/

Stafford, P. (2017, May 11). The four basic ebook models for K-12 libraries. Retrieved from http://www.noshelfrequired.com/the-four-basic-ebook-business-models/

Stafford, P. (2017, May 18). Choosing ebook platforms for K-12 libraries. Retrieved from http://www.noshelfrequired.com/ebook-business-models-in-k-12-libraries-part-3-choosing-a-combination-of-ebook-platforms/

TOON Books. (2010). School collections. Retrieved from https://www.toon-books.com/school-collections.html

Valenza, J., & Boyer, B. (2015). Top reasons to use subscription databases (infographic). Retrieved from https://magic.piktochart.com/output/4021098-top-reasons-to-use-databases

Web2MARC (web-based MARC record generating tool). Retrieved from http://dl2sl.org/records

CHAPTER 9

Acquisitions and Processing

Key Learnings

- Budgets, curriculum, and existing district and school policies are main guides for acquisition and processing decisions.
- Most libraries use jobbers, materials wholesalers, to acquire their materials. Jobbers often will also process materials for a small fee.
- Materials should be described for use. Digital resources require special description and organization considerations.
- Resource sharing is a cost-effective means of making resources in other libraries available to your users.

Acquisition is the process of obtaining materials: confirming that materials are available, verifying order information, identifying and selecting sources of materials, arranging for orders to be sent, allocating funds, keeping records, and producing reports on funds expenditures. Obtaining digital products, reviewing license agreements, and negotiating for leases are also included in the acquisition procedures. Speed, accuracy, and value are common goals of the acquisition process.

The school librarian can acquire materials through purchase, lease, or solicitation of free materials, gifts, or exchanges. Schools participating in resource-sharing programs also borrow and lend materials that are available through interlibrary loan.

This chapter focuses on the components of the acquisition process that are most likely to involve the building-level person directly. It also reviews the relationship of acquisition procedures to acquisition policy, identifies the distribution systems for materials, describes procedures for acquiring materials (including digital materials), discusses the relationship between library professionals and vendors, and describes possible processing and cataloging procedures. Obtaining materials through resource sharing is also discussed.

POLICIES AND PROCEDURES

As Chapter 5 covered, school library collection development policies establish procedures to follow and document the rationale for such procedures. Procedures describe how a process will take place and who will be responsible for implementing the steps in the process. An acquisition policy might state that materials will be purchased from the least expensive and most efficient source, for instance, a jobber. The policy might also indicate that a school librarian may buy an item locally if the need is immediate. In a high school, a policy could state that a paperback or eBook format is preferable to buying fiction books in hardback format.

The acquisition plan for school library materials must match curricular priorities. The school librarian must be able to show that the selection of new materials meets the collection development plan. Once items have been identified that meet the needs of the school librarian and the selection criteria, and those items prioritized for purchase, the school librarian must acquire those items and make them available as quickly and efficiently as possible. An acquisition plan includes determining budget allotments for the current year, identifying sources for wished-for items, selecting vendors, determining which services to purchase, preparing purchase orders, checking in orders, and processing materials.

Budgetary constraints are probably the greatest factor to consider when determining what materials to acquire for a school collection. Some items, because of cost or limited use, may be more appropriately borrowed from another building within the district, from a public library or through interlibrary loan. Pending curriculum adoptions and changes must also be considered before acquiring new materials. Items that will be used for several years should be given priority over items that may be unused after one year. Priority must also be given to items that will be used by a large number of students and staff members.

Based on the analysis of the current collection and the budget allotment, the school librarian identifies materials to purchase that will meet the needs of the curriculum as well as the district selection criteria. A vendor must be identified who can provide the items at the best price and or the urgency at which the item(s) is needed. When selecting a vendor, the school librarian will also want to evaluate the services that each vendor can provide, such as cataloging and processing. After the vendor has been selected, school librarians should follow procedures for making purchases through the school's purchasing mechanisms. It may be useful for the school librarian to compare how the budget is spent from year to year.

In many school districts, acquisition policies are uniform throughout the schools. The school district might also dictate the acquisition procedures. For example, the district's purchasing agent may specify the order forms that one should use. Some school districts may have agreements to use a particular jobber or to order their materials from an online catalog. Procedures for accounting and record keeping are frequently established at the district level. As a new school librarian, you should ask the director of the district school library program or a school administrator for a copy of district policies and procedures that affect the school library. In some school districts, you can find this information online.

To obtain input from teachers, administrators, and students, you may want to create a materials request form. Figure 9.1 is an example of such a form.

Materials Acquisition Request

Requestor:

Name:

email: Phone:

Status (please check one):

Teacher   ☐

Administrator   ☐

Student   ☐

Source of Citation (where you found information about the material):

Book (complete as much information as possible):

Author or Editor:

Title:

Publisher: Year of Publication:

ISBN#:   Price:

Magazine or Journal (complete as much information as possible):

Title:

Publisher:

ISSN#:   Price:

Audio-Visual Material (complete as much information as possible):

Type of Material (audiocassette, video, CD, DVD, etc.):

Producer:

Distributor:

Price:

Figure 9.1. Materials Request Form

VOICES FROM THE FIELD

I am continually reminding librarians that collection development should be community need/interest focused. This should lead us a little away from mainstream lists created by individuals. I am still using Follett software to analyze my collection to see where things need to be updated. Likewise I use it to build lists based on what teachers are teaching, what students request, etc.

—Carrie Betts, school librarian, Michigan

A form like the one featured in Figure 9.1 can be printed out and made available to school library users, perhaps at the circulation desk or at faculty meetings. Ideally, the form should be available digitally through the school library website so users can access the form from classrooms or homes.

DISTRIBUTION SYSTEMS

Choosing the best source for ordering materials or equipment is an important decision in the acquisition process. Chief distributors of materials include jobbers, distributors, publishers, producers, subscription agencies, dealers, and local sources such as bookstores. Any for-profit organization that markets a product or service to libraries can be considered a *vendor*. Other possible sources for materials include museums, online businesses, and garage sales. *Remainders* (publishers' overstocks) and out-of-print materials can sometimes be obtained from online vendors and from both new and used bookstores. Websites that can help you identify some of these sources are found at the end of the chapter under Helpful Multimedia.

Using Jobbers

Jobbers, wholesalers, and distributors are intermediaries between publishers or producers and the buyer, the school librarian. The term *jobber* is used interchangeably with the word *wholesaler*. Jobbers buy materials from publishers and producers and sell them to bookstores and libraries. For example, one can buy books and videocassettes directly from the publisher or producer, but the same items are often available at a lower price from a jobber or a distributor. The word *distributor* is often used for audiovisual materials. Distributors may serve a region of the country or the entire country. Some jobbers and distributors provide newsletters, product hotlines, and websites.

The many advantages for dealing with jobbers are:

- You avoid the cost and paperwork of ordering through many publishers or producers.
- You have only one source to contact for follow-up on orders.
- Libraries receive better discounts from jobbers than from publishers or producers.
- You obtain indirect access to publishers who refuse to deal directly with libraries or give poor service to small orders.
- Most jobbers provide full processing, cataloging services, security devices, and plastic jackets for materials.
- Preselection plans (approval plans in which the librarian examines new titles at the usual discount rate, with full return privileges) are sometimes available.
- Many jobbers offer online ordering services.

Utilizing the services of jobbers also has disadvantages:

- It sometimes takes a month for jobbers to fill orders, whereas publishers can deliver in one to two weeks.
- The availability of older titles depends on the wholesaler's inventory.
- No wholesaler can supply every available title. Some titles, such as materials that professional organizations produce, can be purchased only through direct order.
- Policies on the return of defective or damaged copies may say that credit or replacement is not granted until the wholesaler has received the returns.

Many school districts have established relationships with jobbers and an approved vendor list for you to use. Librarians can expect jobbers or wholesalers to have a large inventory of titles, to fill orders promptly and accurately at a reasonable cost, and to report on items not in stock. If you receive an order and do not obtain satisfactory information about whether a book is out of print, out of stock indefinitely, or temporarily out of stock, you should contact the publisher or producer to inquire about why an item was not received.

If a librarian has a standing order with a publisher, it is not necessary to initiate orders for titles that the publisher delivers under the conditions of the standing order. A *standing order* is an agreement that is made to purchase all items that match certain terms, such as Caldecott Medal Award-winning books or materials on a particular subject. Many school librarians have standing orders to renew their magazine subscriptions with vendors, such as EBSCO or WT Cox. In such a case, the vendor sends the librarian a list of all the subscriptions (either by mail or online) that are to be renewed, and the librarian can delete items or add items to the list. As a new school librarian, you need to check to see if your library has any standing order agreements in effect.

Selecting Jobbers

Selecting jobbers who meet the needs of your library can be critical. Thus, you should do some research about the various jobbers before making a selection. You can ask a jobber to provide you a list of schools in your state that use their services and then inquire with other school librarians about their satisfaction with the use of that jobber. This can also be done on school library e-mail lists. The following are some questions that you might want to ask:

- What types of discounts does the jobber offer?
- Does the jobber change prices of items without prior notice?
- On the average what percentage of an order gets filled?
- How long does it take to get an order filled?
- Does the jobber provide information about items that are not received?
- If the jobber is a magazine vendor, is there a claim procedure in place and how long does it take to obtain missed issues?
- Does the jobber follow your specifications for processing and cataloging?
- Is the cataloging information accurate?
- Are the items packaged well and in good condition when you receive them?
- Are you able to return items?

Some websites that will help you identify possible jobbers, distributors, and publishers who deal with library materials, supplies, and equipment are listed under Helpful Multimedia at the end of this chapter and in this book's Appendix. These companies can also

VOICES FROM THE FIELD

I am noticing a shift toward digital resources to reach students where they are and a shift toward allowing outside companies to do the development (e.g. Junior Library Guild). An ongoing shift toward getting materials pre-processed from one place (e.g. Follett) to allow them to curate the collection [quickly]. My supposition is that less help and fewer available hours in the day are steering [school librarians] away from "old school" collection development.

—Lisa Kelley, school librarian, Michigan

be found by looking for advertisements in professional school library and other library journals. Some jobbers that are frequently used by school librarians include Baker & Taylor, Brodart, Follett, Mackin, Ingram, Bound to Stay Bound, and Perma-Bound. When you obtain your first school library position, you will also find that you automatically begin to receive catalogs and advertising brochures from companies that deal with library items. It is wise to keep these catalogs in an organized file and replace old catalogs as you receive newer versions.

Establishing and maintaining good working relationships with jobbers and distributors is partially your responsibility. You need to make certain that your requests are reasonable, that you keep jobbers informed about your collection needs, and that invoices are processed promptly. To stay in business and provide quality services to libraries, vendors need to have large volumes of sales and have good cash flow. Thus, any way that you can contribute to these goals will be appreciated by the vendors with whom you do business.

A class of vendor does exist between a jobber and a subscription service. These vendors are usually the publishers of the works they sell and they customize each subscription installment to the needs of the particular school library. For example, Junior Library Guild (JLG), a book review and collection development service for school and public libraries, was founded in 1929 as the Junior Literary Guild, and is a commercial book club devoted to juvenile literature. To use JLG, a school librarian signs up and selects topic categories and formats of resources from JLG's website. The school librarian also defines the number of titles and frequency of shipment. JLG's professionals curate shipments based on these preferences. Many school librarians find this service to be a painless, time-saving way to add quality new titles to the collection without having to spend time searching through vendors' offerings.

ACQUISITION ACTIVITIES

An initial goal of acquisitions is to avoid duplication, both of effort and of the item itself. Thus, the first step that should be performed when receiving a material request from a teacher or student is to check to see if the library already owns the item or whether it is on order. The school library catalog can provide information about current holdings, as well as materials that are on order (as long as this information has been entered into the school library catalog). If on-order materials are not entered into the library catalog, then you will need to refer to all orders that you have made to check for duplicates.

Bibliographic Verification

When teachers or students request that you purchase an item for the library, they often do not include the full information needed for ordering or they may even provide some inaccurate information (the title might not be exactly correct or they do not remember the publisher correctly). Thus, it is necessary to verify the bibliographic information needed to order the item. The verification procedure consists of two steps. The first is to establish the existence of a particular item. The second is to identify the correct author, title, publisher or producer, and other necessary ordering data, such as ISBN (International Standard Book Number) or ISSN (International Standard Serial Number).

To learn whether an item is available, one can start with a special type of bibliography called a *trade bibliography*. These tools provide ordering information for materials that are currently in print or otherwise available. Bibliographic tools that indicate availability may also state additional information such as whether the item is available through purchase, rent, or loan and the purchase or rental price, whether one must order the item directly from a publisher or producer or whether it is available through a jobber, distributor, or vendor, and if there are postage or delivery charges. The Appendix to this book contains more information about bibliographic tools.

The information included for each item may vary from one tool to another. For print formats, the bibliographic entry usually includes the author, title, editor, publisher, date of publication, series title and number, available bindings, price, and ISBN or ISSN. For audiovisual items, the bibliographic entry usually includes the title; production and release dates; producer or distributor; physical characteristics (e.g., color or black and white, captioned or sound, audiocassette or videocassette, length or running time, and special equipment needed); number of pieces included (e.g., four study prints and one teacher's guide); languages; price; and special conditions of availability.

Many bibliographies can be used for the verification process. *Books in Print* (Bowker), *Books in Print Supplement* (Bowker), and *Children's Books in Print* (Bowker) are frequently used to verify information for books. These resources are available in book format. *Books in Print* and *Children's Books in Print* are also available online. Other Bowker products that can be used to verify information include *The Complete Directory of Large Print Books and Serials, Bowker's Complete Video Directory, Books Out Loud,* and Ulrich's *Periodicals Directory.* You should use the latest edition of these tools for the most current information on price and availability.

If you do not have access to these tools that need to be purchased or subscribed to online, other options are available. One place to find out whether titles are correct and whether a work is in print is through commercial online bookstores like Amazon. A word of caution, however, is that the bibliographic information in these online bookstores is not always completely accurate. Another option is to look on the publishers' or producers' websites. The bibliographic information for ordering will be available, as well as frequent listings of forthcoming titles.

Publishers' and jobbers' catalogs can also assist in bibliographic verification. Catalogs provide price and availability information, but they should not be used for reviews. Remember that catalogs exist to sell materials, not to offer evaluative reviews. When catalogs do quote reviews, full citations to the reviews are usually not given, so the librarian needs to consider the limitations of incomplete reviews, words taken out of context, and the absence of more critical comments that reviews offer.

Ordering

After a jobber or other vendor is selected, materials then need to be ordered. Each school or school district has a procedure that must be followed in order to purchase items. This consists of filling out standardized purchase orders (POs). Some jobbers and publishers provide online access to ordering. Follett's Titlewave is an example of an integrated catalog, review source, and ordering tool that can save you much time. You can find the website information for Titlewave under Helpful Multimedia at the end of this chapter. You should contact financial personnel at your school to determine whether you are able to use online ordering opportunities and how that should be coordinated with the school's purchasing process.

Common information that vendors need to provide materials include shipping address, author or editor, title, publisher, date of publication, price, number of copies, order number, instructions regarding processing and shipping, invoicing, and method of payment. Vendors may also request ISBNs or ISSNs.

Receiving

Care must be taken when unpacking shipments of materials. Special training might be necessary for clerical personnel, volunteers, and student assistants. The first item to locate is the packing slip or invoice (itemized list). This may be attached to the outside of the package or buried underneath the materials. If you do not find the packing slip, you should keep all the items in that shipment separate from those in other shipments.

As each item is received, check it against the packing slip or invoice for title match. In the case of audiovisual or computer materials, this step must take place before you remove the shrink wrap because many jobbers and distributors will not accept returns of unwrapped digital materials. Check the item for damage or missing parts. Know the jobber's or vendor's policy on returns and whether they will give credit for damage that occurred in shipping.

Common problems include wrong editions, items added to or deleted from the list, wrong number of copies, and damaged or incomplete items. After all items have been checked, stamp the school library name on them. Then enter the barcode into the database. Finally, approve the invoice for payment.

Record Keeping

Acquisition activities involve large amounts of detail work. You can handle the tracing of orders either manually or digitally. Manual systems often consist of keeping binders or files for POs by categories such as *outstanding, completed,* or *to be paid.* Another possible organizational category is using budget account numbers.

Computer software can simplify accessing information and generating records. *Consideration files* (the record of desired items) can be organized with a database management program, enabling one to print, in priority order, a list of items to be ordered from a single vendor. As materials are ordered and received, you can update these records. Some systems allow you to transfer the information to a different file, such as outstanding orders or new arrivals. Some systems also allow the administrator to create categories, such as a subject area, a specific format, back orders, or specified jobbers. You can use word processing programs to create a template to print specific information on preprinted continuous forms, including POs. You can also use a spreadsheet program to keep track of budget reports and projections.

If your school district is not using computer programs for management activities, consider the following questions: What jobs can best be handled through the use of computer programs? What equipment resources are available? What are the implications for staffing? What is the capability of existing software programs? Does your automated program permit online ordering, digital invoicing, and credit-card payments?

Online Subscriptions

Most school libraries purchase databases through online subscriptions and it may become necessary to negotiate licenses with vendors. Such a license is a legal agreement of acceptable understandings and commitments that is often negotiated between the vendor and the school librarian. Of course, be sure to check whether your state makes subscription databases available for free. The Helpful Multimedia list at the end of this chapter should help you find out what your state offers.

Both the cost and the terms of a license can usually be negotiated with a vendor. The cost often depends on the enrollment of your school, the number of users who can simultaneously access the materials, and whether you want remote access to the materials from classrooms and users' homes. It is important that you read through any license agreement and understand the terms. If you do not understand the terminology used in an agreement, you should ask the vendor to define the terms in vocabulary that is appropriate to school library use.

If the quoted cost for access is more than your budget allows, you should not automatically give up on the idea of subscribing to online materials. Rather, you should explain your situation to the vendor representative and ask how the cost can be reduced. The online subscriptions are well worth obtaining since it makes access to materials much easier and also saves valuable space in the library.

Equipment

In most school districts or schools, equipment that costs over a certain amount must be put out for bid. In such instances, specifications for the bids must be drawn up. It is important to include every characteristic that you wish to have for the piece of equipment, for instance, the amount of memory needed in a computer, the size of the monitor, the size of the processor, and any other specifications you require. You should instruct bidders not to include taxes in their bids since schools are usually tax-exempt institutions. The business office of the school district or a regional center will handle the bidding process and the awarding of bids. You will be provided with the name or names of vendors from whom you must order the equipment. If for any reason you know that a vendor does not provide quality products or service, you should share this information with the business office so the vendor is not included in the bids that are considered.

For equipment that costs less than those requiring bids you should check with your business office to see if there are any requirements regarding vendors. For instance, in some schools you may not be able to purchase from local dealers but must order from catalogs. In other instances, you may not be able to order from online vendors. Regardless of the way you order equipment, you will need to keep records of your purchases.

In most instances, materials in a school library are either purchased outright or obtained through licensing agreements. Although equipment is usually purchased, large, costly equipment, such as a copy machine, are sometimes leased from a commercial vendor. In these cases, the school librarian must read the leasing agreement carefully and keep track of the cost-effectiveness of leasing the equipment in comparison to purchasing the item.

PROCESSING ACTIVITIES

The final stage in the acquisition process is preparing the materials for use. This involves cataloging and classifying each item, identifying the library as owner, adding security strips and circulation barcodes, putting needed labels on the materials, and providing protective cases or other packaging for circulation of the materials. You should place copyright warnings on audiovisual and computer materials.

Some school districts have their own central processing of materials, particularly of books. In these cases, the books are sent directly to the central processing office where they are cataloged, have barcodes placed on them, and have the name of the school stamped on the items. If there are no such central processing services, then you should definitely have the vendor provide as much processing as you want, particularly the cataloging, which is a very time-consuming process. All major vendors of library books and many who deal with audiovisual materials offer commercial processing for reasonable costs (often from $1.00 to $2.00 per item). This is a bargain when you consider the amount of time that it takes to fully process a book (generally between 30 minutes to an hour, depending on the difficulty of cataloging and classifying the item). You will need to fill out a specification form that indicates your processing requests so that the items match your current cataloging and you receive all the processing services that you need.

Some school librarians order their materials processed, but ask that the school library stamp not be added to the item. This makes it much easier to return materials that are not wanted after examining the items.

If you are employed in a school that is required to do its own processing of materials, it is possible for you to purchase software to help with the cataloging. Many of the vendors of library automation systems provide software for this purpose.

Almost all school libraries use the Dewey Decimal Classification System (DDC) for classifying materials. Chapter 18 discusses some alternatives to DDC that some libraries have begun to use. The *Abridged Dewey Decimal System Classification* (OCLC) will usually fill the needs of a school librarian who needs to do original cataloging. Other tools that will assist in original cataloging are: *Anglo-American Cataloging Rules* (American Library Association, Canadian Library Association, and Chartered Institute of Library and Information Specialists) and *Sears List of Subject Headings* (H. W. Wilson). These tools are all available in print or online. Machine-readable catalog records (MARC) are also available for purchase of free download from the Library of Congress or other union catalogs and from a number of commercial sources. Librarians can download these records, import them into their OPACs, and adapt the records to local needs.

DESCRIBING DIGITAL RESOURCES

Integrating digital resources into a physical collection poses particular challenges for description. Librarians customarily catalog items with a definite beginning and end, such as books and journal articles. Many of these resources have tables of contents, indexes, or abstracts that can inform the descriptive record. Many others have records that can be purchased from publishers or downloaded from other catalogers. Also, users understand that if a book is a textbook about a course, then they will have to search the book for a chapter on a particular topic. For digital resources, the resource is not a physical entity and it can difficult to define a discrete beginning and end, and harder to accommodate for various uses.

This situation makes it a challenge to determine exactly what constitutes the digital resource to be cataloged (granularity, as depicted in Figure 7.1). For instance, if an engineering course module that has applets and animations about dynamite that can be used in several contexts, then the librarian must decide whether to catalog the course as a whole and then make separate catalog entries for the applets and animations, or choose some other descriptive strategy.

To solve this dilemma, librarians might wish to first catalog the enveloping resource for its intended use. Regardless of whether a librarian loves to catalog or hates it, chances are very good that the librarian either buys MARC records; "copy catalogs" the MARC records by downloading them from another source; or creates MARC records from scratch.

For units or graphics within a resource, librarians can create additional catalog records tailored to that reflect the various educational, technical, or pedagogical applications of the granular item. So for the example given above, the librarian first would create a metadata record to describe the course, and then catalog the individual applets and animations, relate them, and note these relationships within the related records (Mardis, 2015). Best practices include:

- Create a single catalog record for resources as a whole. Create additional metadata records for a whole resource if individual parts of a resource differ substantially in technical requirements, descriptions, and educational information.
- Create relationships between resources using the fields of relation and, occasionally, learning resource type and description. Be careful in using description and learning resource type so as not to give information that should be cataloged in a second catalog record.
- Apply the relationship concept described above to strike a balance between supporting resource discovery with reasonable user effort and avoiding potential user frustration with retrieving many redundant records (Mardis, 2015).

Although this process might seem laborious, solutions are on the horizon that should make it easier to create and share records for both physical and digital resources (see inset box). While the professional fully transitions to RDA/BIBFRAME, a few other options for importing and creating descriptive records for the library catalog are available.

Cataloging can be one of the most time-consuming tasks a librarian undertakes. The process of understanding a work and determining how to describe it for others in a way that is not only consistent, but also intellectually accessible, however, is important. After all, as librarians, aren't we responsible for helping our library users find information in ways that are empowering and translate to other contexts?

RESOURCE DESCRIPTION AND ACCESS (RDA) AND BIBFRAME: A SOLUTION FOR INTEGRATED COLLECTIONS

The American Library Association, Canadian Library Association, and Chartered Institute of Library and Information Professionals (CILIP) launched RDA: Resource Description and Access as the new standard for resource description and access designed for the digital world. Built on the foundations established by the Anglo-American Cataloguing Rules, Second Edition (AACR2), RDA provides a comprehensive set of guidelines and instructions on resource description and access covering all types of content and media. Benefits of RDA include:

- A structure based on the conceptual models of functional requirements for bibliographic data (FRBR) and functional requirements for authority data (FRAD) to help catalog users find the information they need more easily
- A flexible framework for content description of digital resources that also serves the needs of libraries organizing traditional resources
- A better fit with emerging database technologies, enabling institutions to introduce effectiveness in data capture and storage retrievals

The Library of Congress' BIBFRAME Initiative is a foundation for the future of bibliographic description that happens on the web and in the networked world. It is designed to integrate with and engage in the wider information community and still serve the very specific needs of libraries. The BIBFRAME Initiative brings new ways to:

- Differentiate clearly between conceptual content and its physical/digital manifestation(s)
- Unambiguously identify information entities (e.g., authorities)
- Leverage and expose relationships between and among entities

In a web-scale world, it is imperative to be able to cite library data in a way that differentiates the conceptual work (i.e., a title and author) from the physical details about that work's manifestation (e.g., page numbers, whether it has illustrations). It is equally important to produce library data so that it clearly identifies entities involved in the creation of a resource (authors, publishers) and the concepts (subjects) associated with a resource.

Find out more at: http://www.rdatoolkit.org/ and http://www.loc.gov/bibframe/

RESOURCE SHARING

Another way in which materials can be acquired (temporarily) is by borrowing them from another library. This is generally referred to as *interlibrary loan*. Some types of interlibrary loan are formalized with networks to which libraries belong. A school that belongs to such a network has access to a plethora of resources and possibly to some additional services. Resource sharing networks include:

VOICES FROM THE FIELD

It's a passion of mine. I started our program in 2009 and it's expanded to two campuses. We have national ILL borrowing, with a local courier who delivers and picks up book packages. We don't get articles and DVDs as readily as books, and the books we get are almost always scholarly. The program is not complicated or challenging to operate, and it provides a richness in resources for any student with a curiosity about a book that isn't on our shelves. I am reluctant to buy more obscure titles to satisfy quirky curiosities, but with ILL the sky's the limit—I get students literally anything they want.

—Jess Hinds, Bard H.S. Early College

- Other schools in the district—Your catalog may be part of a district-wide union catalog.
- Regional catalogs through intermediate school districts—Many of these intermediate service agencies act as interlibrary loan coordinators for school libraries within a specified region.
- Local public libraries—Many public libraries welcome collaborative relationships with school librarians and are able to facilitate sharing of library resources to students.
- Local community colleges and universities—Similar to public libraries, nearby community colleges and universities may offer students limited borrowing privileges.
- Statewide library systems—Most states have a union catalog of material available throughout the state for any citizen to request.

You may also be able to use a service like OCLC's WorldCat to locate and request items. However, participation carries responsibilities and perhaps financial obligations. Interlibrary loan may also require a "quid pro quo" in that libraries that lend items also expect to borrow items. Some school librarians also use informal methods of interlibrary loan by e-mailing or phoning librarians in local schools to see if particular items can be borrowed. This is very helpful when multiple copies of an item are needed or when an item is requested very infrequently. Figure 9.2 is a sample of an interlibrary loan request form that could be used in a school library. It is important to remember, however, that interlibrary loan should not be used in place of purchasing books or other materials that are frequently requested.

CONCLUSION

Acquisition activities consume time and energy. Much of the work involved is detailed and should not be performed in haste. Although clerical assistants can perform some of the acquisition activities, they need to receive training in which accuracy is emphasized. A librarian's organizational abilities, mathematical skills, and business sense frequently come into play during acquisition activities. Errors or misjudgments can be costly. Using computer management systems can simplify procedures, while controlling the information in a timely manner.

Interlibrary Loan Request Form

Please fill in details below and return to your school librarian. Thank you!

Requestor:

Name:
Grade:
Homeroom Teacher:
Your E-mail (for arrival notification):

Date needed:

Please indicate your status:

Teacher ☐

Administrator ☐

Student ☐

BOOK LOAN

Book Title:

Author:

Publisher:
Publication Date:
Edition or Volume Number:

Where did you find this item?

ARTICLE COPY:

Title of Journal/Periodical:

Title of Article:

Author:
Volume:
Issue No.:
Date:

Where did you find this item?

If article is available as a pdf, I would like it sent directly to my e-mail address:

Yes ☐   No ☐

Figure 9.2. Interlibrary Loan Request Form

DISCUSSION QUESTIONS

1. What are the pros and cons of cataloging websites into your library catalog? Which would you choose to do and why?
2. What are the pros and cons of ordering your books to arrive cataloged?

REFERENCE

Mardis, M. A. (2015). *The collection's at the core: Revitalize your library with innovative resources for the Common Core and STEM*. Santa Barbara, CA: Libraries Unlimited.

ADDITIONAL READINGS

Houston, C. (2015). *Organizing information in school libraries: Basic principles and new rules*. Santa Barbara, CA: Libraries Unlimited.

Kaplan, A. (2015). *Catalog it! A guide to cataloging school library materials*, 3rd edition. Santa Barbara, CA: Libraries Unlimited.

Rush, E. B. (2020). *The efficient library: Ten simple changes that save time and improve service*. Santa Barbara, CA: Libraries Unlimited.

Williams, V. K. (2010). Assessing your vendors' viability. *The Serials Librarian, 59*(3/4), 313–324.

HELPFUL MULTIMEDIA

Follett Library Resources. Titlewave. Retrieved from http://www.titlewave.com

Junior Library Guild. https://www.juniorlibraryguild.com/

Lamb, A., & Johnson, L. (2010). The school library media specialist: Program administration: acquisitions. Retrieved from http://eduscapes.com/sms/administration/acquisition.html

Library of Congress. (2013). MARC record services. http://www.loc.gov/marc/marcrecsvrs.html

Nebraska Library Commission. (2013). Cataloging on a shoestring: Sources of free MARC records. Retrieved from https://www.youtube.com/watch?v=Dat3yzRCa9Y

PMA, the Independent Book Publishers Association. (n.d.). Remainders book expo. Retrieved from http://www.pma-online.org/remaindr/remain.cfm

Valenza, J. (2015). Subscription databases: A state-by-state look at available premium content. Retrieved from http://www.thinglink.com/scene/628624327662632960

Web2MARC: A free tool to create MARC records for digital resources. Retrieved from http://dl2sl.org/records

CHAPTER 10

Maintenance and Preservation

Key Learnings
- School libraries should have maintenance policies that address repair, replacement, preservation, and removal of materials.
- Weeding (deselection) is aided by clear policies that guide when materials should be removed.
- Inventory is an essential element of collection development that should be performed on a regular basis.

An effective collection maintenance program serves two purposes. First, materials and equipment should be readily available for use. Second, policies and procedures for preventive maintenance help ensure economical and efficient management of the collection. Maintenance activities include keeping accurate records of what is in the collection (an inventory); inspecting materials; and repairing, replacing, or removing items.

Policies and procedures of the maintenance program are the focus of this chapter. The Additional Readings and Helpful Multimedia listings at the end of this chapter identify works with more specific information about the preservation and maintenance of items in the collection.

MAINTENANCE POLICIES

Maintenance policies, particularly those relating to equipment, sometimes exist at the district level, rather than at the building level. However, if such policies are not present, you need to create them at the school level.

The overall policy should specify who repairs materials and equipment, whether the school library personnel do any troubleshooting with equipment, who replaces equipment bulbs and conducts preventative computer maintenance, what preventative measures are taken to maintain equipment, who is responsible for weeding the collection, the criteria used to weed the collection, what is done with discarded materials, whether an inventory is taken of the collection, and who is responsible for the inventory.

In preparing the budget, developmental items (those increasing the size of the collection) can be distinguished from replacement items (those maintaining the current level of service). The librarian can base the replacement of materials and equipment on the rates at which the items become unusable because of wear or dated content.

Another factor to consider is loss. A loss rate greater than 2 percent suggests that a replacement or loss factor must be a budget item. Woolls and Coatney (2017) offered two budget formulas for materials and equipment replacement. For example, to replace lost, damaged, and out-of-date books, one formula multiplies by 5 percent the number of books in the collection times the average price of a book. The example uses the following illustration: for a collection with 6,000 volumes, 5 percent of the volumes (300 books) should be replaced. If the average cost of a book is $15, then 300 times $15 means $4,500 is needed to cover the replacement costs. Although this formula can be helpful, it is important to remember that the average cost of a hardback book fluctuates. Be sure to research the most current cost of library materials to ensure that your estimates reflect what you are actually likely to spend. *Information Power: Guidelines for School Library Media Programs* (AASL & AECT, 1988) also provides a formula for replacing equipment. These formulas, along with other valuable information in the appendices, are in themselves good reasons to purchase or locate a copy of this book, despite its copyright date. Later national school library standards unfortunately do not include these valuable appendices. However, by just benchmarking the formulas to current item costs, these approaches should provide a usable rough cost approximation.

Equipment

Policies related to equipment maintenance address the following issues:

- When and why equipment will be traded in or discarded
- The type of repairs and maintenance that will be handled at the building level, at the district level, and through repair contracts
- The records to be kept on equipment usage, repair, and maintenance
- The quantity and type of usable pieces of equipment to be provided, including a replacement schedule
- How school librarians should handle the transfer or disposal of equipment

Materials

With tight budgets in most school libraries, it is essential to make efforts to preserve materials that are in the collection. Maintenance policies for materials should include who is responsible for the maintenance of materials, as well as addressing the weeding and inventory of materials. *Weeding* of materials refers to the removal of the resources from the collection. Often this is referred to as deselection or reevaluation of the existing collection.

The process of carefully weeding a school library to remove outdated and unused materials is as important as the process of selection. A weeding policy should include who is responsible for weeding the collection, the criteria for weeding materials, and what is done with weeded materials.

The school librarian is responsible for weeding a collection, but the expertise of faculty from various fields or grade levels should be enlisted. Classroom educators can provide information relating to the curriculum that can assist the librarian in making professional judgments about which materials can be discarded without affecting curriculum needs.

Physical qualities of a material, suitability of the content, recentness of the material, and accuracy of the information are all factors to be considered when making decisions to withdraw resources from a collection. In general, materials should be weeded from the collection for the following reasons:

- Poor physical condition
- Unattractive appearance
- Poor circulation record
- Old copyright date, with outdated or inaccurate information
- Duplicates of titles no longer in demand
- Subject matter unsuitable for users
- Topics no longer of interest
- Biased or stereotypical portrayals
- Inappropriate reading levels
- No longer needed because of a change in the curriculum

Some librarians like to use what is known as the CREW (Continuous Review, Evaluation, and Weeding). The CREW method uses an acronym, MUSTIE, to help librarians decide when an item should be weeded or removed from the collection.

- Misleading—In other words, factually inaccurate. This may include materials that fail to include substantive periods of time because of the age of the material.
- Ugly—Tattered or worn out and beyond mending.
- Superseded by a newer edition or better source. This may include use of the Internet resources that provide more up-to-date sources.
- Trivial—Meaning having no obvious literary or scientific merit and/or without sufficient reason or use to justify keeping it.
- Irrelevant to the needs and interests of the library patrons and/or not used even though it may be deemed interesting.
- Elsewhere—Meaning the resource may be easily borrowed from another source or found by using an electronic resource and/or the Internet.

Having guidelines for materials also assists in adhering to the weeding criteria that you establish for your library. CREW also includes additional considerations, known as **WORST**, for multimedia materials:

- Worn out
- Out of date
- Rarely used
- Supplied elsewhere (available through ILL)
- Trivial and faddish

For all materials, monitor circulation statistics of use for all materials and view/listen to them periodically to determine their condition. Table 10.1 provides an overview of some suggested guidelines for weeding according to the CREW method. Each Dewey Decimal Classification (DDC) range or media type is followed by a formula. The formula in each case consists of three parts:

1. The first figure refers to the years since the book's latest copyright date (age of material in the book);
2. The second figure refers to the maximum permissible time without usage (in terms of years since its last recorded circulation and assuming that the item has been in the library's collection for at least that period of time);
3. The third refers to the presence of various negative factors, called MUSTIE factors, which will influence the weeding decision.

For example, a call number with the formula "8/3/MUSTIE" assigned to it means that, in this particular area, discard when its latest copyright is more than eight (8) years ago; and/or, when its last circulation or in-house use was more than three (3) years ago; and/or, when it possesses one or more of the MUSTIE factors. Remember that the period of time without use presumes that the book has been in the collection at least that long. Most formulas include a "3" in the usage category because few libraries can afford to keep items in the collection that have not circulated on been used in-house within a three-year period. Exceptions relate mainly to items with local history value. The figure in the age category will vary considerably from subject to subject (and for subcategories within subjects). Most formulas also include the MUSTIE factors because items that are in poor condition or no longer relevant should not be kept in the collection. If any one of the three

TABLE 10.1. OVERVIEW OF CREW FORMULAS

Dewey Class	Dewey Call Number	CREW Formula
000	004	3/X/MUSTIE
	011	10/X/MUSTIE
	020	10/3/MUSTIE
	030	5/X/MUSTIE
	Others	5/X/MUSTIE
100	133	15/3/MUSTIE
	150	10/3/MUSTIE
	160	10/3/MUSTIE
200		10/3/MUSTIE or 5/3/MUSTIE
300	310	2/X/MUSTIE
	320	5/3/MUSTIE (Topical)
		10/3/MUSTIE (Historical)
	330	5/3/MUSTIE
	340	10/X/MUSTIE
	350	10/X/MUSTIE
	360	5/X/MUSTIE

(Continued)

TABLE 10.1.   CONTINUED

Dewey Class	Dewey Call Number	CREW Formula
	370	10/3/MUSTIE
	390	5/3/MUSTIE (Etiquette)
		10/3/MUSTIE (Folklore/Customs)
400		10/3/MUSTIE
500	510	10/3/MUSTIE
	550	X/3/MUSTIE
	570	10/3/MUSTIE
	580	10/3/MUSTIE
600	610	5/3/MUSTIE
	630	5/3/MUSTIE
	635	10/3/MUSTIE
	640	5/3/MUSTIE
	649	5/3/MUSTIE
	690	10/3/MUSTIE
	Others	5/3/MUSTIE
700	745	X/3/MUSTIE
	770	5/3/MUSTIE
	790	10/3/MUSTIE
	Others	X/X/MUSTIE
800		X/X/MUSTIE
900	910	5/3/MUSTIE (Geography and Guide Books)
		10/3/MUSTIE (Personal Narratives)
	Others	15/3/MUSTIE
B or 92 (Biography)		X/2/MUSTIE
F (Fiction)		X/2/MUSTIE
E Fiction (Picture Books)		X/2/MUSTIE
JF (Juvenile Fiction)		X/2 MUSTIE
YA (Young Adult) Fiction		3/2/MUSTIE
J & YA Non-Fiction		Use General Criteria
Periodicals/ Newspapers		3/X/X
VF (Vertical File)		1/2/MUSTIE
College Catalogs		2/X/MUSTIE
Nonprint Media		WORST
Videocassettes		2/X/WORST

parts of the formula is not applicable to a specific subject, the category is filled with an "X." For example, in some categories, like literature or picture books, the copyright date is not a major consideration in the weeding decision.

You may want to alter the table to fit the needs of your school. The policy can also identify materials that are not to be discarded. Examples are local and state history materials; major publications of the school, such as yearbooks or school newspapers; classics (unless newer versions are available); and items incorrectly classified or poorly promoted that might circulate under changed circumstances.

The policy might recommend continuous, intermittent, or periodical weeding. The continuous plan, which takes place on a daily basis, may be difficult to handle without disrupting established routine. The intermittent plan calls for designating specific times of the academic calendar for reevaluating and weeding specific areas or types of media. The periodic plan makes use of days when the school library is not scheduled for use. Careful planning can and should avoid disrupting services to learners and educators.

Inventory

Some school districts have policies that require a complete, annual inventory of school library materials and equipment. You need to inquire about district policies related to this topic. If there is not a district-level policy in place, you should create written policies to address when and by whom inventory of materials and equipment will take place. Usually the librarian, with assistance from school library staff, supervises inventory. Technologies, which include portable scanners capable of reading barcodes that have been placed on materials and equipment, make it possible to use responsible learners or adult volunteers to assist in the process.

You may also want to include in your policy a requirement that the school librarian submits a report of each inventory to the school principal. Discussing an inventory report with a principal is also a wise idea as it will help an administrator understand the process and possible problems, such as large numbers of lost items. Future budget needs for replacement of books or a security system are more apt to be met if a principal is kept aware of inventory results. A copy of each inventory report should be filed in the library and included in your annual report.

MAINTENANCE PROCEDURES

Working within parameters of the district policies, the school librarian is responsible for establishing collection maintenance procedures for systematic inspection of all materials and equipment. While technicians and aides can repair and clean materials and equipment, the librarian identifies maintenance problems, diagnoses causes, establishes corrective measures, and monitors the quality of the work completed by staff or an outside contractor.

Routine internal maintenance procedures include the following:

Books and Print Materials: Replacing protective jackets, repairing torn pages, reinserting separated pages, eliminating minor scribbling, taping and labeling spines, and purchasing heavily used books in library bindings;

Audiovisual Materials: Wiping CDs and DVDs, storing discs and videos upright (book style) in plastic cases, returning materials to storage cases immediately after use, and storing materials in cool, dry environments;

Digital Materials: Checking links, replacing broken links or missing web pages, creating backup copies of library web pages;

Library Facility: Checking behind books on shelves for food or other items that may have been hidden, dusting and vacuuming, emptying trash cans and recycling bins, changing lightbulbs, removing graffiti from tabletops, removing gum from beneath tables, cleaning upholstered furniture;

Equipment: Cleaning areas of heavy use such as device surfaces and lenses, using antistatic wipes on monitors and screens, keeping warranties, manuals, and repair records in an accessible file, training library staff and learners in the proper operation and care of equipment (including replacement of bulbs), covering machines when they are not in use, ensuring that moveable equipment is securely attached to carts, not allowing learners to transport equipment, maintaining an area or workspace with basic tools for minor repairs, replacing, and properly disposing items such as light bulbs and printer cartridges, preventative computer maintenance such as defragmentation, data back up, and virus scans, and keeping equipment in climate-controlled areas.

During the COVID-19 pandemic, OCLC, with funding from the Institute for Museum and Library Services (IMLS), conducted cleanliness tests on a variety of library surfaces (leather to glass and plastic) to determine how long the virus could survive on them (OCLC, 2020). This project's output provides important cleaning procedures and processes.

You and your school library staff should also educate learners and educators about the proper care of library materials and equipment. You can offer professional development workshops to educators on the proper use of equipment, especially if new equipment is purchased.

When learners first begin to use the library, they should be taught to handle books carefully by turning pages only by the corners, keeping books in safe locations out of the reach of young siblings and pets, not writing or placing objects in books, and refraining from reading books while eating or drinking beverages. Older learners should be instructed on how to properly copy pages of materials on a copy machine, emphasizing not pressing down forcefully on the spines of books. If learners are using CDs or DVDs, they should be shown how to handle these items properly, holding the discs carefully by the edges and making certain they do not get scratched.

Providing bookmarks at the circulation desk will alleviate the use of inappropriate items being used to mark places in a book or *dog earring* pages for the same purpose. Librarians have reported finding gum, tobacco, pickles, and numerous other strange items in books returned to their libraries. Additionally, keeping a supply of plastic bags near the exits of the school library can reduce damage to books caused by rain or snow.

If your library adopts the "coffee house" model of serving refreshments in the library, consider limiting the items allowed into the seating area to magazines and newspapers. If food and beverage is allowed into the library, be sure to monitor the cleanliness of table tops and add waste baskets to allow for easy disposal of food, cups, and wrappers.

Having access to a copy machine in the library will cut down dramatically on damage to books when learners tear out pages that they want for research. Installing security systems, particularly in secondary schools, will also help maintain the collection by reducing the loss of materials through theft.

Ensuring appropriate temperature and humidity in the school library to preserve materials and equipment is also one of your maintenance responsibilities. This is particularly important during the summer in hot, humid climates. In such environments, custodial personnel should be instructed to operate air conditioning systems for a part of every day. Not doing so can result in mold and mildew damage and possibly leave equipment inoperable.

Weeding

Psychologically, one of the most difficult tasks of beginning school librarians is weeding a collection. You, like most librarians, are probably a lover of books and other materials that are found in libraries. Librarians give many reasons and excuses for avoiding weeding. Typical attitudes are these:

- Books are sacred objects; only vandals destroy books.
- Someone may need this in the future.
- Our library will look empty if we don't have books filling all of the shelves.
- I don't have enough time to examine every item in the collection.
- There will be a scene if educator X wants this item.
- I don't have time to remove the bibliographic and holding records for all these items.
- Our policy doesn't justify the removal of materials bought with public funds.
- I cannot decide when a fiction title is out of date.
- Kits are expensive to replace, and this one has at least half of the original items.
- This software package has gone through several revisions, adding features we could learn to use, but many of us already know how to use this version.

Weeding a collection has many benefits including the creation of more space, ensuring accurate materials, avoiding the cost of maintaining unwanted items, obtaining and keeping a reputation as a source of reliable information, and saving time in locating items. After weeding a collection of dull or drab materials, you will also find that you have created a more attractive collection and an orderly, neat environment.

In your policies and procedures manual, you should make a step-by-step listing of how to remove weeded items from the collection. This can vary somewhat from one library to another, but generally it involves removing the school identification marks from each item, writing with a permanent marker "Discard" on the items (generally in large letters on the front-end pages of a book), removing the items from the library catalog, and finally discarding the items. In some cases, the items can be recycled or usable materials that can be transferred to another school or given to an organization. Some states do not allow you to sell the items since they were purchased with tax monies, but you might be able to donate useable items to a nonprofit organization, such as Boys Club or Girls Club. Most librarians have found that it is not a good idea to put library materials into a school library trash can since parents and educators often do not understand why the items are being thrown away, and it may create the impression that the school library is not in need of funds for materials. It is better to box the items, tape up the boxes, and have them placed directly into a dumpster or arrange for them to be picked up for recycling. For report purposes, you will need to keep a listing of the number of items that you have discarded, and in some school districts you also need to maintain the title and barcode number of each item.

As in other aspects of collection management, school librarians should involve educators and others in the decisions about what items to remove. Classroom educators and their learners can provide subject area expertise. For example, high school science learners can help spot inaccurate information in science materials. Teachers can be encouraged to bring to your attention materials that are no longer useful. Different techniques are used for involving users in the decision-making process about which items to remove. One technique is to display materials with tags on them on which the faculty can check off "retain," "discard," or "don't know" and then initial the item. Another technique is to use the *book slip* method. In that approach, you put a colored label on duplicate or low-use titles. The call number, the date, and a notice of the intent to remove the item from the collection should be clearly visible. Users are asked to remove the slip and turn it in at the circulation desk if they think the item should be kept. Six months or a year later, the staff checks for materials with slips and removes those materials from the collection, following the procedures written in the policies and procedures manual.

Services like Follett Library Resources' free Titlewave services can also help with weeding tasks through TitleWise, its collection analysis tool. TitleWise will analyze records in the library catalog and create a report that highlights titles that are candidates for weeding, as well as potential replacement titles. Mackin Educational Resources has a similar tool called Collection Analysis Plus.

Digital Resources

Digital resources also require maintenance and this issue can be complex because of the wide range of digital resource formats, access schemes, ownership conditions, and sources. School librarians should consider three aspects of maintaining digital resources: storage, access, and preservation. Storage refers to the location of library materials and access to the ability to view, alter, update, or change the materials. Very often, school librarians do not have administrative access to district servers and cannot maintain their own websites. In this case, a procedure should be devised to check and report broken or changed links to the website administrator. Many librarians circumvent these constraints by maintaining a minimal presence on the school or district website and creating content hosted on other sites, like LibGuides. While this approach allows for easier maintenance, the tradeoff is that school librarians do not control site-wide policies and may find their content taken down or moved without notice. Maintenance of digital resources may also extend to the applications or browser plug-ins required to use digital resources. School librarians will also want to ensure that browsers and plug-ins are up to date on library computers and devices.

Digital resource archives are a place to access materials that have been recorded and preserved. The school librarian will want to preserve items that have value and retain evidence and information about the individuals and sources from which they came. Preservation would include ensuring that the library catalog and any other pertinent library computer data are regularly scheduled for backup and that these backups are retained for a specified amount of time.

Inventory

The importance of establishing and holding to a designated time for inventory cannot be overemphasized. *Inventory* is the process of verifying holding records. During the process the school librarian assesses the physical condition of each item. In this context, inventory is more than mere matching of barcodes with records to obtain a count of the holdings. Inventory, as described here, is the process of examining each item physically and also checking the records for accuracy. A video may be in the wrong container, or an educator's guide for a DVD may be missing. A detailed examination of materials can uncover problems overlooked during the routine checking of items at the circulation desk.

Some schools close collections for inventory, thus freeing the staff from other duties so they can review the collection in depth. However, closing the collection during the school year is in direct conflict with efforts to work collaboratively with school personnel. Some school districts recognize this conflict and hire library personnel for a period when schools are not in session. In one school district a team is appointed to inventory and weed various collections throughout the summer months. This practice can help prevent the emotional strain on school librarians that removing items sometimes entails. The disadvantage of this practice is losing the insight of the person who knows the needs of the school.

Other districts rotate sections of the collection for inventory, including reevaluation, over a three-year period. Inventory can take place when items are in circulation. Through notations on the holdings by checking circulation records in the electronic management systems, librarians can determine whether unexamined materials are on the shelves or circulating. The size of the staff, the size of the collection, available time, and user demands influence the decision whether to evaluate the entire collection at once or one section at a time.

Again, in your policies and procedures manual there should be a listing of the steps to conduct an inventory. This procedure usually includes putting the books or other materials in proper order on the shelves, passing a scanner over the barcodes on each item, running a report of the inventory to show which items are missing, attempting to locate the missing items (checking circulation records, items on display, or items in an area for repair), removing from the report any items that are successfully located, and printing out a final report. It is a good idea to share the record of missing items with educators in case some of the materials can be located in classrooms. Also, one can check learner lockers when learners clean them out at the end of a school year. Providing boxes near the lockers with labels that ask learners to place library materials in the boxes can also help retrieve missing items.

Today, most school libraries have automated circulation and card catalogs, which makes inventory and weeding much easier. If you are in a school that is not automated, the inventory process will be much lengthier as each item must be manually matched to the shelf list of the print card catalog. The weeding process will also take more time as all catalog cards (author, title, and subject) will need to be removed when an item is discarded.

Emergency Planning and Security

Although hopefully you will never need to use them, you should have procedures in place for emergencies, such as fires, floods, hurricanes, or break-ins. It is important to find out if the school district has such plans and to make copies of those plans. It is wise to keep copies of the plans at home, as well as in a file in the library. Emergency telephone numbers of people who can give advice on how to deal with fire or water-damaged materials should be in the plan. The plan should also include which school personnel have a copy of insurance policies, and what evidence is needed to make a claim.

Most school library automation systems can produce holding records of materials and equipment, although they will take a long time to print if your collection is large. Copies of electronic or printed holding records should be kept in a location outside the school, in a school safe, or on a secure server. These holding records need to be updated periodically to include new materials and to exclude discarded items so the holdings of the library are accurate. In an emergency, such as a fire that destroys the library, a listing of all materials and equipment can be produced for both insurance and replacement purposes. Chapter 18, "Opening, Reclassifying, Moving, or Closing the Collection," includes more information about school libraries and disasters.

CONCLUSION

Policies and procedures need to be created for the maintenance of school library equipment and materials. Educating learners and educators on the proper handling of materials and operation of equipment will help preserve these items. Weeding the collection will improve the appearance and use of the collection, as well as ensure that the information in school library materials is accurate and up-to-date. An inventory of the collection is needed to verify that the records in the OPAC are accurate and to help librarians plan for replacement and security needs. Teachers and learners can assist in both the weeding and inventory of a collection, but a librarian should supervise these procedures. Emergency plans should also be available to assist school librarians in case of disasters such as fires, floods, hurricanes, or major thefts. Copies of a library's holdings should be kept in a secure place in case such emergencies occur. Disaster preparation and response are addressed in Chapter 18.

DISCUSSION QUESTIONS

1. Draft three specific policy statements with procedure descriptions that would be included in a school library emergency policy.
2. What are the advantages and disadvantages of inventorying the collection every three years?
3. Find a publicly accessible online catalog for a school library. Browse the items Dewey class 550. Do you see any items that should be weeded? If so, why should these items be removed?

REFERENCES

American Association of School Librarians (AASL) & Association for Educational Communications and Technology (AECT). (1988). *Information power: Guidelines for school library media programs.* Chicago, IL: American Library Association.

OCLC. (2020). Reopening archives, libraries and museums (REALM). Retrieved from https://www.imls.gov/our-work/partnerships/reopening-archives-libraries-and-museums

Woolls, B., & Coatney, S. (2017). *The school library manager,* 6th edition. Santa Barbara, CA: Libraries Unlimited.

ADDITIONAL READINGS

Goldsmith, F. (2015). *Crash course in weeding library collections.* Santa Barbara, CA: Libraries Unlimited.

Moreillon, J. (2013). Policy challenge: Closing the library for inventory. *School Library Monthly,* 29(8), 26–27.

Zarnosky, S. M., & Evans, G. E. (2019). *Collection management basics,* 7th edition. Santa Barbara, CA: Libraries Unlimited.

HELPFUL MULTIMEDIA

American Library Association. (n.d.). Disaster preparedness and recovery. Retrieved from http://www.ala.org/advocacy/disaster-preparedness

American Library Association. (2015, December). Weeding library collections: A selected annotated library collection evaluation. Retrieved from http://www.ala.org/tools/libfactsheets/alalibraryfactsheet15

Davis, K. (2015). The 12 days of weeding. Retrieved from https://www.youtube.com/watch?v=zCd1H4eOTvc

Larson, J. (2012). CREW: A weeding manual for modern libraries. Retrieved from https://www.tsl.texas.gov/ld/pubs/crew/index.html

Library of Congress. (n.d.). Digital preservation. Retrieved from http://www.digitalpreservation.gov/

Library of Congress. (n.d.). Preservation. Retrieved from http://www.loc.gov/preservation/

Little, H. B. (2019, March 12). Weeding without controversy: Part one—Why weed? https://knowledgequest.aasl.org/weeding-without-controversy-part-one-why-weed/

Little, H. B. (2019, April 2). Weeding without controversy: Part two—The process. https://knowledgequest.aasl.org/weeding-without-controversy-part-two-the-process/

National Library of New Zealand. (n.d.). Weeding your school library collection. Retrieved from https://natlib.govt.nz/schools/school-libraries/collections-and-resources/weeding-your-school-library-collection

Pentland, C. (2020, October 19). Revitalizing our school library collection. Retrieved from https://knowledgequest.aasl.org/revitalizing-our-school-library-collection/

CHAPTER 11

Circulation and Promotion of the Collection

Key Learnings

- Circulation can be fostered through clear, consistently applied policies tailored to the needs of the library community.
- Library websites are a fundamental aspect of collection promotion.
- Social media tools can be used to reach library users within and beyond the school day.
- Traditional methods like face-to-face programs and bulletin board remain highly effective ways to promote the collection.

In previous chapters, we have discussed overarching concepts around collections and policies; understanding the school library user community; identifying and selecting materials; and organizing, describing, and maintaining collections. As Figure 11.1 suggests, the curatorial enterprise comprises resource identification, selection, management, and promotion on a continuum from collection activities that include relatively small amounts of participation to curation, considerations of use the involve interaction between the school librarian and the community.

As Figure 11.1 shows, community participation increases in curation activities like circulation. In this chapter, we will focus on these two primary activities in the use of school library collections. Policies and procedures related to them are essential to an effective collection program. The best school library collection is of little use unless the materials are curated for learners and educators, the community for whom they have been collected.

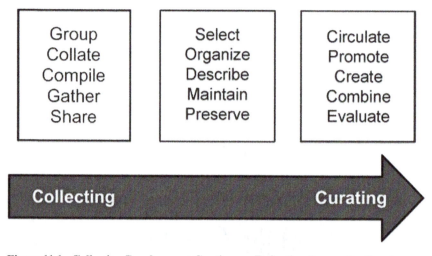

Figure 11.1. Collection Development Continuum Reflecting Increasing Levels of Community Participation

CIRCULATING THE COLLECTION

Circulation Policies

Circulation policies that require consideration include which items should circulate, to whom the materials should circulate, whether there should be limitations on the number of items that circulate to an individual, and how long the materials should circulate. These questions have no right answers since circumstances in your library will affect how you respond to these questions. Such circumstances include the level of your school, the number of items in the collection, curriculum needs, access to online information, and your budget (particularly funds for replacement of items).

Formats

Books, often even reference books, circulate to learners, educators, and administrators. High-demand books can have different circulation periods, waitlists, or multiple copies to meet demands. Educators may request that the school librarian assemble a collection of materials on a specific topic for classroom use or for reserved use in the library.

More differences may be in place regarding circulation of formats other than audio-cassettes and books. For instance, some librarians allow learners to check out DVDs, while other policies limit DVD checkout to educators. Sometimes educators request that learners not be allowed to check out DVDs since the educators use the items in their classroom instruction. Learners who were absent on the day that the video was viewed in a classroom, however, were allowed an overnight checkout of the video. Learners at all grade levels are especially fond of these items and will appreciate a circulation policy that allows their circulation. Undoubtedly it is an effective means of attracting reluctant readers to a school library.

Differences are found in policies related to the circulation of periodicals. Often, elementary school libraries have fairly generous policies, allowing learners to check out back issues of magazines. In secondary schools, the periodical titles are usually indexed, and back issues may be kept in the library for research purposes. In both elementary and secondary schools, current issues of periodicals are available for use in the library and usually do not circulate.

Digital audiobooks and eBooks may have circulation limitations imposed by their suppliers. Digital content providers are able to track the number of simultaneous users or file downloads and control access by prohibiting further use. As mentioned in Chapter 7, the content providers' access policies should be considered in purchase.

In some schools, parents are allowed to check out materials, usually books. Often, this policy exists in schools that collect materials that are aimed at parents, and the items are placed in a special, labeled section of the library. Allowing parents to check out materials, however, can complicate automated circulation by requiring parents to have patron barcodes or identification cards similar to those used by the learners. In order to avoid this added task, parents can be allowed to check out materials on the learners' cards, but if there are limitations on the number of items that a learner can check out, this may affect a learner's use of materials.

Number of Items

Unless you have a large collection in comparison to your enrollment, you may need to consider a limitation on the number of items that learners check out. Sometimes a limitation is set to help learners keep track of the materials checked out and to be responsible for them. In elementary libraries, the lower grades often are allowed fewer books than the upper grades. These policies should be developed in response to learners' wants and needs.

In secondary libraries, policies usually allow for a larger number of items to be checked out by learners. Some high school libraries have no limitations on the number of items, unless there is high demand for the books that are being checked out.

Educators should be considered circulation policies as well. This is particularly true if educators are checking out materials that are being used by learners in their classrooms. In such cases, the educators will need to be able to check out large numbers of materials. Educators may need to be reminded that they must check out materials and return them when they are done using them.

Time Limitations

Policies related to time limitations for the circulation of materials depend on the needs of library users. Usually, learners in an elementary school have a one-week checkout period for materials, with the date due being the day that the class comes to the library if the school is on a fixed library schedule. Sometimes, the upper elementary grades are given a longer checkout period, perhaps two weeks. If you have a flexibly scheduled library and a large collection where there is not frequent demand for titles, it is advantageous to consider a longer circulation period. It is important to remember that you want to have circulation policies that will encourage the use of materials.

Secondary schools tend to have a longer checkout periods, especially when books are being used for research purposes. If research assignments are stretched out over a long period in a high school, it makes sense to have at least a four-week circulation period for books. Having less time will result in very long overdue lists and will frustrate learners, educators, and librarians. Options for renewing materials should be made at all school levels. The number of times an item can be renewed, however, may be limited, particularly if titles are in high demand.

Educators appreciate not having time limitations on materials they check out from a school library. However, it is advantageous to let faculty know what materials they have checked out since it is easy for educators to put materials into a cabinet or closet and forget that they have not returned items to the library. Most library automation systems allow individual patrons to view which items they have checked out, but many educators neglect to use this feature.

Overdue, Lost, and Damaged Materials

Collecting fines for overdue materials is controversial. Charging overdue fines contrasts with the school library's mission to provide free and equitable access to information, especially for low-income children, and can encourage learners to connect the library with penalties. Learners who are ashamed of their overdue fines or financially unable to pay them may stop using the library entirely. Today, most elementary schools do not collect such fines, partly because of the time and effort it takes to deal with the collection of small amounts of money and also because elementary librarians should be encouraging reading and the use of the library. In some cases, charging fines has the effect of leading parents to not allow their children to check out books if they are consistently forgetting to return books and having to pay fines! Having positive methods to encourage the return of materials is a better alternative for young children. This might be giving out a small reward (e.g., allowing kids to stamp their own due dates in books) to all children who return books on time or maintaining a record of classes in which all children return books each week. Some school librarians do not let children check out other books until the learners return the materials that are due.

Secondary libraries sometimes collect fines from learners. Some school librarians and also educators think that older learners need to learn responsibility for the return of materials on time. Other librarians like to have the monies collected in fines to use for special purposes, such as purchasing holiday gifts for learner volunteers or developing a special collection (such as graphic novels) that would not be possible within the general library budget. It is the author's opinion that even at the secondary level it is preferable to use positive means, rather than punitive, to encourage the return of materials. The collection of fines at any grade level should be discussed with administrators and educators before a policy is implemented or revised.

All learners and sometimes educators should be responsible for damaged or lost materials. Assessment for damaged or lost materials can be made either at replacement value (including processing charges), cost of original purchase, or percentage of replacement, depending on how long the item has been in the library collection. Some policies do not charge educators for damaged or lost items unless there is obvious irresponsibility and unreasonable loss. In such instances it is wise to involve the principal and inform the administrator of the monetary amount of such loss.

Sample Elementary School Library Circulation Policies

➢ The following items may be checked out by students:
  - ○ Books
  - ○ Audiocassette kits
  - ○ DVDs
  - ○ Back issues of magazines
➢ Students in kindergarten may check out one book at a time during the first semester and two during the second semester.
➢ Students in first and second grades may check out three items at a time. Students in third, fourth, and fifth grade may check out four items at a time. Parents may check out four items at a time.
➢ Library materials are checked out to students and parents for a two week period.
➢ Reference books and current issues of magazines are generally to be used only in the school library.
➢ Reference books may be checked out by teachers for classroom use and by parents for overnight use.
➢ Teachers may check out a set of 25 books for students to use in the classroom for one month. Special circumstances can be arranged to provide additional materials to support classroom curriculum.
➢ Materials can be placed on reserve by teachers if used for a student assignment. These materials can be used only in the library and will be returned to the library collection after the assignments have been completed.
➢ No overdue fines are charged.
➢ Any lost or damaged books must be paid for.
➢ The library will abide by the State Confidentiality Law, Act XXX, regarding overdue notices.
➢ Overdue notices will be sent home folded and stapled periodically on excessively late due dates.

Figure 11.2. Elementary School Library Circulation Policies

Figure 11.2 is a sample of circulation policies for an elementary school library. Sample circulation policies for a high school library center can be found in Figure 11.3.

CIRCULATION PROCEDURES

The procedures for circulating materials should be included in your policies and procedures manual. If a school library is not automated, then checkout cards and pockets to hold the cards will need to be ordered from a library supply company and attached to all library materials that circulate outside the library.

With today's automation software, librarians can catalog materials, handle circulation, include book recommendations, integrate digital subscriptions, and allow user contributions of ratings and reviews in a single "one-stop shop" online public access catalog portal to search for digital and print resources. These systems even often include advanced reporting tools that can tell librarians the most commonly read genres and the age of books in the library. Specific circulation procedures vary according to the library

Sample High School Library Circulation Policies and Procedures

The following policies are used to ensure fair access to information for all library patrons.

Students

> ➢ Students must present their school identification card in order to check out library materials. At the initial time that a student requests to check out an item, a patron barcode will be placed on the back of the school ID card.
> ➢ Ten items (books, DVDs, CDs, and back issues of magazines) can be checked out at one time.
> ➢ All items are checked out for four weeks.
> ➢ All items may be renewed one time. Renewals can be done in person or by using the "My Account" feature of the library's online catalog.
> ➢ Reference materials are generally to be used in the school library, but can be checked out overnight.
> ➢ Students are responsible for lost or damaged items. Any item that is overdue for more than 30 days will be considered lost. The cost will be based on the amount of damage or the price paid for the item plus a processing fee. A receipt will be issued. If the item is found and returned in good condition within the school year, a portion of the collected fee will be returned.
> ➢ Students withdrawing from the school need to present a withdrawal form for the librarian's signature. The librarian will note on the form any outstanding obligations.

Teachers

> ➢ Teachers are responsible for all materials borrowed, whether the items are for class use or for personal use. Teacher patron barcodes are kept in a file at the circulation desk.
> ➢ There is no limit on the number or types of items that teachers can borrow from the school library.
> ➢ Teachers may put materials on reserve for use by their students in the library. Teachers should contact the librarian or library clerk for assistance in this procedure.
> ➢ All items must be returned to the library at the end of the school year.

Interlibrary Loan

> ➢ Teachers and students may request items that are not available in the school library by filling out the interlibrary loan form.
> ➢ If the item requested is available at another school in the school district, it will be delivered to the high school library.
> ➢ The librarian will notify the teacher or student when the item has arrived and is ready to be checked out. The process generally takes 3-5 school days.
> ➢ If the item is not picked up by the patron within five school days, it will be returned to the loaning library.

Figure 11.3. High School Library Circulation Policies

automation system that is used. Many systems also include apps for tablets or smartphones that allow users to search for materials, check items out, and add comments for their preferred device without having to wait in line at the library desk.

Generally, each learner and educator has an identifying barcode, which is referred to as the patron barcode and serves as a library card. The barcodes that are placed on library items are material barcodes and are different from patron barcodes. Although the same laser reader is used for all the barcodes, the automated library system will be able to identify whether the barcode that is being read by the laser is a patron or material barcode.

In some libraries a card file is kept at the circulation desk with identifying patron barcodes attached to the file cards or on a Rolodex; sometimes the barcodes are covered with a special, thin plastic made specifically for that purpose. When a patron wishes to check out an item, the library staff member finds the learner's name in the file and passes the laser reader over the correct barcode.

Barcodes can also be placed on sheets of paper and retained in files, with the classroom educator's name on the outside of each file. This works well for school libraries that are on fixed schedules. In one school that the author of this book visited, learners decorated bookmarks on which their patron barcodes were placed. Each time the class came to the library, the librarian placed the bookmarks on a small table next to the circulation desk and all the children found their own bookmarks when ready to check out books. The librarian collected all the bookmarks before the learners left the library so they would be available the next time the class came to the library. Learners who had been in the school for several years enjoyed seeing the bookmarks that they had made when they were in kindergarten.

Some schools require that learners bring their own barcodes with them each time they check out items from the library. This is often problematic in elementary schools in which learners are not carrying wallets or book bags where they can safely keep their identifying barcodes.

Large secondary schools usually require learners to have their barcodes with them when they check out materials. These barcodes can be placed on the back of photo identification cards that are issued by the school administration or the library staff can create cards using an automated library management system. Having the barcodes as part of a photo identification system is particularly helpful in large schools where it is difficult to know all the learners. Unfortunately, some secondary learners tend to borrow other learners' library cards and items thus get checked out to the wrong learners.

A growing trend in schools at all levels is computer-based self-checkout, an innovation first used in university and public libraries. With self-checkout, learners either locate their barcodes off directories within the computer's circulation program or scan their library card. Self-checkout not only saves the librarian's time, but it also affords learners a sense of ownership, privacy, and convenience. Learners do need a brief training in the self-checkout system and librarians who do not have security systems to detect when users leave the library with materials that have not been checked out may wish to institute

---

VOICES FROM THE FIELD

I have been using self-checkout with our students for more than 12 years, and it is great. I started it when I didn't have an assistant, but now I do and the process is important for us . . . I have learned over the years that students take ownership in this experience. This is their library and THEY get to checkout their books . . . Students form a line, type their number, see their name on the screen and scan their books. I have set circulation alert sounds so any where in the library I can hear the "good" transaction, a problem or a block for overdue items. There is a rug at the checkout station and only one student can be on the rug at a time. It is a great management expectation.

—Lisa Hunt, Apple Creek Elementary

other safeguards to ensure that materials do not disappear. For younger learners, many librarians ease learners into the process by first allowing them to check in their items and then eventually permitting self-checkout.

Usually, the same patron barcode is used throughout the years that a learner is in a school. If a school library is on a fixed schedule it is necessary for the librarian to get a list of learners in each class at the beginning of the school year in order to organize barcodes into classes. If a library is on a flexible schedule it is still helpful to have class lists so the librarian knows where to send overdue notices. In secondary schools the expected graduation date of a learner is often entered into the automation system, along with the identifying barcode number. This makes it possible to retire large groups of learner barcodes all at once. It is important that each barcode number is unique until learners leave a school.

Material barcodes must also be unique. You can purchase barcodes from library supply companies, but you will need to keep track of the number range that you purchase to make certain you are not purchasing duplicate numbers. Some jobbers will also provide the barcodes and attach them to materials, but again you must provide the number range that is to be used.

In all schools, educators and administrators will appreciate not having to carry their patron barcodes with them each time they come to the library. Instead, their barcodes can also easily be kept on a Rolodex or in a separate file at the circulation desk. School librarians can also locate educator barcode numbers by typing names of educators in the computer program that manages circulation.

If barcodes are not placed on all material formats and equipment, then separate circulation systems will need to be created for those items. These systems might consist of paper forms, checkout cards, or, for equipment, a checkout board, where the names of items and educators can be written with erasable markers.

Procedures also need to be established for requests to reserve materials and equipment. Most library automation systems provide methods of reserving or holding items for patrons. Reserves for equipment that do not have barcodes attached can be handled by having a large laminated calendar on a wall, where educators can write their names, the piece of equipment requested, and the times the equipment is needed. If equipment is checked out permanently to a room, it is best to either barcode the equipment or to keep a separate file for such items. The serial number of each piece of equipment should be indicated on the checkout record.

On many automation systems it is possible for patrons to renew barcoded items on their own, perhaps by accessing the card catalog from a classroom or from home. If you enable such a feature on an automated online catalog, then you will need to inform learners and educators that the feature is available to them.

EBOOK CIRCULATION

eBooks are increasingly popular, especially in secondary school libraries, but also have circulation issues, such as limits on the number of users who can access the eBook at once and time-limited subscriptions. eBooks can be difficult to capture in circulation statistics, too, and often, the school librarian must approximate eBook titles' popularity based on how often the devices used to read them are checked out. Table 11.1 provides an overview of eBook subscription and circulation models that you are likely to encounter.

**TABLE 11.1. COMMON EBOOK PUBLISHER ACCESS AGREEMENTS
(ADAPTED FROM YOUNG, 2020)**

Payment Models	Licenses
• **Metered Access** Access to the eBook is set by a duration of time or a number of checkouts (or a combination of both). When the limit is reached, you have to renew and repurchase the subscription to continue access. • **Pay per Circulation or Checkout** Payment is only made when a patron checks out or uses the eBook. • **Perpetual Access** The library has access to the eBook in perpetuity—there is no end date to access.	• **Single User** Only one user can access the eBook at a time. Similar to a print library book, if the eBook is being used online or is "checked out," it's not available to other patrons. It's the most common license and used for many popular or new titles. • **Class Sets** A set number of users can access the eBook, often rented for a duration of time. • **Unlimited Simultaneous Access** No restrictions and offers concurrent access to an unlimited number of patrons.

As Table 11.1 suggests, eBook access ranges from restrictive models such as metered access and single user approaches, to relatively flexible models that with no time restrictions and simultaneous use. Be sure to investigate which model is most compatible with your needs.

Regardless of the access model, the school community may not realize that the library has an eBook collection, so promotion is necessary with labels on print titles directing users to eBooks, notations in catalog records, and posters or displays. Be sure to let users know about any access limitations in a diplomatic and positive way.

PROMOTING THE COLLECTION

School librarians spend much time and school monies developing collections to meet the needs of learners and educators. Yet in many cases the collections are not used to their fullest. Therefore, librarians should be aware of techniques that can help promote all or certain parts of the collection.

The Library Catalog

A major concept of curation is participation. It's easy to see how learners might recommend or rate resources. Building on the idea of having resource reviews on catalog records in library automation systems such as Follett Library Software's Destiny platform, learners can be encouraged to post their reactions to resources directly on their favorite social media outlets. By allowing learners to post via social media channels directly from the library catalog, as Follett *Library Connections* blogger Ruth Aptaker (2013, para. 2) said,

> [W]e show them that we are current and up to speed with the times. The less our learners think of libraries as going the way of the dinosaur, the better. They will be more apt to come to us with their information needs and trust us as viable resources. Plus your library gets the added bonus of free advertisement!

Most library automation systems also allow users to rate items and make lists. Librarians have the ability with these systems to quickly and easily make lists of topical or popular resources that can be shared widely. Because these systems often involve extensive annual investments on behalf of the school or district, it makes sense to use them as a key part of your promotion plan.

School Library Website

Library websites are now an essential aspect of promoting your collection and services. If the library in which you are employed does not have a website or blog, you should definitely create one on the district's web server, or on a free site like WordPress (https://wordpress.com/) or Tumblr (https://www.tumblr.com/). The advantage of having your website be within the domain of the district or school website is that it may be easier for stakeholders to discover.

Today's learners, educators, administrators, and parents spend large amounts of time accessing information online; if you create a helpful and interesting website, they will use it. Your website should be the default page on the computers in the library so learners and educators are well aware of its existence. You can also advertise its use in newsletters or the school newspaper. The home page should be organized to serve many purposes, including collection development and promotion of the collection.

To promote your collection on a library website, you can feature new materials as they arrive in the library. Also, if you know that a grade level will soon be studying a particular unit, select some of the best resources that are in the library on topics in the unit. Write short, useful annotations on the resources. You can include eye-catching pictures from online sites that provide royalty-free clip art. Spend time locating quality websites on the topics and provide links to those pages.

You can also offer to post classroom assignments on the website on an "Educators' Assignments" page. You can then direct learners to the print and online resources that will assist them in completing the assignments.

You can promote titles by having online book discussion groups in which you list titles of books that can be used in discussions, perhaps selecting a book of the week. Summer reading lists should be posted during the last grading periods, and learners can be encouraged to begin reading the titles on the list. Try to make it possible for learners and educators to check out materials during the summer months. During certain seasons of the year, books on holidays, current sports, or special events can be featured on the website.

If you continuously update the collection information on your website, it will keep the interest of your patrons. Of course, maintaining a library web page can be time consuming so try to recruit the assistance of learners or parents. Parents who cannot ordinarily volunteer during the day because of work or family obligations might be very willing to spend some time in the evening or on a weekend working on website projects that will help promote the collection.

Digital Video Channels

YouTube (http://youtube.com), TeacherTube (http://teachertube.com), and SchoolTube (http://schooltube.com) are free websites that allow you to create a "channel" for video content that you create. The difference between the sites is that YouTube, the largest of the three, is often blocked in schools. However, TeacherTube describes itself as the "The #1 safe educational video community for educators, learners and parents" and SchoolTube "empower[s] learners and educators through the use of video, with a safe, informative, and fun video sharing experience." Both sites contain limited advertising and provide only educator, educational service provider, and learner created content.

Anyone can register (for free) and then upload a variety of content: video, audio, photos, and documents such as PowerPoint presentations. Like YouTube, you do not need to be registered to search and view the content, though if you sign in as a member you can avoid the advertisements that precede every clip.

In addition to using one of these video channels to contain videos that promote your library services and collection, you can also promote your collection by using the many book trailers hosted at these sites. By using QR codes, it is easy to create black-and-white matrixes, typically used for storing URLs for reading by the camera on a smartphone, webcam, or tablet. As one school librarian posted to the LM_NET e-mail list, "We make QR codes and link them to book trailers. We put the codes on the book pocket of our fiction books and the kids can scan them at our QR station to see the trailers . . . My learners really love the trailers and are excited when they find a book with a QR code on it."

Social Media Presences

Most people today use one or all of the big three: Facebook, Twitter, and YouTube. There are dozens more, as we discussed in the context of crowdsourced reviews in Chapter 6, but if you are going to pick a place to begin promoting your collection through social media, start with one of these. Each is different in what they allow you to provide your patrons. Best of all, social media outlets allow you to reach your users with tools many of them already use every day during and beyond the school day.

Pinterest (http://pinterest.com) is a social media tool where you can "pin" pictures from the web or upload them from your computer. You can also drop in a little explanation (500 characters or less) with each picture. Pinterest is great for pinning images book covers, infographics, and pictures of events held in the library. You can also follow Pinterest board created by other school librarians and repin (share on your board) items that appeal to you.

Twitter is an extremely easy to use social media tool for sharing short messages. With its 280-character limit, you can share headlines, newsflashes, and quick tips. All you have to do is get patrons to follow you. Twitter can allow you to have immediate virtual signage that goes directly to your library users. Inspire users to "follow" your library Twitter account with contests and prizes.

Facebook is probably the easiest social media tool to envision using to promote the library. Your Facebook site can be your information sharing space, news feed, and photo album—all for free. Facebook also allows you to integrate and cross-post content from Twitter, Instagram, LinkedIn, YouTube, and other social media platforms.

Instagram, owned by Facebook, is a social networking platform primarily designed for image and photo sharing. Many school librarians have pioneered this space and are using it to promote new books, displays, programs, visitors, achievements in and about their school libraries. Lucas Maxwell, chief blogger at the Book Riot blog, advised school librarians who take to Instagram to consider:

- Post Every Day. Daily posts will let your followers know that you are active.
- Add Hashtags. Consistently adding the same hashtags (e.g., "#librarydisplays") to Instagram posts will make them easy to find. Keep a running list of the hashtags in a document or on your phone so that you don't inadvertently create a duplicate tag and you will save time by copying and pasting, instead of having to repeatedly type hashtags. Be sure to create a hashtag representing your school (or use the one that may exist), use it consistently on each post, and promote it on all library materials to invite your users to tag the library in their posts!
- Repost & Support. Follow hashtags on Instagram. Repost app which notifies the original poster. Use the Repost App to share the work of others and to build a community

VOICES FROM THE FIELD

Twitter may be overwhelming. I know it was for me at first, too. I started by following just a few people. And lurking. I think I was on Twitter for months before I tweeted. Now, I've made connections with many school librarians, public librarians, and teachers, who have become an invaluable PLN [personal learning network] to me.
—Jennifer Underhill, FSU School

among other school librarians on Instagram. Comment positively on other school librarians' posts when you see something you like.
- Stick to Your Instagramming Theme. Your theme is, of course, your school library! Stick to book promotion, student successes in the library author visits, and anything else book related. Stick to one theme and avoid straying from it. Followers will appreciate this consistent identity (Maxwell, 2018).

The key with social media is to keep up with it. Many Facebook "fans" and Twitter "followers" lose interest if you are not updating frequently and providing current material. Another consideration is that many learners are not permitted to access social media during the school day, so your information may not reach their social media feeds until after the school day.

Reading Programs

Sponsoring reading motivation programs is another excellent means of promoting a library collection. The use of digital quiz-based reading programs, such as Renaissance Learning's *Accelerated Reader* or Scholastic's *Reading Counts*, will certainly impact the circulation of books in a library. While widely used, these programs are not without controversy. In letters to the editor about *Accelerated Reader* published on the blog "Rethinking Schools," two education leaders sum up to advantages and disadvantages of using the reading program.

PROS AND CONS OF ACCELERATED READER

I successfully used the Accelerated Reading (AR) software at the junior high level for seven years. If used with fidelity, the program does what it is set up to do: provide students with time to read in a classroom setting, provide teachers with software that helps place students in books that are in their zone of proximal development, and give incentives to students. While the program does have a point system, it is not recommended that the points be tied too closely to a student's grade.
—Carolyn Hondo, Principal, Burley High School, Burley, Idaho

There is no clear evidence that AR works, even in the short term. AR has four components: access to books, time to read, quizzes, and prizes for performance on the quizzes. It is well established that providing books and time to read are effective, but AR research does not show that the quizzes and prizes are helpful. Studies claiming AR is effective compare AR to doing nothing; gains were probably due to the reading, not the tests and prizes.
—Stephen Krashen, Professor Emeritus, University of Southern California

However, you can also easily create your own programs or projects to promote reading (and thus the library collection). The following are a few such ideas:

- Organize book discussion groups that can meet at lunch, or before or after school.
- In collaboration with classroom educators, sponsor fun reading contests where everyone has the opportunity to win a prize or the principal agrees to some outrageous activity (dyeing his hair green or kissing a pig) if a certain number of books are collectively read by the learners.
- Sponsor a poetry reading event, such as a poetry slam; set up a coffee house atmosphere and provide coffee, tea, and pastries.
- Hold programs on a variety of topics such as collecting baseball cards, making films, or physical fitness; invite speakers and provide displays of materials on the featured topics.
- Have a mock Caldecott or Newbery Award election, featuring some of the notable current books.
- Show YouTube clips of movies based on books; have copies of the books available for checkout.
- Encourage your school to have a DEAR (Drop Everything and Read) program for the entire school, including educators and administrators.
- Sponsor an Evening of Stars and invite local celebrities (mayor, sports figures, TV weatherman, etc.) to come in and read aloud from their favorite books.
- Present exciting book talks when you meet with learners in the library or in their classrooms; have multiple copies of the books available for checkout.
- Have learners present book talks on the morning news announcement program.
- Make large Read Posters of educators reading their favorite children's or young adult books and hang the posters in the library and in halls.
- Help organize a Battle of the Books contest.
- Hold a Library Center Preview Party for the faculty when new purchases arrive; provide refreshments and free bookmarks.
- Create attractive handouts or pamphlets of materials on specific topics or genres, mysteries, romances, graphic novels, and books for college-bound learners.
- Enlist the parent educator learner association (PTSA) or a local bookstore to help sponsor an author visit to your school.
- Sponsor a Rock and Read corner in the library, with comfortable rocking chairs and baskets of specially selected books and magazines next to the rocking chairs.
- Practice your informal reading advisory skills by spending time at the circulation desk and making positive comments about each book that is checked out ("This dinosaur book looks interesting; tell me about it when you return it" or "I know another great book about surviving in the wilderness. Would you like to check it out, too?").
- Sponsor a "Catch Them Reading" program in which you give out chocolate candy kisses to learners and educators when you see them reading books outside the library.
- Create a Wall of Readers with photos of educators and learners in various poses reading their favorite books or magazines.
- Sponsor a weekly "Where Is the Principal Reading?" contest in which a photo of the principal reading somewhere outside the school is posted, and the first person to identify the location is given a prize.

Additional ideas for promoting the use of particular collections, such as graphic novels, or digital library materials, can be found in some of the articles listed under "Additional Readings" at the end of this chapter.

Displays and Bulletin Boards

One of the best ways to promote a school library collection is to display items that you would like to have circulated. This can be done in a variety of ways. The glass display cases in many schools, whether in the library or in the hallways, are ideal places to create displays on specific themes or particular authors. If you are not fortunate to have access to such cases, you can make your own displays in the library using the tops of book shelves, tables, file cabinets, or wide window ledges. Library supply companies also have furniture that can be used for displays. The revolving paperback stands are particularly effective for promoting materials in secondary school libraries.

The manner in which you display books on regular bookshelves can promote specific items. This can be done by turning books to show their covers, instead of the book spines. Moving books from very low or very high shelves to eye-level shelves can be effective if certain materials are not circulating.

Learners are sometimes asked to create pictures, dioramas, or models depicting scenes or characters from books. Displaying such learner artwork in the library will create interest in the books.

Eye-catching bulletin boards have always been a great way to promote a library collection. Creating attractive bulletin boards that feature the promotion of books and other library materials is definitely an art. However, if you do not have that special talent, you can easily find ideas for bulletin boards in books or online. Learner aides and parent volunteers can also be of great assistance in preparing materials for bulletin boards.

One of the simplest and yet most successful promotion bulletin boards that the author of this book created in an elementary school library with flexible scheduling was to talk with learners when they returned a book to the library and invite them to write the name of the book on a colorful Post-it®, along with their name, one brief sentence or phrase about the book, and a recommendation of which of their classmates they thought would enjoy the book. The learners were then asked to stick the Post-its® on a bulletin board that was simply covered with white paper. As soon as word about the bulletin board spread, learners came to the library to check the board and see if anyone had recommended that they read specific books. Circulation of books greatly increased during the month of the Post-its® bulletin board.

Professional Collection

Many school libraries have a special collection of professional materials for the educators, support staff, and administrators in the school. This collection is sometimes referred to as the *professional collection* and it may include popular books about educational trends and instructional ideas, educator guides, and current professional journals. Popular K–12 educator professional journals include:

American Educator
Arts & Activities
Education Digest
Education Week
Educational Leadership
Gifted Child Quarterly
High School Journal
Instructor
Phi Delta Kappan

Reading Educator
NSTA Journal
Voices from the Middle

This book's Appendix includes many more publications to consider. Often, it is the professional collection that needs the most promotion, but has the greatest potential to offer spontaneous opportunity to engage with educators about their needs and the library's collection and services.

It is important to have this collection in an area that is easily accessible for educators and staff. If there is an educator workroom located in a room adjacent to the library, that room is an ideal location. If you are fortunate to have an extra room in your library (even a very small room), placing the professional collection in a room with one or two comfortable chairs, a pot of hot coffee, and a plate of cookies will do wonders for the promotion of the professional collection. If you have no extra rooms, then by using low shelving around two or three sides of a large table in the library, you can create a work area for educators. The materials can then be placed on the shelves for easy access, and materials that you want to promote can be put on display on the shelf tops or on the table.

School librarians can also promote the professional collection by e-mailing or using social media to contact educators and invite them to come to the library to view new issues of professional journals or materials that might be helpful in their instructional areas. Presenting brief book talks on professional library materials at monthly faculty meetings is another possibility. An even better idea is to recruit the principal or classroom educators who have checked out professional books or journals to share how they used the information in their work.

CONCLUSION

To encourage the use of library materials, school librarians should develop workable circulation policies and procedures that are positive, rather than punitive. Learners should not link the library with punishment in the form of monetary penalty and deprivation of access. Circulation policies generally vary according to library scheduling and the needs of the learners in a particular school. Taking advantage of the many circulation features of automated library systems can save time for the library staff, as well as for patrons.

Librarians should try various techniques to promote their collections and encourage the use of all types of materials. By working collaboratively with classroom educators to sponsor school-wide reading contests, author visits, and other special events, librarians can promote both reading and the library collection. Making creative displays and bulletin boards that feature library materials are other ways of promoting the collection. Strategically locating the professional collection and bringing educators' attention to the items in the collection can encourage the use of professional materials.

GROUP ACTIVITY

Some areas of the collection get more attention than others, even when they have great resources in them. For this activity, choose a collection area and grade level.

- Lower elementary, audiobooks
- Upper elementary, technology (Dewey 600s)

- Middle School, biographies (Dewey 92, 920, B)
- High School, poetry (Dewey 800s)

Then, in your group, consider these questions:

1. What's your hook? What's the little used or new aspect of your collection you're trying to market?
2. Your target audience;
3. Your three strategies for reaching this audience; and
4. Your plan for determining if your strategy was successful.

REFERENCES

Aptaker, R. (2013, September 13). Destiny as a one-stop shop part 2. Retrieved from https://www .follettsoftware.com/LibraryConnections/archives.cfm/category/learning-library

Maxwell, L. (2018, August 28). Instagramming tips for librarians. Retrieved from https://bookriot .com/instagram-tips-for-librarians/

Young, L. J. (2020, October 22). The ins and outs of buying ebooks: How to bolster virtual collections during the pandemic. *School Library Journal.* Retrieved from https://www.slj.com /?detailStory=the-ins-and-outs-of-buying-ebooks-schools-libraries-librarians-hot-to-bolster -virtual-collections-during-the-pandemic

ADDITIONAL READINGS

Gavigan, K., Pribesh, S., & Dickinson, G. (2010). Fixed or flexible schedule? Schedule impacts and school library circulation. *Library & Information Science Research, 32*(2), 131–137.

Lacey, K. (2014, October). The business of: School library automation. *District Administration.* Retrieved from https://web.archive.org/web/20160408201953/http://www.districtadministration .com/article/business-school-library-automation

Young, T. E. (2010). Marketing your school library media center: What we can learn from national bookstores. *Library Media Connection, 28*(6), 18–20.

HELPFUL MULTIMEDIA

Alexandria. (2020). 7 ways to promote your school library using social media. Retrieved from https://www.goalexandria.com/7-ways-to-promote-your-school-library-using-social-media/

American Library Association. (2015). Implementing library technology. Retrieved from https:// libguides.ala.org/librarytech

Capterra. (n.d.). Library management software. Retrieved from http://www.capterra.com/library -automation-software/

National Library of New Zealand. (n.d.). Social media and the school library. Retrieved from https://natlib.govt.nz/schools/school-libraries/library-services-for-teaching-and-learning /your-school-library-online/social-media-and-the-school-library

Pride, D. A. (2020). Social media marketing for libraries in 2020. Retrieved from https://www .youtube.com/watch?v=FGhtgDX-CKg&t=52s

Valenza, J. (n.d.). The neverending search [blog]. https://blogs.slj.com/neverendingsearch/

Whitehead, T. (n.d.). Mighty little librarian [blog]. http://www.mightylittlelibrarian.com/

CHAPTER 12

Evaluation of the Collection

<div class="box">

Key Learnings

- Evaluating the collection is important for reflecting on current activities and prioritizing future work.
- Evaluation should include a range of quantitative and qualitative techniques in which the program-level and user-level impacts are examined on an ongoing basis.
- Evaluation is also a means of communicating the library's importance of all stakeholders.

</div>

The evaluation of any library collection, including a school library collection, should be based upon how well the collection serves the needs of its users. An evaluation should also take into account the goals and objectives of the library program. The library's policies and procedures manual should include who evaluates the collection, what types of evaluation measures are used, and when evaluation of the collection takes place.

School librarians should oversee evaluation of the collection. However, it is helpful to have input from faculty and learners. Experts in subject areas can also assist with some evaluation methods.

Several different methods of evaluating library collections have been developed. Sometimes techniques are used independently, but more often several methods are collectively used. While there is no one correct method of collection evaluation to use in all libraries, three general types of measures can help school librarians evaluate their collections. Collection-centered measures include checking lists, catalogs, and bibliographies; examining the collection directly; performing age analysis; compiling comparative statistics; applying collection standards; and collection mapping. Use-centered measures include circulation studies, in-house use studies, user-opinion surveys, shelf-availability studies, and analysis of interlibrary loan statistics. Simulated-use studies include citation studies and document delivery tests.

Set aside a time to develop a plan for evaluating the school library collection. The plan should include what methods of evaluation will be used, when data will be gathered, and what will be done with the results of the evaluation.

WHY EVALUATE?

Those who fund library programs need facts on which to base funding decisions, shifts in financial resources, expansion of programs, and cutbacks. As managers, school librarians need information on which to base decisions about collections and for communicating collection needs to administrators. The evaluation process can reveal answers to the following questions: Does the collection meet the users' needs? Is the collection integral to curricular and instructional needs? Does it provide access to materials from outside the school? Does it include formats that users prefer? Does it hinder or facilitate the library program? Is the collection responsive to the needs of all library users? These questions identify general areas of investigation that are broad and complex. One cannot examine all these questions simultaneously; to do so would be an overwhelming task. However, a school librarian can evaluate smaller issues, components of the larger questions. Before beginning an evaluation project, one must identify what information to collect, how to record it, how to analyze it, how to use it, and with whom to share it and why.

The American Library Association (ALA) positions objective collection evaluation as an important aspect of the *Library Bill of Rights*. In ALA's view,

> Libraries continually develop their collections by adding and removing resources to maintain collections of current interest and usefulness to their communities. Libraries should adopt collection development and maintenance policies that include criteria for evaluating materials. Reasons for inclusion or removal of materials may include but are not limited to accuracy, currency, budgetary constraints, relevancy, content, usage, and community interest. The collection-development process is not to be used as a means to remove materials or deny access to resources on the grounds of personal bias or prejudice or because the materials may be viewed as controversial or objectionable. Doing so violates the principles of intellectual freedom and is in opposition to the Library Bill of Rights. (ALA, 2019)

Therefore, evaluation must be ongoing, objective, and systematic.

EVALUATION AND MEASUREMENT

Evaluation is the process of deciding worth or value; measurement, a component of the evaluation process, is the process of identifying extent or quantity. We can count the number of items that circulate in any given period, but that information is not evaluative; counting provides quantitative data, an objective measure. The count gives us information about the number of items that circulated but no information about who used the materials (or whether anyone did) and under what set of circumstances, whether additional materials were used in other places, or even what materials were used within the school library. Merely counting the number of circulated science titles does not measure how adequately the collection supports the science curriculum. One must interpret additional quantitative data and perhaps consider some qualitative assessments before beginning to evaluate. The purpose of evaluating a collection determines whether one should use quantitative or qualitative techniques, or a combination of both. Although quantitative data lack the element of judgment found in qualitative data, quantitative analysis does give us an objective basis for changing a collection policy.

Measurement can lead to meaningful evaluation. Professional judgment helps us decide what to measure, whether we can measure it, and how we interpret the results. The process can provide knowledge about alternatives, possible consequences, the effectiveness of operations, and insight into the managerial aspects of the collection program.

Evaluation produces information that can be judged by four criteria: validity, reliability, timeliness, and credibility. If the information is essential to a decision, it has validity. If we can reproduce the information when repeating the same techniques, the evaluation has reliability. If the information reaches the decision-makers when they need it, it has timeliness. If decision-makers trust the information, it has credibility. One should consider these criteria when planning how and when to evaluate.

BARRIERS TO EVALUATION

As with weeding, school librarians can fall into the trap of finding reasons for putting off or avoiding evaluation. A primary barrier to evaluating the collection is that some people believe library services are intangible and library goals are impossible to measure objectively. However, librarians who use a planning process recognize evaluation as a crucial component in the process. Assessment occurs in the context of each collection's philosophy, mission statement, constraints, users, and environment. Long-range goals guide the direction of the organization. The process also involves short-term, measurable objectives to guide day-to-day activities. Strategies help us to meet the objectives and identify measures for evaluating them (National Library of New Zealand, n.d.).

A second barrier is concern about lack of staff time. Automation answers this argument. Automated circulation systems provide means to easily obtain circulation figures and to analyze use of a collection. This information helps one see patterns in a school library. Library catalog systems can help librarians analyze other aspects of the collection, including the number of books in specific categories and the average copyright date of materials. These analyses can lead to evaluation, which in turn can lead to more efficient and effective operations, thus saving staff time.

Third, school librarians may lack experience with or knowledge about collecting and analyzing empirical data. Some ways can be used to overcome this problem. For example, other members of the school's faculty can be asked to help with these operations. University courses and workshops on research methods provide opportunities to gain confidence in these activities.

Fourth, people who are unfamiliar with evaluation may fear the results. The results should be objective data that identify program strengths and weaknesses. The data can help one make collection decisions. An informed manager can use documented weaknesses to gain additional support of funds.

A fifth barrier is uncertainty about what to do with the results. Those responsible for the collection, including those who provide the funds for collections, must be ready to use the results to make necessary changes. The results of evaluation need to be shared and used, not filed away (Baker & Lancaster, 1991, pp. 4–7).

TECHNIQUES FOR MEASURING COLLECTIONS

The value of a collection can be measured in many ways. The following sections describe the most commonly used techniques for measuring collection value. As you read about them, think about their appropriateness for your purposes. How will the results help you present the school library program to others? What type of data will you collect? What effort must you make to collect the data? How many people will you need to assist in evaluating the collection? What will the costs be? How much time will it take? Once you have obtained the information, how should you organize it? With whom can you share the information? How can you use the information to communicate with others? Analyzing measurement techniques with these questions in mind can help you select the most appropriate technique.

Collection-Centered Measures

To determine the size, scope, or depth of a collection, one can use collection-centered techniques. These are often used to compare a collection with an external standard. They include checking lists, catalogs, and bibliographies; examining the collection directly; performing age analysis; compiling comparative statistics; applying collection standards; and collection mapping.

Checking Lists, Catalogs, and Bibliographies

In this procedure, the titles in the library catalog are compared to a bibliography, list, or catalog of titles recommended for a certain purpose or type of collection. During the procedure, you should record the number of titles the school library owns and does not own. From this data, you can obtain the percentage of recommended titles that the collection contains.

Lists that you can use for this technique include specialized bibliographies; basic subject lists; current lists; reference works; periodicals; lists designed to meet specific objectives; citations in textbooks or curriculum guides; or catalogs from jobbers, publishers, and producers. Examples of current lists are the Association for Library Service to Children's *Notable Children's Books*, *Notable Children's Videos*, and *Notable Children's Recordings*; or the Young Adult Library Services Association's *Amazing Audiobooks for Young Adults*, *Best Books for Young Adults*, *Best Fiction for Young Adults*, *Fabulous Films for Young Adults*, *Outstanding Books for the College Bound*, *Great Graphic Novels for Teens*, *Popular Paperbacks for Young Adults*, *Quick Picks for Reluctant Young Adult Readers*, *Readers' Choice*, and *Teens' Top Ten*. Current lists of this nature identify highly recommended titles, but you must determine whether your collection needs those titles.

If your purpose is to measure the general coverage of titles appropriate for the audience served, standard catalogs, such as the H. W. Wilson series titles *Children's Catalog*, *Middle and Junior High School Core Collection*, and *Senior High Core Collection*, are useful. The Helpful Multimedia section of this chapter and this book's appendix include many more core collection sources. If comparisons reveal that the collection has many of the recommended titles, then, presumably, the collection is successful. The more closely the purpose of the tool matches the purpose of the collection, the more beneficial the comparison will be. The collection development policy can provide a basis for judging the appropriateness of a specific list.

Advantages of this technique to help evaluate a collection are as follows:

- A wide range of lists is available.
- The lists are selective and include informative annotations.
- Lists of this nature are frequently updated and revised.
- Lists can be compiled to meet the needs of a collection.
- Searching lists is a comparatively easy way to evaluate a collection.
- Most compilations have been prepared by competent professional school librarians or subject specialists.

This technique also has some disadvantages for evaluating a collection:

- Some items may be out of print.
- The cost of the list may outweigh the benefit of its use.
- No single list can cover every subject or need.
- Bibliographies cover materials for all ages and may have limited usefulness for evaluating a collection established to serve a specific age group.
- This approach does not give credit to titles in the collection that could be equal to or better than those the list recommends.

In schools where educators use textbooks or curriculum guides that include bibliographies of recommended resources, librarians can measure their collections against the recommended titles. Educators appreciate having lists of titles that are available in the school library, along with the call numbers of the materials. Creating such lists for educators can also alert you to gaps in the collection and simultaneously provide educators with an opportunity to suggest alternate materials. A limitation of this approach is that titles listed in textbooks and curriculum guides may be out of print. However, newer materials may provide the same content.

Examining the Collection Directly

A physical examination of materials can reveal the size, scope, and depth of a collection. An assessment of the timeliness of materials and their physical condition can help identify which items need to be mended, repaired, bound, replaced, removed, or discarded. An examiner can be a member of the school library staff or an outsider. The latter is usually someone knowledgeable about materials on a specific subject.

School library staff can examine the collection on two levels. The more cursory approach is to examine only the shelves while asking yourself questions. Are some shelves consistently empty? Is that a sign of popularity or improper distribution? Are educators giving assignments that call for those materials? Does the collection development policy provide for adequate coverage in this area? Do some shelves have materials that are seldom used? Have learners turned to online forms for this information? This cursory approach takes little time and can indicate a section of the collection that calls for more careful study.

A more in-depth approach is a systematic review of the collection. One examines the materials while considering the collection development policy. If users' needs have changed, a policy change is imperative. For subjects that have low priority in a collection and infrequently used, materials are probably unnecessary. Knowledge of the collection policy and the extent to which materials are added, withdrawn, or replaced can help the librarian establish goals for the review program.

Selection criteria such as those presented in Chapter 7, "General Selection Criteria," can guide these decisions. Ideally, such a review is an ongoing process. It is easy to check the physical condition of books and periodicals when users return them. More time is required to check damage to software or audiovisual materials.

Advantages of directly examining a collection include the following:

- A cursory examination can be accomplished quickly.
- School librarians considering resource sharing can readily identify a collection's weaknesses and strengths.
- Reviewing a collection on a systematic and ongoing basis ensures that both the collection policy and the collection are responsive to school goals and user needs.
- Establishing criteria for decisions about relegating, repairing, binding, replacing, and discarding materials facilitates and standardizes those processes.

Some disadvantages of this technique include the following:

- One must consider all materials that are being circulated during the examination study.
- The process, unless computerized or focused on one aspect of the collection, is time consuming and requires trained personnel.
- If one does not consider the collection development policy and the rate of growth, individual items, rather than the collection as a whole, will be evaluated.
- Resources available through cooperative efforts are not considered. If a library is participating in a resource-sharing program where another collection is responsible for collecting on a specific subject, those materials will not appear in the examination.
- People who are knowledgeable about the school program, as well as a subject area, may be difficult to locate and expensive to hire.

Performing Age Analysis

One method of examining the collection is to estimate the age of the information in the materials. This can be done by selecting a random sample of materials and then computing the average copyright date.

The advantages of utilizing the age analysis technique are as follows:

- Others can easily understand the result.
- It is possible to match the result with anecdotal information, such as noting that the average age of the materials in the collection is 25 years and then recalling what was happening in the world at that time.

Disadvantages of this technique of evaluating a collection are as follows:

- It is difficult for one number to represent an entire set of materials. Sometimes it is better to use one number for fiction and another number for nonfiction.
- One must consider how old is too old for a children's collection. Presently, no standard guidelines determine the appropriate age for children's collections.

Compiling Comparative Statistics

Although the limitations of quantitative methods were discussed earlier in this chapter, there are reasons for collecting these types of data. For example, comparing data collected at various times of the year reveals patterns of use. State and federal agencies, professional associations, and accrediting agencies typically request circulation statistics.

Several types of statistics can be used with local, state, and national policymakers. Statistics can be collected about the following aspects of the collection: size, growth rate (volumes added within a given period of time), expenditures for materials, and collection overlap (how many individual titles are held in common among two or more collections). Advantages of using comparison of statistics to evaluate a collection include the following:

- If records have been kept, statistics are easy to compile.
- If the application is clearly defined, it is easy to understand and compare the statistics.
- The method relates directly to the users in the case of requests filled or not filled.

Disadvantages of using this technique for collection evaluation include the following:

- Standard definitions of the content or quantity of a unit are lacking.
- It is difficult to count nonprint items and sets of materials.
- Significance may be difficult to interpret.
- Possible inaccuracy or inconsistency in data collection and recording exists.
- Statistics are usually nonapplicable to a library's goals and objectives.

The gathering of statistics is commonly used to compare one collection with another, to examine subject balance within a collection, and to decide whether to share resources or to allocate monies. When using data for comparative purposes, the participating agencies need to agree on the definition of each statistical component and use identical measurement methods. You will need to learn what your district or state considers a statistical component and which data-collecting methods are used.

If the collections in your district or state are being compared, data must be gathered in the same way. You should check for the district's or state's guidelines. Are you to use a volume or title count? If you are to count each volume of an encyclopedia set or each record in an album, the total size of the collection may be distorted. Some districts with centralized processing may count an item as it appears in its main entry. For example, because each school may have a separate main entry, a school that owns a kit containing two videos, five books, and an educator's guide might record one kit; another school with only one of the videos and one of the books might record two items, a book and a video. An encyclopedia set cataloged as one item would count as one title. A multivolume set in which each volume is separately cataloged would be recorded as the number of individual titles.

Library catalog systems use barcodes, generally with each volume having an individual barcode. If an item in a kit can be checked out separately, each item would have a separate barcode. However, if the intent is for the kit to be checked out with all items included, one barcode is used for the kit. It is relatively easy to determine the number of volumes in a collection when the items are separately barcoded.

The use of online databases to access titles that are not physically in the school library can also complicate the counting of volumes and titles. Although the materials may not be physically in the school library, they are accessible, and the library budget is being used to purchase their accessibility.

When information is to be used for allocating funds, there is an advantage to having uniform data about the quantity of materials accessible to each learner. One could argue that several learners can use an encyclopedia set; however, circulating materials, such as kits, are usually checked out to one person at a time. Data that include both a title and a volume count reveal more about the accessibility of materials than does a volume count alone. This dual procedure accounts for duplicate titles that can serve more people for a specific item but records the limit of the total resources available.

Statistics about unfilled requests can help determine what materials to add to a collection. It is a good idea to record requests by learners and educators for information or specific items not in the collection. You can then use these records when making selection decisions.

Applying Collection Standards

In this procedure, the collection is compared to quantitative and qualitative recommendations that various standards, guidelines, or similar publications list. The issuing body may be professional associations, such as the American Association of School Librarians (AASL) tend to focus on qualitative standards and a planning approach based on the needs of individual school libraries, and, therefore, can be of limited value because the quantitative characteristics of programs vary in relation to needs and program activities. To assess the whole school library, multiple evaluation inputs are required. AASL's *The National School Library Standards* (2018) noted that the scope and size of each school library depends on the needs of the patrons of the library and have created an evaluation tool that uses the Shared Foundations as an assessment lens (AASL, 2019). However, tools such as reports and surveys from state and national programs can be used to benchmark a school library collection.

Accreditation agencies, such as the Southern Association of Colleges and Schools, are another source of standards. Typically, such standards include basic criteria for evaluation of materials, level of financial support, size and condition of the collection, and access to materials. Accreditation agency standards are based on resources or inputs, such as the amount of money spent per learner.

Advantages for evaluating your collection by applying standards include the following:

- The guidelines generally are relevant to a school library and the school's goals and objectives.
- Educators usually accept standards and guidelines and consider them authoritative.
- They can be used in persuasive ways to solicit support.

Disadvantages of applying standards to evaluate a collection include the following:

- The recommendations may be stated so generally that a high degree of professional knowledge and judgment may be needed to interpret the statements.
- Knowledgeable people may disagree about the application and interpretation of the statements.
- Minimum standards may be perceived as sufficient.

Mapping the Collection

In recent years, collection mapping has been one of the most popular evaluation techniques used by school librarians. It can involve some of the methods already described. Collection mapping is a visual display of the strengths and weaknesses of a library collection. Sometimes, the entire collection is mapped, while in other instances specific areas of the collection are mapped. When mapping only a specific area of the collection, these maps are sometimes called *emphasis maps* or *mini-maps*. Some school librarians try to select one area of the collection each year and create a mini-map project for that area. Often the areas selected correspond with particular areas of the curriculum; therefore, it is important to have knowledge about the curriculum. Frequently curriculum mapping is performed prior to collection mapping. To make certain that a collection meets the needs of a school, a librarian should relate the collection mapping to local, state, and national standards.

Different ways are available to develop procedures for collection mapping and to graphically present a collection. Today, most library catalog systems can create reports that list each item by Dewey number or by copyright date. These reports can be used to create collection maps. Although it has an older copyright date, Loertscher's (1996) book *Collection Mapping in the LMC: Building Access in a World of Technology* can be helpful in learning about several collection mapping techniques. Some of the articles and websites listed at the end of this chapter have additional information about collection mapping.

Figure 12.1 is a sample of a collection map for a middle school. This map provides a graphic representation of the number of books in the collection and the average age of the books. When analyzing the results of this collection map, it can be noted that the number of books per learner (27) is adequate. Generally, a school library should have at least 10 books per learner. Also, since the collection map was made in 2012, we can also conclude that the average age of the sections of the school library collection (2002) could be newer, but it is not nearly as old as many school library collections. The sections that have older average ages (philosophy, religion, and literature) are generally those where the age

Jane Doe Middle School Student Enrollment = 439

January 2012

Category	Number of Books	Average Age of Books
000 General	157	2002
100 Philosophy	142	1995
200 Religion	158	1999
300 Social Science	997	2006
400 Language	153	2000
500 Pure Science	1803	2007
600 Applied Science	1892	2009
700 The Arts	512	1997
800 Literature	304	1992
900 History/Geography	1087	2007
Biography	1601	2002
Fiction	2049	2003
Short Stories	667	2000
Reference	330	2002

Total number of Books = 11852
Books per Student = 27
Average Age of Categories (Sections of the School Library) = 2002

Figure 12.1. Sample Collection Map

of the materials is not as important as in other sections, such as pure science, applied science, and history or geography. This is a collection that has most likely been weeded on a regular basis, and newer titles have been added. Since reference materials also need to be current, the librarian might consider weeding next items in the reference section and replacing them with more current titles. The librarian will need to find out from educators and learners how frequently the print reference titles are being used. It may be a better expenditure of funds to purchase some of the reference titles online than in print format.

Other media formats (eBooks, DVDs, electronic databases, etc.) should also be included in a collection map. Quality components, such as condition of the materials, diversity of formats, cultural representation, and diversity of reading levels, can also be used in a collection mapping project. There are methods to determine what percentage should be recommended for each area of the collection and how well a particular collection is meeting those needs.

Advantages of creating a collection map include the following:

- A collection map can be read and understood fairly easily.
- A collection map can show the strengths and weaknesses of the collection.
- It can be used to indicate areas that need weeding.
- It can demonstrate areas of excellence and areas of need.
- A collection map can be used to develop collection goals.
- Collection mapping can be used to support the curriculum.
- A collection map can be used as a tool to request funding for specific needs.

Disadvantages of collection mapping include the following:

- The process of creating a collection mapping project can be time consuming.
- Knowledge of the curriculum and research assignments must be obtained in order to ascertain curriculum needs.
- Assistance might be needed to analyze the results of a collection map.

Use-Centered Measures

Use-centered measures can be used to determine whether, how often, and by whom materials are used. Circulation studies, in-house studies, user opinion surveys, shelf-availability studies, and analysis of interlibrary loan studies focus on the users and the use of materials.

Circulation Studies

Analysis of circulation data can help you examine the collection as a whole, or any part of it, in terms of publication data, subject, or user group. You can use this information to identify (1) low-usage materials, which may be ready to be removed from the collection; (2) high-usage materials, which may be titles to duplicate; (3) patterns of use in selected subject areas or by format; and (4) materials favored by specific user groups.

The advantages of using circulation studies for evaluating a school library collection include the following:

- Data are easily arranged into categories for analysis.
- Flexibility in duration of study and sample size is possible.
- Units of information are easily compiled.

- Information is objective.
- Data can be readily available with automated circulation systems.
- Types of users can be correlated with the types of materials they use.

Disadvantages of using this technique to evaluate a collection include the following:

- In-house use is excluded, thus underrepresenting actual use.
- It reflects only materials found by users and does not record whether the user did not locate a desired item or whether the collection did not have that item.
- Bias may be present because of inaccessibility of heavily used materials.
- The method is not suitable for noncirculating collections, such as periodicals.

One can use the evidence from circulation statistics to show how well the collection supports the curriculum. Increased circulation of reading for pleasure may result from the introduction of whole language or reading motivation programs. By documenting this increase, a librarian could justify an increased budget allocation for fiction. New school librarians can use this technique to identify which courses and educators make extensive use of which sections of the collection. By identifying weak areas of the collection, educators and librarians can work together to identify materials to fill those gaps.

In-House Use Studies

In-house studies can focus on either the use of noncirculating materials or the users of materials within the school library. During these studies, users are asked not to shelve materials. This allows the library staff to record use of the materials before returning the items to the shelves. You can also request that a database vendor provide you with statistics on how many times learners from your school accessed a particular database. However, this service might add an additional charge to your database subscription.

Advantages of collecting data on in-house use of materials include the following:

- Types of users can be correlated with the types of material they use.
- A circulation study combined with the in-house use study about the same part of the collection provides more in-depth information about the use of that section.
- The method is appropriate for noncirculating materials.
- It can help one determine which journals to keep and for how long, which databases meet learners' needs, areas in which learners need help in developing search strategies, and gaps in the collection.

Disadvantages of this evaluation technique include the following:

- Users' cooperation is needed.
- If conducted during a high- or low-use period, results may be biased.
- Circulating items will not be included, and this may create bias.
- The method does not reflect a learner's failure to locate and find desired information.

User-Opinion Surveys

A survey of users and user groups requires soliciting verbal or written responses through interviews, questionnaires, or a combination of methods. User opinions can be gathered informally to help identify users' needs. Examples of informal surveys are asking learners as they check out materials whether they found what they wanted and recording their answers.

A formal survey is more systematic and thorough. The formal approach involves a series of steps: identifying the objectives, selecting and designing the data collection technique, developing and testing the instrument, selecting the sample (the subgroup of the population), collecting and analyzing the data, and interpreting the results. Questions that could be addressed in a formal survey given to educators include the following:

- Do your learners have available resources to complete their projects and assignments?
- Do learners have adequate resources for pleasure reading?
- Is there a variety of formats to support the learning styles of your learners?
- Is there a balanced collection with a wide range of views on controversial topics?
- Is there sufficient access to electronic information and databases to meet your information needs and the needs of your learners?
- Does the school library have adequate resources to support your curriculum?
- Does the school library have appropriate professional development materials?

Whether using a written questionnaire or conducting interviews, one can use carefully worded questions to identify the strengths and weaknesses of the collection as perceived by the users. The questions should be directed to specific goals, which may or may not be of significance to the user. Formulating questions that solicit the type of information that you need can be time consuming. Interviews, which take longer to administer, can provide more in-depth information. However, the length of time involved may mean that fewer individuals participate in the process. The results of either type of survey can provide the basis for making changes in the collection development policy.

Advantages of using user-opinion surveys to evaluate a collection include the following:

- The survey can be developed to relate directly to the needs of users and to the goals and objectives of the collection.
- The information collected may reflect current interests.
- A survey can be used for most types of users.

Disadvantages of this technique of evaluation include the following:

- The method requires aggressive seeking of opinions.
- Those polled may be passive about participating or lack a point of comparison.
- Users' interests may be narrower than the collection development policy.
- Designing written questionnaires for young children may be difficult.

Shelf-Availability Studies

To determine whether users are finding specific works they seek, users can be interviewed or handed a brief questionnaire that asks them to identify titles they could not find. These data can help identify titles the library does not own, titles for which the library needs duplicate copies, items that have been improperly shelved, and insufficient directions for locating materials. One may also learn that the user had an incomplete or inaccurate citation, copied the call number incorrectly, or did not know where to locate the materials. This information about the collection and the user identifies areas that call for corrective action and changes.

Advantages of using shelf-availability information to evaluate a collection include the following:

- The method identifies failures that users face in trying to find materials.
- Data on possible changes in library policies and procedures are provided.
- The method can be used repeatedly to measure changes in library performance.

Disadvantages of using this technique include the following:

- User cooperation is required.
- Staff time in planning and collecting data is involved.
- The needs of nonusers are not identified.
- Users may not remember titles.

Using a simple questionnaire, a librarian can have learners indicate what they are looking for and whether they find it. The results can indicate areas of the collection that need strengthening or areas where circulation is high and duplicate copies may be needed. Staff members may need to follow up on the survey by determining whether learners had the wrong call number or whether materials were shelved incorrectly.

Analysis of Interlibrary Loan Statistics

Interlibrary loan requests represent materials that people did not find in the collection and sought to obtain from other sources. Analyzing these requests can identify subject or format weaknesses in the collection, identify specific titles needed, and monitor resource-sharing agreements. You should compare analyses of subject areas with similar analyses of acquisition and circulation data to identify areas of heavy use or lack of materials. The results must be evaluated in terms of the collection development policy and existing resource-sharing agreements involving interlibrary loan.

Advantages of analyzing interlibrary loan requests to evaluate a collection include the following:

- The data are often readily available. For example, statistics on requests for periodical titles are usually kept to avoid copyright infringement.
- The items are needed by at least one person.
- Requests may indicate weaknesses in the collection.

Disadvantages of this evaluation technique include the following:

- The significance of the data may be difficult to interpret because it represents the request of only one person.
- Needs of users who personally go to other collections and skip making interlibrary loan requests are not identified.

Records of interlibrary loan requests can be analyzed to identify titles that patrons request. The results can be analyzed in terms of frequently sought subjects in which materials need to be added to a collection. Analysis of requests for articles can reveal heavily used periodicals the collection may need.

Simulated-Use Studies

Information about the use of a collection can be gathered without directly involving users. These simulated situations include citation studies and document delivery tests.

Citation Studies

This method can be used if users of the collection utilize other libraries. If learners write term papers or do independent projects, school librarians can check the bibliographies of learner papers or projects to identify titles cited that are not holdings of the school collection.

Advantages of evaluating a collection by examining citations include the following:

- Lists are easily obtained from the learners' project bibliographies.
- The method relates directly to users.
- The procedure is easy to apply.
- This method identifies works not in the collection.

Disadvantages of utilizing this method include the following:

- The value is limited if learners use only the collection being evaluated.
- Citations are limited to the subject of the paper, a small portion of the total collection.
- The method is limited by the number of learners who write papers.

Document Delivery Tests

This technique is similar to the shelf-availability study; however, members of the library staff, rather than users, perform the searching. Document delivery tests also carry the citation study a step further by determining whether the collection includes a specific title, whether one can locate the item, and how long it takes to do so. The purpose of document delivery tests is to assess the capability of a library to provide users with the items they need at the time they need them. A typical approach is to compile a list of citations that reflects users' needs and determine the time it takes to locate each item.

Advantages of using tests of document delivery to evaluate the collection include the following:

- Objective measurements of the capability of the collection to satisfy user needs are provided.
- Data can be compared between libraries if identical citation lists are used.

Disadvantages of this evaluation method include the following:

- A representative list may be difficult to create.
- Because library staff members perform the searches, the test understates the problems users encounter.
- To be meaningful, tests need to be repeated or compared with studies conducted in other libraries.

Logs can be kept of interlibrary loan requests to record the requested item, the date of the request, the date the item was available to the requestor, and the response time (days between request and availability). The same type of information can be recorded about the response time for an educator requesting a title for purchase. Further information can be obtained by asking whether the requestor still needs the item.

VENDOR SERVICES

Several vendors provide online collection analysis services, often free, that make it easy to analyze a library collection. For example, Follett Library Resources' TitleWise, a tool found within their Titlewave acquisition website, can quickly identify areas of a school library collection that are strong and areas that need weeding. Follett makes TitleWise available to all library users who make a free account. Mackin Library Resources also offers collection analysis tools for customers. These services analyze MARC records from a school library's catalog that must be shared online with the vendor, which then compares the records with a standard based on award-winning library collections. Reporting on a school's collection areas is immediate, and there is no charge for entry-level reports. However, some vendors charge for more in-depth reports that evaluate certain aspects of the collection. The Online Computer Library Center (OCLC) also provides a *WorldCat Collection Analysis*™, which allows libraries to analyze their collections against other WorldCat institutions.

RETURN ON INVESTMENT/VALUE CALCULATORS

School library value calculators allow you to attach a retail price to library materials and services. The tools (two such tools are listed in the Helpful Multimedia section of this chapter) allow school librarians to let their user community how much they would pay out of pocket to acquire the materials and contract for the services they receive for free in the school library. Most library value calculators are based on the one originally developed by the Massachusetts Library Association. The Maine State Library's School Library Use Value Calculator is based on the Massachusetts tool with some special data points for school libraries and has been updated with figures from the Ohio Library Council (2017), as Table 12.1 shows.

Library value calculators use a combination of actual and estimated average costs of library materials and services as well as actual and estimated average costs for equivalent or comparable services available elsewhere. The advantages to these tools are that they are very easy to use and that the output is understandable by all stakeholders, administrators to learners. However, a caution with these tools is that the data sources can be out of date. Another caution is that most calculators do not capture the whole range of collection resources and services school librarians may offer. Be sure to check the date of the data on which the calculator is based (all calculators share their data sources), adjust the numbers for inflation, and let users know your worth!

CONCLUSION

Several techniques can be used to evaluate school library collections. The methods are usually categorized under collection-centered or use-centered approaches. It is important to use both qualitative and quantitative measures when evaluating a school library collection. Generally, two or more methods are used together to obtain meaningful results. In

TABLE 12.1. RETAIL VALUE OF SCHOOL LIBRARY COLLECTION MATERIALS AND SERVICES (ADAPTED FROM OHIO LIBRARY COUNCIL, 2017)

Item	Estimated Retail Value	Values Explained
Books Borrowed	$17.00	Average cost of books (hardcover, paperback, children's)
Audio-Visual Materials Borrowed (audio and/or videos)	$10.00	Average cost to download purchase audio/video materials
Interlibrary Loan Requests (include books borrowed/shared among school district libraries)	$30.00	Average national cost for loans
eBooks/Audiobooks Downloaded	$15.00	Average cost to download an eBook/ audiobook
Magazine/Newspaper Use in Library	$7.50	Average monthly cost of a popular magazines/newspapers issue
Use of School Library as Meeting Room	$50.00	Estimate
Computers Loaned Out and Used in the Library	$12.00	Sample hourly rate at Internet cafes for people using their computers, not their own laptops.
eReader Devices Loaned Out	$150.00	Estimate to purchase an eReader
Reference Questions and Readers' Advisory	$15.00	Estimated cost per question
Direct Class Instruction to Students	$32.00	Based on teacher per diem rate
Professional Development for Teachers	$100.00	Typical hourly rate for a professional consultant
Computer Advice to Staff and Students	$32.00	Based on teacher per diem rate
Troubleshoot/Use of AV Equipment & Computers	$80.00	Estimated cost to troubleshoot technical problems to avoid calling special repair service
Curriculum Development	$32.00	Based on teacher per diem rate
Organizing Enrichment Activities, e.g., author visits	$32.00	Based on teacher per diem rate
Grant Writing	$75.00	Estimated cost to hire outside grant writer and consultant

recent years, collection mapping, graphically representing a collection, has been used to demonstrate the strengths and weaknesses of a collection. Some vendors also provide online free collection analysis to school libraries.

The collection evaluation process provides an opportunity to work with learners, educators, and administrators to ensure that a collection meets their needs. Their involvement can lead to understanding why certain decisions are made.

DISCUSSION QUESTIONS

1. Review Table 12.1. Which items do you feel are missing from the value list? Taking into account that the figures change from year to year, which items do you feel are valued too low or too high?
2. You have been asked to assemble a report about the library collection from the parent-educator organization. Decide what you would want this group to know about your collection and match those information points to collection evaluation activities.

REFERENCES

American Association of School Librarians (AASL). (2018). *National school library standards for learners, school librarians, and school libraries.* Chicago, IL: American Library Association.

American Association of School Librarians (AASL). (2019). Evaluation checklist. Retrieved from https://standards.aasl.org/wp-content/uploads/2018/10/180921-aasl-standards-evaluation-checklist-color.pdf

American Library Association (ALA). (2019, June 25). Evaluating library collections: An interpretation of the Library Bill of Rights. Retrieved from http://www.ala.org/advocacy/intfreedom/librarybill/interpretations/evaluatinglibrary

Baker, S. L. & Lancaster, F. W. (1991). The measurement and evaluation of library services (2nd edition). Arlington, VA: Information Resources Press.

Loertscher, D. (1996). *Collection mapping in the LMC: Building access in a world of technology.* San Jose, CA: Hi Willow.

National Library of New Zealand. (n.d.). Assessing your school library collection. Retrieved from https://natlib.govt.nz/schools/school-libraries/collections-and-resources/assessing-your-school-library-collection

Ohio Library Council. (2017). Updated version of ROI calculator now available. Retrieved from http://olc.org/blog/2018/03/19/updated-version-of-roi-calculator-now-available/

ADDITIONAL READINGS

Adamich, T. (2010). Florida power-library schools and the role of quality library catalogs and collections in 21st century learner achievement. *Technicalities, 30*(2), 13–16.

Cisnek, M. P., & Young, C. L. (2010). Diversity collection assessment in large academic libraries. *Collection Building, 29*(4), 154–161.

Cox, E. (2010). Assessing learner evaluations of resources: Approximation of expertise. *Knowledge Quest, 38*(3), 14–17.

Enochs, E. L. (2010). Features of elementary school library poetry collections: A collection analysis study. *School Libraries Worldwide, 16*(2), 64–79.

Everhart, N. (2021). *Evaluating the school library: Analysis, techniques, and research practices,* 2nd edition. Santa Barbara, CA: Libraries Unlimited.

Greiner, T., & Cooper, B. (2007). *Analyzing library collection use with Excel.* Chicago, IL: American Library Association.

Griffin, G. G. (2011). Steps for evaluating a fifth grade science collection. *Library Media Connection, 29*(5), 26–27.

Howard, J. K. (2010). Information specialist and leader—Taking on collection and curriculum mapping. *School Library Monthly, 27*(1), 35–37.

Hyöodynmaa, M., Ahlholm-Kannisto, A., & Nurminen, H. (2010). How to evaluate library collections: A case study of collection mapping. *Collection Building, 29*(2), 43–49.

HELPFUL MULTIMEDIA

A school librarian's toolkit: Collection analysis tools. (n.d.). Retrieved from http://mottslibtools.weebly.com/collection-analysis-tools.html

American Library Association. (n.d.). Library value calculator. Retrieved from http://www.ala.org/advocacy/library-value-calculator

Ferguson, A. (2014). Accessing Mackin collection analysis. Retrieved from https://www.youtube.com/watch?v=Wdpj45hrMWE

Follett. (2021). Titlewave. Retrieved from https://www.titlewave.com/

Hauser, K. (2013). Collection mapping in a school library. Retrieved from https://www.youtube.com/watch?v=5lUECMzV3aI

Hilling, L. (2014). Analyze collection using Follett Titlewise & Destiny. Retrieved from https://www.youtube.com/watch?v=dRD_MLanU40

Lamb, A., & Johnson, L. (2010). Library Media Program: Collection mapping. Retrieved from http://eduscapes.com/sms/program/mapping.html

Maine State Library. (2015). What are the savings that school libraries bring to their schools? Retrieved from http://www.state.me.us/msl/libs/advocacy/savings.htm

National Library of New Zealand. (2020). Collection Analysis Chart. Retrieved from https://natlib.govt.nz/files/schools/collection-assessment-template.docx

OCLC. (2021). WorldShare collection evaluation. Retrieved from https://www.oclc.org/en/collection-evaluation.html

CHAPTER 13

Legal and Ethical Issues with the Collection

Issues such as intellectual freedom and copyright have been present in school libraries for many years, but others, like the use of Internet filtering, allowing learners to use social networking sites in school, and the importance of physical and emotional safety, are more recent. In order to make both sound and ethical decisions regarding these issues, library policies and procedures must be in place.

Access to information involves intellectual, physical, and cultural access. Intellectual access addresses learners' rights to hear, read, and view information; to receive ideas; to express ideas; and to develop skills to receive, examine, analyze, synthesize, evaluate, and use information. Physical access refers to an environment that permits the unimpeded location and retrieval of information. This involves provision of adequate library staff, access to the library during and after regular school hours, use of interlibrary loan, provision of assistive and adaptive technologies, collection elements that can be used by learners with a range of physical and emotional needs and/or challenges, and access to computerized information networks or databases. Physical access is addressed throughout this book in many ways, with Chapter 15 exploring ways in which the collection can serve a range of physical access matters. Cultural access, addressed also in Chapter 15, refers to ensuring that the school library collection reflects the heritage and environment in which learners live, communicate, and learn. Cultural access involves ensuring access to information and resources for users of all ethnicities, socioeconomic statuses, genders, ages, sexual orientation, and disability. Each of these areas of access includes the librarian exercising responsibilities guided by legal and ethical considerations.

Ethical responsibilities exist not only with the selection of materials, but also with other processes of collection development: the acquisition of materials and equipment, learners' access to materials, preserving and maintaining the collection, circulating materials, and evaluating the collection. This chapter discusses some issues and ethical responsibilities that involve decisions on the part of school librarians. For some of the issues, there are definite legal and ethical guidelines, but in other instances there may be more than one acceptable opinion about an issue. Therefore, the items listed in Additional Readings or Helpful Multimedia are designed to facilitate further exploration and consideration. At the end of this chapter are scenarios involving intellectual freedom, confidentiality, access equality, the use of Internet, and copyright, which will give you an opportunity to work through the chapter's issues in context. As you study them, bear in mind the very real possibility that you may one day face such situations.

ISSUES WITH INTELLECTUAL ACCESS

Intellectual freedom is the overriding theme of legal and ethical responsibilities relating to access. The school librarian's commitment to intellectual freedom and sensitivity to individual needs influence the extent of intellectual, physical, and cultural access that is provided to learners, educators, and administrators.

Intellectual freedom is a principle upon which almost all library collections are based. However, when collections are to be used by children or teens, the concept of intellectual freedom becomes much more controversial. Two questions that need to be considered are as follows:

- How does the concept of intellectual freedom apply to children and young adults?
- Should there be limits on learners' rights to read, view, and listen? If so, who has the right to impose those limits?

Minors' Rights and Intellectual Freedom

The information you make available to learners reflects the value you place on intellectual freedom and learners' rights. In the United States, the First Amendment serves as the basis of intellectual rights. Intellectual freedom is the basis of the First Amendment's three major sections: freedom of religion, freedom of expression, and freedom of association. These three rights have been topics of controversy and court cases. A young person's intellectual rights can be viewed as legal rights, as well as ethical rights. The application of the First Amendment to minors generally arises in matters dealing with public education, particularly in court cases concerning censorship.

How does the First Amendment apply to young people and to intellectual freedom? Moshman (1986) edited a book on the intellectual rights of children in which he addressed this subject. He lists the following legal intellectual rights as they apply to children:

- *Free expression*—Government may not control a child's right to form or to express ideas.
- *Freedom of nonexpression*—Government may not require a child to adopt or express belief in a particular idea.
- *Freedom of access*—Government may not restrict children's access to ideas and sources of information.
- *Free exercise of religion*—Government may not restrict children from acting according to their religious beliefs.
- *Distinction of child from adult*—Limiting First Amendment rights must be based on compelling reasons by showing that harm would occur because the children in question are less competent than the typical adult (p. 27).

In many instances, Moshman's principles have been at the center of legal battles. Table 13.1 provides an overview of some of the cases that reflect how courts have interpreted the rights of minors.

The representative court case for young people's First Amendment rights is *Tinker v. Des Moines* (1969). This is the first time the U.S. Supreme Court declared a government action unconstitutional because it violated minor learners' rights to freedom of expression. The Supreme Court said:

> School officials do not possess absolute authority over their learners. Students in school as well as out of school are "persons" under our Constitution. They are possessed of fundamental rights which the State must respect, just as they themselves must respect their obligations to the State. (*Tinker v. Des Moines*, 1969)

In 2007, the *Tinker v. Des Moines* ruling was attacked by the U.S. federal government in *Morse and the Juneau School Board et al. v. Frederick* when the Supreme Court ruled that a school board can place restrictions on certain areas of speech (in this case, glorification of illegal drugs) within a school environment.

Another important U.S. Supreme Court ruling dealing with young people's rights is *Board of Education, Island Trees, New York v. Pico* (1982). In this case, the Court ruled that a board of education cannot simply remove books from a school library because of the ideas, values, and opinions expressed in them.

Although older, an excellent discussion of some of the Supreme Court cases that deal with learners' rights appears in Lukenbill and Lukenbill's (2007) article "Censorship: What Do School Library Specialists Really Know?" In this article, the authors also report on the findings of a study to determine the knowledge levels of a sample of school librarians concerning what they know about court rulings that affect learners' First Amendment rights and how the librarians support the rulings.

Librarians tend to take one of two positions in response to the question "What intellectual rights do children have?" One position, the protector, assumes that adults know what is best for children, what will harm them, what information they need, and how their needs should be met. The other position, the advocate, assumes an open stance, perceiving children as capable of defining both their information needs and their resource needs. The first position strives to protect learners from themselves, from others, and from ideas. The second strives to help learners identify, evaluate, retrieve, and use information.

TABLE 13.1. SUPREME COURT CASES RELATING TO PUBLIC SCHOOLS

Case Name	Case Cite (Year)	Topic	Court Ruling
Tinker v. Des Moines Independent Community School District	393 U.S. 503 (1969)	First Amendment Freedom of Speech	Seminal case involving students who were expelled after wearing black armbands to school in symbolic protest of the Vietnam War. The U.S. Supreme Court held that "students do not shed their constitutional rights at the schoolhouse gate" and that the First Amendment protects public school students' rights to express their social and political views
Board of Education v. Pico	457 U.S. 853 (1982)	First Amendment. Removal of controversial books from school library	The U.S. Supreme Court held that the school board's attempt to remove controversial books from the school library was unconstitutional. The Court stated that "the right to receive ideas is a necessary predicate to the recipient's meaningful exercise of his own rights of speech, press, and political freedom"
Hazelwood School District v. Kuhlmeier	484 U.S. 260 (1988)	First Amendment. Removal of content considered controversial from school materials	The U.S. Supreme Court held that a school principal acted reasonably after he removed pages dealing with controversial issues from school materials. The Court concluded that "educators do not offend the First Amendment when exercising editorial control over the style and content of student speech in the school-sponsored expressive activities so long as their actions are reasonably related to legitimate pedagogical concerns"
United States, et al. v. American Library Association, Inc., et al.	539 U.S. 194 (2003)	First Amendment. Internet filtering	The U.S. Supreme Court upheld the Children's Internet Protection Act, which requires libraries receiving federal funds for their Internet access, to install filters so that neither adult or children patrons can access materials that are considered obscene, child pornography, or "harmful to minors"

Digital Divide

The disparity between Internet "haves" and "have nots," otherwise known as the digital divide, exists in schools in multiple dimensions: access, skill, policy, and motivation to use the Internet (Mardis, Hoffman, & Marshall, 2008). In many schools, bandwidth capacity dictates how the Internet is used in school libraries and classrooms. While 99 percent of public schools in the United States report having Internet access, classroom connections are less frequent (Deye, 2015). Even if classroom access is available, many building-level policies impeded the integration of the Internet into teaching and learning. Many of school connections were reportedly not meeting school officials' needs because they were overloaded and poorly managed, leading to slow performance or restricted use (Federal Communications Commission [FCC], 2020). For example, in a study done in Michigan, education officials reported having to develop and enforce bandwidth-use policies that limited video streaming and other high-capacity uses; the Michigan finding was confirmed by the overwhelming majority of a nationwide survey of school officials who reported that their networks were too slow to support video streaming. This factor influenced educators' use of the Internet in their classrooms as much as their skills with technology integration (SETDA, 2019). The FCC (2020) noted that poor network performance and problematic connectivity were especially present in rural communities.

Despite the money available for broadband connections in schools, most ($n = 827$ or 78 percent) of the 1,060 school officials surveyed cited that, despite a strong desire to improve their schools' Internet access, a lack a funding for equipment and installation as a barrier (FCC, 2020). For these reasons, adoption is not instant and cannot be assumed. Targeted marketing to community members and parents was required to gain essential support that led to broadband adoption that would enhance education as well as other community services (LaRose, Strover, Gregg, & Straubhaar, 2011).

More than ever, schools are seen as community anchor institutions, along with health care facilities, public libraries, and other community agencies, in which Internet access is not only a key vehicle for the delivery of services to constituents who may not be able to physically engage with the institution. Indeed, many calls have been made to fundamentally redefine the meaning of schooling and re-envision the infrastructure of education to include immersive experiences, informal opportunities, and greater continuity between home, school, and workforce participation, all of which are enhanced by ubiquitous, reliable high-speed networks (SETDA, 2019). Mardis (2016) found that in rural communities where home broadband was absent, learner achievement tended to be low. However, when schools in those communities had school librarians and adequate broadband, learner reading achievement tended to be much higher.

Rural areas are hit hardest by a lack of connectivity, and this rural-to-urban variation has perpetuated a digital divide that once fell solely along economic lines. Increasingly, learning with technology has gone beyond mastering curriculum into real-life opportunities like job application, college enrollment, and driver's training. Moreover, bandwidth is a key aspect of parental involvement as many schools have created networks for information distribution through the use of e-mail lists, broadcast messages, and blogs. It is commonplace to access school websites featuring newsletters, calendars, lunch menus, and school and faculty contact information (Mardis, Everhart, Johnston, Baker, & Newsum, 2010). All of this information serves to keep schools in touch with the communities they serve. In rural areas, schools function as community anchor institutions when public libraries are not available or users' language skills cause them to be reticent to engage with a wide range of community sources (Adkins, Brendler, Townsend, & Maras, 2019).

Fiscal Limitations

Despite the numerous studies that have demonstrated that schools with appropriately staffed and well-resourced school libraries had fared well on standardized reading tests, library staff and budgets have fallen significantly in the last several years (ALA, 2020). At the same time, school librarians are expected to not only add digital resources and eBooks to their collections, but also keep pace with rising print book prices (Jacobson, 2018). Lack of a materials and equipment replacement plan encourages librarians to hold onto out-of-date materials and equipment. School librarians who automate circulation and cataloging systems or expand software and online services without outside funding are likely to have fewer funds available for books and audiovisual materials. In these situations, it is essential that school librarians ensure intellectual access to adequate resources through resource sharing, curating free and open digital resources, and interlibrary loan.

PRIVACY AND PROTECTION

State and federal laws can be confusing and a lack of understanding about them can lead school librarians to inadvertently erect barriers to intellectual access to library resources. Unlike materials selection policies, few school libraries have regulations that address privacy issues—and that can make it difficult for you to respond authoritatively when asked about learner records. There are also mixed feelings about saying no to parents, who have fiscal and personal responsibility over their children's library use and feel they have a right to know more about the kinds of books and materials their kids check out.

Most states safeguard the confidentiality of school library records of minors. No state law gives educators or principals the right to access learners' library circulation records. In many states, parents do not have rights to see circulation record either. On the federal level, the 1974 Family Educational Rights and Privacy Act (FERPA) protects the confidentiality of learner education records. Library circulation records are considered education records under FERPA and cannot generally be disclosed absent consent of the parent unless there's a "legitimate educational interest" (such as an educator checking a learner's standardized test scores or previous year's attendance), an emergency in which information is needed to protect a learner's health and safety, or a court order or subpoena. State and federal library record privacy laws that apply to learners are often confusing and incomplete; school librarians should work with their colleagues to ensure that a clear district-level library privacy policy is crafted to further protect learners' rights. ALA (1986) advises all librarians to:

- Formally adopt a policy that specifically recognizes its circulation records and other records identifying the names of library users to be confidential.
- Advise all librarians and library employees that such records shall not be made available to any agency of state, federal, or local government except pursuant to such process, order or subpoena as may be authorized under the authority of, and pursuant to, federal, state, or local law relating to civil, criminal, or administrative discovery procedures or legislative investigative power.

- Resist the issuance of enforcement of any such process, order, or subpoena until such time as a proper showing of good cause has been made in a court of competent jurisdiction.

Besides treating all users fairly when enforcing circulation rules, the major ethical concern in the area of circulation is confidentiality. American Library Association's (ALA) Code of Ethics addresses this important principle of librarianship by noting that "We protect each library user's right to privacy and confidentiality with respect to information sought or received and resources consulted, borrowed, acquired or transmitted" (ALA, 2008). Almost all states have confidentiality laws that apply to libraries. Some of the state laws include school libraries, while others do not. Whether or not you live in a state that has passed legislation on the confidentiality of school library circulation records, it is important to try to protect the privacy of learners and educators. Displaying overdue lists of materials by linking them to learner names is not ethical. Supplying information about a learner's or an educator's reading habits is also not appropriate. If a person asks who has a particular book checked out, it is not ethical to provide that information, but you may tell the person requesting that information that you will try to *recall* the material. Such a recall will let the person who has the material checked out know that someone else is requesting the use of that particular item.

Sometimes there may be legitimate reasons to share information about the materials that a child has checked out of the library. In the lower grades, educators or parents may need to help learners locate the books they have checked out. However, the privacy rights of older learners, particularly teenagers, should be protected, and any circulation issues should be discussed directly with these learners. If you fear that a learner may be checking out information that might be used to injure themselves or someone else, then obtaining some guidance from the school administrator or guidance counselor is warranted.

Although rare, there are times when a school librarian may feel compelled to violate a learner's privacy rights out of a concern for his well-being. In fact, educators are required by law to report suspected child abuse, but there are also other potential dangers, such as bullying or severe depression. As a school librarian, you're in a unique position to observe kids outside the classroom and are likely to notice significant changes in their personality, circle of friends, or degree of sociability. Address these actions directly, gently, and with an assurance of confidentiality. Explain your concerns and possible alternative actions the learner could take. If the behavior persists, refer the matter to the school counselor.

Placing materials on restricted shelves and only allowing certain learners to check out the items or requiring a parental signature to let a learner see restricted materials also infringes on the intellectual freedom of patrons by restricting access to information. Additionally, if a learner is checking out a book that a librarian thinks may be too difficult or may contain advanced information, it may be appropriate to provide some reading guidance, but the final decision on whether to check out a book should rest with the learner.

As Table 13.2 shows, FERPA is but one law that governs children's privacy. The Child Internet Protection Act (CIPA) requires schools to have technology measures and policies in place that protect learners from harmful materials including those that are obscene and pornographic. Any harmful content contained within inappropriate sites will be blocked. Students must be educated about digital citizenship and adhere to an

TABLE 13.2. KEY LEGISLATION PERTAINING TO INFORMATION ACCESS, PRIVACY, AND SAFETY

Legislation Name	Definition	Notes
Children's Internet Protection Act (CIPA)	Schools and libraries subject to CIPA may not receive the discounts offered by the E-rate Internet service discount program unless they certify that they have an Internet safety policy that includes technology protection measures to block or filter Internet access to pictures that are: (a) obscene; (b) child pornography; or (c) harmful to minors. Before adopting this Internet safety policy, schools and libraries must provide reasonable notice and hold at least one public hearing or meeting. CIPA has two additional requirements: (1) Internet safety policies must include monitoring the online activities of minors; and (2) schools must educate minors about appropriate online behavior, including interacting with other individuals on social networking websites and in chat rooms, and cyberbullying awareness and response.	• According to Supreme Court Justice Rehnquist "[a]ssuming that such erroneous blocking presents constitutional difficulties, any such concerns are dispelled by the ease with which patrons may have the filtering software disabled. When a patron encounters a blocked site, he need only ask a librarian to unblock it or (at least in the case of adults) disable the filter."
Children's Online Privacy Protection Act (COPPA)	COPPA is a law passed by the U.S. Congress in 1998 to specifically protect the privacy of children under the age of 13 by requesting parental consent for the collection or use of any personal information of website users.	COPPA allows schools to act as agents for parents in providing consent for the online collection of students' personal information within the school context. COPPA allows website operators to collect personal information from participating children where a school has contracted with an operator to collect personal information from students for the use and benefit of the school.

TABLE 13.2.   CONTINUED

Legislation Name	Definition	Notes
The Family Educational Rights and Privacy Act (FERPA) (20 U.S.C. § 1232g; 34 CFR Part 99)	FERPA protects the privacy of student education records. FERPA gives parents certain rights to their children's education records. These rights transfer to the student when he or she reaches the age of 18 or attends a school beyond the high school level. Students to whom the rights have transferred are "eligible students." FERPA allows schools to disclose those records, without consent, under specific educational conditions (34 CFR § 99.31).	FERPA prohibits the sharing of library circulation and request records with parents, teachers, and administrators without compelling legal or educational reason.

acceptable use policy (AUP), like the one featured in Figure 13.1, when they use school technology.

Children's Online Privacy Protection Act (COPPA) applies to commercial companies and limits their ability to collect personal information from children under 13. For example, due to COPPA, by default, Google advertising is turned off for Apps for Education users. No personal learner information may be collected for commercial purposes.

How can you protect learners' right to privacy in the library while responding to information requests from parents, educators, and administrators? These steps, suggested by Adams (2011), can help:

- Talk to your principal about learner privacy in the library and how the district adheres to state and federal laws
- Request that your board of education adopt a privacy policy stating who can access library patron records and the circumstances under which they may be released
- Conduct a privacy audit to determine what learner data you've collected, stored, shared, and used—and then determine what records should be purged
- Develop a library records retention policy, written into your library policy manual, that includes a records-removal schedule and conscientiously maintain it
- Be proactive and educate administrators, educators, and all persons working in the library about the need to keep learner library records confidential
- Create and retain as few learner library records as possible
- Password-protect circulation records and provide different levels of access for the adult library staff, learners, and volunteers
- Fold and staple overdue notices so that only the learner's name—and not the book's title—is visible
- Make sure that learners' reference questions, reserve and interlibrary loan requests, and the types of books they check out are kept confidential

- Don't label and arrange library books by reading levels (a common practice in some schools that use Accelerated Reader) so that learners can observe their classmates' reading levels
- Teach learners how to protect their privacy and to respect the privacy of others
- Encourage parents to speak directly with their children about their reading choices and what they've checked out from the school library

Many commercial companies have produced filters for the Internet, which, according to the companies, eliminate objectionable materials. A problem with some of the filters is that they do not always work as intended, for they sometimes block potentially educational sites while permitting access to other inappropriate sites. Software programmers, however, have continually improved the filters and have made them much more sophisticated. The filters can now allow administrators to determine categories of materials to block and to allow various levels of access determined by user passwords. They also allow librarians to override a blocked site.

Many states and school districts have passed legislation dealing with the use of filters on individual computers in schools. Other districts and some states have moved to proxy servers (on external computers) that filter all files before they arrive at individual computers. Some Internet service providers also offer a filtering service for a small fee in addition to their regular Internet service fee.

Much controversy in recent years has been about the use of social networking sites in schools. The ALA addressed the issue in *Minors and the Internet Interactivity: An Interpretation of the Library Bill of Rights* (ALA, 2009) by noting if children and young adults are not allowed to use these sites, they will not learn safe online behavior. These sites are used in many school districts to make it possible for learners to work in groups and to create and exchange information on the web. It is important for school librarians to advocate for the use of social media, content creation, and content sharing in their schools, and to join with educators, administrators, and parents in teaching learners to use the tools and resources in responsible and safe ways.

Regardless of whether a filter on each computer or a proxy server controls Internet access, whether there is open access to the Internet, or whether learners are allowed to use Web 2.0 tools, it is important that a school have a written Internet policy or an acceptable use policy (AUP) that includes parental consent on the use of the Internet. It is essential that school librarians be well acquainted with any policies (state, district, or school) that relate to Internet access in their school libraries.

As Figure 13.1 shows, AUPs should reflect the following considerations:

- A statement addressing the educational uses and advantages of Internet access in the school
- The responsibilities of educators, administrators, and library staff
- The responsibilities of learners
- The role of parent(s) or guardian(s)
- A code of conduct describing how the Internet should be used in the school
- A description of acceptable and unacceptable uses of Internet
- A description of network etiquette
- A description of the consequences for violating the policy, including first offenses and loss of the privilege of using the Internet
- A statement regarding the need to maintain personal safety and privacy while accessing the Internet
- A statement regarding the need to comply with copyright fair use guidelines

STUDENT ACCEPTABLE USE POLICY (AUP)

Technology in the School District is provided to promote educational excellence through resource sharing, innovation, and communication. Access is provided to users who agree to act in a responsible manner consistent with the educational mission of the School District. Students may not use technology at school unless a signed, current AUP has been submitted.

Due to a federal mandate, filters are used on computers in the School District. The filters are not foolproof and students need to continue to use search engines and websites appropriate for school use.

Network Accounts:
- Users must always log off the network when leaving a computer for any period of time.
- Users may not trespass in any other person's folders, work, or files.
- Users may not log into two computers at the same time.
- Users may not allow another student access to their account.
- Users may not download application programs.
- Users may not stream music/audio/video, play games, or access social media unless under a teacher's supervision.
- Users are responsible for keeping backup copies of their data.
- Users may not employ the network/Internet for commercial purposes.
- Users will adhere to the Bring Your Own Device (BYOD) Policy when using personal technology at school.
- School district employees are not liable for any data or device lost, damaged, or unavailable due to technical or other difficulties

Ethical Use:
- Users may not cause malicious or intentional damage to school technology.
- Users may not tamper with default or teacher-created settings on any school owned computers.
- Users may not plagiarize or violate copyright law in any way from any source (see Honor Policy on next page).
- Users may not send, display, or receive messages, pictures, or other content which are abusive, obscene, sexually inappropriate, threatening, racially offensive, considered harassment, or offensive to human dignity.
- Users must comply with state laws regarding cyber bullying. Cyber bullying is willful and repeated harm inflicted through the use of computers, cell phones, and other digital devices.
- Users may not intentionally waste limited resources (paper, ink, toner, CDs, DVDs, etc.).
- Inadvertent access to inappropriate content at school must be reported to a teacher or administrator immediately.
- Users should never reveal their personal information or that of others.
- The School District cannot be held responsible for improper student use of the technology or for data or device loss or damage unavailable due to technical or other difficulties.
- When using technology, students will adhere to the School District's Academic Honor Code.

Cell Phones:
- No phone may be used during the school day unless an administrator approves a teacher's specific educational application.
- Cell phones must be off, or set to silent to minimize distractions. Cell phones should be stored during school hours unless being used for classroom

It is the users' responsibility to abide by the rules set forth in this policy. Violations will result in an immediate loss of access and will be referred to an administrator for disciplinary action.

We have read, understand, and agree to follow the guidelines set forth in this Acceptable Use Policy. Please return this signed document to the School Office or the school library.

Student's Signature _____

Parent / Guardian: _____

Date: _____

Figure 13.1. Student Acceptable Use Policy

- A statement explaining that the use of the Internet is a privilege and not a right
- A signature form that will be signed by the Internet user (and usually by a parent or guardian)
- Assurance that the policy will be enforced
- A disclaimer absolving the school or school district from responsibility
- A statement that the policy is in compliance with state and federal telecommunication rules and regulations

Many actual Internet policies of school districts are available online. Some of these are listed at the end of the chapter under Helpful Multimedia. Ideally you should have your Internet policy examined by a lawyer. Many school districts have consulting lawyers for such tasks.

The agreement form that users are asked to sign before using computers or the Internet in a school should be clearly written and easy to understand.

SELECTION AND CENSORSHIP

What is the difference between selection and censorship? Selection is by nature exclusive. In choosing materials to include in the collection, the school librarian excludes the materials not chosen. Selection and censorship can be differentiated. Selection is a process of choosing among materials. The choices are relative as one item is compared with others. In choosing materials, the librarian strives to give each item fair consideration and makes a concerted effort to suppress personal biases. In censorship, an individual or a group attempts to impose certain values on others by limiting the availability of one or more items. By examining definitions of selection and censorship, one can see how censorship creates barriers to intellectual freedom and how selection can promote intellectual freedom.

Reichman (1993) described the differences between selection and censorship by explaining that selection is conducted by trained professionals who are familiar with resources and choices, as well as being guided by meeting educational purposes. Censors, on the other hand, look for reasons to exclude materials from a collection.

Censorship can be described in terms of who is doing the questioning, which materials they are questioning, what is being questioned in those materials, and how the questions are handled. Policies and procedures to guide these situations are described in Chapter 6, "Selection."

Common objections to materials include sexuality (including sexual orientation), profanity, obscenity, immorality, witchcraft, nudity, occultism, and violence. Less frequently cited reasons include incest, mental illness, and slavery. Censors state family values and the immaturity of learners as reasons for their challenges. The list of those who initiate challenges is long. Individuals include parents and other members of learners' families, educators, learners, principals, and other school administrators, school support staff, community members, school library supervisors, library support staff, and even librarians. Groups include school boards, local government officials, and organized groups who share political or religious beliefs.

Self-Censorship

Unfortunately, some school librarians' choices are colored by their personal values, rather than commitment to intellectual freedom. Setting aside one's biases or special interests when making selections for a school library collection is not easy for some librarians. However, it is necessary that this be done if school librarians are to follow ALA's Code of Ethics, which states that "We do not advance private interests at the expense of library users, colleagues, or our employing institutions" and that "We distinguish between our personal convictions and professional duties and do not allow our personal beliefs to interfere with fair representation" (ALA, 2008).

Knowing one's self is a prerequisite for selection. School librarians should be aware of their own biases and preferences so that personal prejudices do not inadvertently affect selection decisions. A school librarian with a strong belief in higher education may be tempted to purchase more college-oriented materials than items for vocational courses. A librarian who advocates online searching as a major teaching tool may be overzealous in budgeting for online services. A librarian whose hobby is cinema may buy numerous materials about movies and equipment for movie production. College preparatory materials, online databases, books on cinema, and movie production equipment are all worthy resources; however, the librarian's personal interests should not unduly influence selection decisions.

When you next visit a school library, examine the collection. Can you detect any bias on the selector's part? Does this indicate the need to involve others in the selection process? One purpose of the collection is to fulfill the needs of everyone in the school. If you sense that your personal views may be outweighing your professional judgment, seek other people's opinions.

Intellectual Safety

One of the movements very influential in the writing of AASL's recent standards was ASCD's Whole Child initiative (AASL, 2018). One of the basic tenets of this document was that every child has a right to be educated in an environment in which they are healthy, safe, challenged, and engaged (ASCD, 2019). A school librarian's aim is to establish a library with a collection that allows a child to feel comfortable and relaxed, stimulated and challenged, and joyful and creative. The collection should contain a variety of activities and visual aids to engage learners while educating them. In this library, there are plenty of cozy spaces for children to explore a book or other resource, worry free, to allow their imaginations to soar. Warm and friendly school librarians help learners feel comfortable asking any question. A school library is a space where learners should not have to fret over the prospect of not being able to find or do what they need (e.g., get a book, read, learn, do homework, use the Internet, attend a program) because of proximity, bullies, an unhelpful staff, a lacking collection, or a cold and uninviting atmosphere.

Learners should never feel lost or frustrated to the point of giving up when they are in the library working on an assignment. School librarians are there to give them strategies for completing assignments that their educator may not have thought of. Learners will likely come to the library for assigned research and projects, so it is really important that it have materials that fit not just learners' immediate information needs, but also their learning styles. Effective school librarians help and encourage learners through foster anxiety-free library visits through activities that allow learners to work together, understand books and resources deeply, and share their love of the library and its collection in multiple ways.

Copyright and Intellectual Property

As respecters of creative contributions, school librarians have a responsibility to ensure that copyright laws are honored. Because school librarians now foster learner creation of information with the collection's resources as well as learner consumption of these resources, a detailed understanding of various approaches to copyright and intellectual property has become very important. These professional responsibilities include educating learners and educators and learners about fair use guidelines and the copyright laws, placing copyright notices near copy machines and computers, identifying copyrighted materials, helping learners and educators secure appropriate protections for their works;

and monitoring the use of copyrighted materials. Chapter 8, "Criteria by Format," describes copyright regulations for various formats.

Copyright is granted to the creators of works to protect their interest in the work and to encourage people to disseminate information. Copyright law is intended to protect against unauthorized printing, publishing, importing, or selling of multiple copies of a work. A fair use law was developed to provide guidelines in the use of copyrighted materials.

The "fair use" aspect of copyright is intended to balance the interest of the copyright owners with the needs of the users. It is a concept that recognizes that certain uses of copyright-protected works do not require permission from the copyright holder or its agent. There are four requirements that must be passed to meet the law: the purpose and character of use; the nature of the work; the amount, substantially or portion; and the potential market. However, fair use "Creative Commons" is a licensing approach that creates a modified copyright zone rather than copyright-free public domain zone or restricted traditional copyright zone for creators who want to be generous and give their works away. All Creative Commons licenses impose some conditions, and some impose more than others. Table 13.3 compares the three approaches.

Educators are allowed to make copyrighted material available to learners in class, workshops, informal teaching, and school-related websites. They should use material relevant to the topic, and provide proper attribution and citation. All educators are allowed to use copyrighted materials to create lesson plans, materials, and so on to apply the principles of media literacy in an educational context. They should credit and cite sources and use only what is necessary for the educational goal.

Students strengthen their creative and digital citizenship skills by creating content in which they express themselves and communicate their learning. Content creation can foster a deeper understanding of knowledge construction, which is a key element of learning. School librarians should ensure that learners do not use material as a substitute for their own creative efforts; learners should be able to understand and demonstrate how their use of a copyrighted work transforms or repurposes the original.

Students learn most when they are expected to behave in a responsible manner as creators of media and are encouraged to reach audiences beyond the classroom. Student work incorporating the use of copyrighted material may be distributed to wide audiences if it meets the transformational standard of fair use. Educators should explore with learners the differences between material that is Creative Commons licensed, material that is in the public domain or otherwise openly available, and copyrighted material subject to fair use. Providing proper attribution also should be emphasized. If learners wish to distribute their work more broadly, then educators should model the real-life permissions process and emphasize both how the process works and how it affects the creation of media.

More information about each of these sets of guidelines can be found in Helpful Multimedia section at the end of this chapter. Sources for copyright guidelines for resource sharing are included in this chapter under Additional Readings.

ISSUES WITH PHYSICAL ACCESS

Physical barriers to access limit the use of resources and restrict the number of people who can use them. The physical environment of the school library can create limitations: lack of seating and workspace, shelving beyond people's reach, lack of electrical outlets for equipment, or an insufficient number of terminals. Barriers created by administrative decisions include rigid schedules, limited hours for use, and limited learner pass systems.

TABLE 13.3. COMPARISON OF INTELLECTUAL PROPERTY APPROACHES

Fair Use	Creative Commons	Public Domain
• Certain uses of copyright-protected works do not require permission from the copyright holder or its agent.	• Creative Commons is a nonprofit organization that provides free licenses and other legal tools to mark creative work with the freedom the creator wants it to have.	• Works that are not protected by intellectual property laws may be used by anyone without obtaining permission, but no one can ever own them.
• Copyright-protected works for may be used for commentary, parody, news reporting, research and education.	• Works alongside copyright, so you can modify your copyright terms to best suit your needs.	• Collections of public domain material may be protected by the "collective works" copyright. For example, you may use individual images within a collection without permission but not the entire collection.
• To decide whether a use of copyrighted material is fair use, courts consider the following guidelines and best practices:	• Creators choose a from set of conditions they wish to be applied to their work:	• Works arrive in the Public Domain in four ways: expiration of copyright; failure to renew copyright; dedication (the owner deliberately places the work in the public domain); or no copyright protection is available for the type of work.
• What is the purpose and character of the use?	**Attribution:** Others may copy, distribute, display, and perform your copyrighted work—and derivative works based upon it—but only if they give credit the way you request.	
• What is the nature of the copyrighted work?		
• What is the amount of the portion used?	**Share Alike:** Others may distribute derivative works only under a license identical to the license that governs your work.	
• What is the effect of the use upon the potential market for, or value of, the copyrighted work?		
• Did the unlicensed use "transform" the material by using it for a different purpose than that of the original, or did it just repeat the work for the same intent and value as the original?	**Noncommercial:** Others may copy, distribute, display, and perform your work and derivative works based upon it for noncommercial purposes only.	
• Was the material used appropriate in kind and amount, considering the nature of the copyrighted work and of the use?	**No Derivative Works:** Others may, distribute, display, and perform only verbatim copies of your work, not derivative works based upon it.	

Many states have set requirements for school library facilities to ensure that the library space meet minimum access requirements. Examples of those guidelines are in the Additional Readings section of this chapter.

Beyond these policy-level considerations, school librarians are legally required to provide their collections in physically accessible environments. In 1975, the U.S. Individuals with Disabilities Education Act (IDEA) delineated the inherent rights and special needs of children with disabilities. This act allocated billions of dollars for individual states to provide a free and appropriate education in a least restrictive environment (LRE) (U.S. Department of Education, n.d.). The latest revision to this law took place in 2004 when IDEA was changed to the Individuals with Disabilities Education Improvement Act (IDEIA). IDEIA's impact on school library programs has been well described by Helen R. Adams, "Because of this federal legislation, learners meeting the various definitions of 'disabled' are educated with their peers instead of being isolated and they have the right to be active users of the library media center" (2009, 54).

The physical facilities of a school must accommodate learners with disabilities by providing an LRE. An LRE has led to many complementary federal regulations including those that mandate that any facilities built with federal funds, such as libraries and schools, be accessible to persons with disabilities. The combined ADA–ABA guidelines (U.S. Access Board, 2004) prohibit discrimination against persons with disabilities and increased access features in public places. Because of these laws, public schools must provide learning environments with counters and workspaces to accommodate learners in wheelchairs, facilities that are wheelchair-accessible with elevators or ramps of appropriate gradient, and signs that include Braille. In 1998, Section 508 of the amendment to the Rehabilitation Act of 1973 mandated publicly funded institutions make all methods of information and communications technology, including the Internet, accessible, via design, format, or assistive technology to persons with disabilities.

Formats and Assistive Technologies

Learners with special needs use the same range of formats that other learners use, but in some cases alternatives or adaptations are necessary. For instance, paperback books are ideal for learners with upper extremity weakness. Learners with cognitive disabilities may find audio, video, toys, and multimedia formats useful. Large print books and magazines are helpful to learners with visual disabilities.

Students with visual disabilities can participate in all school library activities. Useful pieces of equipment include rear projection screens, which permit learners to get close to the screen without blocking images; tape recorders; speech compressors, which eliminate pauses between words and thus reduce the time needed to access recorded materials; talking calculators; and computers with voice recognition software.

In recent years many technologies have been adapted to assist persons with special needs. Frequently these technologies are referred to as *assistive technologies*, which are defined by IDEIA (2004) as "any item, piece of equipment or product system, whether acquired commercially, off the shelf, modified, or customized, that is used to increase or improve functional capabilities of individuals with disabilities." *Assistive Technology: Access for All Students*, 2nd edition (Carpenter, Johnston, & Beard, 2015) discusses the most recent assistive technology for learners who require special accommodation. A chapter on universal design is included in the book. *ATNetwork: Assistive Technology . . . Tools for Living* (Ability Tools, 2010) is a website that provides a variety of information and resources about assistive technologies.

CONCLUSION

This chapter addressed *how* legal and ethical considerations affect learners' access in the collections' materials; Chapter 15 addresses *what* is in the collection to meet all learners' needs and interests. All selection policies should uphold the principle of intellectual freedom for all the users of the library collection. The Code of Ethics of the American Library Association addresses this topic: "We uphold the principles of intellectual freedom and resist all efforts to censor library resources" (ALA, 2008).

As professionals, school librarians' responsibilities for intellectual freedom and access extend to collection activities other than selection. As selectors, school librarians need to be aware of their own biases. As managers of the collection, they need to ensure adequate funds to support the collection. As respecters of the creative contributions of authors, illustrators, and producers, librarians need to ensure the enforcement of copyright practices. Commitments to intellectual freedom and balance in the collection come into play in all of these areas.

A school librarian's professional responsibilities include obtaining funding that will support and strengthen a collection. This may mean presenting facts about the collection, noting its condition, anticipating replacement costs, informing those who make the budget decisions of the average costs of materials, deciding how much of the budget should go toward the purchase of online databases, or seeking outside funding through grants.

Ethical situations and potential dilemmas of collection development are inescapable. School librarians need to be prepared to face these dilemmas, whether they involve challenges to materials in the library, equality of access to needed information, or protecting the intellectual freedom rights of young people. Every school librarian should be familiar with the Code of Ethics of the American Library Association and be ready to support the principles on which librarianship is based. It is important to have written policies and procedures for any potential collection development issue that might be encountered. Considering possible scenarios that involve ethical issues and discussing professional responsibilities with other professionals will help prepare school librarians for the real situations that occur in their schools. Students need to know that their privacy will be respected and their records kept confidential in the school library. At the very least, they should be able to read and borrow materials free from the scrutiny of others. They should also be able to seek information on a topic without disclosing the subject of their research.

DISCUSSION QUESTIONS

Think about how you would handle the following situations and discuss them with your colleagues:

1. A school board member removes books from a high school library because a citizen said the books contain offensive language. Neither the citizen nor the board member has read the books in question.
2. A learner who rides a bus to school tells you that he does not have Internet access at home and he has no study hall period in which to complete a research assignment that his social studies educator has given.
3. The principal checks out some books that have gay and lesbian characters in them. He fails to return them, but offers to pay for them.

4. Your library clerk tells a high school parent that the parent's daughter is checking out books about abortion.
5. One of your educators is checking out numerous DVDs and returning them the following morning. You suspect that she is making copies of the DVDs at home.
6. The band director is using a copy machine in the school library to make copies of a piece of music that is going to be played by learners at an upcoming school concert.
7. A high school educator comes into the school library after school hours and tries to access pornographic websites.
8. A parent comes into your middle school library and asks that you restrict her son from checking out any graphic novels.
9. The school board informs you that it wants the materials budget to be spent on online databases this year, with no new purchases of print materials.
10. The assistant principal, whose hobby is antiques, has requested that you purchase 15 books on various types of antiques and antique collecting.
11. A parent comes to the library to inform you that her family is moving and she needs a list of all the books checked out by her high school son so she can make certain all books that have been checked out are returned before the family moves.
12. Two high school learners come to the library and ask you to help them obtain some interlibrary loan materials that will describe how to build a bomb.

REFERENCES

Ability Tools. (2010). ATNetwork: assistive technology . . . tools for living. Retrieved from http://abilitytools.org/

Adams, H. R. (2009). Access for learners with disabilities. *School Library Media Activities Monthly, 25*(10): 54.

Adkins, D., Brendler, B., Townsend, K., & Maras, M. (2019, December). Rural school libraries anchoring community mental health literacy. *Qualitative and Quantitative Methods in Libraries, 8*(4), 425–435. Retrieved from http://www.qqml-journal.net/index.php/qqml/article/view/520.

American Association of School Librarians (AASL). (2018). National school library standards for learners, school librarians, and school libraries. Chicago, IL: American Library Association

American Library Association (ALA). (1986). Policy on confidentiality of library records. Retrieved from http://www.ala.org/advocacy/intfreedom/statementspols/otherpolicies/policyconfidentiality

American Library Association (ALA). (2008). Code of Ethics of the American Library Association. Retrieved from http://www.ala.org/advocacy/proethics/codeofethics/codeethics

American Library Association (ALA). (2009). Minors and internet interactivity: An interpretation of the Library Bill of Rights. Retrieved from http://www.ala.org/advocacy/sites/ala.org.advocacy/files/content/intfreedom/statementspols/otherpolicies/minorsinteractivityD.pdf.

American Library Association (ALA). (2020). State of America's libraries 2020: School libraries. Retrieved from http://www.ala.org/news/state-americas-libraries-report-2020/school-libraries

ASCD. (2019). The learning compact renewed: Whole child for the whole world. Retrieved from http://files.ascd.org/pdfs/programs/WholeChildNetwork/2020-whole-child-network-learning-compact-renewed.pdf

Board of Education, Island Trees, New York v. Pico (1982).

Carpenter, L. A., Johnston, L. B., & Beard, L. A. (2015). *Assistive technology: Access for all Students*, 3rd edition. Boston, MA: Pearson.

Deye, S. (2015). Expanding broadband access for all learners. National Council of State Legislatures. Retrieved from https://www.ncsl.org/Portals/1/Documents/educ/broadband_final.pdf

Federal Communications Commission (FCC). (2020). 2020 broadband deployment report. Retrieved from https://docs.fcc.gov/public/attachments/FCC-20-50A1.pdf

Individuals with Disabilities Education Improvement Act of 2004. Pub. L. No. 108–446, § 118 Stat. 2647.

Jacobson, L. (2018, March 1). Big fish, small budget: Insights from SLJ's spending survey. *School Library Journal.* Retrieved from: https://www.slj.com/?detailStory=big-fish-small-budget-insights-sljs-2017-spending-survey

LaRose, R., Stover, S., Gregg, J., & Straubhaar, J. (2011). The impact of rural broadband development: Lessons from a natural field experiment. *Government Information Quarterly, 28*(1), 91–100. doi:10.1016/j.giq.2009/12.013

Lukenbill, W. B., & Lukenbill, J. F. (2007). Censorship: What do school library specialists really know? A consideration of learners' rights, the law and implications for a new education paradigm. *School Library Media Research, 10.* http://www.ala.org/aasl/sites/ala.org.aasl/files/content/aaslpubsandjournals/slr/vol10/SLMR_Censorship_V10.pdf

Mardis, M. A. (2016). Beyond the glow: Children's broadband access, digital learning initiatives, and academic achievement in rural Florida. *Journal of Educational Multimedia and Hypermedia, 25*(1), 53–74.

Mardis, M. A., Everhart, N. E., Johnston, M., Baker, S., & Newsum, J. (2010, September 1). From paper to pixel: Digital textbooks and Florida schools. Retrieved from http://www.palmcenter.fsu.edu/documents/digitaltextbooks_whitepaper.pdf

Mardis, M. A., Hoffman, E. S., & Marshall, T. E. (2008). A new framework for understanding educational digital library use: re-examining digital divides in U.S. schools. *International Journal on Digital Libraries, 9*(1), 19–27. doi:10.1007/s00799-008-0035-z

Morse and the Juneau School Board et al. v. Frederick, 551 U.S. 393 (2007).

Moshman, D. (1986). Children's intellectual rights: A First Amendment analysis. In D. Moshman (ed.), *Children's Intellectual Rights* (pp. 25–38). San Francisco, CA: Jossey-Bass.

Reichman, H. (1993). *Censorship and selection: Issues and answers for schools.* Chicago, IL: American Library Association; Arlington, VA: American Association of School Administrators.

State Educational Technology Directors Association (SETDA). (2019, November). Broadband imperative III: Driving connectivity, access and student success. Retrieved from https://www.setda.org/wp-content/uploads/2019/11/SETDA_Broadband-Imperative-III_110519.pdf

Tinker v. Des Moines Independent Community School District, 393 U.S. 503 (1969).

U.S. Access Board. (2004). American with Disabilities Act and Architectural Boundaries Act Accessibility Guidelines. Retrieved from https://www.access-board.gov/aba/

U.S. Department of Education. (n.d.). About IDEA. Retrieved from https://sites.ed.gov/idea/about-idea/

ADDITIONAL READINGS

Adams, H. (2011, April 1). The privacy problem. *School Library Journal.* Retrieved from https://www.slj.com/?detailStory=the-privacy-problem

Adams, H. R. (2011). Solo librarians and intellectual freedom: Perspectives from the field. *Knowledge Quest, 40*(2), 30–35.

Barber, R. (2011). My experience with library censorship and some suggestions. *Library & Media, 39*(1), 11–13.

Butler, R. P. (2009). *Smart copyright compliance for schools: A how-to-do-it manual.* New York: Neal-Schuman.

Chmara, T. (2012). Privacy and e-books. *Knowledge Quest, 40*(3), 62–65

Hill, R. (2010). The problem of self-censorship. *School Library Monthly, 27*(2), 9–12.

Kurtts, S., Dobbins, N., & Takemae, N. (2012). Using assistive technology to meet diverse learner needs. *Library Media Connection, 30*(4), 22–23.

Mates, B. T. (2010). Assistive technologies. *American Libraries, 41*(10), 40–42.

Scales, P. R. (2010). The blame game. *School Library Journal, 56*(1), 16.

Scales, P. R. (2010). *Protecting intellectual freedom in your school library*. Chicago, IL: American Library Association.

Simpson, C. (2010). *Copyright for schools: A practical guide*. Santa Barbara, CA: Linworth.

Simpson, C. (2011). *Copyright catechism II: Practical answers to everyday school dilemmas*. Santa Barbara, CA: Linworth.

Stripling, B., Williams, C., Johnston, M., & Anderton, H. (2010). Minors & internet interactivity: A new interpretation of the LBOR. *Knowledge Quest, 39*(1), 38–45.

HELPFUL MULTIMEDIA

American Library Association. (2008). Professional ethics. Retrieved from http://www.ala.org/tools/ethics

American Library Association. (2011). Intellectual freedom issues. Retrieved from http://www.ala.org/advocacy/intfreedom

American Library Association. (2017). Privacy. Retrieved from http://www.ala.org/advocacy/node/466/#statements

American Library Association. (2017, January 21). Library privacy checklist for students in K–12 schools. Retrieved http://www.ala.org/advocacy/privacy/checklists/students

American Library Association. (2020, December 11). Library privacy guidelines for students in K–12 schools. Retrieved http://www.ala.org/advocacy/privacy/guidelines/students

American Library Association and Privacy Revolution. (2015). Choose privacy every day. Retrieved from https://chooseprivacyweek.org/

Coalition for School Networking (CoSN). (n.d.). Protecting privacy in connected learning. Retrieved from http://cosn.org/focus-areas/leadership-vision/protecting-privacy

Crash Course. (2013). Introduction to intellectual property: Crash course IP (6 videos). Retrieved from https://www.youtube.com/playlist?list=PL8dPuuaLjXtMwV2btpcij8S3YohW9gUGN

Federal Communications Commission (FCC). (2019, December 13). Children's Internet Protection Act. Retrieved from http://www.fcc.gov/cgb/consumerfacts/cipa.html

Gaffney, L. (2018, May 11). Librarians, youth reading and intellectual freedom: Historical and contemporary views. Retrieved from https://knowledgequest.aasl.org/librarians-youth-reading-and-intellectual-freedom-historical-and-contemporary-views/

Henderson, C. C. (n.d.). Libraries as creatures of copyright: Why librarians care about intellectual property law and policy. Retrieved from http://www.ala.org/advocacy/copyright/copyrightarticle/librariescreatures

Little, H. B. (2019, November 13). Teaching digital ethics. Retrieved from https://knowledgequest.aasl.org/teaching-digital-ethics/

National Council of Teachers of English. (2011). Censorship by committee. Retrieved from https://ncte.org/blog/2016/09/censorship-by-committee/

Phillips, A. (2014). More than just books: Librarians as a source of support for cyberbullied young adults. *Journal of Research on Libraries and Young Adults, 4*. Retrieved from: http://www.yalsa.ala.org/jrlya/2014/05/more-than-just-books-librarians-as-a-source-of-support-for-cyberbullied-young-adults/

Scholastic. (2011). *Using technology: Why have a technology policy in your school library?* Retrieved from https://www.scholastic.com/librarians/tech/techpolicy.htm

Schrader, A. M. (2009). *Internet access policies: School libraries*. Retrieved from http://www.ualberta.ca/~aschrade/internet/school.htm

Swanson, L., & Schaino, J. (2013). IDEA basics: Least restrictive environments. Retrieved from https://www.youtube.com/watch?v=sc5pgXhyLoQ

CHAPTER 14

The Curriculum

Key Learnings

- Local, state, and national trends affect school curriculum and the school collection.
- Programs that take place beyond the school day often include the school library and should be supported by the collection.
- Using targeted selection materials can help to ensure that the collection supports the curriculum for a range of users.

A major purpose of the collection is to support the school curriculum. The collection should comprise a variety of materials that can be used for inquiry-based learning and for the needs and interests of its users (American Association of School Librarians [AASL], 2018).

The wide range of instructional programs and practices in a school creates many demands upon its library collection. To be well versed about instructional programs, a school librarian must understand the school's approaches to education, be knowledgeable about the curriculum, and be aware of any educational trends that might affect the curriculum.

School librarians are able to help teachers align their instructional focus by providing the necessary technology to locate curriculum-relevant primary sources. This may involve some shifts in budget allocations to make certain that the necessary technology and nonfiction print materials are available.

THE SCHOOL'S PURPOSE

A look at a high school mission statement can illustrate the complexity of demands for educational support. Some high schools serve a single, overriding purpose. Sometimes this purpose is expressed in the name of the institution, with adjectives such as "magnet," "technical," "preparatory," or "alternative." For some schools the purpose is narrowly defined, and thus the role of the school library program can be relatively narrow in scope. More often, a high school serves more than one purpose. A multipurpose or comprehensive high school exerts varied demands on the library collection and presents added challenges to the school librarian. In some comprehensive high schools, the purposes may not be clearly defined, which may lead to problems for budget allocations.

To determine the type or purpose of a school, one should ask the following questions. Is the school a comprehensive high school with both academic and practical courses and departments? Is it a technical school emphasizing specific career-related courses? Is the school a performing arts or technical school offering special programs for talented students? Is there a nontraditional or an alternative program? A school librarian needs to consult with administrators, teachers, curriculum coordinators, and students to learn about the school's purposes and programs. The school board's annual report to the community can also offer additional insight into the purposes of the school and its place in the district's overall education plan.

Middle schools and elementary schools also have mission statements. Like high schools, some of these schools have specific purposes that can affect a school library's program and collection. For instance, the Meredith Nicholson Elementary School in Indianapolis has the following mission statement: "We believe in preparing students for their future impact on the world by providing a loving, safe environment of high expectations and best instructional practices so that students grow academically and socially." (Meredith Nicholson Elementary School, n.d.). The school's library website notes that it has a unique video and book collection that highlights their position as an elementary school that primarily facilitates English as a Second Language (ESL) learning.

A school's purpose has implications for the collection. Each of the schools described requires different sources in its collection. Some general materials, such as reference works, may be in the collections of all the schools. In the case of a relatively expensive multivolume work, such as *The New Grove Dictionary of Music and Musicians* (Oxford University Press), all schools may not need to own a copy; however, a school that emphasizes performing arts may want its own copy. The full text of the hardback version (plus other music reference tools) is also available by database subscription at *Grove Music Online*. Being aware of materials available in other schools in the district or through interlibrary loan, as we also discussed in Chapter 4, will also guide collection development tailored to your unique school community.

EDUCATIONAL PROGRAM

A school achieves its purpose through its educational program, the curriculum. The curriculum may be in response to mandated standards of the school district or state, professional organizations, and even federal government issues. The standards may call for specific content, establish sequencing of experiences, prescribe the teaching methods, and define the learner. If a school is teaching to specific standards that have been established

		Math	L. L.	Social Studies	Science
Aug. 30 – Sept. 3	M	*Standard 1: Mathematical Processes* How do American inventions connect to Math? GLE 0606.1.7	*Standard 8: Literature* Short Story **Hatchet** Literary Terms Intro to Theme: Technology. Intro to Literary Terms (Character, Theme, Plot/Conflict, Setting, POV)	*Standard 1: Culture* The influence of science and technology on the development of culture through time. GLE 6.1.06	*Embedded Technology & Engineering* **What kind of engineers are there?** GLE 0607.T/E.1
	T	*Standard 4: Geometry & Measurement* Circumference, diameter, & perimeter GLE 0606.4.3, 0606.4.11	*Standard 8: Literature* Short Story **Hatchet** Literary Terms A closer look: Characterization (Direct & Indirect)	*Standard 1: Culture* The influence of science and technology on the development of culture through time. GLE 6.1.06	*Embedded Technology & Engineering* **Who are Inventors?** GLE 0607.T/E.1
	W	*Standard 4: Geometry & Measurement* The meaning of Pi 0606.4.12	*Standard 8: Literature* Short Story **Hatchet** Literary Terms A closer look: Conflict (Types: Man vs. Man, Nature, Technology, Self)	*Standard 1: Culture* The influence of science and technology on the development of culture through time. GLE 6.1.06	*Embedded Technology & Engineering* **Consequences of technology on social, economic, and political needs of society** GLE 0607.T/E.3
	R	*Standard 1: Mathematical Processes* Build own Ferris Wheel GLE 0606.1.8	*Standard 8: Literature* Short Story **Hatchet** Literary Terms A closer look: Setting How does setting manifest itself in a story?	*Standard 1: Culture* The influence of science and technology on the development of culture through time. GLE 6.1.06	*Embedded Technology & Engineering* **Engineering Design Process** GLE 0607.T/E.2
	F	*Standard 1: Mathematical Processes* Geometry & Measurement Build on Ferris Wheel GLE 0606.1.8	*Standard 8: Literature* Short Story **Hatchet** Literary Terms A closer look: Theme *Standard 2: Communication* Discussion **Discussion of Hatchet & Theme**	*Standard 1: Culture* The influence of science and technology on the development of culture through time. GLE 6.1.06	*Embedded Technology & Engineering* **Experiment on Design** CHK 0607.T/E.1

Figure 14.1. Sample Theme-Based Curriculum Map (Headrick, 2012)

by the state, such as the Common Core State Standards (CCSS), it is essential that you obtain copies of those standards for each of the subject areas and grade levels taught in your school. You need to make certain that you have the print and nonprint resources available to support the teaching of all standards in your state or school district.

Most schools develop curriculum plans to meet the school's purpose or particular standards. A typical curriculum plan includes a statement of goals and objectives, the content teachers must cover, the organization (or sequencing) of that content, scheduling of content, teaching strategies designed to meet the objectives or organizational requirements, and a program for evaluation. Curriculum plans may emphasize one or more of these elements. Each element of the curriculum plan has implications for the library program and its collection. Figure 14.1 illustrates a sample week-long theme-based curriculum plan for sixth grade.

Examine the curriculum plans for your school. This task may be time-consuming since curriculum plans vary in scope, and there may be plans for all subject areas. Some plans are comprehensive, covering all educational programs; others cover specific subjects or specific learning situations. They may also be called curriculum maps, schedules, and five-day thematic units. Curriculum plans may be general or give very specific directives to teachers. The general approach outlines the broad tasks of the school and identifies the teachers' responsibilities. More specific curriculum plans prescribe when, how, to whom, with what, and under what conditions teachers are to function. Specific plans may also offer more direct practical information for the school librarian than the general curriculum. However, both types of plans will be helpful guides for deciding material purchases for the school library collection.

An analysis of a curriculum plan can indicate what content or subject matter is required or recommended, when and to what depth it will be covered, and how it will be presented. If several classes will be studying the same unit simultaneously, you most likely will need to have duplicate copies of some materials. In other cases, the school librarian can work with teachers to decide whether certain units can be taught at different times of the year. The curriculum plan might indicate why a unit is recommended for a specific time and whether altering its sequence would be detrimental to the learning process.

Many school staff go through an involved process of curriculum planning and present their curriculum in a graphic representation called a *curriculum map*. Generally, all members of the teaching staff, including the school librarian, participate in the planning. Curriculum maps present data about implemented curriculum, using data collected from individual teachers. These may then be integrated into grade levels or subject areas. The maps offer a scope of what is taught, the sequence of the content taught, the processes involved, and the assessments that are utilized to evaluate student learning. By reviewing curriculum maps, educators can determine if there are redundancies or gaps in the curriculum, as well as documenting the relationship of components of the curriculum with intended student learning outcomes. The maps also can help identify interdisciplinary opportunities. Curriculum maps are reviewed and updated on a regular basis. For further information about curriculum mapping, including website links to actual curriculum maps, refer to listings under Helpful Multimedia at the end of this chapter.

RANGE OF COURSE OFFERINGS

To explore a school's unique demands on its collection, you should examine the range of courses the school offers. A high school may offer basic courses in art, computer education, dance, drama, foreign languages, health, humanities, language arts, library media, mathematics, music, physical education, safety and driver education, family and consumer services, science, and social studies. The social studies department may offer anthropology, economics, global studies, and history. History courses may include African, Asian, U.S., and world history. The school may offer courses in agribusiness, natural resources, business, health occupations, industrial occupations, marketing, public-service occupations, and technology. Additional courses may be designed to meet the needs of exceptional students, including gifted students and students with disabilities.

The state department of education in each state most likely has lists of approved courses. This information may be available through the department's website or obtained from the principal or curriculum coordinator.

If a collection is to support a wide variety of courses, it must provide some level of coverage for all subjects. Again, you will need to ask some questions. Is the subject covered at an introductory, advanced, or remedial level? Are there honors courses? Do honors students have access to a nearby college collection? Has a shift in the local population created a need for materials that present concepts in simple English or bilingual formats? How are the subjects organized or approached? For example, is art history taught as a separate course, or is it integrated into a study of humanities?

Extracurricular groups and programs create demands for specific subject materials. A debate society needs timely information and opinions on controversial issues. A drama club needs plays, information about costumes, and ideas for set designs. After-school programs require information about crafts and sports. As coding (writing computer code) becomes more popular, you'll need to support these students with resources and equipment.

New programs or changes in organization create new demands. An example is the case of an actual school district in which it was decided to open a centrally located high school library to serve students from all schools in the district during after-school hours and on Saturdays. School librarians from various schools took turns overseeing the school library. They found that the reference collection needed to expand in order to meet the needs of students from diverse programs. In another community, students in adult education programs began meeting in a high school during evening hours. They had access to the high school library. Although the students used some of the materials that daytime students used, they also needed materials to support additional subjects taught in the adult education programs; thus other resources were added to the collection.

SPECIAL PROGRAMS AND EVENTS

Often, schools initiate special programs that will influence the school library collection and activities. Usually these occur after much discussion and planning at the district level. It is important for school librarians to be involved in these discussions. Sometimes, the programs are long term, lasting several years; in other cases, a program may be in place for only a year or two. Examples of such programs are literature-based reading programs and electronic reading programs.

In a literature-based reading program, trade books (the types of books found in libraries and bookstores in contrast to instructional textbooks) are used to teach reading to students. In these programs, large amounts of print materials must be made available to teachers and students. If a literature-based reading program is used across disciplines, as is usually the case, then these materials must include both fiction and nonfiction materials. Often, these programs are set up around thematic units developed by individual teachers or more frequently by grade-level faculty. It is essential that a school librarian be aware of these themes and the teachers' plans to use library materials in thematic units. Figure 14.2 is a sample of a form that could be used to maintain records of units taught each year. This form can be put online using a service like Wufoo (http://www.wufoo .com/) or Google Drive so that teachers can complete the forms from anywhere and the forms are automatically stored for you.

As Figure 14.2 suggests, when the librarian is armed with a clear idea of the learning needs and outcomes as well as the resource needs, they can be better prepared to assist students and teachers. The school library collection may not be adequate to support the themes the teachers select; thus, the librarian may need to order special materials. Sitting

VOICES FROM THE FIELD

Here is what we do. Each grade level has its own set of goals for the students to reach per nine weeks. There are no limits on what type of book they can read beyond [beyond grade level appropriateness]. The points are part of their English grade; English teachers often let them take tests over books that they read as part of their English class curriculum. The reason we have and still use AR [Accelerated Reader] is just to make sure students are reading. They are required to read 30 minutes a day in advisory. The combination of having a set reading time every day in addition to the required AR points makes reading a very successful program K-12.

—Anonymous LM_NET poster

Unit Information Form

Please help us be prepared to assist your class by providing the following information prior to your unit's start:

Unit Theme:

Grade:

Teacher:

Unit Objectives:

End-of-Unit Student Products (check all that apply):
- ☐ Paper
- ☐ Oral Presentation
- ☐ Powerpoint
- ☐ Web page

- ☐ Image
- ☐ Audio
- ☐ Video
- ☐ Other (please describe)

Information Literacy Skills Required:
- ☐ Identify information need
- ☐ Locate information in a variety of formats
- ☐ Evaluate information quality and applicability
- ☐ Synthesize information and draw conclusions
- ☐ Communicate information via various means
- ☐ Properly cite sources
- ☐ Translate findings for a variety audiences

Student Considerations:

Information Resources Required:

Call # or Source (if known)

Special Resource needs:

Date Needed for Resources:
Unit Due Date:

Library Delivery Format
- ☐ Reserve
- ☐ Classroom Cart
- ☐ Pathfinder
- ☐ Facilitated Student Search

Please attach unit plan and any additional information. Thank you!

Figure 14.2. Unit Resource Form

in on grade-level curriculum planning sessions will enable you to know in advance what types and quantities of materials might be needed (frequently sets of particular titles are used in literature-based reading programs). Such a program will greatly affect the monetary demands on the school library budget. It is advisable that you address this topic as early as possible. A meeting with school administrators and faculty may make it possible to shift textbook funds to the school library budget to meet the needs of the literature-based reading program.

Another program that has had great impact on school library collections and programs is the use of electronic reading programs, such as *Accelerated Reader* (produced by Renaissance Learning) and *Scholastic Reading Counts* (produced by Scholastic). In these programs, students read specific books with designated reading levels and take computer tests on those books. Thus, there is much pressure on the school librarian to have specific titles in the library and to have them labeled with reading levels. This may not make it possible for the school librarian to purchase other materials that are needed by the curriculum or that would be of particular interest to students. Also, a school librarian may have a philosophical problem with labeling books that teachers say are to be read by only certain students. These programs exist with much controversy about them including their long-term effects on improving student reading and their impact on collections in school libraries. It is important for you to be aware of these programs and the controversy. If there is discussion about initiating such a program in your school, you should participate in the discussions. Share your views on the programs and the ways that they might impinge on both students and the school library collection. Be thoughtful about how you can implement the reading program in a way that is beneficial to your school—sometimes, this way may not be the "by the book" approach recommended by the program's creator!

Schools often hold special events that need to be supported by the school library resources. Examples of such events are author visits, science fairs, and participation in the Battle of the Books. For such events you will often need to collaborate with classroom teachers to plan the event and provide the necessary library resources.

Whenever there is discussion at your school about initiating a new program, be prepared to share your views by participating in discussions and serving on committees.

EDUCATIONAL REFORMS AND TRENDS

The education standards movement gained momentum with the Clinton administration's Goals 2000 education plan, and that momentum continued with state-level standards prompted by the George W. Bush administration's revision of the Elementary and Secondary Education Act (called No Child Left Behind), which provided an imperative for K–12 curriculum development. Standards-based reform is one of the biggest issues in American K–12 education today, and has been since at least 1989, when the nation's governors met with President George H. W. Bush in Charlottesville, Virginia, to set national education goals (Finn, Petrilli, & Julian, 2006), which are largely still reflected in the current Elementary and Secondary Education Act, the Every Student Succeeds Act (ESSA).

The standards documents produced by various levels of local education agencies and professional teaching associations represent the efforts of education stakeholders to communicate the content and skills necessary for student success. Standards often are written in the format of what students should "know" (content) and "be able to do" (skills and abilities) in particular grades. Standards began in the five core curriculum areas of history, science, mathematics, English/language arts (ELA), and geography, although some states later added other disciplines such as government (civics), economics, and technology.

Standards implementation efforts have always been fraught with complication. Approximately 10 years after the call for states to draft standards, their implementation processes were uneven, at best. The Fordham Institute's *State of State Standards* report (Finn & Petrilli, 2000) includes an analysis of the extent to which national standards had made their way into state curriculum frameworks. For the five core subject areas, most states fared poorly and received failing grades. The Fordham Foundation's third state standards survey (Friedberg et al., 2018) reported that although most states had revised or replaced their standards in many subjects, academic standards were no better in content or execution in 2018 than they were in 2000.

To complicate matters further, the U.S. Department of Education has been unable to establish a relationship between state standards and student achievement on standardized tests such as the National Assessment of Education Progress (NAEP). The state standards movement has yielded a very mixed bag of standards having varying degrees of quality and similarity. Most states that either failed to adopt or made nontrivial changes to the CCSS replaced them with standards that were weaker in both subjects (Friedberg et al., 2018). Because no one could determine the true effect of the standards, the quest for comparability between states began.

Early attempts to fit the standards into the existing educational system were plagued by problems due to competing economic, social, political, and institutional pressures on school administrators, teachers, and parents. The *State of the Standards* surveys (Finn & Petrilli, 2000; Finn, Petrilli, & Julian, 2006; Friedberg et al., 2018) included analyses of the barriers to standards implementation. This closer look at each state's implementation revealed a common set of challenges. In many instances, education officials reported feeling that standards documents were a federal attempt to control the curriculum in schools at the local level. Moreover, educators reported that standardized emphasis on curriculum content did not fit well with the constructivist learning environments they favored and that were promoted by national organizations such as National Council of Teachers of Mathematics (NCTM), National Science Teachers Association (NSTA), and the National Council of Teachers of English (NCTE).

Beyond that, educators were overwhelmed by the amount of curriculum material in the state standards documents. Because many state standards were authored through committee, group compromises often resulted in material that was unrealistic to implement given the length of the school day and year, the availability of qualified teachers, and existing graduation requirements. Add in local politics and a lack of articulation between states and local school districts, and successful implementation was blocked from many directions (Friedberg et al., 2018).

Three states—Massachusetts, California, and Indiana—successfully implemented curriculum frameworks because educational leaders in those states supported it with funding for local districts; allowed external organizations such as companies and higher education institutions to review and endorse standards documents; and reflected a single agreed-upon ideological and pedagogical orientation in each curriculum area. The standards that emerged from these states were clear and jargon-free, and reflected a strong and consistent commitment to learning and teaching each curriculum area (Friedberg et al., 2018). The successes of these three states laid the foundation for national common standards. The adoption of the CCSS and the Next Generation Science Standards (NGSS) by most of the U.S. states has had a great impact on the curriculum of schools.

The Common Core State Standards

Despite political rhetoric during the Trump administration, the U.S. Department of Education did not "kill" the CCSS because it was not their product to eliminate (Greene, 2020). The CCSS has provided a clear and consistent understanding of what students are expected to learn in their K–12 education in order to be prepared for success in college and careers. The CCSS were developed in collaboration with teachers, administrators, and other education experts and were built upon the strengths and lessons of state and international standards. They include rigorous content and the application of knowledge through high-order skills.

The current version of the CCSS is research and evidence based and internationally benchmarked. The standards aim to be understandable and consistent, aligned with college and career expectations, and based on rigorous content and application of knowledge through higher-order thinking skills. The intent of the CCSS authors was to build upon the strengths and lessons of current state standards and look to other top-performing countries to determine how best to prepare all students for success in our global economy and society. To date, 41 states have adopted the CCSS, as Figure 14.3 illustrates. States now are focusing on implementation of the standards. Because it is a state-driven effort, implementation timelines vary.

Figure 14.3. States' 2020 Status for CCSS Adoption

The CCSS are based on the assumption that schools exist to develop competencies in children. The CCSS are expressed as contextual competencies but assume academic competence. Academic competence is what we think of as traditional subject-area mastery; that is, individual competence in the procedures and factual recall within a specific discipline, such as the formula used to determine area in mathematics or spelling in English/language arts. Contextual competence, on the other hand, is based on collaborative work that allows students to infer and apply an appropriate range of interdisciplinary procedures and facts to solve problems or to express and defend a position. This competence might be expressed, for example, through using the formula for area to determine how much tile it requires to cover a floor. Knowledge of word stems might help a student determine the meaning of an unfamiliar word in a text. Both types of competencies are viewed as essential requirements for students to graduate from high school and be prepared to succeed in entry-level careers, introductory academic college courses, and workforce-training programs.

Instructional Shifts for the Common Core

The shift in emphasis from academic to contextual competence required a shift in instructional strategies. Table 14.1 provides an overview of these shifts.

English/language arts includes six main shifts in strategies. The first, "Balancing Informational and Literary Text," requires teachers to help students build competence with a range of texts including—but beyond—novels and short stories. Informational text includes nonfiction work and periodicals. Graphic novels are emphasized as important texts to bring into learning activities. The CCSS concludes with a special section focused on building textual literacy in a number of content areas, including science.

In "Building Knowledge in the Disciplines," students are asked to expand their understanding of the world through text. This shift is directly supported by the expanded use of informational text. To increase the "Staircase of Complexity," students are encouraged not just to read at grade level, but also to challenge themselves to read more-complex texts. Teachers are to provide the time, space, and support for this type of advanced reading. When teachers focus on "Text-Based Answers," students learn to use a variety of texts as evidence from which they synthesize content and construct answers to questions; with a focus on "Writing From Sources," students translate that use of evidence to persuasive writing in which they use evidence from texts to build and express arguments in a written format. Finally, when teachers "Increase Academic Vocabulary," through exposure to increasingly complex texts that are analyzed and synthesized for persuasion, students learn to understand and apply new vocabulary (CCSS Initiative, [n.d.]-b).

TABLE 14.1. INSTRUCTIONAL SHIFTS IN THE COMMON CORE

English/Language Arts	Mathematics
1. Balancing literary and informational text	1. Focus
2. Building knowledge in the disciplines	2. Coherence
3. Staircase of complexity	3. Fluency
4. Text-based answers	4. Deep understanding
5. Writing from sources	5. Applications
6. Academic vocabulary	6. Dual intensity

The CCSS mathematics standards also call for instructional shifts that build and extend the National Council for Teachers of Mathematics (NCTM) processes of problem solving, reasoning and proof, communication, representation, and connections, and the National Research Council (NRC) emphasis on adaptive reasoning, strategic competence, conceptual understanding, procedural fluency, and productive disposition. The CCSS mathematics standards have a new emphasis on application and "habitual inclination to see mathematics as sensible, useful, and worthwhile, coupled with a belief in diligence and one's own efficacy" (CCSS Initiative, [n.d.]-a, 6).

The mathematics standards include fewer topics but a more concentrated focus. Rather than racing to cover many topics in a "mile-wide, inch-deep curriculum," (CCSS Initiative, [n.d.]-a, 3), the standards enable teachers to focus on helping students gain a solid understanding of concepts, a high degree of procedural skill and fluency, and the ability to apply the math they know to solve problems both inside and outside of the class-room. The standards also ask teachers to emphasize coherence by linking topics and thinking across grades so that students do not see mathematics as a list of disconnected topics. Teachers are asked to present mathematics as a coherent body of knowledge com-posed of interconnected concepts. This idea of coherence involves connecting mathematics work to ideas learning in prior grade levels and in other curriculum areas.

To help students meet the standards, educators must pursue three aspects of rigor in the major work of each grade: conceptual understanding, procedural skills and fluency, and application. Teachers should help students access concepts from a number of perspectives; build students' competence, calculation speed, and accuracy through practice; and help students to apply mathematics to problem solving (CCSS Initiative, [n.d.]-c).

Common Core Controversies

Although states are not required to adopt the CCSS, and 45 states signed on before the assessments even were created, some states are beginning to question these decisions. Four states have rescinded their acceptance of the CCSS, leaving a total of 41 states that have formally adopted the standards as of 2020. Objections range from the cost of retooling tests to fears of government control over education and concerns about states being compared to one another and penalized. Often, states are just rebranding the CCSS with their own name to avoid citizens' criticism and concern.

Many states have questioned the cost of implementing the CCSS. States that have to adopt the CCSS must have an 85 percent degree of fidelity. Many states therefore are finding that the time and expertise required to perform this customization require an investment beyond what they can afford (Bauerlein & Stotsky, 2012). As a result, many states are adopting the online tests—e.g., Partnership for Assessment of Readiness for College and Careers or SmarterBalanced—which already are geared toward assessing college and career readiness. These tests are expensive, however, and also require significant technology and bandwidth expenditures (Strauss, 2014).

Another driver of CCSS resistance is a lack of instructional materials that are explicitly linked to the standards (Jobrack, 2012). Commercial textbooks have been found to be inadequate (Samuels, 2012), and although the market potential for educational publishers is enormous (Mickey & Meaney, 2013), many states and districts cannot afford to switch to a new textbook series and instead are turning to free digital materials known as open educational resources (OERs) as a cost-saving approach to accumulating sufficient educational content (Ash, 2012). Even this approach is aspirational, however, because few state education leaders feel that they have access to the curatorial expertise required to ensure an appropriate supply of high-quality OER (Ishmael, 2020). Since the CCSS emphasizes reading in all content areas, school librarians have a great opportunity to provide an abundance of nonfiction materials that support the curriculum.

Next Generation Science Standards

Mirroring the CCSS, in July 2011 the NGSS were published. Created with input from a range of stakeholders including states, the NRC, the NSTA, and the American Association for the Advancement of Science (AAAS), this new set of standards aims to provide consistent science education through all grades, with an emphasis on engineering and technology. The NGSS describe what each student should know in the four domains of science—physical science; life science; earth and space science; and engineering, technology and science application. To date, 20 states have formally adopted standards while 24 states have developed standards derived from the NGSS (NSTA, 2020). Those states are listed in Figure 14.4.

As with the CCSS, the NGSS are focused on helping students become literate in applying scientific concepts and principles so that they will have the skills and knowledge to tackle real-world issues such as water quality and energy conservation. The NGSS are explicitly aligned to the CCSS so that when students are learning about science, they also are enhancing their skills in reading, writing, and math. Figure 14.5 depicts an example of a NGSS standard.

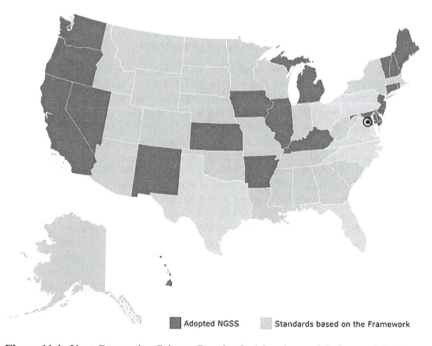

Adopted NGSS   Standards based on the Framework

Figure 14.4. Next Generation Science Standards Adoption and Influenced States (NSTA, 2020)

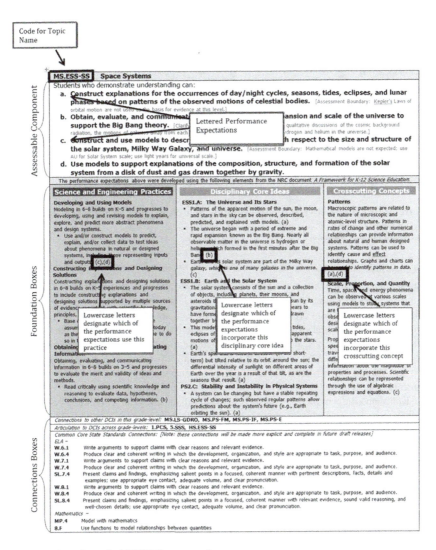

Figure 14.5. Sample NGSS Framework

As Figure 14.5 shows, within each disciplinary area the NGSS standards are internally organized framework is divided into three parts.

- Practices: Describe how scientists build theories and models about the way the world and systems within it work.
- Cross-cutting concepts: Concepts that apply to all four science domains.
- Disciplinary core ideas: The foundational ideas needed for every student to be able to begin their own inquiries and practices.

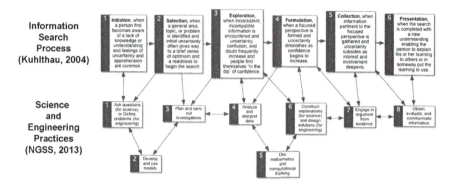

Figure 14.6. Links Between the Information Search Process and Science and Engineering Practices

Each standard begins with performance expectations and provides links between those performance expectations and aspects of each of science and engineering practices, disciplinary core areas, and crosscutting concepts. Each standard concludes with links to specific mathematics and ELA CCSS elements. The NGSS has been lauded for this construction based on the individual performance expectation and its built-in implementation support that links the CCSS to the NGSS. Even on an implementation level, "doing" science and "doing" information searching have an enormous amount of congruence, as Figure 14.6 shows.

Kuhlthau's information search process (Kuhlthau, 2004) is a foundational framework for information seeking in the library that includes a progression through:

- initiation, when a person first becomes aware of a lack of knowledge or understanding, and feelings of uncertainty and apprehension are common;
- selection, when a general area, topic, or problem is identified and initial uncertainty often gives way to a brief sense of optimism and a readiness to begin the search;
- exploration, when inconsistent, incompatible information is encountered and uncertainty, confusion, and doubt frequently increase and people find their confidence flagging;
- formulation, when a focused perspective is formed and uncertainty diminishes as confidence begins to increase;
- collection, when information pertinent to the focused perspective is gathered and uncertainty subsides as interest and involvement deepens; and
- presentation, when the search is completed with a new understanding enabling the person to explain their learning to others or in some way put the learning to use.

Similarly, the NGSS (Achieve & AASL, 2013) explicates eight science and engineering practices that are essential for all students to learn:

- asking questions (for science) and defining problems (for engineering);
- developing and using models;
- planning and conducting investigations;
- analyzing and interpreting data;
- using mathematics and computational thinking;

- constructing explanations (for science) and designing solutions (for engineering);
- engaging in argument from evidence; and
- obtaining, evaluating, and communicating information.

Both frameworks begin with identifying an information need and conclude with an opportunity for self-assessment and reflection.

Although objections to the NGSS have not reached the extent of the criticism engendered by the CCSS, the NGSS has elicited some concerns. Some opponents say that the science standards are vague and stress scientific practices too much instead of covering more theory, and that some states already have standards that are superior to the NGSS. Most notably, the Fordham Institute, producers of the *State of State Standards* reports, gave the NGSS a "C" grade, because the standards lacked essential content, such as the topic of covalent bonding in high school chemistry; overemphasized engineering practices, such as coming up with problems and models to solve them; and failed to integrate sufficient mathematics into science learning (Gross et al., 2013).

Some critics have expressed concern that basic content knowledge is needed before students can understand scientific and engineering practices, or how scientists "do science." Coupled with the lack of clarity specifically in what is expected from teachers, critics are concerned that the standards stress too many things at once and have the potential to overwhelm students (Asif, 2013).

Learning Environments for the Common Standards

Because they reflect a shift in instructional practice and a focus on interdisciplinary connections and applications, the CCSS and NGSS thrive in learning environments that are student-centered, immersive, and provide intuitive access to an adequate quantity and comprehensive range of academically rigorous and relevant learning resources. As Figure 14.7 depicts, there are some learning environment that particularly well suited to the learning tasks of the NGSS and CCSS.

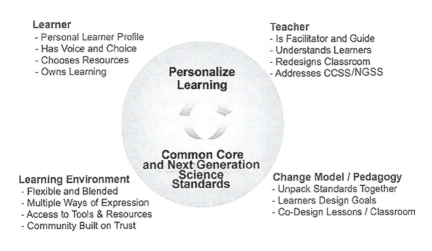

Figure 14.7. Elements of an Optimal CCSS/NGSS Learning Environment

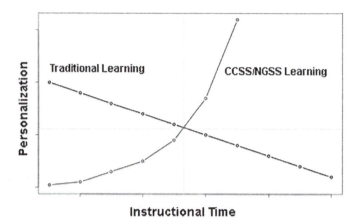

Figure 14.8. Instructional Time and Effort in Common Standards–Based and Traditional Learning

As Figure 14.7 shows, optimal learning environments for the common standards include several key components. The common standards are based on the notion of building not just personal mastery, but personal relevance for the standards. The personalized learning environment requires interplay between the learner, the teacher's role, the learning environment, and the learning approaches employed. The learner should be in an environment that supports metacognition through discussion and individual contemplation regarding what information or topics should be considered, understood, or researched. Students should have a sense of why the learning activity is occurring. Likewise, an environment conducive to the common standards supports self-actualization. Students require the opportunity to reflect and realize the extent to which their own problem-solving abilities are growing as a result of newly acquired knowledge and experiences. Figure 14.8 gives an overview of the shift in instructional effort.

As Figure 14.8 shows, the object of a shift to a common standards–based learning environment is to increase the amount of time students engage in personalized learning and decrease the amount of time teachers spend on traditional explicit instruction. When knowledge is both constructed and deconstructed in the course of a learning activity, students are able to enhance and express the abilities that result from newly acquired knowledge and experiences that displace prior knowledge and experiences.

Contextual or application competencies and their associated instructional shifts provide great entry points for librarians. The introduction of the English/language arts standards document sets the scene for librarians' involvement by stating that students who meet the standards:

> habitually perform the critical reading necessary to pick carefully through the staggering amount of information available today in print and digitally. They actively seek the wide, deep, and thoughtful engagement with high-quality literary and informational texts that builds knowledge, enlarges experience, and broadens worldviews. They reflexively demonstrate the cogent reasoning and use of evidence that is essential to both private deliberation and responsible citizenship in a democratic republic. (National Governors Association & Council of Chief State School Officers, 2010, 3)

The CCSS authors go on to state that the ELA standards have information and media skills woven throughout—just the type of contextual learning promoted by the AASL *Standards for the 21st Century Learner*. The crosswalks and standards associations in the NGSS make it easy for teachers and librarians to see links to information skills in practices and crosscutting concepts. The CCSS and NGSS give teachers and learners a framework in which to place information; information can help learners see that literacy is a matter of not just how, but also of why.

In 2013, AASL produced *Implementing the Common Core State Standards: The Role of the School Librarian*, a report that included an explanation of the CCSS and their instructional shifts as well as the role of the school librarian in supporting them. The report authors concluded school librarians in CCSS schools take the lead by:

1. Building reading, writing, speaking, and listening skills together across the curriculum
2. Building appreciation of the best literature and informational materials together across the curriculum as a part of a literate culture
3. Creating a school-wide participatory culture
4. Building co-taught research projects in blended learning experiences
5. Promoting interdisciplinary real problems, projects, and learning experiences that take advantage of rich information resources and useful technology tools
6. Using technology to boost teaching and learning together
7. Creating cultural experience across the school, community, and the world
8. Fostering creativity, innovation, play, building, and experimentation
9. Assessing the results of collaborative learning experiences
10. Managing the integration of classroom, library learning commons, and technology tools (Achieve & AASL, 2013, 12)

These 10 initiatives rely heavily on the collection and also position the collection as a school-wide resource that goes far beyond print materials.

The widespread adoption of the NGSS and CCSS represents a rare alignment of the legislative, pedagogical, and technology trends currently impacting education. This provides an opportunity to dramatically and positively evolve K–12 education. Pressures to adopt digital tests, cut instructional materials costs, and comply with accountability and reporting requirements might compel K–12 leaders to quickly embrace proprietary solutions to meet the NGSS and CCSS. As Escambia County (Florida) chief technology officer Don Manderson pointed out, "Putting in place a next generation, interoperable digital learning ecosystem is key to positively impacting the core competency of K–12 by empowering teachers to be more efficient and effective in delivering . . . personalized instruction" (Manderson, 2012, 8).

The key item to know about commons standards is that they focus on competency. Yet standards often end up in the background, mostly ignored because teachers must prepare students to excel on tests and also to protect teachers' high-stakes evaluations. Textbook publishers could make the most superficial changes and assert that their instructional materials are "aligned" with the standards. Teacher preparation programs might simply ignore them. But it doesn't have to be this way. As researchers from Fordham pointed out,

> Standards are the foundation upon which almost everything else rests—or should rest. They should guide state assessments and accountability systems; inform teacher preparation, licensure, and professional development; and give shape to curricula, textbooks, software programs, and more. Choose your metaphor: Standards are targets, or

blueprints, or roadmaps. They set the destination: what we want our students to know and be able to do by the end of their K–12 experience, and the benchmarks they should reach along the way. If the standards are vague, watered-down, or misguided, they can point our schools down perilous paths. If there are no standards worth following, there is no education destination worth reaching. (Finn, Petrilli, & Julian, 2006, 10).

Science, Technology, Engineering, and Mathematics

An examination of the professional guidelines for both science teachers and school librarians also suggests that, despite the lack of current cooperation, these roles arise from similar beliefs about the school community and student learning.

To give science teachers—with their diverse backgrounds and experiences—a common language, multiple efforts have been undertaken to create instructional guidelines and goals. Despite the spread of new national science and mathematics learning standards, STEM (science, technology, engineering, and mathematics) teaching standards are well established and new professional standards have not yet been released. In 1985, the American Association for the Advancement of Science (AAAS) established Project 2061, a long-term initiative to improve science literacy, and the NSTA contributed to benchmarking and dissemination efforts. Finally, in 1996, the NRC unified the AAAS and NSTA efforts into the National Science Education Standards. These standards proceed from a belief in high student expectations, teaching for depth of understanding, science literacy, and active learning; the National Science Education Standards recognize that diversity in approaches and perspectives will exist within its framework (Ellis, 2003). The standards also strongly promote professional development to increase awareness of different teaching and learning ideas.

The National Science Teaching Standards—the portion of the National Science Education Standards that addresses classroom practice—begin with encouraging teachers to develop a long-term plan for science teaching that facilitates inquiry-based learning, includes formative and summative assessments, and creates a conducive physical setting (NRC, 1996). Although the imperative to balance and integrate immediate demands (such as state-mandated standardized tests) with professional standards is an ongoing challenge, the National Science Teaching Standards give educators a lens through which to examine their own practice as well as their role in the school community.

An overview of the roles and their mutually reinforcing nature is depicted in Figure 14.9. Each of the National Science Teaching Standards is delineated across the top of the figure; each of the school librarian roles (AASL, 2018) is listed across the bottom of the figure.

Figure 14.9 reflects that the roles of science teachers and of school librarians enjoy a fair amount of commonality. Depending upon the school context in which these educators work, the overlap can be even greater. These relationships are described in more detail below. Within each of these sets of guidelines, activities for science teachers and school librarians are broken down into role elements.

Barriers to Connecting

Teaching philosophy influences instructional practice, but other forces such as teacher preparedness and preservice teacher education affect the classroom environment. Teachers at all levels report feeling unprepared to teach life, earth, or physical science, with elementary teachers at a particular disadvantage (Morrell et al., 2020). Preservice science teachers also are not uniformly receiving the exposure to science teaching methods and

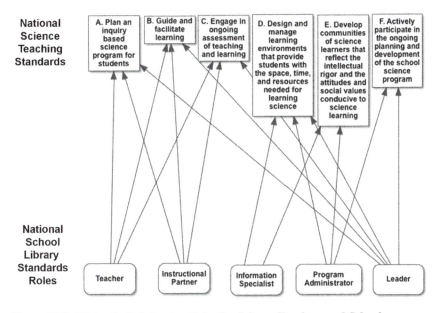

Figure 14.9. Mutually Reinforcing Roles for Science Teachers and School Librarians

approaches that enable them to develop their own perspectives on teaching and learning (Morrell et al., 2020).

Although the potential exists for positive outcomes in school librarian–STEM teacher collaborations, previous research has identified barriers that remain. STEM teachers reported that their school libraries tended to have old and small collections to support their subjects, and that their school librarians did not seem fluent in science and mathematics topics (Subramaniam et al., 2012). School librarian–focused studies (e.g., Godwin, 2015) pointed to a lack of school library–focused professional development in STEM as a barrier to closer work with STEM teachers and students. School librarians might not be permitted to attend professional development events because they are not considered teachers, are not welcomed on curriculum committees, and are not permitted to engage in tasks that leave the library unstaffed.

Other Educational Trends

Myriad educational trends affect schools and the role of the school library collection. Probably the most profound effect on the school curriculum has been the COVID-19 global pandemic (Kuhfeld et al., 2020). The COVID-19 pandemic has introduced uncertainty about how school closures will impact student achievement, as well as how the rapid conversion to virtual instruction will continue to affect achievement. While some students have now returned to in-person learning and educators have more experience with remote instruction than when the pandemic forced schools to close in spring 2020, recent data (Kulfeld et al., 2020) have made clear that there is work to be done to help many students get back on track, especially in math, and that the long-term ramifications of COVID-19 for learning—especially in underserved communities—remain unknown (Middleton, 2020). School librarians may find their roles more important than ever, helping learners regain ground and supporting teachers transition to hybrid or online instruction. AASL (n.d.-a) has assembled resources to support and promote school librarians during the pandemic uncertainty.

The national pivot to K–12 virtual learning is, in many ways, an operational extension of homeschooling. The increase in the number of students who are being homeschooled is another educational trend that can affect school libraries. In recent years, some school districts have partnered with parents of homeschooled students so that the students can take part in various school activities and use some of the public school facilities and resources. Thus, there can be increased demand for the resources in a school library. In some cases the homeschooled students follow a different curriculum so additional materials may need to be added to the collection.

With the increased pressure from high-stakes testing, school librarians have been asked to take on an additional role in reading. While school librarians have always had responsibility in motivating students to read, this additional role includes helping teach specific reading skills, such as comprehension, predicting, and synthesizing. AASL (n.d.-b) has developed a reading tool kit for school librarians to assist with this role. Several articles about the role of school librarians in teaching reading and motivating students to read are listed in Additional Readings at the end of this chapter.

Other educational trends or reforms that can affect the school library program and collection include site-based management, charter schools, school choice, technology innovations, distance education, inclusion, and school-to-work programs. You should become knowledgeable about educational trends and issues and consider how they impact school libraries.

ASSESSMENT OF STUDENT LEARNING

With the introduction of national and state standards, many states developed their own state-wide student tests. National assessment programs were also implemented, with the NAEP, which is sometimes referred to as the nation's report card. Like the adoption of the CCSS, it will be up to states to develop a common assessment system that will make it possible to allow comparisons across states and to provide information to support more effective teaching and learning (National Governors Association Center for Best Practices & Council of Chief State School Officers, 2011). High academic standards and accountability have become the emphasis in education, and much pressure from the new standardized tests has been put on both teachers and students. These tests and the standards upon which they are based have greatly affected curriculum.

Some educators disagree with the emphasis on standardized testing; they have advocated alternative assessments of student learning, such as performance-based learning experiences that involve higher order of thinking skills. The use of student projects and portfolios of students' works are two alternative assessments that are sometimes utilized in schools.

No matter what type of assessment of student learning is used in a school, school librarians need to work collaboratively with classroom teachers to ensure that the resources needed to prepare the students for assessment are available. Many of the standardized tests emphasize information skills; thus, school librarians should work with classroom teachers to make certain students can fulfill the learning standards summarized in the *National*

School Library Standards for Learners, School Librarians, and School Libraries (AASL, 2018). These standards include inquiring, thinking critically, and gaining knowledge; drawing conclusions, making informed decisions, applying knowledge to new situations, and creating new knowledge; sharing knowledge and participating ethically and productively as members of a democratic society; and pursuing personal and aesthetic growth. Chapter 12, "Measuring Learner Growth" in the AASL *Standards* is a great way for school librarians to bring the new standards to learner and professional assessment.

School libraries and school librarians have also been affected by the recent trend of standardized testing, student learning, and accountability. Many school districts have cut budgets for any programs that cannot demonstrate that they are directly affecting student test scores. The school library profession has become much more proactive and has been demonstrating their impact on student learning through research studies and positive public relations. You should be aware of the findings of such studies and share them with teachers, administrators, and parents. Citations for some of the studies are listed under References in Chapter 4, "The School Library Program."

DISTRIBUTION OF LEARNING MATERIALS

As Chapter 4 indicated, another factor influencing subject and program-oriented materials is the location of the materials themselves. When departmental libraries or resource centers are established to support particular subject areas, their relationships to the collection housed in the school library must be determined. Are the centers' materials purely instructional? Are the materials considered part of the school library collection, but housed conveniently near the classrooms?

Another pattern of housing occurs when materials are stored in the classroom or teaching areas where they are used most frequently. For instance, cookbooks might be housed in a family and consumer services classroom or materials on woodworking could be in a woodworking shop. A tour of the school helps you identify the distribution pattern. If materials are not housed in the school library, you need to determine who is responsible for them. You may need to ask some additional questions. What are the circulation procedures? Who is responsible for inventory, maintenance, and control? Have the materials been entered on the online public access catalog? Are separate funds used to buy these materials, or are they purchased with school library funds?

VOICES FROM THE FIELD

I am trying very hard to keep our school from thinking of classroom libraries by putting rotating collections of library books in English classes. I emphasize ALA Quick Picks (http://www.ala.org/yalsa/quick-picks-reluctant-young-adult-readers) in these "collections." I set them up in prominent places—face out. One teacher lets me put them down the "chalk" tray. Another lets me line up along a cabinet. I check the books out to the teacher, and I change them out about every 10 days . . . Quick Picks are perfect because they are "guaranteed to grab the reader in the first ten pages." If a kid picks up one and wants to take it from the classroom, the teacher just e-mails me the kid's name and the book's name. I can check it out to the kid then and get another book down to the collection.

—Anonymous LM_NET poster

PROFESSIONAL COLLECTION

Provide professional resources for staff members in your school. Staff members include people with teaching responsibilities, as well as those who work with learners in other ways: administrators, guidance counselors, social workers, nurses, speech therapists, aides, secretaries, and technical staff. The portion of the collection designated to fulfill these people's needs is usually called the *professional collection*. Frequently a professional collection is housed in a specified area in the school library; other times the collection is in a separate room, such as a teacher workroom. The professional collection should be placed in a location that is convenient for teachers and where it can get adequate exposure.

As is true with the rest of the collection, a variety of formats and resources should be available. If the collection does not contain the materials the school staff needs for their professional duties, then the school librarian should know where one can obtain those materials. Some best practices for establishing a popular professional collection include the following:

- Put the books in an area separate from the library altogether, like the teacher workroom or a conference room or keep the materials in the library but separate from the rest of the nonfiction.
- Set up a paper sign out sheet or a computer station with a scanner. Even if your system is primarily an honor-based system, it's better that teachers borrow them without correctly checking them out, rather than spend money on books that no one will ever use!
- Advertise the books to teachers to raise awareness of the collection. Reminding helps!
- Set up a theme table with books on it for classroom use that changes weekly/monthly.
- Send out professional book reviews monthly.
- Constant reminding seems to help some of them.
- Weed the bad, old, and outdated ones.
- Take professional collection titles to faculty meetings and spend one minute telling teachers about one title that might help them.

Some of the resources that compose a professional collection should relate to the student standards for the various subjects. If a school is participating in special programs, such as block scheduling, literature-based reading, or distance education, then the materials dealing with those programs should be in the professional collection.

Resources for Particular Grade Levels

Resources are also available that will assist teachers at the various grade levels. People who are responsible for preschoolers will find *A to Zoo: Subject Access to Children's Picture Books*, 8th edition (Libraries Unlimited, 2018) by Rebecca L. Thomas to be a helpful guide for selecting materials and activities for young children that include picture books.

Teachers in elementary or middle schools that utilize thematic units for instruction will especially appreciate a subscription to *Book Links: Connecting Books, Libraries, and Classrooms* (American Library Association), which reviews old and new materials for individual units and provides suggestions for using the materials with children. provides information relating to book-based webbing with young children. Remember to review your materials for links to the CCSS and/or NGSS and record these standards in your catalog records!

Literature and Genre Materials

Survey books about children's and young adult literature can be helpful to teachers and school librarians as they work with students in classrooms and in the school library. Rebecca J. Lukens's *A Critical Handbook of Children's Literature*, 9th edition (Pearson, 2013) is a classic survey of children's literature. The second part of each chapter in Donna and Saundra Norton's *Through the Eyes of a Child*, 8th edition (Prentice Hall, 2011), includes activities on how to use each genre of children's literature in the classroom, while the first part deals with the books themselves. Carol Lynch-Brown and Carl M. Tomlinson's *Essentials of Children's Literature*, 9th edition (Pearson, 2018), interweaves the history of each genre with the selection and evaluation of such materials. Their chapter on multicultural and international literature is particularly useful. *Children's Literature in Action: A Librarian's Guide*, 3rd edition, by Sylvia M. Vardell (Libraries Unlimited, 2019) and *Young Adult Literature in Action: A Librarian's Guide*, 3rd edition, by Rose Brock are both useful tools that include lively annotations and activities for numerous titles.

Elementary classroom teachers dealing with the genre of picture books will find over hundreds of picture eBooks in over 73 languages organized into categories at the free and easy-to-use International Children's Digital Library (http://icdlbooks.org). *Popular Series Fiction for K–6 Readers: A Reading and Selection Guide*, 2nd edition (Libraries Unlimited, 2008), by Rebecca L. Thomas and Catherine Barr covers selected series books, which are annotated and arranged alphabetically by the series name. Include award-winning books in your collections for teachers to use. *Newbery and Caldecott Awards: A Guide to the Medal and Honor Books* (American Library Association, 2011) provides annotations for all the winning and honor titles since the inception of the awards.

Teachers interested in working with particular genres will find *Teen Genreflecting: A Readers' Advisory and Collection Development Guide, 4th Edition* by Sarah Flowers and Samuel Stavole-Carter (Libraries Unlimited, 2020), valuable as it contains over 5,000 titles and is a well-organized resource that can be used as a reading advisory tool for middle school and high school students. *The Girl-Positive Library: Inspiring Confidence, Creativity, and Curiosity in Young Women* by Mary Ann Harlan (Libraries Unlimited, 2018) provides a bibliography titles that empower girls, with annotations and grade levels included. *Connecting Children with Classics: A Reader-Centered Approach to Selecting and Promoting Great Literature* by Meagan Lacy and Pauline Dewan (Libraries Unlimited, 2018) can be especially helpful in recommending titles for young readers. A few books are designed to connect literature and specific subject areas. These books are especially helpful to educators who want learners to use school library resources. *Young Adult Nonfiction: A Readers' Advisory and Collection Development Guide* by Elizabeth Fraser (Libraries Unlimited, 2020) groups nonfiction books into themes.

Reviewing Journals and Magazines

Journals produced by professional organizations provide worthwhile information. Many carry reviews and produce bibliographies. Titles you might consider for a professional collection are *Language Arts, School Talk*, and *English Journal* (National Council of Teachers of English); *American Music Teacher* (Music Teachers National Association); *Educational Leadership* (Association for Supervision and Curriculum Development); *History Teacher* (Society for History Education); *Journal of Geography* (National Council for Geographic Education); *Journal of Family & Consumer Services* (American Association of Family & Consumer Sciences); *Journal of Physical Education, Recreation & Dance* (American Alliance for Health, Physical Education, Recreation, and Dance); *Teaching Children Mathematics, Mathematics Teaching in the Middle School,* and *Mathematics Teacher* (National Council of Teachers of Mathematics); *Reading Teacher* and *Journal of Adolescent & Adult Literacy* (International Reading Association); *Science & Children, Science Scope,* and *The Science Teacher* (National Science Teachers Association); and *Social Studies and the Young Learner* and *Social Education* (National Council for the Social Studies). Several of the associations have journals specific to either elementary, middle, or high schools so you should select the journals that are most appropriate for the level of your school. This book's Appendix includes many more review sources.

CONCLUSION

A school librarian is responsible for ensuring that a collection meets a school's curricular and instructional needs. To carry out this responsibility, one must be knowledgeable about the purpose of the school and the curriculum. A school librarian should be aware of conditions for use of materials, including who will use the resources and for what purposes. As curricula and teaching methods change, librarians must reevaluate items in the collection in terms of how effectively the resources contribute to the teaching and learning process. Standardized testing, educational reforms, extracurricular activities, special events, and programs adopted by a school can also affect a school library collection.

School librarians should provide a professional collection for the school staff so that classroom teachers are able to obtain materials that support their instruction. They should have a budget that can be used to purchase some of the resources described in this chapter. Through cooperative efforts, teachers and school librarians can make selection decisions that will meet the school's curricular needs.

As school librarians get caught up in the day-to-day administrative activities and are busy coping with technological advances, they should not forget that the common goal shared by educators is to create an effective environment for the educational experience.

DISCUSSION QUESTIONS

1. Select and research a K–12 educational trend. What are its implications for school library collection development?
2. Design an outreach and marketing strategy for a professional collection in an elementary school. Think about what you will collect, where you will house the materials, and how you will raise awareness about the collection.

REFERENCES

Achieve, Inc. & American Association of School Librarians (AASL). (2013). Implementing the Common Core State Standards: The role of the school librarian. Action brief. http://www.achieve.org/files/CCSSLibrariansBrief-FINAL.pdf.

American Association of School Librarians (AASL). (n.d.-a). Pandemic resources for school librarians. Retrieved from http://www.ala.org/aasl/about/pandemic

American Association of School Librarians (AASL). (n.d.-b). School librarian's role in reading toolkit. Retrieved from http://www.ala.org/aasl/advocacy/tools/toolkits/role-reading

American Association of School Librarians (AASL). (2018). *National school library standards for learners, school librarians, and school libraries*. Chicago, IL: American Library Association.

Ash, K. (2012). Common Core drives interest in open education resources: Spurred by the adoption of common-core standards by nearly every state, the movement for open digital resources is growing as educators realign curricula. *Digital Directions, 6*(1), 42. Retrieved from http://www.edweek.org/dd/articles/2012/10/17/01open.h06.html?tkn=NTOFMxrZ1BSvAwIeHWdbG7nRcERE8nd99JI3&print=1

Asif, A. (2013, September 4). States are slow to adopt controversial new science standards. Retrieved from http://hechingered.org/content/states-are-slow-to-adopt-controversial-new-science-standards_6355/

Bauerlein, M., & Stotsky, S. (2012, September 19). How Common Core's ELA standards place college readiness at risk. Retrieved from http://pioneerinstitute.org/?wpdmdl=282&

Common Core State Standards Initiative. (n.d.-a). Common Core State Standards for mathematics. Retrieved from http://www.corestandards.org/wp-content/uploads/Math_Standards.pdf

Common Core State Standards Initiative. (n.d.-b). Key shifts in English/language arts. Retrieved from http://www.corestandards.org/other-resources/key-shifts-in-english-language-arts/

Common Core State Standards Initiative. (n.d.-c). Key shifts in mathematics. Retrieved from http://www.corestandards.org/other-resources/key-shifts-in-mathematics/

Ellis, J. D. (2003). The influence of the national science education standards on the science curriculum. In K. S. Hollweg & D. Hill (eds.), *What is the influence of the national science education standards? Reviewing the evidence, a workshop summary* (pp. 39–63). Washington, DC: National Academies Press.

Friedberg, S., Barone, D., Belding, J., Chen, A., Dixon, L., Fennell, F., Fisher, D., Frey, N., Howe, R., & Shanahan, T. (2018, August). *The state of State Standards post-Common Core*. https://fordhaminstitute.org/sites/default/files/0822-state-state-standards-post-common-core.pdf

Finn, C. E., & Petrilli, M. J. (2000). *The state of the standards 2000*. Washington, DC: Thomas B. Fordham Foundation.

Finn, C. E., Petrilli, M. J., & Julian, L. (2006). *The state of the standards 2006*. Washington, DC: Thomas B. Fordham Foundation.

Godwin, A. E. (2015, September 1). School librarians and STEM in the digital age: Faculty advance a new program integrating OER. Retrieved from https://www.iskme.org/our-ideas/school-librarians-and-stem-digital-age-faculty-advance-new-program-integrating-oer

Greene, P. (2020, January 20). Common Core is dead. Long live Common Core. https://www.forbes.com/sites/petergreene/2020/01/30/common-core-is-dead-long-live-common-core/?sh=10f8ebff5e65

Gross, P., Buttrey, D., Goodenough, U., Koertge, N., Lerner, L. S., Schwartz, M., & Schwartz, R. (2013, June 13). Final evaluation of the Next Generation Science Standards. Retrieved May 10, 2014, from http://edex.s3-us-west-2.amazonaws.com/publication/pdfs/20130612-NGSS-Final-Review_7.pdf

Headrick, E. (2012). Grade level curriculum planning. Retrieved from https://emilyheadrick.weebly.com/grade-level-curriculum-planning.html

Ishmael, K. (2020, November 2). Making connections: PreK–12 OER in practice. Retrieved from https://www.newamerica.org/education-policy/reports/making-connections-prek12-oer-in-practice/

Jobrack, B. (2012). Solving the textbook-common core conundrum. *Education Week, 31*(37), 31, 36. Retrieved from http://www.edweek.org/ew/articles/2012/08/08/37jobrack_ep.h31.html?tkn=WXRF2N9OKd0Fpb%2Bd%2FK0gxFrFO%2FnR8Qij9Mln&cmp=ENL-EU-NEWS2

Kuhfeld, M., Soland, J., Tarasawa, B., Johnson, A., Ruzek, E., & Lewis, K. (2020, December 3). How is COVID-19 affecting student learning? Initial findings from fall 2020. Retrieved from https://www.brookings.edu/blog/brown-center-chalkboard/2020/12/03/how-is-covid-19-affecting-student-learning/

Kuhlthau, C. C. (2004). *Seeking meaning: A process approach to library and information services.* Santa Barbara, CA: Libraries Unlimited.

Manderson, D. (2012, May). Evolving personalized learning: Maximizing K-12 expenditures to support instructional reform. Retrieved from http://www.imsglobal.org/i3lc/201211-Evolving K12PersonalizedLearning-FNL.pdf

Meredith Nicholson Elementary School. (n.d.). About us. Retrieved from https://myips.org/meredithnicholson/

Mickey, K., & Meaney, K. (2013). *Getting ready for the Common Core 2013–2014.* Stamford, CT: Simba Information.

Middleton, K. V. (2020). The longer-term impact of COVID-19 on K–12 student learning and assessment. *Educational Measurement, Issues and Practice.* doi: 10.1111/emip.12368.

Morrell, P. D., Park Rogers, M. A., Pyle, E. J., Roehrig, G., & Veal, W. R. (2020). Preparing teachers of science for 2020 and beyond: Highlighting changes to the NSTA/ASTE standards for science teacher preparation. *Journal of Science Teacher Education, 31*(1), 1–7. https://doi.org/10.1080/1046560X.2019.1705536

National Governors' Association & Council of Chief State School Officers. (2010). Common Core State Standards for English language arts & literacy in history/social studies, science, and technical subjects. Retrieved from http://www.corestandards.org/assets/CCSSI_ELA%20 Standards.pdf

National Governors Association & Council of Chief State School Officers. (2011). Frequently asked questions. Retrieved from http://www.corestandards.org/frequently-asked-questions

National Research Council (NRC). (1996). National science education standards. Washington, DC: National Academy Press.

National Science Teachers Association. (2020). About the Next Generation Science Standards Retrieved from https://ngss.nsta.org/about.aspx

Samuels, A. C. (2012). Big districts push for teaching texts aligned to Common Core. *Education Week, 36*(10). Retrieved from http://elibrary.bigchalk.com

Strauss, V. (2014). Everything you need to know about common core—Ravitch. *Washington Post.* Retrieved from http://www.washingtonpost.com/blogs/answer-sheet/wp/2014/01/18/everything -you-need-to-know-about-common-core-ravitch/

Subramaniam, M., Ahn, J., Fleischmann, K., & Druin, A. (2012). Reimagining the role of school libraries in STEM education: Creating hybrid spaces for exploration. *The Library Quarterly: Information, Community, Policy, 82*(2), 161–182. doi:10.1086/664578

ADDITIONAL READINGS

Knowles, L., and Smith, M. (2018). *Boost your STEAM program with great literature and activities.* Santa Barbara, CA: Libraries Unlimited.

MacDonald, M. R., Whitman, J. M., & Whitman, N. F. (2014). Storytelling your way into the Common Core and beyond. *Knowledge Quest, 42*(3), 78–80.

McCracken, B. J. (2014). Common Core from the outside looking in. *Knowledge Quest, 42*(3), 8–9.

McLees, T. (2017). *YALSA's top reads: STEM and making.* eBook. Chicago, IL: American Library Association.

HELPFUL MULTIMEDIA

American Association of School Librarians. (2018). Standards crosswalks. https://standards.aasl
   .org/project/crosswalks/
American Association of School Librarians. (2019). The instructional role of the school librarian.
   Retrieved from http://www.ala.org/aasl/sites/ala.org.aasl/files/content/aaslissues/position
   statements/AASL_Position_Statement_Instructional_Role.pdf
Education World. (2011). Curriculum mapping. Retrieved from http://www.educationworld
   .com/a_curr/virtualwkshp/curriculum_mapping.shtml

CHAPTER 15

Equity, Diversity, and Inclusion and the Collection

Key Learnings
- The collection should reflect the needs and interests of your school community, not your personal preferences.
- The collection should include resources in formats that address the needs of all learners and demonstrate that the school library includes them.
- Needs assessment and environmental scanning must be ongoing to ensure that the collection reflects emerging trends in the school community.

Equity, diversity, and inclusion in school library collections refers to ensuring that the collection represents the entirety of the school community's culture and participants as Figure 15.1 illustrates.

As Figure 15.1 suggests, equity is an approach that ensures everyone access to the same opportunities and diversity is the presence of difference within a given setting. These two forces culminate in inclusion, which means creating a school culture in which different identities and perspectives and contributions are reflected and valued. Culture defines how a person lives, thinks, and creates meaning. Culture is complex, extending beyond foods, traditions, language, and religion to include daily experiences influenced by myriad social factors defined by a particular community or region as well as larger national, personological, and external influences. Ethnicity, race, family composition, ancestry, ability, sexual orientation, socioeconomic status, language fluency, citizenship status, religious preference, age, gender expression, education level, and domicile are all aspects of a person's culture (Naidoo, 2014).

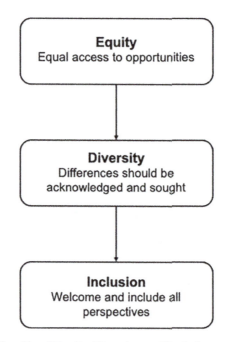

Figure 15-1. Relationship of Equity, Diversity, and Inclusion

The *National School Library Standards for Learners, School Librarians, and School Libraries* (AASL, 2018) provides an important social justice imperative for school librarians. A fundamental building block of the Standards in the Shared Foundation of Include, which calls on school library users to "demonstrate an understanding of and commitment to inclusiveness and respect for diversity in the learning community" (p. 75) because "when learners' community includes members with diverse experiences, they are aware of a range of viewpoints and anticipate the challenges often encountered in reaching consensus" (p. 29). This mastery is known as "cultural competence."

When school librarians include equity, diversity, and inclusion principles in their work, they are operationalizing "social justice" for their communities. Social justice is composed of actions action intended to create genuine equality, fairness and respect among people. The most tangible expression of social justice in the school library is the collection (Fitzgerald et al., 2020). Library collections must represent the diversity of people and ideas in our society. Librarians have an obligation to select and support access to content on all subjects that meet, as closely as possible, the needs, interests, and abilities of all persons in the community the library serves. A balanced collection reflects a diversity of content, not an equality of numbers. Content should represent the languages commonly used in the school library's community and should include formats that meet the needs of users with disabilities.

This chapter features some general guidelines for balancing and evaluating a collection. Because cultural diversity encompasses so many considerations, this chapter will feature a few examples of school community members who should be considered in collection development, but these illustrations should serve only as templates and starting points for you to develop your own strategies to ensure a balanced and diverse collection. A note about language—school librarians should be conscious of the way in which the school library's users are described and avoid dehumanizing language. For example, describing a person as having autism, rather than "autistic" is an important aspect of providing welcome through recognition and eliminating stigma.

DETERMINING A COLLECTION'S EQUITY, DIVERSITY, AND INCLUSION

Many people state that their motivations to be librarians related to their love of books. While a desire to promote the love of reading is important, it's also important to remember that you are the leader and steward of the school library and its collection—it's not your library. Too easily, a school librarian can fall prey to selecting materials based on his/her own personal interests. Rather, school librarians must remove themselves from the process, consider the community, and provide the users with diverse reading and informational resources to support the school's developmental, cultural, social, and linguistic needs.

To determine the extent to which you are inheriting a diverse collection or have been successful in building a diverse collection, consider following these steps:

1. Review recent data about your community, locale, and school population. Sources of these data are suggested in Chapter 3 of this book.
2. Review recent data for your library user needs assessments. If you do not have needs assessment data, either take the time to conduct a needs assessment with an online or paper survey. Examples of library needs assessments are in Chapters 3 and 4 of this book.
3. Review local, state, and national data for current characteristics and trends affecting your school community and its larger information needs.

    As you review the data, be sure to note any community trends or learner needs that you do not recall considering in your collection decisions. Note overall the breadth of diversity and needs expressed in the date—they will form the basis for your collection diversity analysis guide (see example guide in Figure 15.2).

Figure 15.2 is just an excerpt of what your analysis guide might look for. As the sample guide illustrates, you may want to bold those areas in which you want to pay special attention to the collection's content.

4. For each subject area listed on the template, ask yourself, "do we need/have any resources relating to this topic?"
    - If there are no resources—highlight the topic on the template.
    - If there are resources relating to the topic, ask yourself the following questions:
      ○ Are they relevant to the curriculum and school programs?
      ○ Do they cover a range of reading levels?
      ○ Do they provide easy access to up-to-date information?
      ○ Will they appeal to learners?
      ○ Are they in good condition?
    - If you answer NO to any of the questions, then highlight the topic on the template and add a clarifying comment.

You will also want to review content in all formats and the contents of your fiction collection. As you review your fiction content, think about these questions (adapted from Ehrlich, 2014).

1. Does your book list or collection include books with characters that reflect the diversity of your school community or the community-at-large?
2. Does it include books with *main* characters who are diverse?

Subject area		Comments
100 – 199		
133	Supernatural	
133	Magic	
150	Human behaviour, psychology	
152.4	**Emotions / feelings**	
153	**Thought and thinking**	
155	**Myself / self esteem**	
155.9	Death	
160	Logic	
170	**Values (bravery, courage, honesty)**	
190	Philosophy and philosophers	

Subject area		Comments
200 – 299		
200	Religion	
220	Bible/bible stories	
230	Christianity	
294	Buddhism	
296	Judaism	
297	Islam	

Subject area		Comments
300 – 359		
301	People (anthropology, sociology)	
302.2	**Communications**	
302.2	Body language	
302.3	**Friendships**	
302.3	**Relating to others**	
302.3	Bullying	
303.3	Leadership, propaganda, prejudice	
303.6	Conflicts/conflict resolution	
303.6	Peace	
305	Age groups (youth, adults, elderly)	

Subject area		Comments
380 – 394		
391.6	**Body decoration**	
392	Customs (birth, death, marriage etc)	
394	**Festivals**	
394	**Holidays**	
395	Etiquette / manners	

Subject area		Comments
400 – 499		
411	Alphabets	
411	Braille	
419	Sign language	
420 – 499	Languages: Pacific Islands languages, French, Spanish, German, Japanese etc	

Subject area		Comments
600 – 629.8		
612	**Human body**	
612.6	**Growing up/puberty**	
613	Health and hygiene	
613.2	**Healthy eating**	
613.6	Personal safety	
613.7	Physical fitness	
614	Disease prevention (including immunisation)	
616	Illnesses	
617.6	Dental health	

Figure 15.2. Sample Collection Diversity Analysis Guide

3. Does it include books written or illustrated by diverse authors?
4. Does any book have diverse characters on the cover? Do the characters on the book covers accurately reflect the characters in the books?
5. Can your learners see themselves reflected in books from which they can learn about others?
6. Do you have any books featuring diverse characters that are not primarily about race or prejudice?
7. Do your classic books contain hurtful racial or ethnic stereotypes, or images? If so, how will you address those stereotypes with learners? Have you included another book that provides a more accurate depiction of the same culture?

Collection analysis approaches like those discussed in Chapter 12 may also help you determine the answers to these questions. Even with digital collection analysis tools, be sure to follow up those reports with a personal examination of the materials in your collection to ensure that they meet the standards of appearance and presentation you desire for your library community.

Balancing a Collection

Once you know the extent to which your collection reflects the diversity of your school community, you may need to balance your collection for scope, focus, or topic. Some people define a balanced collection as one that contains materials that represent all sides of various issues. Advocates of this position express the belief that young people should learn to gather and evaluate information; they believe these skills are necessary to preserve democracy. Opponents argue that learners need to be directed or guided to materials selected by adults to reflect the adults' beliefs and values.

Another debate centers on whether it is possible to objectively present any controversial subject. Would oversimplification and generalization result? Attempting to be objective may put constraints on the writer who is well informed about an issue and cares about the outcome. Authors who attempt to present both sides may become bogged down in phrases such as "some experts believe." Fortunately, many writers achieve objectivity while stimulating curiosity.

A more realistic goal of collection development is to maintain objectivity by including works that present differing views and covering a wide range of topics. Some learners may not be aware of the wide range of viewpoints that exist about a particular subject. School librarians should encourage learners to seek many sources of information and not stop at the first source encountered.

When examining materials about controversial subjects, you should consider not only content, but also presentation. Excluding relevant facts is only one way to slant information. Word choice and connotations, use of visuals, vocal inflection, or filming techniques may be used to elicit emotional responses.

One benefit of a balanced collection containing many diverse viewpoints is that there will be materials on hand to counter criticism of controversial works. For example, one can anticipate questions about contemporary works on creation science, sexuality, birth control, and homosexuality. One response to critics is to refer them to works that present a different perspective on adolescents' problems. To address this situation, some librarians may select works that reflect traditional, conservative, or various religious views.

To achieve balance within a collection, librarians must grapple with the conflict between popular appeal and literary value. At one end of this spectrum is a collection that includes only popular items lacking literary merit. At the other end is a collection that contains classic works of little or no interest or relevance to many young people. Proponents on both sides argue vehemently, generating lively debate in conversations and in print. Some say that appeal is more important than quality; others promote the role of libraries in preserving and providing quality materials.

The issue of demand selection versus literary selection cuts across the boundaries of content, format, reading level, and intellectual freedom. The selection tools discussed in Chapter 4 as well as in the Additional Readings and Helpful Multimedia sections of this book will guide you to sources of high-quality materials to help you to build your collection's diversity.

Because diversity is a dynamic topic that is ever changing and growing, the following sections will illustrate a few areas in which your collection will need to reflect the school community and community-at-large. Let's take a closer look at building a collection for and about learners in relation to particular themes: different abilities; multiculturalism and internationalism; and lesbian, gay, bisexual, transgender, queer, intersexual, and asexual (LGBTQIA+) perspectives, and reading encouragement. For each of these examples, this chapter includes a definition; grounds the area in community trends that may affect the library community; presents booklists and good sources of materials along with selection considerations; and provides additional considerations.

DIFFERENT ABILITIES

School librarians should have as one of their goals ensuring that learners, educators, and staff members with disabilities have access to both print and digital resources in the collection. Likewise, learners should have the opportunity to learn and understand that people have a range of abilities, some of which require special consideration but still deserve equal understanding and opportunity.

As we saw in Chapter 13, two pieces of national legislation of particular relevance for this discussion are the Education for All Handicapped Children Act of 1975 (Public Law 94–142), now called the Individuals with Disabilities Education Act (IDEA), and the ADA (Public Law 101–336). IDEA addresses the needs of the child and calls for an individualized education program (IEP) based on each child's needs. School librarians should cooperate with educators to learn about the methods educators are using for IEPs in order to offer support. *Building the Legacy* produced by the Center for Parent Information and Resources (2010) is a training curriculum intended to help all persons involved with children with disabilities understand and implement IDEA, the U.S. special education law. All parts of the modules are available in both English and Spanish. Other books dealing with special education and IEPs include *The Special Educator's Survival Guide* (2015) by Roger Pierangelo, *Special Education and the Law: A Guide for Practitioners*, 2nd edition, by Allan G. Osborne and Charles J. Russo (2014), and *The Every Day Guide to Special Education—A Handbook for Educators, Parents and Other Professionals*, 2nd edition, by Randy Chapman (2008).

Information about the characteristics of disabilities and the materials recommended to meet the needs of people with disabilities can guide collection activities. The characteristics of a specific disability, however, might not apply to everyone with that disability. Also, many children have needs identified with more than one type of disability.

In working with these learners, you have a responsibility to learn about the different characteristics and the implications for resources. Table 15.1 illustrates disability classifications that you may encounter.

TABLE 15.1. CATEGORIES OF DISABILITY IN FEDERAL EDUCATION LAW

Federal Disability Term	Alternative Terms	Brief Description
Learning disability (LD)	Specific learning disability	A disorder related to processing information that leads to difficulties in reading, writing, and computing; the most common disability, accounting for half of all students receiving special education.
Speech or language impairment	Communication disorder (CD)	A disorder related to accurately producing the sounds of language or meaningfully using language to communicate.
Intellectual disability (ID)	Cognitive impairment (CI)	Significant limitations in intellectual ability and adaptive behavior; this disability occurs in a range of severity.
Emotional disturbance (ED)	Behavior disorder (BD). emotional disability	Significant problems in the social-emotional area to a degree that learning is negatively affected.
Autism	Autism spectrum disorder (ASD)	A disorder characterized by extraordinary difficulty in social responsiveness; this disability occurs in many different forms and may be mild or significant.
Hearing impairment	Deaf, hard of hearing (DHH)	A partial or complete loss of hearing.
Visual impairment	Low vision, blind	A partial or complete loss of vision.
Deaf-blindness		A simultaneous significant hearing loss and significant vision loss.
Orthopedic impairment (OI)	Physical disability	A significant physical limitation that impairs the ability to move or complete motor activities.
Traumatic brain injury (TBI)		A medical condition denoting a serious brain injury that occurs as a result of accident or injury; the impact of this disability varies widely but may affect learning, behavior, social skills, and language.
Other health impairment (OHI)		A disease or health disorder so significant that it negatively affects learning; examples include cancer, sickle-cell anemia, and diabetes.
Multiple disabilities		The simultaneous presence of two or more disabilities such that none can be identified as the primary disability; the most common example is the occurrence of mental retardation and physical disabilities.
Developmental delay (DD)		A nonspecific disability category that states may choose to use as an alternative to specific disability labels for identifying students up to age nine needing special education.

You need not compile all of this information alone. School staff members can help. Educators can describe learners' behavior management programs, abilities, and learning styles. The school librarian can learn which disabilities call for modifications or adaptations and how to implement them. Specialists at the district or state level can also provide information and advice.

The Association for Library Services to Children recommends several books that deal with children with disabilities. The resources, which include working with autistic children, providing disability etiquette tips, including families with special needs, and mainstreaming services in school and public libraries, are particularly useful for educators and librarians. The website that lists and annotates the resources is listed at the end of the chapter under Helpful Multimedia.

Other sources of information are national organizations and clearinghouses. The U.S. Council for Exceptional Children (CEC) provides information about education for both children with disabilities and gifted children. CEC provides suggested resources and professional development opportunities, advocates for appropriate governmental policies, and sets professional standards. The Canadian CEC assists educators, support personnel, and parents who work with special learners. CECs also provide professional development and blogs, as well as helping develop responsible legislation. The National Information Center for Children and Youth with Disabilities is a central source of information on disabilities in children and youth, IDEA, and how No Child Left Behind (NCLB) relates to children with disabilities. They also provide research-based information on effective educational practices. The home pages for these organizations are listed under Helpful Multimedia at the end of this chapter. Journals of interest to adults working with special education children include *Exceptional Children*, *Teaching Exceptional Children*, and *Teaching Exceptional Children Plus* (CEC), and *Exceptional Parent Magazine* (Exceptional Parent).

Neurodiversity

Autism, an example of neurodiversity, is a complex developmental brain disorder with different levels of severity. In the United States, 1 percent of children have been diagnosed with an autism spectrum disorder. The rate of increase in recent years has been 10–17 percent annually. It is the fastest growing serious development disability in the United States, surpassing juvenile diabetes and childhood cancer. Boys are generally four times more likely to be diagnosed with autism than girls. In the United States, 1 of 70 boys is diagnosed with autism (Autism Speaks, 2011).

The increase in neurodiversity in young people is a growing opportunity for schools. In some school districts, neurodiverse learners are educated in special schools or classes with special education educators. Many neurodiverse learners attend regular classrooms, and the special services needed by the learners are brought to the classroom. In the United States, schools must first consider the option of inclusion in a regular classroom. School librarians should use the same types of instructional strategies for autistic children as those used by special education educators. A list of resources for professionals and for learners is included in the book. Some websites that contain resources about autism, including books for professionals, books for teens, and books for children, are listed in Helpful Multimedia at the end of this chapter. Articles that discuss how school librarians can help meet the needs of learners with autism can be found under Additional Readings.

Visual Impairment

Persons who have vision problems may require special types of materials. Some people with partial sight can use regular print materials, whereas others need large print materials. One cannot make the assumption that large print materials are appropriate for all learners with partial sight. Low-vision aids, handheld magnifiers, or closed-circuit televisions can magnify standard print materials. Trained learners can use Braille books, games, and outline maps. A blind person can read printed materials by using optical machines that allow users to feel sensation on their fingertips. For others, audio recordings may be most useful.

People with visual and other physical disabilities can use audiobooks (talking books), textbooks, and magazines (available in English and other languages, including Spanish).

COOL TOOL: PROJECT ENABLE

Project ENABLE (Expanding Non-discriminatory Access by Librarians Everywhere) provides foundational, self-paced, web-based training for librarians to learn (or refresh their learning of) the concepts and skills required to provide effective library and information services, programs, and resources to students with disabilities. The training's primary target audience is librarians and library paraprofessionals but is open to all who wish to participate.

The tested site design, based on sound instructional and motivational theories and models, consists of five learning modules: (1) Disability Awareness, (2) Disability Law & Policy, (3) Creating an Accessible Library, (4) Planning Creative Programs & Instruction, and (5) Assistive Technology in Libraries. Registration is free.

The innovative Project ENABLE training is customized according to type of library setting (school, academic, public) and library location (state) to account for individual differences and provides an option for librarians to register solely as individuals or for administrators, trainers or professional developers to register a group of individuals.

The site incorporates a variety of formats including text, videos, graphics, photos, audio files, links to relevant sites, games, interactive activities, evaluation checklists, fill-in templates for creating action plans for ensuring an accessible library and designing inclusive lesson plans and even a facilities blueprint template for redesigning a library facility. There are also module quizzes and overall pre- and post-assessments with immediate feedback to allow trainees to monitor their learning progress. The "My Ideas" feature allows participants to take notes or jot down ideas within a password-protected personal page while progressing through the training.

Upon completion of all training and assessments, a printable certificate of achievement, designating 20 hours of professional development, is available to each trainee. Project ENABLE is funded by three successive grants from the Institute of Museum and Library Services (IMLS) and developed and maintained by researchers at the Center for Digital Literacy, Syracuse University.

Visit Project ENABLE at http://projectenable.syr.edu/

Talking books are a free service of the National Library Service for the Blind and Physically Handicapped (NLS), part of the Library of Congress. Arrangements can be made through a local public library. Titles can be found in plaintext catalogs and bibliographies obtained from the NLS, or they can be downloaded online. Information on the books can be found in the print and online versions of *Braille Book Review* (1932–) and *Talking Books Topics* (1935–) from the NLS. These titles are available free to the blind or people with other disabilities. In 1998 the titles in the audiobooks program became available in digital format.

In 1999, the Library of Congress introduced the Web-Braille service, which offers many books in electronic format, as well as some music scores, and all Braille magazines produced by NLS. Because of copyright laws, access to Web-Braille is limited to NLS patrons and eligible institutions that provide services to the blind. Links to Web-Braille books are included in the NLS online catalog. The American Foundation for the Blind develops, publishes, and sells useful books, pamphlets, periodicals, videos, and electronic materials for learners and professionals. It also publishes the *Journal of Visual Impairment and Blindness*. The American Printing House for the Blind publishes Braille books, magazines, and large print texts, as well as materials in recorded and computer disk formats. It also produces an online monthly newsletter, which includes brief reviews of new recreational books in Braille.

Deafness or Hearing Impairment

Captioned DVDs and videos are useful for persons with hearing impairments and can be used by everyone in the library. These materials can be obtained free through a loan program of open captioned materials provided by the Described and Captioned Media Program (DCMP), whose services are available through the National Association of the Deaf and are funded by the U.S. Department of Education. The materials can be found on the DCMP website, which lists captioned media that can be borrowed by deaf and hearing-impaired people. Check with your local educational television station for information about captioned programming and the equipment necessary to receive it.

You can provide materials to learners who have learned sign language. Books, videos, and other materials in sign language are available from the Alexander Graham Bell Association for the Deaf and Hard of Hearing online bookstore. Weston Woods produces audiovisual adaptations of several children's books with sign language narration. These materials are intended for young children who cannot yet read captioned media. The American Speech-Language-Hearing Association publishes the newsletter *The ASHA Leader*, which includes articles for persons working with the deaf and hard of hearing. These and many more resources are located in the appendix to this book, as well as in the Additional Reading and Helpful Multimedia sections of this chapter. School librarians who take a course in sign language can greatly increase rapport with learners who are deaf or have hearing impairments.

School librarians should include in their collections materials appropriate for all learners, including those with disabilities. The learners should be guided to the materials that will fit their special needs and interests. Librarians may need to modify assignments and materials when teaching library skills to learners with disabilities.

One of the most important ways of serving learners with disabilities is to provide books and other materials that deal with disabilities. School library collections should include not only nonfiction resources about disabilities, but also fiction titles in which persons with disabilities occur as main or minor characters. All learners with disabilities need to see themselves represented in books and other library materials. Additionally, other learners need to be exposed to materials that have in them persons with disabilities so they can better understand their peers with special needs. Mason Crest Publishers has produced *Living with a Special Need* (2015), an entire series of books (16-volume set) on youth with special needs. The books, which are geared for ages 10 and up, address the challenges and triumphs of youth with special needs, including physical, mental, and emotional disabilities.

Not only do school librarians need to know the materials in the collection that are appropriate for children with disabilities, but they also have a responsibility to be aware of the resources available in the community. These may include rehabilitation agencies, information agencies, and other educational or recreational programs. School librarians should make information about such facilities available to educators, parents, and other members of the school community.

MULTICULTURALISM AND INTERNATIONALISM

Multiculturalism refers to the conditions surrounding people joining cultures other than their own and fusing, to a range of extents, those cultures together. Internationalism refers to exploring a culture other than ones' own in situ. Joining that culture is not a direct theme of internationalism, but awareness is. Multicultural and international materials support individual needs as well as the curriculum. These materials help learners learn about people whose backgrounds are different from their own. Seeing their own culture represented in materials helps raise the self-esteem of members of minority groups. It is important for the school librarian to be aware of the diversity of a school's population and to make certain that materials are available to meet those learners' needs. If there are large numbers of non-English-speaking learners in the school population, the library needs to have materials available in languages other than English.

The topic of multicultural materials can raise heated debate. Questions center on a few issues:

- *Definition of multicultural materials:* Does it include books from or about other nations? How does it define a cultural group? Should Vietnamese, Cambodian, Chinese, and Japanese materials all be labeled "Asian American" when the differences between these cultures are significant?
- *Background of authors:* Who is qualified to write about ethnic and cultural experiences? Should only those who are actually members of a culture write about that group? Can an author successfully write about a culture if they have gained insight into it through extensive research or experience in the culture?

Because you will want to select high-quality multicultural and international materials to include in your collection, a third issue, the quality of the literature, deserves your special attention as a school librarian. It is important to remember that the standards for any good literature also apply to multicultural and international literature. However, additional criteria should be considered:

- The materials should be culturally accurate. This includes the illustrations in a book as well as text.
- Ethnic materials should contain authentic dialogue and depict realistic relationships.

- The materials should avoid racial and cultural stereotyping. Characters should be regarded as distinct individuals.
- The materials should not contain racial comments or clichés.
- Details in a story should help the reader gain a sense of the culture.

The Appendix to this book contains several resources address multicultural materials. For example, Donna E. Norton's *Multicultural Children's Literature: Through the Eyes of Many Children,* 4th edition (2013), can help school librarians evaluate and select multicultural literature for children and young adults. Book awards can also be a great source of titles to diversify your collection. To help you select African American titles for your collection, consult *The Coretta Scott King Awards: 50th Anniversary* (American Library Association, 2019), which features annotations of winning and honor titles, as well as biographies of their authors and illustrators. Helpful review and selected websites like The Brown Bookshelf and African-American Voices in Children's Fiction are listed in this chapter's Helpful Multimedia section.

Rose Z. Trevino's *The Pura Belpré Awards: Celebrating Latino Authors and Illustrators* (2011) covers the first 15 years of the Pura Belpré Awards. The book includes annotations of the award-winning titles and provides biographies of the authors and illustrators. Another helpful resource for selecting Latino titles for your collection and using them in lessons is *Celebrating Cuentos: Promoting Latino Children's Literature and Literacy in Classrooms and Libraries* (2010) edited by Jaime Campbell Naidoo. Isabel Schon's *Recommended Books in Spanish for Children and Young Adults: 2004–2008* (2008) is an essential selection aid for purchasing materials in Spanish.

Recent selection tools for Native American Indian materials are more difficult to locate. In this case, librarians may wish to consult online sources for recent First Nation-focused titles and critical analysis of popular books. Established in 2006, Debbie Reese's American Indians in Children's Literature (AICL) website provides critical perspectives and analysis of indigenous peoples in children's and young adult books, the school curriculum, popular culture, and society. Websites and additional resources for Native American books for children and young adults are listed in Helpful Multimedia at the end of this chapter.

Bibliographies of multicultural materials for the groups discussed, as well as many not mentioned here, can be found on several websites. Some of the sites are listed under Helpful Multimedia at the end of this chapter. Public libraries are also great sources of relevant literature, with the added benefit of being accessible without purchase. Additionally, the websites for some awards that are given for books that deal with minorities are also listed. These lists can be helpful selection aid resources since the winning titles are some of the best books published about the represented minorities. It is important for school librarians to purchase these books and give these award-winning titles the recognition that they deserve.

READERS NEEDING ENCOURAGEMENT

Encouraging reluctant and struggling readers has always been a challenge for educators and school librarians, especially when the reader reads below expected levels. This is not a reflection of that person's potential to read. A reluctant or a resistive reader is one who has the skills needed to read, but prefers not to read. Books with high appeal and appropriate reading levels can help these learners. Some helpful criteria for evaluating such books include:

- Catchy and attractive cover
- Good blurb
- Appropriate format with an appealing balance of text and white space
- Clear writing without long, complex sentences or sophisticated vocabulary
- Direct and simple narrative
- A few well-defined characters
- Use of dialogue and action
- Well-organized, direct information
- Repetition of main points
- Illustrations to explain the text
- Humor when appropriate
- Presented in chronological order

The topic of reluctant readers has been addressed in library literature during the last few years. Orca Book Publishers in Victoria, British Columbia, publishes *Orca Currents: Middle-School Fiction for Reluctant Reader*, which includes paperback titles for developing readers and a resource guide for educators and parents. Each year, the Young Adult Library Services Association selects quick picks for reluctant young adult readers. The website for this list, as well as other lists for reluctant readers, can be found under Helpful Multimedia at the end of this chapter. Books that often appeal to reluctant readers include graphic novels, series books, and picture books for older readers.

Unfortunately, some educators equate reading only with books. Some even think of reading as only the reading of fiction. In reality, children are doing much reading in formats other than books. Magazines, newspapers, and comics are appealing not only to reluctant or resistive readers, but also to teenagers in general. It is important to remember that the time that learners spend on computers and playing video games also involves reading. If we want to motivate learners to read, we must first find out their interests, including what they are reading. We can then be more successful in matching their interests to reading materials.

For multicultural learners with ESL learning needs, some of the same considerations should go into choosing materials. According to McGaffery (1998, p. xiv), these books should have the following:

- An appealing format
- Appropriate reading and content levels
- Appropriate illustrations
- Accurate text and illustrations
- Access to information through an index
- A glossary of terms
- Bibliographies for further exploration

ESL books need to be representative of the culture they describe and effectively explain that culture. Public libraries are often excellent sources of multicultural books, especially by local authors and award winners.

LBGTQIA+ LEARNERS

Following the June 26, 2015, U.S. Supreme Court decision to strike down state bans against gay marriage in the United States (*Obergefell v. Hodges*, 576 U.S. 556), much attention has been paid to the history and extent to which LGBTIA+ individuals have always been represented among children, parents, and community members. For the most part, school library services for LGBTQIA+ learners have been grossly inadequate. Internet filtering on school library computers has seriously affected these learners' capabilities to access information about their sexual orientation, and some school librarians are hesitant to include gay literature in their collections because they fear controversy and book challenges. Yet without vital books and resources, LGBTQIA+ learners can often end up in high-risk situations. Having information available on LGBTQIA+ individuals not only can provide the information needs of LGBTQIA+ learners, but can also discourage the teasing and harassing of LGBTQIA+ learners that exist at many schools. Reading gay-themed books can help LGBTQIA+ learners realize there are other young people like them. Learners, including young children, living in families with LGBTQIA+ parents should be able to see their families represented and accepted in literature.

A growing number of quality gay-themed titles are available, so it should not be difficult to find materials to purchase. Many blogs and review publications include annual lists of materials that appeal to LGBTQIA+ youth.

CONCLUSION

One of the responsibilities of school librarians is to provide materials and services to meet the needs of learners, including learners who have special needs. Several changes in our society and in education have resulted in many special groups of learners in our schools who have needs that impact the school library collection. Such groups include learners with physical disabilities, such as sight or hearing impairments; young people with learning disabilities or health problems; gifted and talented learners; learners from ethnic minority groups; youth whose first language is not English; LGBTQIA+ learners; transient young people; and at-risk learners. School librarians should purchase materials that address the needs of all these groups, including books that have these young people as major characters. Additionally, school librarians should provide safe, welcoming environments in their libraries for all of these learners who often face challenging situations with their peers.

One of the primary purposes of school libraries is to meet the needs of all learners in a school. Thus, it is important to understand and address the needs of special groups of learners. Trends in our society and in public education in the last few decades have resulted in many more learners designated as having special needs. Some of these trends include the mainstreaming or inclusion of learners with disabilities; acknowledgment that gifted and talented learners have specific needs; an increase in ethnic and cultural diversity in the population, including the addition of large numbers of families whose first language is not English; a decrease in some learner reading test scores; recognition of LGBTQIA+ persons in society; and the inclusion of preschool programs in some public schools.

Materials for particular groups of learners may be tempting to shelve separately (Yorio & Ishikuza, 2018). While shelving separately might make it easier for students and patrons to find those books, drawing attention to these materials by segregating them from the main collection can be perceived as just that—segregation. Before placing materials in any kind of special location (e.g., dedicated labeled shelves or behind the circulation desk) should be carefully considered. Be sure you are not practicing de facto censorship by making the books inaccessible to browsing. If you are concerned about school library users not being aware that the collection contains these materials, use displays, bookmarks, and other promotions to make their presence known.

Although each person is unique, some learners are part of groups sharing characteristics that require special consideration in the collection. Meeting the needs of special groups of learners affects selection of resources, as well as accessibility of materials. Consideration of the needs of these learners can also impact circulation policies. School librarians should also be attentive to learners and educators who represent more than one kind of diversity; this intersectionality should also be considered in selection and programming.

All learners benefit from materials geared to their needs and interests as well as to learning about the learners and community around them. All of these learners need to see themselves represented in nonfiction and fiction materials. As school librarians, educate yourselves to welcome all children to the library with storytelling programming and learning experiences that reflect the "doors and windows" to the world that your collection can provide.

REFERENCES

American Association of School Libraries (AASL). (2018). *National school library standards for learners, school librarians, and school libraries.* Chicago, IL: American Library Association.

Autism Speaks. (2011). Facts about autism. Retrieved from http://www.autismspeaks.org/what -autism/facts-about-autism

Center for Parent Information and Resources. (2010). Building the legacy/Construyendo el Legado: A training curriculum on IDEA 2004. Retrieved from http://www.parentcenterhub.org /repository/legacy/

Ehrlich, H. (2014, May 4). Checklist: 8 steps to creating a diverse book collection. Retrieved from http://blog.leeandlow.com/2014/05/22/checklist-8-steps-to-creating-a-diverse-book -collection/

Fitzgerald, M., Mignardi, D., Sturges, J., & Walker, S. (2020, January/February). School libraries and social justice education. *Knowledge Quest, 48*(3), pp. E1–E6.

McGaffery, L. H. (1998). *Building an ESL collection for young adults.* Westport, CT: Greenwood Press.

Naidoo, J. (2014, April 5). *The importance of diversity in library programs and material collections for children.* An ALSC whitepaper. Retrieved from http://www.ala.org/alsc/sites/ala .org.alsc/files/content/ALSCwhitepaper_importance%20of%20diversity_with%20graphics _FINAL.pdf

Yorio, K., & Ishikuza, K. (2018, October 26). Shelving debate: To separate or integrate? *School Library Journal.* Retrieved from https://www.slj.com/?detailStory=shelving-debate-separate -or-integrate

ADDITIONAL READINGS

Castro, R. (2021). *Chicano folklore: An A–Z of beliefs, rituals, folktales, and more.* Santa Barbara, CA: Greenwood.

Collins, K. (2015). What do elementary school librarians know and believe about learners with color vision deficiencies? *School Libraries Worldwide, 21*(1), 108–120. doi: 10.14265.21.1.007

Froggatt, D. L. (2015). The informationally underserved: Not always diverse, but always a social justice advocacy model. *School Libraries Worldwide, 21*(1), 54–72. doi: 10.14265.21.1.004

Garry, C. P. (2015). Selection or censorship? School librarians and LGBTQ resources. *School Libraries Worldwide, 21*(1), 73–90. doi: 10.14265.21.1.005

Hudiburg, M., Mascher, E., Sagehorn, A., & Stidham, J. S. (2015). Moving toward a culturally competent model of education: Preliminary results of a study of culturally responsive teaching in an American Indian community. *School Libraries Worldwide, 21*(1), 137–148. doi: 10.14265.20.1.009

Hughes-Hassell, S., & Stivers, J. (2015). Examining youth services librarians' perceptions of cultural knowledge as an integral part of their professional practice. *School Libraries Worldwide, 21*(1), 121–136. doi: 10.14265.21.1.00

International Board on Books for Young People (IBBY). *Bookbird: A journal of international children's literature.* Retrieved from http://www.ibby.org/1497.0.html

McLees, T. (2017). *YALSA's top reads: Community engagement and collaboration—eEditions e-book.* Chicago, IL: American Library Association.

Naidoo, J. (2012). *Rainbow family collections: Selecting and using children's books with lesbian, gay, bisexual, transgender, and queer content.* Santa Barbara, CA: Libraries Unlimited.

Naidoo, J. (2016). *A world of rainbow families: Children's books and media with lesbian, gay, bisexual, transgender, and queer themes from around the globe.* Santa Barbara, CA: Libraries Unlimited.

Osborne, A. G., & Russo, C. J. (2014). *Special education and the law: A guide for practitioners, 3rd edition.* Thousand Oaks, CA: Corwin Press.

Phoenix, J. (2020). *Maximizing the impact of comics in your library: Graphic novels, manga, and more.* Santa Barbara, CA: Libraries Unlimited.

Pierangelo, R. (2015). *The special educator's survival guide,* 2nd edition. San Francisco, CA: Jossey-Bass.

Richmond, K. J. (2018). *Mental illness in young adult literature: Exploring real struggles through fictional characters.* Santa Barbara, CA: Libraries Unlimited.

Subramaniam, M., Oxley, R., & Kodama, C. (2013). School librarians as ambassadors of inclusive information access for students with disabilities. *School Library Research, 16.* Retrieved from: http://www.ala.org/aasl/sites/ala.org.aasl/files/content/aaslpubsandjournals/slr/vol16/SLR_SchoolLibrariansasAmbassadorsofInclusiveInformationAccess_V16.pdf

Takahashi, D. K. (2019). *Serving teens with mental illness in the library: A practical guide.* Santa Barbara, CA: Libraries Unlimited.

HELPFUL MULTIMEDIA

American Library Association. (2011). Coretta Scott King Award. Retrieved from http://www.ala.org/emiert/cskbookawards

American Library Association. Equity, diversity, and inclusion. Retrieved from http://www.ala.org/advocacy/diversity

Association for Library Service to Children. Welcome to the (Mildred L) Batchelder Award home page. Retrieved from http://www.ala.org/alsc/awardsgrants/bookmedia/batchelderaward

Association for Library Service to Children. Welcome to the Pura Belpré Award home page! Retrieved from http://www.ala.org/alsc/awardsgrants/bookmedia/belpremedal

Association of Jewish Libraries. Sydney Taylor Book Award. Retrieved from https://jewishlibraries.org/content.php?page=Sydney_Taylor_Book_Award

Autism Society. About autism. Retrieved from http://www.autism-society.org/about-autism/

Autism Speaks. Resource guide. Retrieved from https://www.autismspeaks.org/resource-guide

Beckstrand, K. (2014). Multicultural children's books. Retrieved from https://www.youtube.com/watch?v=q1NdQ1-aFs0

The Brown Bookshelf. https://thebrownbookshelf.com/

Bookshare: Books without barriers. Retrieved from http://www.bookshare.org/

Clegg, L. B., Miller, E., Vanderhoof, B., Ramirez, G., & Ford, P. K. (n.d.). How to choose the best multicultural books. Retrieved from https://www.scholastic.com/teachers/articles/teaching-content/how-choose-best-multicultural-books/

Glaser, K. (2015). The ultimate guide to books for reluctant readers ages 12 to 13. Retrieved from https://bookriot.com/ultimate-guide-books-reluctant-readers-ages-12-13/

ICDL. (n.d.). International Children's Digital Library. Retrieved from http://en.childrenslibrary.org/

Los Angeles Public Library. Native American young adult fiction you need to read. Retrieved from https://www.lapl.org/teens/books/native-american-young-adult-fiction-you-need-read

Orca Currents: Middle-school fiction for reluctant reader. Retrieved from https://us.orcabook.com/Series-for-Reluctant-Readers.aspx

Reading Rockets. Retrieved from http://www.readingrockets.org/

Reese, D. American Indians in children's literature (AICL) [blog]. Retrieved from http://americanindiansinchildrensliterature.blogspot.com/

San Francisco Public Library. Our Asian heritage: Children's books on the Asian American experience. Retrieved from https://sfpl.bibliocommons.com/list/share/378225037/399427447

Smith, C. L. (2012). Native American themes in children's and young adult books. Retrieved from http://www.cynthialeitichsmith.com/lit_resources/diversity/native_am/NativeThemes_intro.html

Smith, R. F. (n.d.). Celebrating cultural diversity through children's literature. Retrieved from http://multiculturalchildrenslit.com/

Social Justice for Change: Teaching for Change Books. (n.d.). Recommended booklists: Booklists by theme. Retrieved from https://socialjusticebooks.org/booklists/

Stepaniuk, C. (2017, May 11). 100 must-read LGBTQIA YA books. Retrieved from https://bookriot.com/100-must-read-lgbtqia-ya-books/

Tomás Rivera Mexican American Children's Book Award. (n.d.). Retrieved from https://www.education.txstate.edu/ci/riverabookaward/

University of Wisconsin–Milwaukee. Center for Latin American and Caribbean Studies (CLASP). Américas Book Award for Children's and Young Adult Literature. Retrieved from http://www.claspprograms.org/americasaward

Walling, L. L. (2010). Linda Lucas Walling collection: Materials for and/or about children with disabilities. Retrieved from https://sc.edu/study/colleges_schools/cic/library_and_information_science/literacy/south_carolina_center_for_community_literacy/collections/walling_collection/index.php

CHAPTER 16

Fiscal Issues Relating to the Collection

Key Learnings

- Budgeting requires an established process to ensure responsible funds management.
- Purchasing through consortia is a cost-effective way to add collection resources.
- Funds can be supplemented through a number of means including crowdsourcing.

School librarians face the reality that a single collection cannot comprise all available resources, nor can it meet all of its users' demands. In meeting this challenge, school librarians must address some issues. Among these is the question of ownership versus access. Should a school librarian use funds to purchase an item, or should the librarian obtain a license so patrons can use that item? Other questions deal with technologies. Should one add new formats such as eBooks to the collection? How often is it necessary to upgrade the current technology?

School library budgets are declining as resource costs continue to increase (Jacobson, 2018). Unfortunately, in many school libraries there are not enough funds to even purchase basic print materials. Thus, school librarians are faced with the challenge of how to raise additional monies, perhaps through fundraising projects or by applying for grants.

THE BUDGET

Given these situations, how do school librarians plan a budget and allocate funds for acquiring or accessing resources? Very few persons become school librarians because they have a special interest in developing budgets; however, budgeting is an important

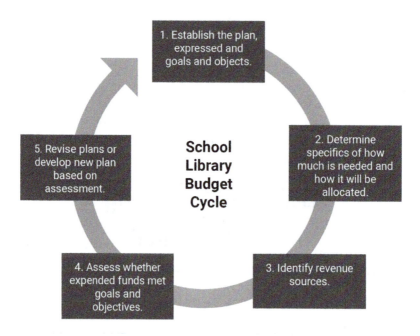

Figure 16.1. School Library Budget Cycle (adapted from Morris, 2010).

part of the program administration role of school librarians. Morris (2010) noted that the school library budget is part of an ongoing cycle, as shown in Figure 16.1.

As Figure 16.1 suggests, school library budgeting is an ongoing cycle founded on specific goals and objectives; ongoing assessment of the extent to which expenditures help to meet the specified goals is key to the ongoing process.

Kimmel (2014, p. 105) detailed the school library cycle with a series of questions that are applied to collection development:

1. Are there budget estimates for each of the long-range collection goals that emerge from collection evaluation?
2. Is there a budget to meet short-term collection goals?
3. Does the detailed budget include:

    a. a variety of formats including print and digital materials?
    b. estimates based on current, actual costs?
    c. likely vendors or suppliers?
    d. processing, handling, and shipping fees?
    e. equipment, storage, devices, peripheral devices, supplies, and infrastructure?
    f. recurring costs such as updates, subscriptions, or licenses?
    g. professional development or training?
    h. a timeline for submitting orders?

4. Do long-range collection budget goals address likely replacements, repairs, and recurring costs?

5. Are there purchases that can be covered by grants, title monies, donations, community partners, or other sources?

Although this list seems daunting, considering the following aspects will help you approach the process one piece at a time.

Knowledge of the Budget Process

School library budgets are usually one of two-types: needs based or lump sum. Needs-based budgets allow the school librarians to detail all of the needed expenditures (subscriptions, materials acquisition costs, processing supplies, etc.) and attach budget amounts to them. Then, the school librarian and school administrator review the requests and agree on items and allocations. In a lump-sum budget, school librarians are given a fixed amount of funds and must determine how to spread the budget over identified library needs. Most school librarians prefer the needs-based budgeting approach since it is the most responsive for current needs and allows for dialogue between the school administrator and school librarian (Morris, 2010; National Library of New Zealand, n.d.; Woolls & Coatney, 2017).

In most schools, the principal has a major role in deciding how funds will be dispersed. Some states require that a certain amount of money based on student enrollment be allocated for library resources, but this is generally a minimum amount. In some instances, particularly in schools using site-based management, a school committee also has input into how monies are allocated in the school. In many cases you will be competing with other units in the school for the same funds. Therefore, it is essential that you understand the funding process and are able to clearly communicate in writing the needs of the library, with well-documented costs of the resources that you think need to be purchased for the library.

Planning and Implementing

In order to decide which resources or services to purchase, you should decide on some collection management goals and establish yearly budget priorities. The collection must be assessed to determine how closely the current resources respond to curriculum needs. A collection development plan should then be created to fill any gaps in the current resources. This plan should be reviewed annually. When requesting funds for resources, it is important to include the dollar amount needed to replace old and worn items, in addition to filling any identified gaps.

Budget requests can be presented in various formats, but all budgets should include itemized dollar amounts and justification for the purchase of each item or service. In today's educational setting, it is wise to relate justification to student learning and achievement.

Allocation of funds can be based on curriculum areas, subjects, curriculum mapping, formats, and users. Other approaches include historical (how allocations were handled in the past), anticipated loss or replacement, and age of the collection. Allocation of funds also reflects a librarian's stance on the amount of electronic access versus ownership (the more traditional position).

Escalating costs is another factor that school librarians face. The average cost of books continues to increase, but digital resource costs are remaining static or falling. One can consult the April issue of *Publishers Weekly* or the latest edition of the *Bowker Annual Library and Book Trade Almanac* for an annual update on this type of information.

It may be possible that the amount of money requested to fully fund the needed resources is not well received; however, it is our responsibility as school librarians to submit a well-justified budget each year. Even if the initial request for funding is not completely fulfilled, that is not a reason to quit asking for funding or to lower the amounts requested. As long as you are basing requests on documented facts, you should continue in your pursuit of requesting funds. It may be necessary for you to become proactive and gather support from others—parents, teachers, and students—who can benefit from the resources that you think should be in the library. Good public relations including attending parent/teacher association (PTA) meetings, sponsoring extracurricular activities, and presenting staff development workshops will also aid in increasing the chances that the school library program will be funded (Morris, 2010; Woolls & Coatney, 2017).

Licensing

In the future and in many school libraries today, licensing or access fees for digital resources may make up the major portion of the library's nonpersonnel budget. With the advent of being able to access digital information, rather than obtain outright ownership, school librarians are learning to negotiate licensing agreements. These agreements define appropriate use and specify a given time period. Both the school library as buyer (licensee) and the vendor (licensor) are bound by the negotiated terms. Common issues in licensing electronic resources are the following:

- Resolving the issue of ownership and access
- Defining how the content may or may not be used (fair use)
- Determining whether the content is to be accessed within the library or remotely
- Defining who is authorized to use the resource

When examining access licenses, other practical advice includes the following:

- Select the clauses in license agreements with which you agree.
- Create a licensing template of those terms.
- Develop a checklist of terms and conditions that are appropriate for your situation.
- Be sure the license follows the copyright laws.
- Avoid licenses that hold the school library liable for each and every infringement by authorized users.
- Avoid noncancellation clauses.
- Avoid nondisclosure clauses.
- Make certain time limitations are clearly defined.
- Avoid licenses that permit subcontracting to an agent.

Resource Sharing

The basic concept of sharing bibliographic information and collections is not new. However, the advent of telecommunications and other technologies has increased the opportunities to share resources. Although location of information is an important aspect, delivery of the desired items is of greater concern. Changes in technological delivery systems make it possible to address the needs of individual learners more effectively regardless of geographic location. These multitype library organizations, that is, academic, public, school, and special libraries, establish formal cooperative organizations of independent and autonomous libraries or groups of libraries to work together for mutual benefit. Networks or consortiums are not limited to regions; they can be found within a school system or at the community, county, state, national, and international levels.

The traditional library network was a cooperative in which participating members shared resources on formal and informal bases. These early consortia shared union lists of serials, provided loans through their interlibrary lending network, or jointly owned a film collection. The current use of the term *networking* acknowledges the development of online infrastructures through which members are linked to resources through some type of telecommunications connection. The participants include multistate and multitype libraries.

Successful networks are characterized by a financial and organizational commitment from the members, who agree to perform specific tasks and adhere to specific guidelines. In return, the member library has immediate access through computer and communications technology to databases that originate in the public or private sector. Commonly held beliefs about networks are the following:

- Opportunity to access information is the right of each individual.
- Networks do not replace individual collections; rather, they enhance existing ones and expand their range of services.
- Participating libraries are responsible for meeting the daily needs of their users and for contributing to the network.
- Networking is not free. Costs include equipment, materials, computer time, postage, telephone, copying expenses, and staff time.
- Effective communication among participants is essential.
- Commitment to participation is made at the school district level.
- Local, district, and regional levels of service must be clearly defined.
- School-level personnel need to be notified early in the process and kept informed about plans.
- Decisions must be made as to which services such as bibliographic retrieval, cataloging, or interlibrary loan the network will provide.
- Delivery systems for bibliographic data and information retrieval must be spelled out.
- Remuneration to or from systems must be mutually agreed upon.
- Legislative issues and governance must be agreed upon.

Several states have developed network projects that can be used by school librarians. Wisconsin's BadgerLink (https://badgerlink.dpi.wi.gov/) is a project begun in 1998 by the Wisconsin Department of Education whose services are available in the state's public, school, academic, and special libraries. It contracts with vendors to provide users' access to articles from newspapers and periodicals, image files, specialized reference materials, and websites. INFOhio, a virtual K–12 library, is funded by the state of Ohio. Its resources are available to all of Ohio's K–12 students and teachers. Many states have similar networks for subscription database access (see the map created by Valenza [n.d.]) and group purchasing.

Some states provide funds for databases that can be accessed electronically. To stretch their dollars, school libraries need to take advantage of these state-provided databases.

ALTERNATIVE FUNDING

It is a sad time in education when schools are not able to provide the funds to purchase the necessary materials and equipment to support the curriculum of a school and to provide resources for the personal interests of young people. Nonetheless, this is the reality in many communities. Besides fulfilling the major roles of school librarians in recent years, librarians have also needed to develop skills in both fundraising and grant writing.

Fundraising

With rising costs of materials and tightening of budgets, many school librarians have taken up projects for fundraising. While it is possible to sell school supplies out of the school library office or hold garage sales to obtain alternative funding, the author of this book does not recommend such endeavors. Rather, it seems more appropriate to undertake projects that can contribute to the goals of a school library and at the same time raise monies. Sponsoring a book fair is a good example of such a project. Book fairs, however, can be very time consuming, so you should solicit the help of parent volunteers or the PTA organization. While the profits can sometimes be very large for schools with large enrollments or where the economic status of the students is high, in other instances the profit share can be low compared to the amount of time and effort necessary to conduct a book fair. Scholastic and Troll are two publishers who provide book fair materials to many school libraries. Bookstores in a community are sometimes willing to provide materials for a school book fair. If you are a school librarian in a parochial school, you can ask a local religious bookstore if it is interested in collaborating with you on a book fair. Most companies or bookstores that help sponsor book fairs provide either a small monetary cash profit, typically 20–30 percent of the sales, or a larger amount if you purchase materials from them with a share of the profits.

Another creative idea for fundraising is to conduct a *read-a-thon* in which students get pledges from family and friends for the number of books that the students read. Students often earn prizes for their fundraising efforts. Local merchants can be asked to provide prizes. Such a project can raise monies for the library while also encouraging reading.

If your school plans an author visit, you should contact a local bookstore to see if it would like to collaborate with you by having multiple copies of the author's books available for sale, providing you with a share of the profits, of course. Most authors are happy to autograph their books, making them even more special to students. Remember to provide adequate time in an author visit for the sale and autographing of the books.

Most of the fundraising projects that you may want to sponsor will take much extra time and effort. Organizing a Friends of the Library group or meeting with the PTA to share your ideas about fundraising can result in finding able helpers for your projects.

Grant Writing

School librarians can obtain outside funding through grant proposals, with monies coming from local, regional, or national sources. Many of the grant opportunities can be found by searching on the Internet. Some school districts also hire professional grant writers to be in charge of researching possible grants and assisting in the writing of grant proposals. You should be proactive and ask your administrator and classroom teachers to provide you with information on possible grants that could enhance your collection. Do not simply wait for announcements or calls for grant proposals.

Most grants are very specific, and the funds can be used only for specific purposes. Some of the possible funding opportunities include adding new technologies, upgrading technology, purchasing computer software and audiovisual materials, financial support for resource sharing, subscribing to online databases, and improving facilities. Since student reading test scores have been emphasized in recent years, several grants provide funding for materials and projects that can improve literacy.

Each grant has its own specifications that must be carefully followed in order for a school library to be considered as a possible recipient of funds. Typical elements in a proposal are:

- *Cover sheet*: Brief identification of project, goals, and beneficiaries of the project.
- *Abstract*: Brief summary of project.
- *Table of contents.*
- *Introduction*: Description of applicant, purpose, programs, constituents, credibility of organization and its accomplishments, and credibility of the proposed program.
- *Needs statement*: Need, support data, and experiences.
- *Goals and objectives*: Intent and anticipated outcomes of the proposed project.
- *Project design*: Plan of action, activities, and methods planned to achieve the project objectives.
- *Budget*: Costs and expenditures for personnel (includes wages, salaries, and fringe benefits) and nonpersonnel (includes equipment and supplies).
- *Evaluation design*: Plans for determining whether goals are met, assessing process and product, and identifying who will monitor and evaluate.
- *Dissemination*: Identification of what will be reported to whom and how that information will be distributed.
- *Plans for the future*: Outline of how the project will be supported after outside funding runs out.
- *Appendix (you should refer to these items in the narrative)*: Examples of items to include are the mission statement, bibliography, vitae of personnel, and letters of commitment and endorsement.

The Foundation Center (http://foundationcenter.org) established in 1956 is a national nonprofit organization whose mission is to strengthen the nonprofit sector by advancing knowledge about U.S. philanthropy. The center maintains a comprehensive database on U.S. grant makers and their grants. Fundsnet Services.com (http://www. fundsnetservices .com) is another useful website that provides grant seekers with opportunities to obtain information on financial resources. School librarians can also check for grant opportunities from the American Association of School Librarians (AASL), which offers the Inspire grant for various library activities. Check AASL's Grants and Awards website to find the most current emphases for the Inspire grants.

The Additional Readings and Helpful Multimedia listings at the end of this chapter identify additional sources.

Crowdfunding

Crowdfunding is a new funding mechanism that uses small amounts of capital from a large number of people to finance a new business or venture. Crowdfunding makes use of the easy accessibility of vast networks of friends, family, and other stakeholders through social media websites like Facebook and Twitter and to get the word out about a new business or funding need. Products and services that may have never reached the market in the past are finding new audiences through websites like Kickstarter (http://kickstarter .com) and Indiegogo (http://indiegogo.com). As we mentioned earlier in this chapter, librarians are no strangers to asking for assistance through donations. In fact, library projects are becoming so popular that Kickstarter had a link to library-related projects from its home page at the time of writing this book. Do a library search on Indiegogo and you will find a variety of projects.

In 2019, the EveryLibrary Institute unveiled FundLibraries (http://fundlibraries.org) the first and only crowdfunding website dedicated to innovative projects in school, public, and academic libraries. Fundlibraries.org is a one-stop fundraising platform for libraries and library support organization that connects ideas in need of crowdsourced funding with many potential donors across the country.

If you're thinking of using one of these websites as a funding possibility, here are a few things to consider. If you don't achieve your goal on Kickstarter, no one who signed up to contribute will be charged, and you don't receive any of the pledges. The company states that this model makes the process less risky for the creator and the funders, as well as providing strong motivation to get your campaign out there and visible. It charges a small fee for the money collected by creators. You can find more information on its FAQ page.

On the other hand, Indiegogo has two funding options: fixed or flexible. Like Kickstarter's method, the fixed funding is an all-or-nothing approach. The Indiegogo website offers the flexible funding option because in most instances any amount will help you toward your goals. If you reach your goal, you are charged 3 percent as a nonprofit. If you chose flexible funding and don't reach your goals, you are charged 9 percent. Fixed funding options that aren't met are not charged anything. Indiegogo is easy to use with templates and outlines.

Aimed at teachers, nonprofits, and parent-teacher organizations, PledgeCents is an education-focused crowdfunding site that offers an easy, efficient, and secure new service that will maximize fundraising capabilities, so schools can offer better education to tomorrow's youth. You purchase your own items with the funds it collects. For example, you might run a PledgeCents campaign to purchase college-and-career-readiness materials.

TABLE 16.1. SUCCESSFUL CROWDFUNDING STRATEGIES

1. Be Realistic with Your Goal	Be conservative when setting your goal. It is recommended that goals be set at 75 percent of what you need to raise. You can always raise more than your goal; there is no limit!
2. Be Creative	An attractive title will entice investors to support you! Share your goal through social media, email marketing, and apply methods that have worked for others. Don't be afraid to get creative when marketing your cause. Any idea you have is worth a try!
3. Use as Much Detail as Possible	The more a potential investor knows about your cause, the more likely they will be to contribute. Include a detailed explanation of why you are raising money and the impact it will have on your students.
4. Add a Video along with Uploading Your Photos	Creating a video will help investors connect with your cause on an emotional level and allow you to convey the importance of reaching your goal.
5. Include Your Students	Your students can be your best fundraising resource. Get them excited about helping with your cause, and teach them about planning and implementing a fundraising effort.
6. Promote Your Cause	Do not create your cause and expect it to fund itself. The more ways you market it and get the word out, the more likely you will be to reach your goal!
7. Keep Your Investors Informed	People contribute to your cause because they believe in you and your students. Your investors want to know where their contributions are going and how they are being used.

Crowdfunding has the potential to meet school library funding needs for specific improvements by making school and community members aware of the need and soliciting help in whatever increments supporters want to donate. Crowdfunding allows librarians to help their needs achieve greater visibility in the community and beyond through the reach of the Internet, especially if the best practices outlined in Table 16.1 are used.

As the table suggests, crowdfunding is most successful when it is carefully planned and energetically executed. The strategy is one in which the entire school and community can be engaged to ensure success. Be sure to do your homework before choosing a crowdfunding site. It's important to know if the service will give the funds directly to your school (like PledgeCents or FundLibraries will) or if you must have the funds deposited into your personal account (like Kickstarter does). Having to declare the funds as personal income and/or figure out how to get the funds from your account to the school's account can add an additional layer of complexity to the process.

CONCLUSION

School librarians face fiscal issues when dealing with their collections. They must have knowledge relating to budgeting processes and how to request the funds needed to administer effective school library programs. Since it is not possible to purchase all available resources that are desired or needed, alternative methods of obtaining materials should be considered. One means of obtaining use of materials is to subscribe to online electronic resources. With such subscriptions, licenses must be negotiated. Many issues should be considered when agreeing to licenses. Some issues include who is authorized to access materials, whether remote access outside of a school is needed, and deciding how content of the materials can be used.

To make more materials available to their users, some school librarians participate in resource sharing, which is generally set up through electronic networks with libraries in their own school district or state, or perhaps with other types of libraries. In this way, they are able to provide their users with materials through interlibrary loan. Other means of obtaining the funds needed for a school library collection include fundraising (sponsoring book fairs or read-a-thons), writing grants, and engaging in crowdfunding campaigns.

REFERENCES

Jacobson, L. (2018, March). Big fish, small budget. *School Library Journal, 64*(3), 26–30.

Kimmel, S. C. (2014). *Developing collections to empower learners*. Chicago, IL: American Library Association.

Morris, B. (2010). *Administering the school library media center*. Santa Barbara, CA: Libraries Unlimited.

National Library of New Zealand. (n.d.). School library budget. Retrieved from https://natlib.govt .nz/schools/school-libraries/leading-and-managing/managing-your-school-library/school -library-budget

Valenza, J. (n.d.). Subscription databases: A state-by-state look at available premium content. Retrieved from http://www.thinglink.com/scene/628624327662632960

Woolls, B. & Coatney, S. (2017). *The school library manager: Surviving and thriving*, 6th edition. Santa Barbara, CA: Libraries Unlimited.

HELPFUL MULTIMEDIA

American Library Association of School Librarians. (2020). *Awards & grants*. Retrieved from http://www.ala.org/aasl/awards

Candid. (2020). Retrieved from https://candid.org/

Ellis, L. (2019, July 24). The changing winds of grant writing. Retrieved from https://knowledge quest.aasl.org/the-changing-winds-of-grant-writing/

Everylibrary.org. http://everylibrary.org

Fundsnet Services.com. (2020). Grants fundraising.com. Retrieved from http://www.fundsnet services.com

Hakala-Ausperk, C. (2020, February 28). 9 steps to writing successful school and library grants. Retrieved from https://www.demcointeriors.com/blog/9-steps-writing-library-grants/

INFOhio: The information network for Ohio schools. (2011). Retrieved from http://www.infohio .org/

Lewis, C. (2013, May 15). Crowdfunding the library. *Library Journal, 138*, 15.

PebbleGo. (2018, October 2). 3 tips for crowdfunding your school library. Retrieved from https:// pebblego.com/blog/3-tips-crowdfunding-your-school-library

Wisconsin Department of Public Instruction. (n.d.). *What is BadgerLink?* Retrieved from https:// youtu.be/DIcNoSmxx4c

Witteveen, A. (2019, November 7). 5 grant writing tips. *School Library Journal*. Retrieved from https://www.slj.com/?detailStory=5-Grant-Writing-Tips-libraries

CHAPTER 17

Learning Environment

Key Learnings

- The infusion of digital resources is affecting learning environments, not just resource collections.
- Learning commons represent a transition to library facilities that are open, flexible, and self-directed.
- Makerspaces allow student the opportunity to create artifacts that represent their learning.
- Librarians should track trends in education and society to anticipate their users' needs for resources and services.

School libraries' facilities create a learning environment that has an impact on the resources that they house and the use of the library collection. As school libraries have added digital resources, there has been a change in the requirements for both physical and virtual space. A primary role of today's school librarian is to provide in those spaces a learning environment where the focus is on helping student learners gain and use media skills ethically and productively.

FACILITIES

Making better use of space in a school library sometimes results in having smaller onsite collections. However, directing students and teachers to the use of items in the physical collection remains critical in a school library. One of the best ways this can be done is through effective signage that is geared toward the age level of the students. When students or teachers enter your school library facility, there should be clear, large signs that easily direct them to locate the materials they are seeking. If there are many ESL (English as a Second Language) students in your school, you should consider adding images or appropriate languages to the signs. Although many types of attractive signs can be purchased from library supply vendors, computer-generated signs with clip art or photographs can also be effective. Student volunteers sometimes enjoy creating such signs that can be used to announce award-winning titles or the availability of new digital resources (Sullivan, 2010).

Shelving that is too high for young students to reach needed materials can not only frustrate students as they seek access to materials in a collection, but also be a safety hazard if children stand on chairs or climb on shelves to reach desired items. Unstable rotating racks used for paperback books or the removal of all books from one side of such a rack can also cause a safety problem. The needs of students with disabilities must also be considered when placing materials on shelves. Although the suggested maximum bookshelf height is 72 inches, the maximum reach up from most wheelchairs is 54 inches from the floor. Aisles between bookcases should be at least 36 inches for wheelchair accessibility and at least 42 inches if a student in a wheelchair needs to turn and face the opposite bookcase or if other students want to pass a wheelchair in an aisle. Shelves more than 36 inches wide cannot safely hold books without supplementary support. Adjustable shelving makes it possible to more easily accommodate different size materials and shift materials when needed. Slick shelf surfaces like those on metal bookcases make it difficult for bookends and materials to stay in place. Shelves that are overcrowded with books or other materials can also make it difficult for students to remove the desired resources. Mobile shelving can be especially effective in shifting attention to a particular part of the collection.

Setting up displays of library resources in the library or in glass cases in school halls also can draw attention to the materials you want to promote. Using a kiosk with large monitors and looping information on available computer software are ideal ways to introduce students and teachers to new books or materials.

Lighting can not only add ambience to your school library, but also impact the use of materials in a school library. Accent lighting can be used to bring attention to a display of books or to a thematic bulletin board featuring books and other materials. Good lighting in the areas where students read or work on projects makes it easier and more comfortable to use resources. Taking advantage of the sun's natural lighting from windows or skylights can add beauty to the environment and at the same time reduce the need for artificial lighting.

Arrangement of a school library facility should motivate students to learn. Keep in mind that there is one common piece of school furniture you rarely see in a school library: the study desk with the attached chair! From the moment a person enters a school library, its arrangement of chairs and tables rather than individual desks signals that it is an exciting place for collaborative learning. Long bookcases of shelves tend to make a library look like an uninviting warehouse. Instead, try using smaller groups of bookcases that are broken up with tables for group work or comfortable chairs for leisure reading. Visiting a successful local bookstore and taking note of its furniture, signage, and display arrangements can give you possible ideas to use in your school library to make the environment more inviting.

Consider also the availability of empty space in your library. Mardis (2007) reported that when the school library had space to accommodate science fair displays and special installations like portable fish tanks and planetaria, science teachers, students, and parents visited the library more frequently. Many school librarians find that mobile shelving allows them to rearrange the space as needed without sacrificing storage. If your furniture is already in place and not designed to be mobile, you can attach "gliders" (flat pieces of plastic used to make large pieces of furniture movable) to the bottoms of the table legs so that they can be moved easily by one person.

CHARACTERISTICS OF AN INNOVATIVE SCHOOL LIBRARY LEARNING ENVIRONMENT (adapted from National Library of New Zealand)

An innovative library space is a:

- welcoming, vibrant, and culturally inclusive environment;
- large, flexible, adaptive learning space;
- place for end-to-end learning: consuming, creating, producing, and sharing new knowledge;
- balanced access to print, digital and multimedia collections; and
- place of exploration and curiosity.

These characteristics will:

- encourage readers to develop a passion for reading and become critically capable, self-directed, discerning learners;
- allow school library staff, educators, and learners to collaboratively find, use, share, and create information;
- provide seamless access to information resources, advice and support to the classroom, home, and mobile devices 24/7;
- strengthen the connection between home and school; and
- create a meeting place for the school community.

DIGITAL RESOURCES

School libraries are not simply warehouses for books and other materials as some may have been in the past. More and more digital resources are being integrated into school libraries and are being utilized by students and teachers for both school assignments and special interests. School librarians are also using digital resources and a wide range of technologies in their instruction. Thus, collections are being vastly expanded to include digital resources and virtual spaces. Digital libraries are now launched from school library websites and can be accessed from classrooms and homes. Databases with numerous resources are available to students online, and eBooks and audiobooks are being added to school library networks. In many cases, more than one student is able to access these digital resources simultaneously, a distinct advantage over print materials.

Myriad educational digital library projects have exemplary collections for elementary and secondary educators and students. The prevalence of digital media available in these collections offers new opportunities to diversify school library collections with open educational resources (OER): downloadable and editable digital video and audio, data sets, interactives, simulations, and hypertext resources. Questions you may consider include:

- What are the considerations, such as quality, accessibility, and curation that might make them more challenging to manage than traditional library resources?
- How do you begin to work with classroom teachers to introduce and integrate OER into their arsenal of classroom resources?
- How do you link selection of OER to your school's curriculum?
- What role does OER play in the larger concept of new styles of pedagogy?

A key actor that has not targeted by many digital library and OER projects is the school librarian, however, this absence is being addressed by groups like Institute for the Study of Knowledge Management in Education (ISKME, 2019) and AASL's OER Task Force, which was convened 2017 (AASL, 2017). School use of digital open educational resources remains nascent, but is growing. To achieve deep and lasting digital library content integration in schools, support beyond professional development is needed and school-based actors beyond learners and classroom educators must be included (Larsen, 2020). School librarians need to know more about the complications inherent in the process of integrating open content in school library activities.

With the advent of the first online public access catalogs (OPACs) in the mid-1970s, libraries started to replace traditional card catalogs (Nisonger, 2000). Librarians, in essence, began building and maintaining their own vast metadata repositories that included bibliographic information, with features like holdings information and request services (Okerson, 2000). Traditionally, OPACs only have pointed to physical resources, but they have the technical capacity to include records that point to a range of media. Today, library catalogs thus are a building block for greater distribution and increased awareness of open content.

We should not assume that all librarians know how to leverage their resource expertise and collaborative roles to foster engaged learning through open educational resources. Recent studies have shown that, although many students best learn STEM (science, technology, engineering, and mathematics) concepts with digital resources, few teachers infuse then into practice (Bikson et al, 2017). By adding arts, thus expanding STEM activities to STEAM activities, school librarians blend science, technology, engineering, and/or math with art to provide learners with an inquiry-based interdisciplinary approach to learning. STEAM projects do not need to be time or labor intensive, making them a perfect fit for school librarians with busy schedules and/or supporting online learning (Rinio, 2020).

Digital resources also call for an abundance of electrical outlets and careful planning of where computers are placed in a school library. Consolidating the student computers and printers in one area of the library makes it easier to supervise and instruct students as they access digital resources. Laptops and handheld devices need recharging so providing some eight-outlet power sources is appreciated by both students and staff.

BRING YOUR OWN DEVICE

Bring Your Own Device (BYOD) is gaining popularity in many schools as a way of increasing access to technology without the cost of purchasing a device for each student. BYOD allows students to bring their personal laptops, tablets, and smartphones from home and use them for educational applications in the classroom.

At a time when budgets are shrinking, school districts are considering BYOD programs to integrate cost-effective technology into their educational programs. It's a promising idea, especially for schools that lack sufficient technology budgets. BYOD takes advantage of the technology that students already own and are familiar with. However, BYOD programs have been met with some concerns from staff and administrators who believe the challenges outweigh the perceived benefits.

BYOD is especially important for school librarians because numerous researchers (e.g., Everhart & Mardis, 2010; Everhart, Mardis, & Johnston, 2011) have demonstrated that regardless of the technology policy innovation, school librarians are often the on-site managers of the implementation. Because managing school computers and devices in BYOD implementations to use information resources are often seen as by school administrators as extensions of collection development tasks, school librarians should be aware of the advantages and disadvantages of BYOD. Some of these considerations are listed in Table 17.1.

As Table 17.1 shows, moving to BYOD requires many considerations within and beyond the curriculum that present a great likelihood to impact the school librarian's role and the school library collection. While you will not be in control of many of these factors, be involved with the policy development and adoption process to ensure that you are in the best position to make the most of BYOD. Your best contribution may be to help your administration develop usage contracts like the one featured in Figure 17.1.

In order to ensure that both students and parents understand the rights and responsibilities that accompany using school-owned and personal devices in school, it may be helpful to use a contract like the one illustrated in Figure 17.1 that covers a range of uses. Sometimes such a contract is drafted by a school committee and enforced throughout a school.

LEARNING COMMONS

The infusion of digital technologies and ubiquitous Internet connectivity in many schools offers additional pathways to learning and content acquisition. Students and teachers no longer need a library simply for access. Instead, they require a place that encourages participatory learning and allows for co-construction of understanding from a variety of sources. In other words, instead of being an archive, libraries are becoming a learning commons.

TABLE 17.1. BRING YOUR OWN DEVICE CONSIDERATIONS

Device Limitations	Curriculum
Although mobile devices offer many advantages, there are times when students will require a computer. Many software programs require a computer with a file structure and mouse input, even if they offer a companion mobile app to supplement the software program. Not all software features and file types are supported on mobile devices. • What will students use when they require a keyboard? • How will students use software programs that require a "real" computer? • What will students use when they need a larger screen? • How will students access files that are not supported on their mobile device?	A BYOD program requires a significant amount of curriculum analysis and redesign in order to take full advantage of mobile device features. Teachers need to be aware of the impact teaching to an array of devices will have on their plans. BYOD also requires a school to rethink its digital citizenship and information literacy curricula. • How will teachers be supported with BYOD implementation? How will they learn about new software applications and devices? • Do students know about Internet etiquette and safety? Who will be responsible for teaching this information? • What about teachers who choose not to participate in BYOD?

(Continued)

TABLE 17.1. CONTINUED

Logistics	Communication
Device considerations and logistical planning requires both time and energy from school staff. • Will students be responsible for keeping their devices charged? How/where will students charge devices if needed? • How will devices be secured when not in use, for example during lunch, tests, or sports? • What about students without devices? How will students check out a loaner device? How long will they be able to keep it? Can they take it home?	Implementing a BYOD program requires time and energy devoted to maintaining ongoing communication between district administrators, staff, parents, and students. If a mobile device is purchased, maintained, repaired, and managed by parents and students, it's going to be important to communicate well and communicate often. • Are parents involved in the planning and decision making process? How will they continue to be involved in the program? • Do parents know how the devices are being used at school? How can they follow-up at home?

Security	Network Infrastructure
BYOD brings with it a host of security concerns, including data protection and compliance with the Children's Internet Protection Act (CIPA). • How will you protect student information and avoid data security conflicts? • How will you protect your network from viruses and malware? • Will students be protected from unsolicited email and inappropriate sites? • How will you monitor Internet usage?	Many devices will create heavy demands on your network infrastructure. • Will the network be able to handle large a number of devices simultaneously? • Will students be able to rely on network access 24/7? • How will you ensure enough bandwidth to handle multimedia applications? • Does your network infrastructure have the capacity for growth?

Budget

At first glance, a BYOD program may appear to save money by passing the cost of devices on to parents. However, there are many costs associated with BYOD implementation that must be considered.

• What needs to be done to update the network infrastructure? How will you ensure that students will have reliable, fast network service 24/7?
• How often will you update the network to maintain its viability?
• How many loaner devices will you purchase? How often will they be replaced? How will you pay for repairs?
• Mobile devices are designed to supplement, not replace, the work done on "real" computers. How many computers will the school purchase? Where will they be located?
• Will you have mobile device charging stations?
• How will that impact the school's energy budget?

Personal Electronic Device Contract

As a member of the XXX school community I will follow the following guidelines regarding my own and school-owned devices:

- I will respect others by not writing or saying anything that is hurtful or not true.
- I will respect the work of others by identifying the author and where it came from (source), whether online or in print.
- I will respect other people's computer files and not open, move, or delete them.
- I will respect other people's user information and will not use it or share it with others.
- I will take care of the school computers and other technology tools so that others can use them, too. (Technology tools include flash drives, printers, headphones, microphones, cameras, scanners, SmartBoards, graphics tablets, and other items.)
- I will log into the school network using only the assigned username and password given to me by the school librarian, technology coordinator, and/or my teacher.
- I will use my school student account only as directed by the Lower School school librarian, technology coordinator, and/or my teachers.
- I will only use the Internet when given permission by the school librarian, technology coordinator, and/or my teacher.
- At school, I will only use the wikis, blogs, or other social networking sites that are assigned by the school librarian, technology coordinator, and/or my teacher.
- When using the Internet, I will notify the school librarian, technology coordinator, and/or my teacher immediately if I accidentally access "inappropriate" websites.
- I will not use my school student account (i.e. email address) to register for any Internet website, service, or activity unless requested to do by the school librarian, technology coordinator, and/or my teacher.
- I will not change or modify any computer, in any way, unless asked to do by the school librarian, technology coordinator, and/or my teacher.

Personally-owned Electronic Devices

If I choose to bring in and use my personal laptop and/or other electronic device (Nook, Kindle, iPad, Cell phone, etc.), I understand that I may use it only when given permission by the school librarian, technology coordinator, and/or my teacher. This includes using the camera on my device, accessing the internet, and/or any apps or programs on my devices. I also understand that:

- I am responsible for the safety and security of my laptop and/or electronic device, including bringing in the appropriate power adapters so that my device(s) can be charged, if needed.
- I may post pictures/videos taken during school, at school-sponsored activities or events, and on school-provided buses only when given permission by a teacher.
- I may not post any pictures/videos on any non-school-approved media site.
- I may not take photos or videos using any device while in transit to/from school on school-provided transportation.
- I may be asked to demonstrate that I know how to use my e-reader and/or laptop (i.e. connect to the wireless network) in order to continue bringing my personal devices to school.

Cell Phones

If I use my cell phone for any activity, I understand that:

- My phone must be set to vibrate and that I may not answer calls, at any time during the school day.
- I may only make phone calls when I have been given specific permission.
- I may not read and/or send e-mail or text messages from personal accounts during the school day.
- I may not post photos/videos taken during school and/or school events on any non-school-approved social media site.
- I may not take photos or videos while in transit to/from school on school-provided transportation.

Student Signature: _____ Parent Signature: _____

Date:_____

Figure 17.1. Personal Electronic Device Contract

The learning commons, sometimes called "information commons," has evolved from a combination library and computer lab into a full-service learning, research, and project space. The modern commons is a meeting place, typically offering at least one area where students can rearrange furniture to accommodate impromptu planning sessions or secure a quiet place to work near a window. In response to course assignments, which have taken a creative and often collaborative turn in the last two decades, the learning commons provides areas for group meetings, tools to support creative efforts, and on-staff specialists to provide help as needed. The successful learning commons does not depend solely upon adaptable space configuration or the latest digital equipment. Its strength lies in the relationships it supports, whether these are student-to-student, student-to-faculty, student-to-staff, student-to-equipment, or student-to-information. Effective learning commons is alive with the voices of students working together, establishing the kinds of connections that promote active, engaged learning.

Learning commons typically reflects several considerations:

User-centered: Does your library focus on user needs or storing equipment and materials?

Flexible: Are your policies, resources, and facilities available in ways that are adaptable and scalable to a variety of uses?

Self-Directed: How do you handle frequently asked questions and performed tasks? How do you enable users to help themselves? How do you create an atmosphere of trust and empowerment with tools, services, and resources?

Join Resources: Have you streamlined access to resources and services? Are they available from one central point?

Remove Barriers: Do users have request resources from special areas? Do you require forms to be completed by teachers and students before delivering materials and services?

Publicize: How do you measure and share your successes? How do you reach new users? How do you retain existing users? (Adapted from Harland, 2011)

Many libraries already contain elements of a learning commons approach, but just require rethinking and rearrangement. However, for those libraries that have traditional materials, furniture, and policies, the initial drawback to a learning commons is its expense. The cost of new equipment and furniture can be substantial, and some spaces may be difficult or costly to reconfigure. Another often-encountered problem is that of choosing the right services to offer in a new commons. Since there is no single model of the ideal learning commons, it can be anything designers conceive to suit each institution's unique needs and culture. This flexibility is an opportunity, but it also means institutions might have to experiment with features and services based on the results of a needs assessment. Even when a commons is well designed and executed, the space can become overcrowded, especially during peak periods. As a result, some librarians have had to adopt scheduling procedures, making their gathering areas less available for just-in-time learning.

MAKERSPACES

Makerspaces, sometimes also referred to as hackerspaces, hackspaces, and fablabs, are creative, do-it-yourself (DIY) spaces where people can gather to create, invent, and learn. In libraries they often have 3D printers, software, electronics, craft and hardware supplies and tools, computing/coding resources, and more. Makerspaces in school libraries are part of the evolving debate over what school libraries' core mission is or should be. Some librarians are moving to providing the tools to help patrons to facilitate the production of their own works of art or information and sometimes also collecting the results to share with other members of the community. From a collection development perspective, school librarians will want to consider how to manage the collection of equipment and output from makerspaces.

VOICES FROM THE FIELD

I'm on a four day, fixed rotation, so my "Maker Space" is a subset of the stations that I put out on Fridays and let students pull out after they've checked out but are waiting for classmates to finish. I don't have any specific rules outside of our general library expectations and "keep yourself busy doing something productive." I do ration the amount of supplies that I put out for each class. I find that more practical and less stressful than trying to enforce per student limits on things like origami paper and stickers for bookmarks. The perception of scarcity can work wonders in controlling waste. The students and I both LOVE our Friday choice days.

—LM_NET member

Makerspaces promote learning through hands-on experience. In this way, they have the potential to build student confidence through trial and error and spark interest in STEM and other creating-oriented careers. Makerspaces also tie into the growing trend of independent artistry in every medium—including books—that are bypassing traditional modes of accessing production, taking advantage of new tools to produce professionally polished products, and going direct to the web to share, gather feedback, and gain new ideas.

Makerspaces can take a range of forms—not all require advanced equipment. Quite often, a makerspace can be composed of hands-on activities you already do in the library or done in conjunction with the art teacher. If you are interested in establishing a makerspace in your library, you may wish to consider the following:

1. Funding: Who pays for the makerspace? Is it part of the library budget or school budget or are outside sources such as grants or other monies used? Who pays for the equipment? What is the budget to remodel or outfit the space?
2. Staffing: Who staffs makerspace? Is it separate staff from the library, or the library's staff? Is this an additional duty for library staff?
3. Equipment: What types of equipment are available in the makerspace? What supplies are provided? Are users expected to bring any supplies? Are there safety issues to be aware of? How will staff and students be trained to use equipment?
4. Location: How large will the space be? Will the space be located in the library or elsewhere?
5. Hours of operation: Will the space be open after school, on the weekend, or during the summer? Will students be allowed to visit during the school day, or just with a class?

Thanks to virtual learning tools like Zoom and Microsoft Teams, makerspaces can thrive online or offline. For example, during pandemic-related school closures, many school librarians turned to using virtual learning platforms to engage learners in creating via coding, virtual reality, and other activities (SLJ, 2020).

TRACKING THE FUTURE

To meet the ever-changing needs of your school community, follow blogs, and Twitter feeds; read professional publications frequently; be active in your local, state, and national professional learning networks; and cultivate a habit of looking for future trends from elsewhere in society that may inform your ability to stay on the cutting edge. Two key sources of tracking future trends that you may wish to follow are:

Center for the Future of Libraries: Trends (http://www.ala.org/tools/future/trends)
The Center for the Future of Libraries works to identify trends relevant to libraries and librarianship. This collection is available to help libraries and librarians understand how trends are developing and why they matter. Each trend is updated as new reports and articles are made available. New trends will be added as they are developed. Trends are organized into seven categories: Society, Technology, Education, the Environment, Politics (and Government), Economics, and Demographics.

Project Tomorrow *Speak Up* Reports (http://tomorrow.org)
The Speak Up reports from Project Tomorrow provide an easy way for students, parents, and educators to participate in your local decisions about technology, as well as contribute to the state and national dialogue about educational technology. Since 2003, Project Tomorrow has collected the viewpoints of almost 4 million students, educators, and parents—the Speak Up data set represents the largest collection of authentic feedback from these key educational stakeholders. The free downloadable reports aim to:

- Provide a means for local schools and districts to easily and effectively listen to and act upon the ideas of their stakeholders
- Provide a conduit for the voices of education stakeholders, most notably students, to inform national and/or state/provincial policies and programs
- Stimulate new local discussions around the use of technology within education

CONCLUSION

Making better use of school library facilities to house and promote the collection is essential. This also includes making certain that students with disabilities have equitable access to materials. The integration of technology and digital resources into school libraries has affected both the physical and virtual space requirements. School libraries continue to change to meet the needs of 21st-century learners. School librarians, in turn, are providing environments where students can develop effective and responsible media literacy skills.

Students need to use a variety of informational resources and technologies as they learn to formulate meaningful questions, work on collaborative projects, and create information. *Learning commons* is a term that has been recently used in the school library profession; however, it has been present for the last couple of decades in higher institutions of learning. It refers to transformation from traditional library space to facilities and instruction where students and teachers can master information technology (Mihailidis & Diggs, 2010). *Makerspaces* allow students to create tangible items that depict their learning that can be shared with others. *Media literacy* aligns with the learning commons approach. It refers to the ability to exhibit critical thinking skills in relation to information media and technology. Although students in today's libraries have a world of information at their fingertips and are often called *digital natives*, they are still in need of learning how to evaluate resources, problem solve, and use information to appropriately engage with others.

The learning environment in a school library includes not only young people reading books, magazines, and newspapers, but also students who are actively engaged in connecting to resources and persons outside the walls of the school library. Librarians can provide direction to these students by helping them become engaged, safe, and responsible media users in their daily lives.

DISCUSSION QUESTIONS

1. Design and draw a learning commons and design a makerspace floorplan. Review the considerations in the makerspace section, as they apply to both types of facilities. What are the advantages and disadvantages of each type of facility? How do you feel that you can support the curriculum with activities, programs, and/or services in each type of facility?
2. Choose two trends from the Center from the Future of Libraries. How do these trends apply to school libraries? How might you act on these trends in your school library.
3. Create a policy for the archiving and preserving of makerspace output. What will you need to consider?

REFERENCES

American Association of School Librarians (AASL). (2017, March 17). Open educational resources and school librarians—The right fit! Retrieved from https://knowledgequest.aasl.org/open-educational-resources-school-librarians-right-fit/

Bikson, T. K., Straus, S. G., Agnew, G., Kalra, N., McArthur, D. J., Crompton, H., Kase C. A., & Leuschner, K. J. (2017). *Digital resources for STEM educators and recommendations for cyberlearning initiatives: Results from the National Science Foundation digital library/distributed learning program evaluation.* Santa Monica, CA: RAND Corporation, 2017. Retrieved from https://www.rand.org/pubs/research_reports/RR414.html

Everhart, N., & Mardis, M. A. (2010). The leadership role of the teacher librarian in technology integration: Early results of a survey of highly certified teacher librarians in the United States. Paper presented at the *Diversity Challenge Resilience: School Libraries in Action Proceedings of the 12th Biennial School Library Association of Queensland, the 39th International Association of School Librarianship Annual Conference incorporating the 14th International Forum on Research in School Librarianship, 27 September—1 October, Brisbane, QLD, Australia.*

Everhart, N., Mardis, M. A., & Johnston, M. (2011). National Board Certified school librarians' leadership in technology integration: Results of a national survey. *School Library Media Research,* 14. Retrieved from https://files.eric.ed.gov/fulltext/EJ955799.pdf

Harland, P. (2011). Toward a learning commons. *School Library Monthly, 28*(1), 34–36.

Institute for the Study of Knowledge Management in Education (ISKME). (2019). School librarians as OER curators: A framework to guide practice. Retrieved from https://tinyurl.com/SL-OER-Curation

Larsen, M. (2020, February 20). Ten lessons for school librarians leading district OER initiatives and curation efforts. Retrieved from https://knowledgequest.aasl.org/ten-lessons-for-school-librarians-leading-district-oer-initiatives-and-curation-efforts/

Mardis, M. A. (2007). School libraries and science achievement: A view from Michigan's middle schools. *School Library Media Research, 10.* Retrieved from: http://www.ala.org/aasl/sites/ala.org.aasl/files/content/aaslpubsandjournals/slr/vol10/SLMR_SchoolLibScienceAchievement_V10.pdf

Mihailidis, P., & Diggs, V. (2010). From information reserve to media literacy learning commons: Revisiting the 21st century library as the home for media literacy education. *Public Library Quarterly, 29*(4), 279–292.

National Library of New Zealand. (n.d.). Think about your learners and school community. Retrieved from https://natlib.govt.nz/schools/school-libraries/place-and-environment/designing-library-spaces

Nisonger, T. E. (2000). Collection development in an electronic environment. Special issue. *Library Trends, 48*(4), 639–922.

Okerson, A. (2000). Are we there yet? Online E-resources ten years after. *Library Trends, 48*(4), 671–693.

Rinio, D. (2020, May 1). Full STEAM ahead. Retrieved from https://knowledgequest.aasl.org/full-steam-ahead/

School Library Journal (SLJ). (2020, April 23). What librarians are doing to support students and teachers in the shutdown. Retrieved from https://www.slj.com/?detailStory=slj-covid-19-response-survey-shows-librarians-preparation-and-response-to-school-closures-coronavirus-COVID19

Sullivan, M. (2010). Merchandising your library resources. *Teacher Librarian, 38*(2), 30–31.

ADDITIONAL READINGS

Bdeir, A., & Richardson, M. (2015). *Make: Getting started with littleBits: Prototyping and inventing with modular electronics.* San Francisco, CA: Maker Media.

Briggs, J. R. (2012). *Python for kids.* San Francisco, CA: No Starch Press.

Diana, C. (2013). *LEO the maker prince: Journeys in 3D printing.* San Francisco, CA: Maker Media.

Doorley, R. (2014). *Tinkerlab: A hands-on guide for little inventors.* Boston, MA: Roost Books.

Everhart, N. (2021). *Evaluating the school library: Analysis, techniques, and research practices,* 2nd edition. Santa Barbara, CA: Libraries Unlimited.

Fleming, Laura. (2015). *Worlds of making: Best practices for establishing a Makerspace for your school.* Thousand Oaks, CA: Corwin.

Gabrielson, C. (2013). *Tinkering: Kids learn by making stuff.* San Francisco, CA: Maker Media.

Morgan, N. (2014). *JavaScript for kids.* San Francisco, CA: No Starch Press.

Morgan, R. F. (2012). *Tape it & make it: 101 duct tape activities.* Hauppauge NY: Barron's.

Murphy, M. (2014). *High-tech DIY projects with 3D printing.* New York: Powerkids Press.

Peppler, K., Gresalfi, M., Tekinbas, K. S., & Santo, R. (2014). *Short circuits: Crafting e-Puppets with DIY Electronics.* Cambridge, MA: The MIT Press.

Peppler, K., Gresalfi, M., Tekinbas, K. S., & Santo, R. (2014). *Soft circuits: Crafting e-fashion with DIY Electronics.* Cambridge, MA: The MIT Press.

Rinio, D. (2020). *STEAM activities in 30 minutes for elementary learners* (AASL Standards–Based Learning Series). Chicago, IL: ALA Editions.

Rush, E. B. (2017). *Bringing Genius Hour to Your Library: Implementing a Schoolwide Passion Project Program.* Santa Barbara, CA: Libraries Unlimited.

Sullivan, M. (2014). *High impact school library spaces: Envisioning new school library concepts.* Santa Barbara, CA: Libraries Unlimited.

Valk, L. (2014). *The LEGO MINDSTORMS EV3 discovery book.* San Francisco, CA: No Starch Press.

Weinstein, E. (2014). *Ruby wizardry.* San Francisco, CA: No Starch Press.

Wilkinson, K., & Petrich, M. (2014). *The Art of tinkering.* San Francisco, CA: Weldon Owen.

HELPFUL MULTIMEDIA

Baltimore County Public Schools Library Media Programs. (n.d.). Transforming school library spaces. Retrieved from https://bcpslis.pbworks.com/w/page/112334974/Transforming%20School%20Library%20Spaces

Britton, L. (2012, October 1). The makings of Maker Spaces, Part 1: Space for creation, not just consumption. *Library Journal Digital Shift.* Retrieved from http://www.thedigitalshift.com/2012/10/public-services/the-makings-of-maker-spaces-part-1-space-for-creation-not-just-consumption/

Core77. (2014). The future of learning environments: An issue that concerns the students. Retrieved from http://www.core77.com/posts/26413/the-future-of-learning-environments-an-issue-that-concerns-the-students-26413

Make: Community. (n.d.). Retrieved from https://makerspaces.make.co/

National Library of New Zealand. (n.d.). Designing library spaces. Retrieved from https://natlib.govt.nz/schools/school-libraries/place-and-environment/designing-library-spaces

Peters, A. (2014). Is this the school library of the future? *Fast Company*. Retrieved from http://www.fastcompany.com/3033930/futurist-forum/is-this-the-school-library-of-the-future#1

School Specialty. (2020, May 14). When designing a modern school library, here are some ideas to inspire you. Retrieved from https://blog.schoolspecialty.com/when-designing-a-modern-school-library-here-are-some-ideas-to-inspire-you/

The Sylvia Show: Episodes. Retrieved from http://sylviashow.com/episodes

U.S. Department of Justice. (2010). ADA home page. Retrieved from http://www.ada.gov/

CHAPTER 18

Opening, Reclassifying, Moving, or Closing the Collection

> **Key Learnings**
> - Prior planning streamlines the process of establishing, altering, and/or closing a collection.
> - Ongoing data collections, annual goals, and regular reporting can identify collection challenges that require attention.
> - Various classification schemes exist to help you tailor collection organization to community needs.

When the school community is begun, changes, or concludes an academic year, school librarians respond by creating initial collections, combining collections, reclassifying collections, annually closing, or permanently closing a collection. The school library might also be moved to a different location within the same school campus. Each situation presents different demands upon school librarians' knowledge and skills. A librarian's human relations skills may be tested in the tensions of these experiences. Emotions can run high when a collection is rearranged, a school is closed, or a favorite genre or grade level is lost.

CREATING INITIAL COLLECTIONS

The opening of a new school calls for the creation of an initial collection. When a new building is being planned, various patterns of preparation for the initial collection can occur. The optimal time to begin planning is when the building contract is awarded. In an ideal situation, a school librarian and faculty are hired to plan during the year preceding the opening of the building. This procedure has definite advantages. The school librarians can benefit from participating with faculty members as they identify philosophies and goals, create a curriculum, and develop plans. The librarian's major responsibility during the year is to ensure that the desired types of learning environments will be ready on the opening day. The librarian must place orders early enough to allow for delivery, processing, and time to make any necessary substitutions. Admittedly, school districts rarely have the financial resources or educational foresight to provide a whole year of planning.

Even if an entire faculty is not engaged in planning during the year prior to opening a school, the collection needs to be ready on the opening day. If the school's staff have not been appointed, the responsibility often rests with district-level staff. Those planning the new facility need to be aware of the long-range goals and objectives of the district's educational program and the equipment and materials needed for an initial collection. Planners should design flexibility into plans to accommodate changes that may occur in teaching styles, subjects taught, and the needs of unknown users. An example of such flexibility would be to save a portion of the collection budget so it could be spent by the school librarian in the first few weeks of the school year when more information about the users of the collection is available.

Districts follow various patterns for handling orders for a new building. Some districts use one-third of the initial collection budget to buy materials to have on opening day. One third is reserved for recommendations by the principal and professional staff. The remaining one-third is reserved for orders generated by the school librarian, who works with teachers and students to make selections. Other districts spend the entire first year's budget prior to the opening of the school. When making a budget, school district administrators and staff must also consider the cost of licensing electronic resources for the collection.

School districts with recent student population growth patterns may have lists of recommendations for the initial collection or have electronic holdings records of such collections. In some cases, these districts are willing to share or sell their lists. This type of list is designed to cover the broad scope needed by teachers and students in widely varying school communities and may be revised annually. You should contact district school library supervisors to determine if such lists exist in their school districts.

Major book jobbers also offer prepackaged opening day collections. Even though such a package, or any list developed by other school districts, may not address your school's unique needs, there are some advantages to these packages. Current costs are known, out-of-print titles are excluded, time and effort are saved by not having to consider unavailable items, the librarian can add additional materials, and the printout of online orders saves time. Such a list, however, has disadvantages. Direct order items and standing order items will not be covered, items requiring licensing will not be included, and the unique needs of the school may not be met.

General guidelines about the number of items that should be in an initial collection may also be available from the state's school library consultant or state school library association. These guidelines may outline the formats as well as stages of development, from the initial collection to one considered to be excellent.

By using selection aids, one can identify specific titles for a collection. Useful sources include *Children's Catalog* (H. W. Wilson), *Middle and Junior High School Core Collection* (H. W. Wilson), and *Senior High School Library Catalog* (H. W. Wilson) as well as state and regional book award lists. These tools are found in print format as well as online. Additional helpful resources can be found in this book's Appendix: Resources and Further Reading and this chapter's Additional Readings and Helpful Multimedia. The broad scope and coverage of these tools help librarians identify titles to match the wide range of information needs that will be experienced during the opening days of a collection.

STEPS TO GENREFY A FICTION COLLECTION

1. Do an initial audit of your fiction circulation.

Plan your genrefication process to begin at the end of a school year so that it can be complete and ready to launch when a new school year begins. The first step is to examine your current circulation report for the area to be genrefied. You may also want to formally or informally survey students to find out what they like and/or would change about the current organization. Armed with this information, you'll better be able to see the difference your genrefication efforts make over time.

2. Select a range of genres.

Aside from the common genres like "Romance," think about the initial genres you may be commonly asked about like "Halloween," "Steampunk," or "Fangirl." You may also want to consult free crowdsourcing book review sites like *Good Reads* or *Library Thing* to get an idea of how readers describe the titles.

3. Sort the fiction by genre.

Depending on the size of your collection, this step may take some time. Sorting and grouping titles by genre can be a great activity in which you can include student and/or parent volunteers. Having student input on this process can also be a great way to get free publicity for your efforts!

You may find that some genres are too broad or do not necessitate their own category. Divide, combine, and condense as needed—just be thinking about what will work best for your collection in the long term as items are added and weeded.

4. Shelve, sign, and display.

Once the categories have been assigned in catalog records, with spine labels, and in groups of like genres, guide your users to the new genre locations with exciting signage and displays. An easy integrated display is a bookstore-style "face out," in which you turn one or two titles with attractive cover art outward so that browsers are drawn them. If the book won't stand on its own, you can prop it up with a bookend.

5. Pause and reflect.

Don't forget to systematically check your circulation reports and "spot survey" your library's users to find out the difference your efforts make. Check in with your readers often to make sure that your genres are keeping pace with changing tastes.

RECLASSIFYING COLLECTIONS

Integrating collections can include combining or separating middle school and high school collections; shelving fiction by genre; and intershelving reference works with the circulating collection.

Integrating Collections

Often, school librarians will be faced with decisions about their shelving schemes that require integrating, or intershelving, collections. Noncirculating reference sections can function as a way of protecting high-use, large, or expensive materials like encyclopedias, dictionaries, and atlases. As reference titles become more commonly available in digital form, integrating the reference collection into the circulating nonfiction collection often becomes a consideration. School librarians who have thoroughly weeded their reference sections to eliminate outdated and duplicate materials, intershelved their reference titles with the nonfiction collection, and allowed these materials to circulate on even a limited basis report that they are more widely used by students. Many school librarians also remove the "REF" notation in the catalog record and on the spine label to prevent confusion in shelving and location. In her 2011 *School Library Monthly* article, school librarian Pamela Harland describes intershelving reference and nonfiction as "user-centered . . . trusting . . . flexible, and [as a result] a barrier has been reduced."

Integrating collections can also be a need in school that serve of wide range of grades like schools that move from a junior high (grades 7–8 or grades 7–9) model to a middle school model (grades 6–8). Junior highs were often instituted to help students make a curriculum-based separation between primary school content and secondary level content while middle schools were seen as an alternative that accomplished the same curriculum goals but used more developmentally appropriate groups of students (Dhuey, 2013). As school administrators revisit these divisions, they may opt to make different choices about grade groupings, thus necessitating a change to the school library collection. In the case of a collection adding sixth-graders or ninth-graders as users, librarians will want to think about where to draw the line between grade levels. A common guideline to work from are grade-level book lists provided by state organizations such as the Sunshine State Young Readers Award program lists for grades K–5 and grades 6–8. These lists will help you to determine, for example, the difference between grade 5 content and grade 6 content. The Helpful Multimedia section of this chapter includes references to sources of these lists.

Reclassifying Collections

Genrefication is the act of reclassifying materials according to genre like "Romance," "Horror," or "Mystery." Genres can be denoted by graphical or colorful stickers affixed to the book spine and/or genre notations in catalog records. Genres can be shelved in groups, intershelved with other books, and reflected in displays. Many school librarians genrefy to increase circulation and enable readers to more quickly locate materials in which they are interested. Genrefying a collection can take anywhere from a month to an entire school year.

While genrefying fiction collection is common, less common is gentrifying nonfiction collections. However, the "Ditching Dewey" movement is gaining a lot of attention.

In this approach, librarians assign classifications to nonfiction using self-generated, crowdsourced, or alternative classification schemes.

Two popular alternative classification schemes are Metis and BISAC. Metis is a library classification system developed and implemented in 2011 by librarians at the Ethical Culture School in New York City. The system places the thinking, interests, information needs, and information-seeking behavior of children at its center. It is developed as an alternative to the alphabetical arrangement of fiction by author, and the frequent arrangement of biographies in alphabetical order by biographee. The Metis system (named for Metis the Titan who was the mother of Athena in Greek mythology) was designed to encourage productive independent browsing by children, as well as to allow for successful catalog searching by elementary school students. The 26 main categories and their accompanying subcategories were devised through the research of Queens College CUNY Graduate School of Library and Information Science professor Linda Z. Cooper, who investigated of the categorizing behavior of children from kindergarten through fourth grade. The system does not use traditional call numbers and instead uses its categories in alphabetical order denoted single alphabetical letter, for example, A: Facts; B: Machines, C: Science, D: Nature, E: Animals, and F: Pets. Aside from the categorization letters, the call numbers use whole words and common language.

Some Metis main categories differ markedly from the Dewey main classes. One example is "Making Stuff," which includes arts and crafts, collections, games, cooking, putting on plays, and magic tricks—a perfect category for makerspace materials! Another is "Mystery," which includes nonfiction on code breaking, true crime, puzzles, and unexplained phenomena, as well as mystery and detective fiction. In these categories, one can see the principle of user interest that is at the center of the Metis system.

BISAC subject codes are the North American subject classification standard for physical and digital books. The BISAC system is maintained by the Book Industry Study Group, which classifies books into 52 broad categories, each with additional levels of specificity. Publishers use them to categorize books according to topical content. BISAC subjects identify to retailers where these books should be shelved or in which genre they should be grouped. So that it continually meets the needs of retailers, the list is updated once a year. The complete BISAC subject headings list is available online at no cost for looking up subjects one by one. BISAC is also related to the international book retailers' subject vocabulary called Thema, and modified, word topic driven version called WordThink.

BISAC and its related schemes allow users to browse the library like they do a bookstore. It also allows for combining and recombining topics into categories that shift as the

---

VOICES FROM THE FIELD

Folks who have changed their libraries from Dewey classification to the bookstore model sing the praises of the change touting increases in circulation and happier students. What we need to consider however, is the question, "if I had simply turned the books forward and provided better signage, would that have been enough to excite my students?" Solid research on the matter simply does not exist that justifies the cost in time and materials necessary to make the switch.

—Allison G. Kaplan, Author of *Catalog It!* (Libraries Unlimited, 2015)

list is updated. However, BISAC classification schemes are not widely available and difficult to capture in an online catalog. Librarians who use BISAC find that, without guidance, users often struggle to specific titles.

The decision to reclassify a collection is ultimately a local one; as long as you collect data that evidences a need for change, listen closely to your community to ensure that you understand what kind of change is needed (e.g., you may just need to promote your existing titles more rather than reclassify them), and institute methods of determining the extent to which reclassification efforts address users' needs, then a change may be appropriate for your library. Keep in mind, however, that most successful reclassifications occur in the fiction section rather than in the whole collection and that you will also want to make sure that you are empowering students to find materials in other school, public, and academic libraries.

SHIFTING OR MOVING COLLECTIONS

Sometimes it becomes necessary to shift or move entire collections. This might occur because of redesigning, remodeling, simply outgrowing space for the present collection, or relocating the entire school library. Moving or shifting a collection is no easy task. Planning is essential in order to avoid many frustrations that can result from such a move.

The following suggestions can help you successfully move a collection with a minimum number of problems:

1. Weed the collection before making a move or shift. There is no reason to move books that are not being used.
2. Read the shelves to ensure that all the books are in order.
3. Measure the floor, wall, and shelf space that will be available for the collection.
4. Make a paper model (to scale) of the school library facility to which you are moving. Be sure to draw in windows, furniture, and cabinets. Also indicate the electrical outlets.
5. Measure and log the amount of space needed for each section of books (as they presently line the shelves). Write in the sections on your paper model, making certain you leave adequate space for each section.
6. Choose sturdy boxes that are not too large for packing the books. Books are heavy, and you may need to move some of them yourself.
7. Pack boxes in reverse order, beginning with the last book on each shelf. When you unpack, the books will be in shelf order.
8. In large letters, label the boxes on the side, identifying which books are in each box. For instance, the easy picture books might be labeled "E AAR-ADA." Consider color-coding boxes, using different color marking pens: blue for books that go in the easy section, yellow for fiction, green for nonfiction, and red for computer equipment.
9. Number the boxes and create a database that includes what is inside each box.
10. Put all unpacking supplies (scissors, utility knives, tape, pens, and cleaning rags) in one box. Label it, "Supplies! Open Me First!"
11. Have the movers place all the boxes (in numerical order) near the bookcases where they will be shelved to avoid overlooking a box. If the labels are color-coded it will help the movers quickly locate the part of the library where the boxes should be placed.
12. Choose your unpackers carefully and watch closely over their work.
13. Do not fill all the shelves. Leave at least one-fourth of each shelf to allow for expansion.

14. If space allows, do not use the bottom shelves. It is difficult to read the labels on the spines on the bottom shelves. Also, this will again leave room for expansion in individual sections.

15. Do not forget to plan for your online collection as well. Plan the location of computers so they are accessible to electrical outlets and away from the heavy traffic areas. Be sure adequate work surfaces are available next to each computer.

16. Have technicians install and test the equipment, including the computers that house the circulation system.

If these steps are followed when moving a collection, it should avoid many possible problems, but you should also remember to expect the unexpected and not get frustrated with situations that are out of your control.

ANNUAL CLOSING OF COLLECTIONS

Develop a process of "closing" your collection each year. While this process may not include restricting access to the collection, it can be helpful to determine procedures you need to follow once per year and some activities are better suited to times when students are not in school and teachers have concluded their school-year activities. Some items to consider including in your annual "end-of-year" process include the following:

- Determine whether you would like to allow summer checkout. If you do, then choose an ending date for circulation for annual reporting purposes.
- Do an inventory each year. This information is vital in helping you track issues emerging in the collection. Student and parent volunteers can provide great help in barcode scanning.
- Work with your administration to determine how best to locate items that have been checked out but not returned. Messages communicated via student announcements, and notes sent home to parents and sent to teachers can be very effective in reminding users to return materials. While some librarians choose to charge students overdue or replacement fees, some librarians feel that this practice generates a negative image of the library while not generating a significant source of revenue.
- Weed throughout the year so that this aspect of collection maintenance does not need to be performed during the other tasks at the end of the school year.
- Enter incoming student names into online public access catalog at the end of the preceding school year.
- As you perform end-of-year activities, you'll get a chance to reflect on the past year and will likely have great ideas for displays, reading lists, or other collection promotion activities. Write these ideas down and save them where you will find them in the fall.
- Finalize teacher's fall reading lists so they are ready to go when school starts. If you need to pull books for the list, do as soon as inventory is done. Store the books on a cart for easy access in the fall.
- Update your procedures manual with any "lessons learned" from the school year. Make this reflection an annual activity.
- Prepare your annual report. Each year, you should provide your administration and school community with an annual report that documents library programs and activities, circulation, new items and services, progress toward your annual goals, annual goals for the coming year, and statements of need for collection development and promotion. Gather quotes from students, teachers, parents, and community members and include photos from library events to make the report exciting to read. Make the report available in digital format on the library website, too.

As you spend more time in your library and with your collection, you will develop strategies that work for you and for your environment. The key is to set goals, be systematic about measuring them, and reflect on your practice and your collection regularly to ensure that the collection continues to meet your community's needs.

PERMANENTLY CLOSING COLLECTIONS

When schools are closed, are consolidated, or have attendance districts reorganized, the full impact might not be felt until the formal announcement is made. Someone should be responsible for determining the procedures for removing materials. School librarians must be involved in the planning to avoid confusion and inefficiency.

Consolidation and reorganization of school districts and schools can be hot issues calling for special handling by the school librarian. Knowledge about the situation, diplomacy, and tact will help. Perhaps the loss can be turned into a gain for other schools in the district. Planning is the key factor in retaining items that a collection needs, while also preparing for the transfer of other items. Send information about available items, with plans for their transfer, to the receiving school. Assess each of the newly formed collections in terms of their weaknesses and strengths in meeting the new demands.

When schools close, answers to the following questions can guide the planning process. What will be the disposition of the materials, equipment, and furniture? What legal guidelines are there for the disposition of materials and equipment? Are there local constraints? What are the closing deadlines? Will extra help be available?

Once the target date is known, you should create a timeline with specific goals. This information can be posted to alert users and staff so they will be aware of when the school librarian plans to curtail services. Teachers who are moving to other schools can help you by indicating the titles they want available in the other schools. These items should be allocated first so they can be processed into the collections.

You should refer to your policies to see if there are criteria that might relate to the closing of a collection. For instance, does the policy on gift materials provide for transferring the materials to another school? You also need to check to determine if there are additional materials that other regulations or agreements cover. This should be done before deciding on how to dispose of items.

You can provide a list of remaining materials in your library and distribute the list to other schools in the district so librarians can request specific titles. Any items that are not requested will need to be stored, distributed, or discarded. Distribution possibilities include storing materials at an exchange center where they can be examined, or donating the materials to other agencies serving children, such as youth centers. Policies within the district will govern how you can disperse materials; the district may grant approval for sale to other library collections or to individuals.

PROTECTING THE COLLECTION IN A DISASTER

An unanticipated, but serious, effect on the collection is a disaster. Depending on the nature of the disaster, the school library may be in physical or structural peril or be inaccessible due to repurposing of library space of safety. Throughout this book, we have explored many aspects of library operation that need to be captured in the library's collection development policy; disaster planning is an often-overlooked and critical element of a policy. Disasters are no time to have no guidelines for response!

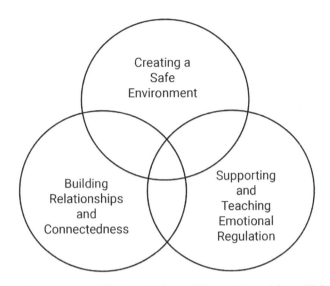

Figure 18.1. Components of Trauma-Informed Care (adapted from Walters, 2018)

In disaster response, schools have an obligation to provide learners and educators trauma-informed care. This care encompasses physical and socioemotional elements, as Figure 18.1 illustrates.

As Figure 18.1 shows, a safe environment is the linchpin of trauma-informed response. Without a space in the school that has been thoughtfully created to support relationships and emotional regulation, trauma-informed response is difficult (Pelayo, 2020). During the onset of the COVID-19 global pandemic and its resulting widespread school closures, many learners reported feeling traumatized and anxiously seeking information resources and personal enjoyment materials to help them cope (Witteveen, 2020). School librarians may wish to be proactive about dealing with trauma their school community may face by developing a section of the collection with fiction and nonfiction materials that explain and provide strategies for coping with crisis (Kaaland, 2015). The collection can provide coping strategies before, during, and after the disaster.

Although schools are likely to encounter a wide range of natural, public health, and social tragedies (e.g., mass shootings, overdoses), this section will focus on occurrences most likely to affect the school library collection.

Natural Disasters

Throughout the world, natural disasters (e.g., hurricanes, floods, wildfires) are increasing in number and severity, thus improving the likelihood that a school librarian will have to respond to at least one tragedy during their career. While disasters are scary and discussing them may raise anxiety, school librarians should look up disaster preparation and response as a leadership opportunity (Kaaland, 2015) in which they can not only act to protect the library, but also further a school-wide conversation about the need to acknowledge and prepare for adverse events. See the Kaaland (2015) book in this chapter's references for an excellent and extensive list of youth and children's books about disasters.

SELECTION CRITERIA FOR BOOKS RELATED TO DISASTER RECOVERY

Consider the following criteria when selecting books to recommend to children following a school crisis or natural disaster event:

- Plot demonstrates respect for the readers' tragedy;
- Characters deal authentically and honestly in their disaster response;
- Plot provides realistic resolution to a disaster or crisis;
- Author shows respect for diverse cultural responses to disasters or crisis;
- Illustrations support the tone of the disaster or event; and
- Plot offers readers constructive ideas for coping with crises

For schools that have been subjected to a major crisis, librarians may want to limit purchases of titles, even popular books, that show unhealthy responses to crisis. (Kaaland, 2015, p. 123–124)

Natural disaster response is usually divided into three phases: preparedness, response, and recovery. Each of these phases have distinct implications for the collection:

Preparedness. This phase relies on policies and practices that have been determined and documented ahead of time. The first step to preparing for a disaster is doing an inventory of the items in the collection (including materials, furniture, and equipment) that might be vulnerable to a disaster. Visually survey the library's physical space. Are there ceiling tiles that look like they may have gotten damp in the past? If so, request that they be replaced. Does the library have a dehumidifier and fans to deal with dampness? Rolls of waterproof plastic and tape? Are there enough gloves and masks for everyone who is going to be participating in the recovery effort? Proactive mitigation, such as moving computers away from windows, can be a starting point with preparation.

Another important aspect of preparation is keeping a list of who to contact when disaster strikes. For example, in your disaster policy, you may wish to keep contact information for "catastrophe cleaners" and other necessary helpers to protect and restore facilities and collections. Know who the school's insurance representative is and how the school library collection is covered by the school's policy. Have contact information and a copy of the policy on hand (Cowick, 2018).

This contact list should also include the library contact for gifts or donations—and be sure that your collection development policy's gifts and donations section includes pertinent information for disaster-prompted community generosity!

VOICES FROM THE FIELD

After Hurricane Charley (2004) we were inundated with donations that we had no space for and sadly were outdated and often not useful at the time. We lost 7 schools from the storm. Cash is definitely the way to go or gift cards. I would also suggest that you designate one person to make the contact and get a sense of what the people you are helping need. Knowing that there are others out there who want to help and who care is also a huge boost to morale.

—Ruie C., Florida school librarian

Response. One of the reasons why preparation steps are so important is that response often must be immediate. Your plan should include a detailed step-by-step prevention list that the school librarians and any helpers can divide and complete. Valuable items should be moved to safe locations. Backup data and software. Relocate fish tanks or any other animal residents of the library. Unplug equipment. Lock doors and windows to prevent vandalism or theft in the disaster's aftermath. Meticulous documentation in the preparation phase should provide a roadmap to follow in the response and recovery phases.

Recovery. Aside from helping library users emotionally recover from a disaster through information provision and storytelling, school librarians lead, often independently, recovery efforts. Again, thorough documentation is an important starting point for recovery and for determining at which hazard control stage from Figure 18.2 the library can operate.

When an event like flood or fire has reached the collection, the school librarian may be in the position of repairing and salvaging the collection. The first step is to require all people helping with the salvage effort to have any personal protective equipment (PPE) they may need. Even if the disaster is not chemical or disease in nature, mold and mildew can be powerful sources of contagion and illness (Cowick, 2018). Call professional disaster mitigators of the cleanup includes any unknown or concerning elements.

Restoring the library may be a lengthy process that includes partial reopening or relocation. Be sure that your disaster plan explicitly accounts for necessary actions in each level of hazard control delineated in Figure 18.2 to avoid any delays or disruptions in recovery and restoration efforts. *Crash Course in Disaster Preparedness* by Carmen Cowick, located in this chapter's references, includes a fantastic type-by-type item salvage and restoration list that will be indispensable to getting your school library and its materials ready to be used again.

One of the key elements of disaster recovery is one of the most difficult—though recovery processes can be lengthy, be sure to reflect on how complete your collection development policy's documentation was for preparation, response, and recovery efforts. Add, improve, and adjust policies as you better understand how they worked in actual practice.

Pandemics

Figure 18.2 provides a hierarchy of hazard control strategies that school librarians will want to consider in a disaster. While the examples here pertain to the COVID-19 global pandemic, these categories are useful for analyzing response to a number of disaster situations.

VOICES FROM THE FIELD

After the storm [Hurricane Michael], the city clerk said "Come and get your stuff." Now here's the thing. We had some wet materials. The workers that they sent in ahead of us . . . took the books from the shelves . . . and they just threw them in huge boxes, willy nilly, from any shelf. When we walked in, we thought what have they done! They thought they'd done a good job, and I thought but [the books are] just crinkled up in boxes. We had to go through the collections in two days and put them all back on the shelves in order.

—Sandra P., public librarian, Florida

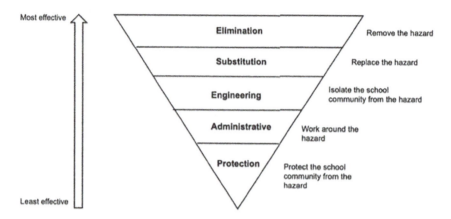

Figure 18.2. Hierarchy of Disaster Controls (adapted from National Academies, 2020)

As Figure 18.2 shows, the hierarchy includes five levels of protection that school librarians will want to consider.

Protective. School librarians protect themselves and school library users from the hazard, while the library remains open and accessible. Requiring students to wear masks and gloves is a type of protection control.

Administrative. In this level, the school librarian changes the way people work, for example, the school library would remain open, but the number of learners and educators allowed into the facility may be limited, tables spread further apart, and some chairs removed. This level may also include activities like cleaning and sanitizing returned materials before they are placed back in the collection. Excellent information about how long the COVID-19 virus lingers on library materials and surfaces is available from OCLC's REALM (Reopening Archives, Libraries, and Museums) Project (OCLC, 2020).

Engineering. To isolation library users from the hazard, the school librarian might close the library all together or not allow students into the library. The school librarian might deliver materials upon request.

Substitution. To replace school library services, librarians might direct users to another school library or public library. Another option is to increase access to digital materials.

Elimination. At the highest level of disaster control, the library facility may be deemed unusable and relocated to another site. Fumigation or furniture and décor replacement is another way of eliminating a hazard.

As we have seen in earlier chapters of this book, library materials are paramount to academic and personal learning. School librarians should strive to ensure that users have access to library resources as much and as soon as possible. In fact, many school librarians reported that disasters' impact on learning had led them to include more digital resources in their collections (*School Library Journal*, 2020). Ensure that your collection development policy includes clearly delineated strategies for each of these levels so that the school library can remain as accessible as possible in each phase of the disaster.

When schools move to all virtual learning, school librarians can still ensure access to the collection by offering story times, readers' advisory, and research assistance online via synchronous or asynchronous video. Whether school is in-person or virtual, school librarians must keep in mind the technology and physical access learners have when devising strategies; all virtual services, for example, may not be accessible to many learners in communities in which learners have low technology and Internet access (AASL, 2020).

CONCLUSION

Instances occur in which a collection may need to be opened, moved, or closed. In each case, a school librarian will need to follow specific guidelines, as well as be aware of the emotions that may accompany the shifting of a grade level to another school or closing down a school. Early preparations for creating a new collection can make it possible for the school library to be open on the first day that a new school begins operation. Useful selection aids can assist in the selection of an initial school library collection. If a grade level leaves a school or a new grade is added to a school, the collection will need to be assessed and adjusted to meet student and curriculum needs. Following specific guidelines and tips for moving an entire collection can save time and prevent much frustration. Set annual priorities for the collection and, at the end of the school year, collect and present data that help you determine if you're meeting your goals. When closing an entire collection, it is essential that school librarians follow any existing policies or regulations for the disposition and disposal of resources.

DISCUSSION QUESTIONS

1. What are important issues to ask the school district or building administration about establishing a new collection?
2. Discuss the pros and cons of reclassifying a high school nonfiction collection. What might be data points you could collect that would drive the decision to reclassify?

REFERENCES

American Association of School Librarians (AASL). (2020, April 10). Snapshot of school librarian roles during school closures. Retrieved from https://knowledgequest.aasl.org/snapshot-of-school-librarian-roles-during-school-closures/

Cowick, C. (2018). *Crash course in disaster preparedness*. Santa Barbara, CA: Libraries Unlimited.

Dhuey, E. (2013). Middle school or junior high? How grade-level configurations affect academic achievement. *Canadian Journal of Economics/Revue canadienne d'économique, 46*(2), 469–496. doi: 10.1111/caje.12020

Harland, P. (2011). Toward a learning commons. *School Library Monthly, 28*(1), 34–36.

Kaaland, C. (2015). *Emergency preparedness and disaster recovery in school libraries: Creating a safe haven*. Santa Barbara, CA: Libraries Unlimited.

National Academies of Sciences, Engineering, and Medicine. (2020). *Reopening K–12 schools during the COVID-19 pandemic: Prioritizing health, equity, and communities*. Washington, DC: The National Academies Press. https://doi.org/doi:10.17226/25858

OCLC. (2020). Lab testing. Retrieved from https://www.oclc.org/realm/research/lab-testing.html

Pelayo, Elizabeth. (2020). Trauma-informed school libraries: A space for all. *Knowledge Quest, 48*(3), 50–55.

School Library Journal. (2020, April 23). What librarians are doing to support students and teachers in the shutdown: SLJ COVID-19 Survey. *School Library Journal*. Retrieved from https://www.slj.com/?detailStory=slj-covid-19-response-survey-shows-librarians-preparation-and-response-to-school-closures-coronavirus-COVID19

Sunshine State Young Readers Award Program. http://www.floridamedia.org/?page=ssyrahome

Walters, J. (2018, January 30). Embedding trauma-informed practices within existing school-wide practices. Retrieved from https://medium.com/@drjimwalters/embedding-trauma-informed-practices-within-existing-school-wide-practices-a17a65256f36

Witteveen, A. (2020, November 2). Ahead of the curve: School librarians innovate and take on new responsibilities: SLJ COVID-19 Survey. *School Library Journal*. Retrieved from https://www.slj.com/?detailStory=ahead-of-the-curve-school-librarians-innovate-take-on-new-responsibilities-SLJ-covid-19-survey

ADDITIONAL READINGS

Bundy, A. (2010). Moving library collections. *Australasian Public Libraries and Information Services, 23*(2), 80.

Fortriede, S. C. (2010). *Moving your library: Getting the collection from here to there*. Chicago, IL: American Library Association.

HELPFUL MULTIMEDIA

A School Librarian on Genrefication—Things to Do, Traps to Avoid, and Surprising Benefits. Retrieved from https://www.youtube.com/watch?v=MKTwcicP1tI

Adcock, D. (n.d.). Closing—school library media centers. Retrieved from http://www.lib.niu.edu/1984/il840292.html

American Association of School Librarians. (n.d.) Pandemic resources for school librarians. Retrieved from http://www.ala.org/aasl/about/pandemic

American Association of School Librarians. (2020, July 13). School librarian role in pandemic learning conditions. Retrieved from http://www.ala.org/aasl/sites/ala.org.aasl/files/content/advocacy/SchoolLibrarianRolePandemic_Resources_Chart_200713.pdf

American Library Association. (2019, January 1). Moving libraries: ALA library fact sheet 14. Retrieved from https://libguides.ala.org/libraryrelocation

American Library Association. (2019, March 18). Cataloging tools and resources: Home. Retrieved from http://wikis.ala.org/professionaltips/index.php?title=Classification

Bales, J. (2019). Moving the school library collection. Retrieved from https://kb.com.au/school-library-collection-relocation/

Bates, N. (2015, Spring). Genrefication infographic: Do you genrefy? Retrieved from https://magic.piktochart.com/output/5927045-genre-survey-spring-2015

Chappell, S. (2006). Moving library collections: Planning shifts of library collections. Retrieved from http://libweb.uoregon.edu/acs_svc/shift/

International Federation of Library Associations (IFLA). (2020, October 13). Key resources for libraries in responding to the coronavirus pandemic. Retrieved from https://www.ifla.org /covid-19-and-libraries

McIlwain, J. (2020, June 16). IFLA disaster preparedness and planning: A brief manual. Retrieved from https://www.ifla.org/publications/node/8068

Metis: Library Classification for Children. https://sites.google.com/site/metisinnovations/

National Library of New Zealand. (n.d.). Tips for moving your library. Retrieved from https:// natlib.govt.nz/schools/school-libraries/library-systems-and-operations/library-operations /tips-for-moving-your-library

State and Regional Book Award Lists. http://archive.hbook.com/resources/awards/state.asp

Appendix:
Resources and Further Reading

This list identifies books, journals, electronic sources, and organizations published in the last decade that are useful for gaining more information about topics introduced in this book, building professional and student collections, as well as collection matters not addressed in this volume. For additional resources, please see the listings at the end of chapters.

BOOKS

A to Zoo: Subject Access to Children's Picture Books. 10th ed. Rebecca L. Thomas. Libraries Unlimited, 2018. ISBN 9781440834349.

Arranges 17,025 picture books (fiction and nonfiction) for children preschool–grade 2 under a vast range of subjects to meet librarians', teachers', and parents' needs and indexed by author, title, and illustrator. Five sections: subject headings, subject guide, bibliographic guide, title index, and illustrator index.

American Reference Books Online. 2019 Edition, Volume 50. Libraries Unlimited. ISBN 9781440869136 (hardcover); ISBN 9781440869143 (eBook).

Reviews print and electronic reference resources published in the United States and Canada. Includes author, title, and subject index.

Assistive Technology: Access for All Students, 3rd ed. Laura Bowden, Linda B. Johnson, and Lawrence A. Beard. Pearson, 2015. ISBN 9780133550948.

Discusses how assistive technology can be used to meet the needs of students with disabilities. Includes a chapter on universal design.

Best Books for Children: Preschool Through Grade. 10th ed. Catherine Barr and Jamie Campbell Naidoo. Libraries Unlimited, 2014. ISBN 9781598847819.

Includes brief annotations for 25,000 titles that had two or three recommendations in leading journals. Helps build collections by topic. Provides bibliographic and order information and citations to reviews. Indexes by author and illustrator, title, grade level, and subject.

Best Books for High School Readers: Grades 9–12. 3rd ed. Catherine Barr. Libraries Unlimited, 2013. ISBN 9781598847840.

Easy-to-navigate resource covering more than 12,000 titles. Includes annotations, plot summaries, reading levels, review citations, and ISBNs. Enables the evaluation of teen literature collections and assists in the creation of thematic and genre-oriented reading lists. Author, title, and subject indexes.

Best Books for Middle School and Junior High Readers: Grades 6–9. 3rd ed. Catherine Barr. Libraries Unlimited, 2013. ISBN 9781598847826.

Evaluates teen literature and enables creation of thematic and genre-oriented reading lists. Includes elements such as annotations, bibliographic data, and plot summaries that can aid in curriculum development and recreational reading selection.

Best STEM Resources for NextGen Scientists: The Essential Selection and User's Guide. Jennifer L. Hopwood. Libraries Unlimited, 2015.

This guide introduces more than 500 STEM resource suggestions for toddlers to young adults; highlights more than 25 detailed library program or activity suggestions to be paired with STEM book titles; provides resource suggestions for professional development; and contains bonus sections on STEM-related graphic novels, apps, and other media. Resources are organized according to the reading audiences for which they are intended, from toddlers through teens, and the book includes annotated lists of both fiction and nonfiction STEM titles, graphic novels, digital products, and online resources. The author also includes a selection of professional readings for librarians and media specialists who wish to further expand their knowledge.

Booktalking Authentic Multicultural Literature. Sherry York. Linworth, 2009. ISBN 978158633008.

Includes 1,010 booktalks of resources by authors of contemporary fiction for young readers (elementary through middle school). Provides indexes for subject, title, and author/illustrator/translator.

Bridges to Understanding. Linda M. Pavonetti. Scarecrow Press, 2011. ISBN 0810881063, ISBN 9780810881068.

Includes nearly 700 listings of annotated books published between 2005 and 2009. Organized geographically by world region and country.

Charlotte Huck's Children's Literature: A Brief Guide. Barbara Kiefer and Charlotte S. Huck. McGraw-Hill, 2019. ISBN 9781259913846.

Based on the classic text, explores the critical skills needed to select and share children's literature in the classroom including researching and evaluation. Provides the reader with evaluative tools, as well as suggestions on how to create and implement curriculum.

Children's Core Collection. 24th ed. H. W. Wilson. ISBN 9781642650235.

A definitive collection development resource. Contains more than 10,000 titles including fiction, graphic novels, magazines, and nonfiction works.

Collection Management Basics. 7th ed. Margaret Zarnosky Saponaro and G. Edward Evans. Libraries Unlimited, 2019. ISBN 9781440859649.

Provides a comprehensive overview, including needs assessment, development policies, the selection process, an overview of publishing, print and electronic serials, other electronic materials, government information, audiovisual materials, acquisitions, distributors and vendors, fiscal management, collection evaluation, resource sharing, collection protection, legal issues, censorship, and intellectual freedom, with focus on the issues and processes of collection development.

Collecting for the Curriculum: The Common Core and Beyond. Amy Catalano. Libraries Unlimited, 2015. ISBN 9781610699679

This book begins with a primer on the CCSS and how curriculum librarians can support them. Discussion of the Standards is then woven through chapters, arranged by content area, that share research-based practices in curriculum development and instruction to guide curriculum selection. Material types covered include games, textbooks, children's literature, primary sources, counseling, and nonfiction. Additional chapters cover the management of curriculum collections, testing collections, and instruction and reference, as well as how to support and collect for special needs learners. The book closes with a discussion of the future of curriculum materials.

The Collection's at the Core Revitalize Your Library with Innovative Resources for the Common Core and STEM. Marcia A. Mardis. Libraries Unlimited, 2014. ISBN 9781610695046
    The book is composed of three sections: an overview of policy initiatives; a thorough exploration of STEM education policy, digital materials, and collection considerations; and detailed explanations of strategies for collection development and promotion. The book also includes instructions for collection analysis to determine the age and extent of your STEM collections and make priorities for enriching them with appropriate digital multimedia resources, as well as how to classify resources using Dewey and Sears and with regard to the Common Core State Standards and the Next Generation Science Standards.

Connecting Boys with Books 2: Closing the Reading Gap. Michael Sullivan. Chicago: American Library Association, 2009. ISBN 9780838909799.
    Discusses what boys like to read and programming ideas. Includes an index.

Connecting Children to Classics: A Reader-Centered Approach to Selecting and Promoting Great Literature. Meagan Lacy and Pauline Dewan. Libraries Unlimited, 2018. ISBN 978-1-4408-4439-3.
    This guide identifies hundreds of books that can help children develop into engaged readers. The detailed descriptions of each book provide plot summaries as well as notes on themes, subjects, reading interest levels, adaptations and alternative formats, translations, and read-alikes.

The Coretta Scott King Awards: 50th Anniversary. Carole J. McCollough and Adelaide Poniatowski Phelps, eds. American Library Association, 2019. ISBN 9780838918692.
    Provides annotation and biographical information about works by African American authors and illustrators for the designated award or honor books. Includes example of each winning illustration. Includes a subject index which may assist with curriculum planning.

Critical Handbook of Children's Literature. 9th ed. Rebecca J. Lukens. Allyn & Bacon, 2013. ISBN 9780137056385.
    Provides readers with examples of quality children's literature to aid in the book selection process. Explains the essential literary elements of literature and suggestions applying these elements to additional readings that are reflective of the current time.

Educational Media and Technology Yearbook. Robert Maribe Branch, Lee Hyewon, and Sheng Shiang Tseng, editors. Springer, 2019. ISSN: 87552094.
    Published annually in cooperation with, and cosponsored by the Association for Educational Communications and Technology. Describes current developments and trends in the field of instructional technology. Highlights the major trends of the previous year and advances in online learning. It identifies instructional technology-related organizations and graduate programs across North America. Includes mediagraphy of journals, books, ERIC documents, journal articles, and nonprint resources. Available at https://www.springer.com/series/8617

Encountering Enchantment: A Guide to Speculative Fiction for Teens. 2nd ed. Susan Fichtelberg. Libraries Unlimited, 2015. ISBN 9781610691130
    This guide includes more than 1,500 books, most published since 2006, organized by genre, subgenre, and theme. Subgenres growing in popularity such as "steampunk" are highlighted. The guide will help three audiences (librarians, teen readers, and teachers/parents) help match students with the right books.

Essentials of Children's Literature. 9th ed. Kathy M. Short, Carol Lynch-Brown and Carl M. Tomlinson. Pearson, 2018. ISBN 9780134532592.

Surveys children's literature, featuring genres, authors within the genre, and recommended titles. Includes a chapter on multicultural and international literature. Includes curriculum and teaching strategies for grades K–6. Combines lists, examples, figures and tables with clear, concise, and direct narrative.

The Everyday Guide to Special Education Law: A Handbook for Parents, Teachers and Other Professionals. 3rd ed. Randy Chapman. Mighty Rights Press, 2015. ISBN 9780977017973.

Provides information from the IDEA regulations and court decisions dealing with special education. An excellent book to have in a professional collection for teachers and parents.

Gay, Lesbian, Bisexual, Transgender and Questioning Teen Literature. Carlisle K. Webber. Libraries Unlimited, 2010. ISBN 1591585066, ISBN 9781591585060.

Provides over 300 fiction and nonfiction titles, including poetry, drama, and graphic novels. Organized by genres and themes, with codes for the types of characters (G, L, B, T, and Q). Reading levels and titles that have video or audio versions are indicated.

Genreflecting: A Guide to Popular Reading Interests. 8th ed. Diana Tixier Herald and Samuel Savole. Libraries Unlimited, 2019. ISBN 9781440858475.

Updated classical text. Contains over 5,000 titles that are classified by genre, subgenre, and theme. Includes new chapters on Christian fiction and emerging genres as well as essays written by experts. Indexes are by subject or author and title.

Graphic Novels for Young Readers: A Genre Guide for Ages 4–14. Nathan Herald. Libraries Unlimited, 2011. ISBN 9781598843958.

Describes the growing number of graphic novels suitable for young readers. Organizes approximately 400 titles by genres, subgenres, and themes.

Historical Fiction for Teens: A Genre Guide. Melissa Rabey. Libraries Unlimited, 2010. ISBN 1591588138, ISBN 9781591588139.

Organizes more than 300 titles by subgenres and themes. Provides annotations, subject lists, and reading levels.

Hooked on Horror: A Guide to Reading Interests in Horror Fiction. 3rd ed. Anthony J. Fonseca and June Michele Pulliam. Libraries Unlimited, 2009. ISBN 9781591585404.

Describes contemporary and classic titles for English literature classes and horror fans. Focuses on widely available titles. Annotated bibliography of adult horror novels and films arranged by 13 subgenres. History of the horror genre. Includes graphic novels, indications of audio, eBook, and large print formats. Identifies additional reading, sources for research on the subject of horror, and lists of award winners.

Instructional Technology and Media for Learning. 12th ed. Sharon E. Smaldino, Deborah L. Lowther, Clif Mims, James D. Russell. Pearson, 2019. ISBN 9780134999722.

Discusses selection and use of media. Includes software package for teachers to use in creating, maintaining, printing, and evaluating lesson plans and the materials used in them. Incorporates technology and media to meet the needs of 21st-century learners and addresses concerns such as copyright, free and inexpensive media resources, learning theory, and instructional models. Updates technology use in schools. Includes educational resources and technology, teaching skills, and techniques.

Intellectual Freedom Manual. 10th ed. ALA Office of Intellectual Freedom. American Library Association, 2021. ISBN 9780838948187.

Includes most up-to-date intellectual freedom guidelines, policies and their interpretations. Offers guidelines for developing policies and practices.

Kids with Special Needs (series). Sheila Stewart. Simon & Schuster, 2011. ISBN 9781422217276.

Ten-volume book series written specifically for young people. Can be purchased as a set or as separate books. Available in hardback and paperback. Topics include: speech impairment, physical challenges, deaf and hard of hearing, intellectual disabilities, blindness and visual impairment, chronic illness, emotional disturbances, attention-deficit/hyperactivity disorder, autism, brain injury, and learning disabilities.

Living with a Special Need. Mason Crest Publishers, 2015. 16-volume set: ISBN 9781422230275.

This series educates young readers about a variety of special needs their peers live with every day. Each book in this set focuses on a different special need, from autism to ADHD, and includes stories about the lives of young people with these needs. (http://www.masoncrest.com/site/index.php/drugs-family-health-740/living-with-a-special-need.html)

Making Libraries Accessible: Adaptive Design and Assistive Technology (Library Technology Reports). Char Booth. American Library Association, 2012. ISBN 9780838958629.

Expert contributors address standards, spaces and services, devices, websites, and collections, offering advice on (1) assistive technology products, including screen readers, literacy software, and speech input; (2) eBooks and eReaders for users with print disabilities, with charts comparing accessibility features of the most common eReaders; (3) the nuts and bolts of using HTML, CSS, JavaScript, or JQUERY for accessibility; and (4) best practices for evaluating vendor database compliance.

Moving Library Collections: A Management Handbook. 2nd ed. Elizabeth Chamberlain Habich. Libraries Unlimited, 2010. ISBN 9781591586708.

Offers suggestions for planning effective moves handled by staff or professional movers. This updated edition includes sections on electronic resources, space limitations, project management software, archival materials, and special guidelines for small libraries, supplemented by illustrations and charts. Includes an updated bibliography of over 230 resources.

Multicultural Children's Literature: Through the Eyes of Many Children. 4th ed. Donna E. Norton. Pearson, 2013. ISBN 9780132685764.

Focuses on incorporating the best multicultural books into the classroom, honoring and respecting both the literature and the cultures in the classroom, and using literature to motivate and nurture a culturally responsive classroom. A chapter each is devoted to the following children's and adolescent literature in the following cultures: African American, Native American, Latino, Asian, Jewish, and Middle Eastern. Includes annotated bibliography.

The Newbery and Caldecott Awards: A Guide to the Medal and Honor Books, 2020 Edition. American Library Association. ISBN 9780838947456.

Annual. Provides background information about the titles and their creators, including selection criteria. Bibliography and index included.

The Picture Book Almanac: Picture Books and Activities to Celebrate 365 Familiar and Unusual Holidays. Nancy J. Polette. Libraries Unlimited, 2015. ISBN 9781440842764

The daily featured book titles cover the classics, such as books in the Paddington Bear series and Cinderella to outstanding current and just-published titles, collectively representing the best choices for collection building over time. This book includes more than 365 recommended picture books selected for their genuine worth as well as for their diversity and offers fun, quick, and easily completed activities coordinated to daily holidays throughout the year.

Popular Series Fiction for K–6 Readers: A Reading and Selection Guide. Catherine Barr and Rebecca L. Thomas. Libraries Unlimited, 2009. ISBN 1591586593, ISBN 9781591586593.

Introduces best and most popular fiction series of today, appropriate for elementary readers. Annotations provide bibliographic information, as well as indicate series and titles accepted by some of the popular electronic reading programs (e.g., *Accelerated Reading, Reading First*). Appendixes include "Books for Boys," "Books for Girls," "for Reluctant Readers/ESL Students," and "Developing Series." Includes index.

Teen Chick Lit: A Guide to Reading Interests. Christine Meloni. Libraries Unlimited, 2010. ISBN 9781591587569

Describes and puts into categories more than 500 titles. Provides bibliographic information, recommended ages, book awards, media connections, keywords, and annotations.

Teen Genreflecting: A Guide to Reading Interests. 4th ed. Sarah Flowers and Samuel Stavole-Carter, Foreword by Diana Tixier Herald. Libraries Unlimited, 2011. ISBN 9781440872723

This guide covers nearly 1,300 titles (1,100 are new) and authors for popular teen genres of historical novels, science fiction, fantasy, mystery, suspense, horror adventure, sports, romance contemporary novels, contemporary realistic to fantasy, and graphic novels. In addition, each genre and subgenre is defined; current trends in publishing and teen interest, readers' advisory services to teens, and collection development are discussed.

Teen Legal Rights. 3rd ed. Greenwood Press, 2015. ISBN 9781610696999.

Updated to include more information for the turn of the century. Includes driving, on the job, parents' divorce, alcohol and drug abuse, gay and lesbian teens, property rights, contracts, and how to find the law.

Through the Eyes of a Child: An Introduction to Children's Literature. 8th ed. Donna E. Norton and Saundra E. Norton. Prentice Hall, 2010. ISBN 9780137028757

Prepares reader to evaluate, choose, and share quality literature with children. Focus on classroom-tested teaching strategies and new teaching ideas. Treats multicultural literature as a separate chapter as well as integrated throughout. Updated edition expands coverage of biography, informational books, and integrated technology, as well as author insights.

JOURNALS AND MAGAZINES

ALAN Review. Assembly on Literature for Adolescents, National Council of Teachers of English, 1979–. ISSN 0882-2840 (Print), ISSN 1547-741X (Online).

Three times per year. Publishes articles that explore, examine, critique, and advocate for literature for young adults and the teaching of that literature. Published pieces include, but are not limited to, research studies, papers presented at professional meetings, surveys of the literature, critiques of the literature, articles about authors, comparative studies across genres and/or cultures, articles on ways to teach the literature to adolescents, and interviews with YA authors. Subscription: http://www.alan-ya.org/publications/the-alan-review/

American Journal of Health Education. Society of Health and Physical Educators (SHAPE), 1991–. ISSN 19325037.

Bimonthly. Multifaceted resource that aims for the advancement of the health education profession. Priorities of the American Association of Health Education include increasing the amount of available, valid research on health education, creating and fostering dialogue among health education professionals, and promoting related policies, procedures, and standards. Subscription: Society of Health and Physical Educators, 1900 Association Drive, Reston, VA 20191 (http://shapeamerica.org)

American Music Teacher. Music Teachers National Association, 1951–. ISSN 00030112.

Bimonthly. Covers earliest music history to the latest developments in music technology. Features articles on teaching methods and techniques. Reviews teaching materials, music publications, videocassettes, music software, and other new technology as well as issues and trends. Subscription: http://www.americanmusicteacher.org/publication/register.php

ASHA Leader Online. American Speech-Language-Hearing Association, 1996–. ISSN 10859586.

Reports on emerging issues and news of the profession. Available online at http://leader.pubs.asha.org/

Assistive Technology Journal. Rehabilitation Engineering and Assistive Technology Society of
    North America (RESNA). ISSN 10400435.
    Quarterly. Seeks to foster communication among researchers, developers, clinicians, educa-
tors, consumers, and others working in all aspects of the assistive technology arena. Available
online at http://www.resna.org/professional-development/assistive-technology-journal/assistive
-technology-journal. Subscription: http://www.resna.org

Book Links: Connecting Books, Libraries, and Classrooms. American Library Association,
    1991–. ISSN 10554742
    Quarterly supplement to *Book List.* Discusses old and new titles. Includes "Quick Tips" with
easy to implement classroom ideas, "Classroom Connections bibliographies" that link literature to
curricular topics, author profiles and author interviews. Subscription: https://www.booklistonline.com

Bookbird: A Journal of International Children's Literature. Johns Hopkins University Press,
    1962–. ISSN 00067377.
    Quarterly. Includes a variety of children's literature topics as well as information on chil-
dren's literature studies and awards. Online subscription: http://muse.jhu.edu/journals/bookbird/

Booklist. American Library Association, 1905–. ISSN 00067385. Also *Booklist Online*
    Semimonthly (22/year). Reviews current books, videos, and software on regular basis.
Reviews foreign language materials and materials on special topics in irregular columns. Provides
monthly author/title index and semiannual cumulative indexes. Includes *Reference Books Bulletin*
with reviews of encyclopedias, dictionaries, atlases, and other books using a continuous revision
policy. Subscription: http://booklistonline.com

Braille Book Review. U.S. Library of Congress, The National Service for the Blind and Physically
    Handicapped (NLS), 1932–. ISSN 0006873X.
    Bimonthly. Free to individuals with visual impairments and physical handicaps. Describes
books for children and adults. Provides title, order code, author, number of volumes, and date of
original print edition. Indexed monthly and annually. Includes news of developments and activities
in library services. Identifies new Braille books and magazines. Subscription: http://www.loc.gov
/nls/bbr.html

Bulletin of the Center for Children's Books. Johns Hopkins University Press, 1945–. ISSN
    00089036.
    Monthly (except August). Summaries and critical evaluations of newly published and forth-
coming books for children. Uses codes to indicate level of recommendation. Author/title index in
each volume. Subscription: https://bccb.ischool.illinois.edu/

Consumer Information Catalog. Consumer Information Center, General Services Administration,
    1977–.
    Quarterly. Free. Delivers useful consumer information from federal agencies to the public.
Available online at http://www.pueblo.gsa.gov/catalog.pdf. Subscription: http://www.pueblo.gsa.gov

Educational Leadership (magazine). Association for Supervision and Curriculum Development
    (ASCD), 1943–. ISSN 00131784.
    Eight times a year. *Educational Leadership* magazine is ASCD's flagship publication and is
an authoritative source of information about teaching and learning, new ideas and practices relevant to practicing educators, and the latest trends and issues affecting prekindergarten through
higher education. Online version has selected full-length articles and several abstracts of articles.
Reviews professional books. Subscription: http://www.ascd.org

English Journal. National Council of Teachers of English, 1912–. ISSN 00138274.
    Bimonthly. Reviews young adult literature, films, videos, software, and professional publica-
tions. Issues examine relationships between theory, research, and classroom practice. Subscription: https://library.ncte.org/journals/ej/

Exceptional Children. Council for Exceptional Children, 1934–. ISSN 00144029.

Four times a year (fall, winter, spring, and summer). Research-based articles. Reviews professional books. Publishes current articles on critical and controversial issues in special education, as well as credible articles on research and developments in the field. Subscribe: https://exceptionalchildren.org/improving-your-practice/cec-publications/exceptional -children

Exceptional Parent: The Magazine for Families and Professionals Caring for People with Special Needs. Exceptional Parent, 1971–. ISSN 00469157.

Twelve issues per year. Provides practical advice, educational information and support for families with children with disabilities and the professionals who work with them. Subscription: http://www.eparent.com

Gifted Child Quarterly. National Association for Gifted Children, 1957–. ISSN 00169862.

Quarterly. For educational researchers, administrators, teachers, and parents of gifted children. Publishes research and theoretical papers on the nature and needs of high-ability children. Supplies information on gifted and talented development. Subscription: https://www.nagc.org /resources-publications/nagc-publications/gifted-child-quarterly

Gifted Child Today. Sage Publications, Inc., 1978–. ISSN 10762175.

Bimonthly. Features information about identifying gifted children, building effective gifted and talented programs, helping gifted children with learning disabilities, building effective gifted education in math, science, language arts, and social studies and designing quality learning activities for gifted children. Includes bibliographies, illustrations, book reviews designed to meet the needs of parents and teachers of gifted, creative, and talented youngsters. Subscription information: https://us.sagepub.com/en-us/nam/journal/gifted-child-today#subscribe

History Teacher. Society for History Education, 1967–. ISSN 00182745.

Quarterly. Reviews books, textbooks, supplementary readers, and professional books. "Features informative and inspirational peer-reviewed analyses of traditional and innovative teaching techniques in the primary, secondary, and higher education classroom" (from website). Subscription: http://www.thehistoryteacher.org

Horn Book Magazine. Horn Book, 1924–. ISSN 00185078.

Six issues per year. Reviews and ratings for hardback and paperback books. Includes books in Spanish. The guide is published two times a year (April 1 and October 1). Subscription: http:// www.hbook.com/magazine/

Journal of Adolescent and Adult Literacy (JAAL). International Reading Association, Inc., 1957–. ISSN 19362706.

Eight times a year (September to May; December/January combined). Classroom-tested ideas grounded in research and theory for published for teachers. Issues include practical ideas for instruction, reviews of student and teacher resources, and reflections on current literacy trends, issues and research. Subscription: https://ila.onlinelibrary.wiley.com/journal /19362706

Journal of Advanced Academics (JOAA). Sage Publications, Inc., 2006–. ISSN 1932202X.

Quarterly. Formerly known as *Journal of Secondary Gifted Education.* This journal contains research programming ideas for gifted students. Subscription: https://us.sagepub.com/en-us/nam /journal/journal-advanced-academics#subscribe

Journal for the Education of the Gifted. Sage Publications, Inc., 1978–. ISSN 01623532.

Quarterly. Reports on the latest research on topics such as the characteristics of gifted children, evaluating effective schools for gifted children, gifted children with learning disabilities, the history of gifted education, and building successful gifted and talented programs Subscription: https://journals.sagepub.com/home/jeg

Journal of Family and Consumer Sciences. American Association of Family and Consumer Sciences (AAFCS), 1909–. ISSN 10821651.

Quarterly (winter, spring, summer, and fall). Reviews professional and trade books covering family relations, children, food and nutrition, household affairs, and teaching methods. Subscription: https://www.aafcs.org/resources/publications-products/journal-consumer-sciences#order

Journal of Geography. National Council for Geographic Education, 1902–. ISSN 00221341.

Bimonthly. Presents innovative approaches to geography research, teaching, and learning. Reviews textbooks and professional materials; has a column on free and inexpensive materials. Subscription: http://www.ncge.org

Journal of Intellectual Freedom and Privacy. Intellectual Freedom Committee of the American Library Association, 2019–.

Reports events relating to intellectual freedom and censorship. Available online. Subscription: https://journals.ala.org/index.php/jifp

Journal of Physical Education, Recreation and Dance. American Alliance for Health, Physical Education, Recreation, and Dance (AAHPERD), 1896–. ISSN 07303084.

Monthly (nine/year). Index. Features bylined articles and short features on all aspects of physical education, recreation, dance, athletics, and safety education as taught in schools and colleges. Covers administration, curriculum methods, and equipment. Subscription: https://www.shapeamerica.org/publications/journals/joperd/subscription.aspx

Journal of Visual Impairment and Blindness (JVIB). American Foundation for the Blind, 1977–. ISSN 0145482X.

Monthly. Articles pertaining to visual impairment and blindness. Available in regular print or in Braille. Available in microform, on audiocassette, and online at http://www.afb.org. Subscription: https://www.afb.org/publications/jvib

Kirkus Reviews. Kirkus Media, LLC., 1933–. ISSN 00426598.

Semimonthly. Available online. Entries provide bibliographic or order information, paging, month and day of release, type of book, and grade level on more than 500 prepublication books. Subscription: http://www.kirkusreviews.com/

Language Arts. National Council of Teachers of English, 1924–. ISSN 03609170.

Bimonthly (September through July). Reviews children's books and professional materials. Issues discuss theory and classroom practice as well as examine current research. Subscription: http://www.ncte.org/journals/la

Library Journal. Media Source, Inc., 1876–. ISSN 03630277.

Twenty times a year, semimonthly except monthly in January, July, August, and December, plus Buyer's Guide, 10 supplements and weekly review. Covers technology, management, policy, and other professional concerns. Available in microform. Reviews books, magazines, videos, CD-ROM, software, audiobooks, and systems that libraries buy. Monthly author index to reviews. Includes annual buyer's guide to hardware and equipment. Also available online at *Library Journal Digital* at http://www.libraryjournal.com/. Subscription information: https://www.libraryjournal.com/?page=subscribe

Mathematics Teaching in the Middle School. National Council of Teachers of Mathematics (NCTM), 1994–. ISSN 10720839.

Nine times a year (September to May, with a combined December/January issue and a yearly focus issue in February). A resource for middle school students, teachers, and teacher educators. The focus is on intuitive, exploratory investigations that use informal reasoning to help students develop a strong conceptual basis that leads to greater mathematical abstraction. Includes ideas for activities, lessons, strategies and practice problems. Subscription: https://www.nctm.org/publications/mathematics-teaching-in-the-middle-school/

Mathematics Teacher. National Council of Teachers of Mathematics (NCTM), 1908–. ISSN 00255769.

Nine times a year (monthly August through May, with a combined December/January issue). Features on the improvement of mathematics instruction in junior and senior high schools, two-year colleges, and teacher education colleges. The column "Reviewing and Viewing" covers teaching materials, including games, videotapes, workbooks, software, and books for teachers. About 100,000 mediagraphic items covered. Also provides a forum to link education research to practice and share activities and strategies. Subscription: https://www.nctm.org/membership/

Online Journal of School Mathematics (ON-Math). National Council of Teachers of Mathematics (NCTM), 2000–. ISSN 15346749.

Peer-reviewed journal developed and designed exclusively for the Internet. An interactive site with ideas for mathematics educators at all levels. Available online at https://library.osu.edu/ojs/index.php/OJSM

Publishers Weekly. Media Source, Inc., 1872–. ISSN 00000019.

Weekly. Reviews books and audiovisual materials. Discusses news and trends in the book industry, including author interviews, advance book reviews, marketing and book design, and manufacturing articles (http://www.publishersweekly.com/).

Quill and Quire: Canada's Magazine of Book News and Reviews. St. Joseph Media, 1935–. ISSN 00336491.

Ten times a year. Available online. Reviews books and has advertisements for tapes and records. Subscription: https://www.quillandquire.com

School Library Connection + reVIEWS. Libraries Unlimited, 2003–. ISBN 9781440842924

Bimonthly. Blending practical information, professional development, and book and technology reviews by educators. Subscription: http://schoollibraryconnection.com/

School Library Journal: The Magazine of Children, Young Adults, and School Librarians. Media Source, Inc., 1954–. ISSN 03628930.

Twelve issues per year. Reviews books (preschool through adult titles for young people, Spanish language, references), videos, recordings, CD-ROMs, and software. Includes checklists, pamphlets, posters, and free materials. Includes monthly index, annual author/title book review index, and audiovisual index. Subscription: https://www.slj.com/?page=subscribe

Science and Children: The Journal for Elementary School Science Teachers. National Science Teachers Association (NSTA), 1963–. ISSN 00368148.

Nine times per year (September through May). Presents ideas and activities for science educators from preschool through middle school. Reviews software, curriculum materials, and children's books. Available online at http://www.nsta.org/pubs/sc/. Subscription: http://www.nsta.org/membership/benefits.aspx?lid=ele

Science Scope: A Journal for Middle-Junior High Science Teachers. National Science Teachers Association (NSTA), 1978–. ISSN 08872376.

Nine times a year. Ideas about how to include science materials in libraries and classrooms. Available online at https://www.nsta.org/science-scope

The Science Teacher. National Science Teachers Association (NSTA), 1934–. ISSN 00368555.

Nine times a year (January, February, March, April, July, September, October, November, December). Reviews software, books for students, and professional books. Available online at http://www.nsta.org/highschool#journal.Subscription: http://www.nsta.org

Social Education. National Council for the Social Studies (NCSS), 1937–. ISSN 00377724.

Seven issues per year. Reviews books for children and young adults, and includes ideas for lessons, teaching techniques, and incorporating instructional technology. Subscription: National Council

for the Social Studies, 8555 16th Street, Silver Spring, MD 20910 or http://www.socialstudies.org
/publications/se/

Social Studies and the Young Learner. National Council for the Social Studies (NCSS), 1988–.
   ISSN 10560300.
   Quarterly. Offers K–6 social studies educators practical tips in all aspects of social studies
instruction. Subscription: http://www.socialstudies.org/publications/ssyl

Teacher Librarian. Kurdyla Publishing, 1973–. ISSN 14811782.
   Five times per year. Available online at http://teacherlibrarian.com. Reviews professional reading, magazines, paperbacks, software, videos, and websites. Subscription: http://teacherlibrarian
.com/subscribe/

Teaching Children Mathematics. The National Council of Teachers of Mathematics (NCTM),
   1994–. ISSN 10735836.
   Monthly August–May. Includes articles on teaching mathematics to elementary-age children.
Articles focus on intuitive and exploratory investigation. Subscription included in membership
dues in pre-K–8 section of The National Council of Teachers of Mathematics. Subscription: http://
www.nctm.org/publications/tcm.aspx

Teaching Exceptional Children. Sage Publications, Inc., 1968–. ISSN 00400599.
   Six times a year. Articles deal with current issues and practical methods and materials for
classroom use. Archives online 2001 to present. Subscription: https://exceptionalchildren.org
/improving-your-practice/cec-publications/teaching-exceptional-children

Technology and Learning. NewBay Media, LLC. 1980–. ISSN 10536728.
   Ten issues a year. Reviews computer software and multimedia for elementary and secondary
students. Provides hardware requirements, emphasis, grade level, publisher, description of software
manuals and guides, rating, strengths, and weaknesses. Subscription: http://www.techlearning.com

The Video Librarian: Video Review Guide for Libraries. Video Librarian, 1986–. ISSN 08876851.
   Bimonthly. Reviews nearly 200 videos for public, school, and university libraries. The magazine's supplement is available online at http://www.videolibrarian.com/. Subscription: http://www
.videolibrarian.com

VOYA: Voice of Youth Advocates. Kurdyla Publishing, 1978–. ISSN 01604201.
   Bimonthly. Reviews books (trade, paperbacks, reprints, professional), reference titles, and
media of materials for or about adolescents. Available online at http://voyamagazine.com. Subscription: http://www.voya.com

REFERENCE WORKS AND DATABASES

American Book Publishing Record. R. R. Bowker, 1960–. ISSN 00027707.
   Reference. Monthly. Compiles titles cataloged by the Library of Congress. Dewey classification arrangement. Provides full cataloging data, LC and DDC numbers, subject headings, and
price. Author index.

AV-iQ.
   Database. AV-iQ is a large, comprehensive database of AV product information and delivers
that information with powerful search tools. Available online at https://www.av-iq.com/

*AV Market Place, 2020: The Complete Business Directory of Products and Services for the Audio/
   Video Industry.* 48th ed. Information Today. ISBN 9781573875608.
   Reference. This annual list includes addresses and services of producers, distributors, pro-
duction services, manufacturers, and equipment dealers.

BIBZ Selection Tool. Brodart Co.

Database. Web-based service for collection development and ordering. Requires Brodart account. Allows user to search and access relevant titles, build customized bibliographies, select best items, and order online. Includes free full-text reviews from *Kirkus Reviews.* Available online at http://www.bibz.com

Book Review Digest. H. W. Wilson, 1905–.

Database. "This essential library tool provides access to book reviews on a wide range of topics from a variety of sources, including newspapers, review journals and popular magazines." Available online at https://www.ebsco.com/products/research-databases/book-review-digest -plus

Book Review Index. Gale.

Database. An online database of more than 4 million books. Available online at https://www .gale.com/c/literature-book-review-index

Bookfinder Database. YALSA, American Library Association.

Database. "While these books have been selected for teens from 12 to 18 years of age, the award-winning titles and the titles on YALSA's selected lists span a broad range of reading and maturity levels. We encourage adults to take an active role in helping individual teens choose those books that are the best fit for them and their families." Free. Available online at http://booklists .yalsa.net

Books in Print. R. R. Bowker, 1947–. ISBN 9781642654967.

Reference. Annual. Serves as the definitive bibliographic resource with more than 1,879,000 titles of the full range of books currently published or distributed in the United States. Various titles available in print and online. See also Books in Print database. Available online at http:// www.booksinprint.com

Books Out Loud: Bowker's Guide to Audiobooks, 2021. Grey House Publishing, 1985–. ISBN 9781642657210.

Reference. Annual in two volumes. Covers more than over 300,000 audiobooks from more than 10,000 producers and 2,100 distributors and wholesalers. Indexes include title, authors, reader/performer, producer, and distributor.

The Bowker Annual Library and Book Trade Almanac, 65th edition. Medford, NJ: Information Today, 2020. ISBN 9781573875639.

Reference. Includes research and statistics such as average prices of books; news about legislation, associations, and grant-making agencies; lists of distinguished books; and directory information.

Bowker's Complete Video Directory. New York: R. R. Bowker, 2021. ISBN 9781642658620.

Reference. Annual. This 7,000+ page reference directory provides details on over 73,000 entertainment and performance titles, as well as educational and special interest videos (documentaries, how-tos, certain sport titles, and other videos directed toward specialized audiences) and educational programs.

Catalog of United States Government Publications
http://catalog.gpo.gov/F?RN=583554046

Database. Washington, DC: U.S. Government Printing Office, 1895–. Identifies publications by major branches, departments, and bureaus of the U.S. government. Provides depository and order information

Children's Book Review Index, 2017 edition. Detroit: Gale Research, 1976–. ISBN 9781410328304.

Reference. Provides review citations for books recommended for children through age 10. Illustrator and title indexes.

Children's Books in Print 2021. 52nd ed. New York: R. R. Bowker, 2020. ISBN 9781642655261.
     Reference. Annual. Three volumes. Children's books for schools and libraries. Provides bibliographic and ordering information and uses Sears subject headings, supplemented by LC headings. Excludes textbooks. Related work: *Subject Guide to Children's Books in Print.* ISBN 9781642655087 (annual).

Children's Core Collection. 20th ed. Hackensack, NJ: Grey House Publishing, 2021. ISBN
     9781642650235
     Reference. A comprehensive guide to 15,000 recommended books for children from preschool through sixth grade. In this information-packed volume, users will find bibliographic data, content descriptions and reviews of 15,000 highly recommended titles, including Picture Books & Easy Readers, Story Collections, Fiction Books, Nonfiction Books, Biographies, and Graphic Novels.

Core Collection. EBSCO.
     Database. Core Collections are impartial, authoritative guides that help librarians build and maintain well-rounded collections of the most highly recommended reference, nonfiction and fiction books. Beloved in print for years, the collections are available in a more comprehensive and more regularly updated online version. Core Collections makes it easy to connect the information to your local collection and compare what your library owns to what our experts recommend. Core Collections include: Children's Core Collection; Graphic Novels Core Collection; Fiction Core Collection; Middle & Junior High Core Collection; Nonfiction Core Collection; Senior High Core Collection.

El-Hi Textbooks and Serials in Print, 2021. Grey House Publishing, 2021. ISBN 9781642658637.
     Indexes over 195,000 textbooks and has additional resources such as reference books, periodicals, maps, tests, teaching aids, and audiovisuals. Titles are listed and cross-referenced in subject, title, author and series indexes. Entries include title, author, grade, publication, date, educational level, price, ISBN, related teaching materials. Includes publisher, wholesaler, and distributor index, with complete contact information.

Encyclopedia of Romance Fiction. Libraries Unlimited, 2018. ISBN 9780313335723.
     Reference. Provides the basics about authors, works, themes, and other topics related to romance fiction using alphabetically arranged reference entries. Offers suggestions for further reading and other works of romance fiction via reading list. Written by contributors who are scholars, librarians, and industry experts with broad knowledge of the genre."

Ferguson's Career Guidance Center. 3rd ed. Ferguson, 2020.
     Database. Ferguson's Career Guidance Center is an award-winning reference database for lifelong career exploration and planning. It offers a wealth of resources for users to assess their career goals and interests, plan their education, learn workplace skills, find apprenticeships and internships, conduct a job search, and much more.

Fiction Core Collection. 20th ed. Grey House Publishing, 2020. ISBN 9781642653168
     Database. Provides expert collection development advice on the most highly recommended works of classic and contemporary fiction. Over 7,600 titles are included, all are popular works deemed to have lasting value to readers as well as new literary and genre titles that have been recognized as significant achievements in their respected areas of literature.

For Younger Readers: Braille and Talking Books. National Library Service for the Blind and
     Physically Handicapped (NLS), U.S. Library of Congress, 1967–. ISSN 00932825.
     Reference. Biennial (every two years). Latest edition covers 2014–2015. Annotates Braille and audiobooks announced in *Braille Book Review* and *Talking Books Topics.* Available in Braille, sound recording, and large type. Free to individuals who are visually impaired and/or physically handicapped. Large print available.

Graphic Novels Core Collection. 3rd ed. Grey House Publishing. ISBN 9781642656473.

    Reference. Includes nearly 2,500 book titles which constitute a shortlist of the essential books in a given category or on a given subject. Each title includes content descriptions and quotes from selected reviews. The graphic novels in this collection cover a wide variety of genres including adventure, biography, fantasy, superhero, horror, mystery, romance, science fiction, and more.

Guide to Reference Materials for School Library Media Centers. 6th ed. Libraries Unlimited, 2010. ISBN 1591582776, ISBN 9781591582779.

    Reference. Covers more than 2,000 titles including electronic resources with age and reading levels, presentation styles, strengths and weaknesses, comparison with other works, and citations to reviews. Includes resources recommended for use by school librarians.

Literary Market Place: The Directory of the Book Publishing (LMP). Information Today, 1973–. ISSN 00001155.

    Database. Lists publishing and publishing-related businesses from the United States and Canada, including distributors, literary agents, small presses, book producers, translators and interpreters, events, editorial and art devices, reference books and magazines, printers, binders and Literary Association, Societies and Awards. Also lists recent mergers and acquisitions and company reportage of publishers, that is, divisions, subsidiaries, and imprints.

Middle and Junior High School Core Collection. 14th ed. H. W. Wilson, 2019. ISBN 9781642652598.

    Reference. Separate sections for nonfiction, fiction and short story collections. Contains entries for more than 10,000 books. Each book entry includes bibliographic description, suggested subject headings, an annotation, and an evaluation from a quoted source (when available). Multiple indexes included.

Pioneer Drama Service.

    Database. Provides sources for one-act comedies, melodramas, and musicals for students. Available online at https://www.pioneerdrama.com/

Readers' Guide to Periodical Literature. H. W. Wilson, 1901–. ISSN 00340464.

    Reference. Monthly. Available in print and online. Author and subject indexes to selected general interest periodicals of reference value in libraries, including book reviews.

Recommended Reference Books for Small and Medium-Sized Libraries and Media Centers. Libraries Unlimited, 2017 edition, Volume 37. ISBN 9781440856617.

    Reference. Based on *American Reference Books Annual*; written by over 200 subject specialists; identifies best, most affordable, and most appropriate new reference materials in any field. Reviews coded to identify titles of interest to school library media centers.

Reference Sources for Small and Medium-Sized Libraries. 8th ed. American Library Association, 2014. ISBN 9780838912126.

    Reference. Comprehensive buying guide. Describes reference sources recommended by the Reference Sources for Small and Medium-sized Libraries Editorial Committee, Collection Development and Evaluation Section, Reference and User Services Association of the American Library Association. Includes different types of affordable resources such as websites, databases, and print. Titles are annotated and include bibliographic information.

Senior High Core Curriculum. 22nd ed. Grey House Publishing, 2020. ISBN 9781642656480.

    Reference. Identifies essential material available for high school libraries and young adult collections. It is a helpful guide to over 8,200 recommended fiction and nonfiction titles for adolescents and young adults (grades 9–12).

University Press Books Selected for Public and Secondary School Libraries. Association of American University Presses, 1991–. ISSN 10554173.

Database. Annual. Selections rated by a committee from the AASL and the Public Library Association (PLA). Rates books in terms of general audience, regional interest, and in-depth collections for students in grades 6–12. Available online at http://aaupnet.org/librarybooks/.

Video Source Book. 59th ed. Cengage, 2017. ISBN 9781410324993.

Reference. Annual. Covers prerecorded video programs currently available on videocassette, videodisc, and videotape. Provides date of release, running time, major plot, theme, closed captions, or signing for individuals with a hearing impairment, and availability. Comprehensive coverage of video offerings with listings for more than 130,000 complete programs, encompassing more than 160,000 videos. All titles arranged alphabetically with bibliographic information included. Multiple indexes. Order from https://www.cengage.com/

WEBSITES

Ability Tools, California's Assistive Technology Act Program.
   http://abilitytools.org
   Services include: AT Exchange marketplace; device lending libraries; financial loan program for AT; information and referrals; and a reuse program in affiliation with organizational partners. The organization also provides in-person and webinar trainings, technical assistance to organizations on AT issues and coordinate the California Assistive Technology Reuse Coalition. Ability Tools offers a free membership to anyone interested in learning more about AT and looking to connect with other like-minded individuals via the Ability Tools listserv

American Foundation for the Blind
   http://www.afb.org
   Produces books, journals, videos, and electronic materials for individuals who are visually impaired and professionals who work with them.

American Printing House for the Blind
   http://www.aph.org
   "The world's largest source for adapted educational and daily living products since 1858." Provides educational materials in a variety of formats for visually impaired students.

Autism Speaks
   http://www.autismspeaks.org/
   Includes information about the largest autism science and advocacy organization in the United States.

Described and Captioned Media Program (National Association of the Deaf)
   http://www.dcmp.org
   A free-loan library that has more than 4,000 described and caption media titles available to members. Created to promote and provide equal access to information for those with auditory or visual impairments. National Association of the Deaf, 1447 E. Main St., Spartanburg, SC 29307. 800-237-6213 (voice) 800-237-6819 (TTY). Site is also viewable in Spanish. Free membership.

Hoagies' Gifted Education Page.
   https://www.hoagiesgifted.org/
   Consists of over 1,000 pages of information on gifted children and adults. Provides information on topics such as Testing and Assessment, Academic Acceleration, and Differentiation of Instruction and Success Stories.

Latest Books in Braille and Audio
   https://www.loc.gov/nls/braille-audio-reading-materials/latest-books-in-braille-and-audio/
   Lists braille books and magazines recently added to the NLS collection and available through a network of cooperating libraries. Library of Congress, National Library Service for the Blind and Physically Handicapped (NLS).

Notable Children's Digital Media–2021
   http://www.ala.org/alsc/awardsgrants/notalists/ncdm
   Helps parents, children, teachers, and librarians evaluate authorship or sponsorship, purpose, design, stability, and content. Recommends sites for children. Association of Library Service to Children (ALSC). Chicago, IL: American Library Association.

Stuff for the Teen Age. New York Public Library, Committee on Books for Young Adults, 1929–.
   https://www.nypl.org/voices/blogs/blog-channels/sta
   In 2010, *Stuff for the Teen Age* became a blog. Includes book picks for teens by teens, as well as selections from the top 100 teen titles from the previous year.

Index

Note: Page numbers followed by *t* indicate tables and *f* indicate figures.

About the Author

MARCIA A. MARDIS, EdD, is Professor, Associate Dean for Research, and Director of the Information Policy, Management, and Use Institute at Florida State University's College of Communication & Information. She has a bachelor's degree and Master of Science in Information degree from the University of Michigan and a Doctorate in Education from Eastern Michigan University. Lead writer of the American Association of School Librarians' *National School Library Standards* (2018), Dr. Mardis' other recent books include *Social Justice and Culture Competency* (2019), a volume edited with Dianne Oberg; *Research Methods for Librarians and Educators: Practical Applications in Formal and Informal Learning Environments* (2018), edited with Ruth V. Small; and an edited volume entitled *Librarians and Educators Collaborating for Success: The International Perspective* (2016).